Late 19th century: the archeologist Maudslay perched on the tower of the "Palacio" at Palenque in the Chiapas ▲ 246.

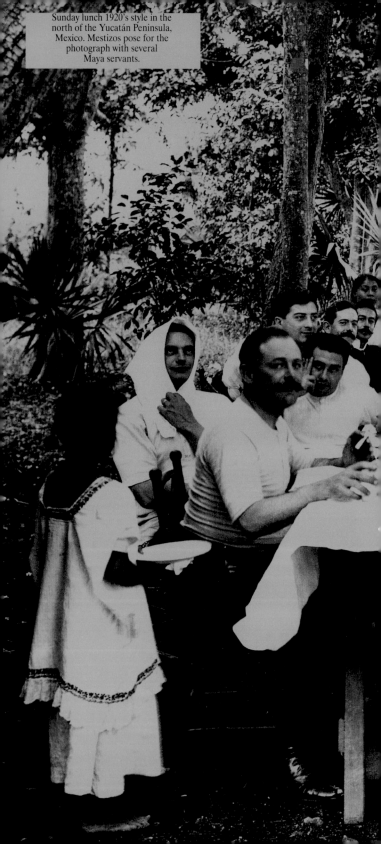

Sunday lunch 1920's style in the north of the Yucatán Peninsula, Mexico. Mestizos pose for the photograph with several Maya servants.

Quirigua, in the Motagua Valley
(Guatemala), where archeologists have
uncovered a giant stele ▲ 306.

NUMEROUS SPECIALISTS AND ACADEMICS HAVE CONTRIBUTED TO THIS GUIDE.

AUTHORS AND EDITORS: Michel Antochiw, André Aubry, Claude-François Baudez, Michèle Bisgambiglia, Michel Boccara, Jean-Luc Braconnier, Alain Breton, Marie-Hélène Carpentier, Danièlle Cavaleri, Isabelle de Couliboeuf, Seymourina Cruse, Nicole Dagnino, Noëlle Demyk, Clarisse Deniau, Philippe J. Dubois, Luisa Galeotti de González, Zipoena de León, Grégory Leroy, Pierre-Yves Mercier, Perla Petrich, Gérard Rocamora, Isabelle Roller, Nathalie Saint-Martin, Odile Simon, Nathalie Victor-Pujebet.

ILLUSTRATORS AND ICONOGRAPHERS: Anne Bodin, Isabelle-Anne Chatellard, Kristof Chemineau, Jean Chevallier, Paul Coulbois, Gismonde Curiace, François Desbordes, Claire Felloni, Stéphanie Girel, Jean-Marie Guillou, Jean-Benoît Héron, Gilbert Houbre, Pierre Hugo, Bernard Hugueville, Patrick Mérienne, Philippe Munch, François Place, Maurice Pommier, Claude Quiec, Christian Rivière, Pascal Robin, Jean-Sylvain Roveri, Amato Soro, Franck Stefan, Olivier Verdy, Flo Villacèque.

PHOTOGRAPHERS: Emmanuel Chaspoul, Jean-Pierre Courau, Seymourins Cruse, Mireille Vautier.

WE WOULD ESPECIALLY LIKE TO THANK:
Michel Antochiw, André Aubry,
Claude-François Baudez, Jean-Luc Braconnier, Alain Breton

WE WOULD ALSO LIKE TO THANK:
Danièlle Cavaleri (Ethnic Comnsultants), Françoise de Tailly (Inguat Paris), Marco Tulio Ordóñez (Inguat Guatemala-Ciudad).

TRANSLATED BY WENDY ALLATSON;
EDITED AND TYPESET BY BOOK CREATION SERVICES, LONDON.
PRINTED IN ITALY BY EDITORIALE LIBRARIA.

EVERYMAN GUIDES
PUBLISHED BY DAVID CAMPBELL PUBLISHERS LTD, LONDON

© 1995 David Campbell Publishers Ltd

© 1995 Editions Nouveaux-Loisirs, a subsidiary of Gallimard, Paris.

ISBN 1-85715-870-9

EVERYMAN GUIDES
79 BERWICK STREET
LONDON W1V 3PF

THE ROUTE
OF THE MAYAS

EVERYMAN GUIDES

CONTENTS

EASTERN YUCATÁN

WESTERN YUCATÁN

CHIAPAS

HIGHLANDS OF
GUATEMALA

SOUTHEASTERN MAYA

PETÉN

BELIZE

▲ THE ROUTE OF THE MAYAS

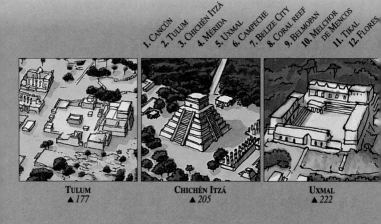

TULUM

CHICHÉN ITZÁ

UXMAL

GULF OF MEXICO

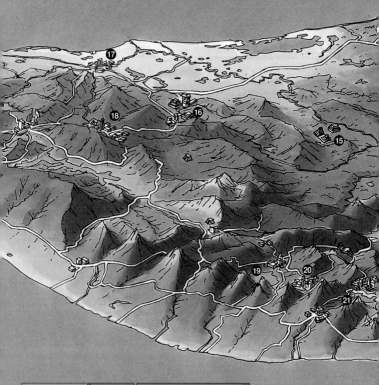

NORTH AMERICA
ATLANTIC OCEAN
WEST INDIES
PACIFIC OCEAN
SOUTH AMERICA

GULF OF MEXICO
CARIBBEAN
MEXICO
BELIZE
GUATEMALA
HONDURAS
PACIFIC OCEAN
EL SALVADOR

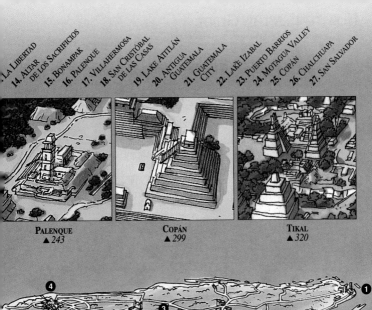

PALENQUE
▲ *243*

COPÁN
▲ *299*

TIKAL
▲ *320*

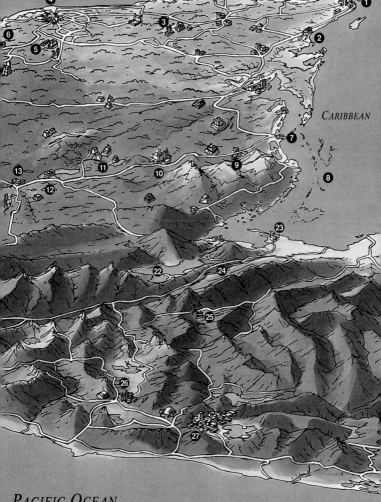

CARIBBEAN

PACIFIC OCEAN

HOW TO USE THIS GUIDE

(Sample page shown from the guide to Venice)

The symbols at the top of each page refer to the different parts of the guide.

■ NATURAL ENVIRONMENT

● KEYS TO UNDERSTANDING

▲ ITINERARIES

◆ PRACTICAL INFORMATION

The itinerary map shows the main points of interest along the way and is intended to help you find your bearings.

The mini-map locates the part itinerary within the wider area covered by the guide.

▲ CANNAREGIO

•The gateway to Venice, after all, is none other than the station, before us, beyond by proptides. *A rabbit in a great river.* Fernand Braudel, *France*

Immediately outside the railway station lies Cannaregio, the first of the six sestieri of Venice. Situated at the north-west end of the city, this is the second largest sestiere after Castello ▲ 155, covering an area of 150 hectares. Nearly a third of the population of Venice is concentrated here, amounting to more than twenty thousand people. There are two theories about the origins of the name Cannaregio, according to one, it comes from Canal regio (the Royal Canal), meaning the broad waterway which once provided convenient access to the city from the mainland (which later derives from canal of San Girolamo (which runs parallel to the railway bridge). The other hypothesis is that the word derives from the reeds and canes which used to abound in this area. In any case, a system of straight, parallel canals, with long derives cross the sestiere, southwards and linked by calli, criss-cross the sestiere, workmen's houses interspersed with magnificent palaces. To the south, behind the palaces of the Grand Canal, a wide street known as the Strada Nuova, built at the end of the last century. Now pedestrianized, it runs from the station to the Campo Santi Apostoli, crossing a number of different names as it goes. Few people lived in this sestiere until the 11th century, and it seems to have taken form only gradually, as the process of draining and consolidating the shore progressed. From the 15th century onwards, Cannaregio was a definable quarter, though it was still peripheral to Venice proper. Before the railway bridge and the station were built, manufacturing was the principal industry in this district, despite attempts to create a new area of green within the Fondamenta Nuove. A similar project in the 16th century, the draining of the Sacca della Misericordia, was also never realized.

Santa Lucia Station

Half a day

THE GATEWAY TO VENICE ★

PONTE DELLA LIBERTÀ. Built by the Austrians 50 years after the Treaty of Campo Formio in 1797 ● 34, to link Venice with Milan. The bridge ended the thousand-year separation from the mainland and shook the city's economy to its roots as Venice, already in the throes of the industrial revolution, saw its dependence on the mainland grow out of all recognition. **SANTA LUCIA STATION.** The present station dates from 1954, but still bears the name of the Renaissance church, demolished in 1861 to make way for it. Opposite is the green dome of the Church of San Simeone Piccolo.

BRIDGES TO VENICE. The Austrians conceived a project for a bridge to connect Mestre and Venice as early as 1841 but it was not until 1846 that the construction of the Ponteminario began. The single span of this new viaduct was almost 11,500 feet, some 222 arches. On April 25, 1933, the Ponte della Libertà was opened. Built in less than two years by motor cars.

260

THE GATEWAY TO VENICE ★

PONTE DELLA LIBERTÀ. Built by the Austrians 50 years after the Treaty of Campo Formio in 1797 ● 34, to link Venice with Milan. The bridge ended the thousand-year separation from the mainland and shook the city's economy to its roots as Venice, already in the throes of the industrial revolution, saw

✖ Half a day

BRIDGES TO VENICE

★ The star symbol signifies that a particular site has been singled out by the publishers for its special beauty, atmosphere or cultural interest.

● ▲ ■ ◆

The symbols alongside a title or within the text itself provide cross-references to a theme or place dealt with elsewhere in the guide.

At the beginning of each itinerary, the suggested means of transport to be used and the time it will take to cover the area indicated:

🚤 By boat
✖ On foot
🚲 By bicycle
🕐 Duration

NATURE

BIOGEOGRAPHY

The *adobe* (sun-dried mudbrick ● *126*) houses of a highland basin, at about 6,500 feet, are scattered among the *milpas* ● *22*.

Maya territory occupies the western half of the Central American isthmus and is divided into highlands and lowlands. The proximity of two coasts, the contrasts of rainfall due to the the tropical climate, and the varied relief explain the different environments which occur. The highlands, bordered by the volcanic cordillera (Sierra Madre) along the Pacific coast and the limestone Cuchumatanes in the north, have hot, temperate and cold regions according to altitude, all with different ecological characteristics. While the narrow Pacific coastal plain suffers prolonged winter drought, the Caribbean slopes and benchlands (piedmont plains) are exposed to the regular flow of the eastern trade winds and have high levels of rainfall.

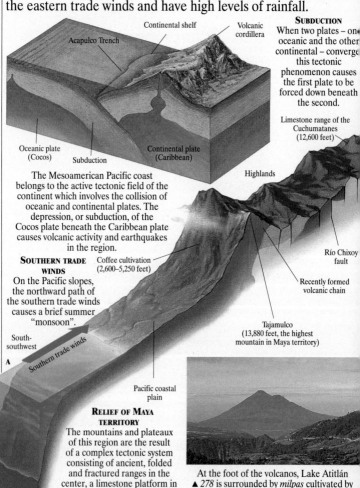

Continental shelf

Acapulco Trench

Volcanic cordillera

SUBDUCTION
When two plates – one oceanic and the other continental – converge this tectonic phenomenon causes the first plate to be forced down beneath the second.

Oceanic plate (Cocos) Subduction Continental plate (Caribbean)

Limestone range of the Cuchumatanes (12,600 feet)

The Mesoamerican Pacific coast belongs to the active tectonic field of the continent which involves the collision of oceanic and continental plates. The depression, or subduction, of the Cocos plate beneath the Caribbean plate causes volcanic activity and earthquakes in the region.

Highlands

SOUTHERN TRADE WINDS
On the Pacific slopes, the northward path of the southern trade winds causes a brief summer "monsoon".

Coffee cultivation (2,600–5,250 feet)

Río Chixoy fault

Recently formed volcanic chain

Tajamulco (13,880 feet, the highest mountain in Maya territory)

South-southwest

Southern trade winds

A

Pacific coastal plain

RELIEF OF MAYA TERRITORY
The mountains and plateaux of this region are the result of a complex tectonic system consisting of ancient, folded and fractured ranges in the center, a limestone platform in the north and a chain of recently formed volcanos in the south.

At the foot of the volcanos, Lake Atitlán ▲ *278* is surrounded by *milpas* cultivated by Indian communities who also live by fishing and traditional crafts.

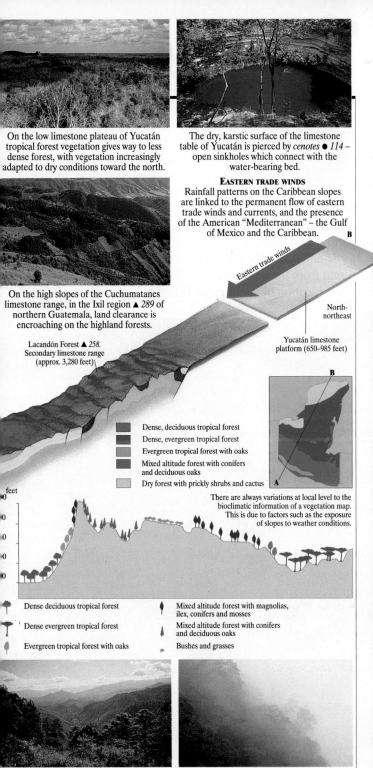

On the low limestone plateau of Yucatán tropical forest vegetation gives way to less dense forest, with vegetation increasingly adapted to dry conditions toward the north.

The dry, karstic surface of the limestone table of Yucatán is pierced by *cenotes* ● *114* – open sinkholes which connect with the water-bearing bed.

EASTERN TRADE WINDS
Rainfall patterns on the Caribbean slopes are linked to the permanent flow of eastern trade winds and currents, and the presence of the American "Mediterranean" – the Gulf of Mexico and the Caribbean.

Eastern trade winds

North-northeast

Yucatán limestone platform (650–985 feet)

On the high slopes of the Cuchumatanes limestone range, in the Ixil region ▲ *289* of northern Guatemala, land clearance is encroaching on the highland forests.

Lacandón Forest ▲ *258.* Secondary limestone range (approx. 3,280 feet)

Dense, deciduous tropical forest
Dense, evergreen tropical forest
Evergreen tropical forest with oaks
Mixed altitude forest with conifers and deciduous oaks
Dry forest with prickly shrubs and cactus

There are always variations at local level to the bioclimatic information of a vegetation map. This is due to factors such as the exposure of slopes to weather conditions.

feet

Dense deciduous tropical forest

Dense evergreen tropical forest

Evergreen tropical forest with oaks

Mixed altitude forest with magnolias, ilex, conifers and mosses

Mixed altitude forest with conifers and deciduous oaks

Bushes and grasses

In the mountainous regions of central Guatemala, the coniferous forest of the temperate layer has been largely cleared by peasants.

Tree-like ferns and epiphytic plants (plants which fix themselves to trees) thrive in the heavy mists and humidity of this north-facing slope in Chiapas (about 6,500 feet).

CORAL REEFS

STONE BASS, OR WRECKFISH
If threatened, the wreckfish changes
color: the lower part of its body turns
white and the upper part almost black.

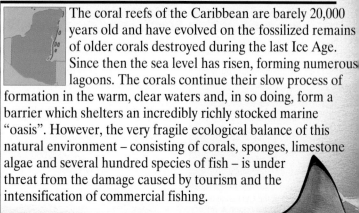

The coral reefs of the Caribbean are barely 20,000
years old and have evolved on the fossilized remains
of older corals destroyed during the last Ice Age.
Since then the sea level has risen, forming numerous
lagoons. The corals continue their slow process of
formation in the warm, clear waters and, in so doing, form a
barrier which shelters an incredibly richly stocked marine
"oasis". However, the very fragile ecological balance of this
natural environment – consisting of corals, sponges, limestone
algae and several hundred species of fish – is under
threat from the damage caused by tourism and the
intensification of commercial fishing.

BLACK-TIPPED SHARK
This coastal shark lives in groups of six to
eight individuals. It is renowned for its
agility and amazing leaps out of the water.

Sand star

Fan coral,
or sea fan

Mombin-eater

Moving basin
sponge

Moray

Sea cucumber

Sea melon

Capitaine

Bonito

Sea urchin

Sea cactus, or sea
candle, a cylindrical,
or "pillar", coral.

Royal gramma
This tiny, timid fish sometimes
swims upside down above the
many places of refuge provided
by the depths of the reef.

ROYAL ANGELFISH
One of the most brightly
colored fish on the reef,
the royal angelfish has a
blue, tiara-like mark on
its head.

ATLANTIC BIG-EYE
Although it prefers
deep water, this
striking fish does
frequent shallower
waters at certain
times of year.

BLACK ANGELFISH
This fish can grow to
almost 12 inches and
weigh up to 5½ lbs.

SQUIRREL FISH
This tiny, nocturnal
predator feeds on
crabs and shrimps.

Royal trigger fish
The trigger fish can keep
one eye on a predator
while looking for
somewhere to hide with
the other.

WHITE-SPOTTED FILE FISH
The file fish sometimes changes
its single-colored livery to one
covered with white spots.

BOXFISH
The boxfish feeds on micro-
organisms which it dislodges
by blowing onto the sand.

19

■ MANGROVES

BIRTH OF A MANGROVE
The leaves and flowers of mangroves are at the
end of the branch (**1**). When it reaches maturity,
the fruit germinates on the tree (**2**).

The coastal strips of marshland around the Yucatán Peninsula and along the Pacific shores of Guatemala are rich in plant and animal life. Between the tropical forest and the Caribbean, impenetrable networks of vegetation – mangroves – invade the muddy deposits which teem with aquatic life. Their long, submerged and intertwined roots provide shelter for fish and shellfish, while their numerous "islets" harbor colonies of nesting birds.

BOA CONSTRICTOR
The boa constrictor is the largest snake in
Central America. Harmless to human beings,
it hunts birds, mammals and reptiles and
crushes them to death.

LOGGERHEAD TURTLE
These turtles live in shallow waters, feeding
on fish, jellyfish, shellfish and algae. Between
May and September they leave the sea to lay
their eggs on the beaches.

Magnificent frigate bird

The mangrove's stilt roots
enable it to grow on the
loose substratum of the
salt marshes.

BROWN PELICAN
Extremely awkward on land, this bird is an
extremely strong flier and a skilled fisherman,
using its beak as a fishing net.

Barnacle
Oyster
Algae

The fruit produces a dart-like plantlet about 11 inches long (**3**) which frees itself from the branch, falls into the mud and takes root (**4**).

Mangrove roots form a sort of buttress around the tree and become inextricably entangled. The animals which seek refuge among the roots attract large numbers of predators.

Fanworms

Sponges

MANATEE, OR SEA COW ▲ *312*

The manatee lives in the fresh waters of estuaries and coastal lagoons. It is disturbed by the turbulence caused by motor boats and has disappeared from areas where this kind of traffic is frequent.

SCARLET IBIS

The scarlet ibis nests in the most inaccessible parts of the mangrove. Overhunted for its superb red plumage, today it is on the verge of extinction.

Male performing his courtship display

MAGNIFICENT FRIGATE BIRD

This superbly aerial bird makes headlong chases to catch a fish that has just surfaced or to snatch another bird's prey.

Brown heron

Great white heron, or American egret

BROWN HERON

This wading bird nests on mangrove "islets" along with other species of heron.

NEOTROPIC CORMORANT

This common bird rarely wanders out to sea. It is also often seen on inland lakes.

21

■ "MILPA"

Milpa – a Mexican word
derived from Nahuatl, meaning
"freshly cleared ground" – is an area of cultivated forest. In
Maya tradition trees are ancestors and cutting them down would
be commiting murder. To ensure that the forest regenerates,
land must be cleared according to precise rules and rituals
which require an excellent knowledge of the environment and
the many species of plant life. Corn is not the only crop grown
on the plot. A number of different crops are developed through
a remarkable combination of archaic techniques and highly
complex systems of irrigation, drainage, terracing and soil
classification, all adapted to the particular region.

"Coa"   **LAND CLEARANCE**
Land is cleared using the axe or *bat* and the
machete-like *coa* or *lotche*, and is usually
carried out in August when the wood is at its
most tender. A hardworking peasant can clear
2–3 *mécates* (960–1,430 square yards) per day.

BURNING. The Maya walk round their plots
lighting fires with a torch at regular
intervals and whistling to invoke
beneficent winds – an act
considered vital for a
successful harvest.

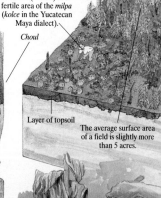

Peasant (*kolkab*) in a
fertile area of the *milpa*
(*kolce* in the Yucatecan
Maya dialect).

Choul

SOWING. Corn is sown "between the stones"
with a sort of dibble called a *choul*, a
traditional tool which has undergone only one
development since prehistoric times: the
point, originally hardened by fire, has been
replaced by a steel tip.

Layer of topsoil

The average surface area
of a field is slightly more
than 5 acres.

Implement for
extracting the cob
from its sheath

WEEDING. Since the 1970's, weedkillers have
gradually replaced the use of the *coa* for
weeding. However, peasants are becoming
increasingly aware of their disadvantages and
are adopting less harsh methods.

HARVEST. The women and children help
with the harvest and, sometimes, other
peasants who in turn enlist help for their
own harvest. The average yield is in the
order of 1,320 lbs of corn per 2½ acres.

Corn

The stems of the cobs are "broken" in September–October to prevent the grain being rotted by rain or pecked by birds.

Beans

Marrow

VARIETIES OF CORN
The several varieties of this starch-rich cereal crop are classified according to color and ripening period (2–5 months). It is almost always grown with beans and marrows, whose seeds are sown in the same hole as the corn seeds.

MIXED CROPS

Red and black beans

Marrow

Gourd

Sweet potato

Tomatoes

Bananas

Chili

In the richer areas of soil – usually located in small, damp depressions known as *k'op* – the peasants plant various food crops: pulses, tubers, fruit and vegetables and, of course, chilies ● 86.

Stony ground where corn is grown "between the stones"

Pasel

Forest canopy

Cenote

Palm tree left during clearance

Permeable, karstic layer

MILLING
After the harvest, the corn has to be turned into flour. Today the millstone has been replaced by a hand- or motor-operated mill.

MAKING TORTILLAS
The rhythmic sound of women slapping corn pancakes into shape can be heard late in the morning in any Maya village.

23

TROPICAL FOREST

Original area of tropical forest
Lowland tropical forest
High altitude tropical forest

Maya territory has the largest expanse of tropical forest in Central America. In the drier parts of Yucatán, the so-called lowlands, this is "dry" vegetation consisting of relatively low-growing, deciduous trees. Further south the rainfall increases and the forest becomes taller and more luxuriant as, for example, in Petén and Chiapas. This wet jungle, or tropical rainforest, is found up to altitudes of around 6,500 feet where it is replaced by conifers. The uncontrolled development of agriculture and stockbreeding and the exploitation of timber in recent decades have destroyed a large part of this ecosystem, in spite of the creation of nature reserves.

The tropical forest constitutes the richest ecosystem in the world and contains almost half the world's flora and fauna. A wide diversity of species is often accompanied by low numbers of individuals in any given area, with the result that populations are small and vulnerable. This biodiversity also gives rise to complex food chains and an appropriate distribution of species within a particular environment, each fulfilling its own ecological function.

AMAZON PARROT ▶
Amazon parrots fly rapidly through the forest in small, noisy bands.

BLUE COTINGA ▶
The brilliant color of the male can look dull when seen against the light.

▲ GREAT CURASSOW
This flightless bird is under threat today from deforestation and hunting.

KING VULTURE ▶
Its keen sense of smell enables this bird to locate animal carcasses, even when in flight.

▲ NINE-BANDED ARMADILLO
The armadillo is hunted for its flesh and skin.

▲ OCELLATED TURKEY
This bird lives on the edge of the forest. It has been hunted to extinction in many regions of Central America.

▲ BAIRD'S TAPIR
The tapir is the largest land mammal in Central America and can weigh up to 440 lbs.

▲ COLLARED PECCARY, OR MEXICAN HOG
The peccary is widely hunted by the Indians.

▲ AGOUTI
This rodent is commonly found in the undergrowth, near water.

◄ **RESPLENDENT QUETZAL**
Mainly found in the mountain forests of Chiapas and Verapaz ▲ *293*.

SCARLET MACAW ▼
Its powerful beak enables it to crack open the shells of the hardest fruit.

KEEL-BILLED TOUCAN ▲
This toucan prefers the high tree-tops where it feeds on fruit.

HARPY EAGLE ▼
This rare, forest-dwelling eagle hunts mammals, reptiles and birds.

BLACK HOWLER MONKEY ▲
Once the sacred animal of the Maya, this monkey is now threatened by the disappearance of the tropical forest.

IRGINIA ►
POSSUM
his small, octurnal mnivore a marsupial.

BLACK-HANDED SPIDER MONKEY ◄
The spider monkey's prehensile tail and long limbs enable it to move from tree to tree with amazing speed and agility.

CELOT ▼
ound only in tropical gions of America, is cat is important Mayan culture.

▼ **PUMA**
One of the most adaptable of all cats, the puma is found throughout the American continent from humid forests to mountains.

▲ **RING-TAILED COATI**
Mainly diurnal, the coati uses its tail to improve its balance when climbing trees.

▲**TAYRA**
Active at night and in the morning, the ayra feeds mainly on rodents. It has become ncreasingly rare as a result of deforestation.

▲ **JAGUAR**
This beautiful big cat is a formidable hunter. For the Maya the jaguar embodied the night sun.

■ FOREST LAYERS

CACAO
The Maya already knew how to prepare the "nectar of the gods" using the beans from the cacao tree, which can reach heights of 50 feet.

The tropical forest of Central America is so rich that in some places there are more than a hundred species of trees in an area of 2 acres. Its various layers of vegetation harbor a wide variety of flora and fauna and have a particularly complex structure, characterized by the profusion of lianas (woody, free-hanging climbing plants) and epiphytes such as orchids and bromeliads. The trees usually have large, rigid leaves and huge buttressed roots, like those of the silk-cotton tree.

Young trees can reach heights of up to 165 feet.

CANOPY

LIFE AT ALL LEVELS
Young trees harbor insects, bats and predatory animals, while the canopy is the domain of monkeys and multicolored butterflies. Snakes and tree frogs live in the intermediate layer and mammals find shelter among the smaller trees and undergrowth.

SAPODILLA
This lactiferous tree produces chicle, a form of latex used to make chewing gum ▲ 330.

Epiphytes

INTERMEDIATE LAYER

"STANTOPEA OCULATA"
This epiphytic orchid with its heady perfume grows "upside down" on the branches of tall trees.

Palm tree forming part of the lower level of smaller trees. Palms do not grow very tall and need a minimum amount of light.

Some lianas strangle and kill their host trees.

SHRUB LAYER

"LYCASTE SKINERI"
This pink orchid, the national emblem of Guatemala, is found mainly in the wet, mountain forests.

The soil on the forest floor is poor and the trees have shallow but extensive root systems.

HISTORY

● History

12000 BC	8000 BC	4000 BC	2000 BC	1500 B

7000 BC
Cereals begin to be cultivated in the Tehuacan Valley, Mexico.

1700 BC
First ceremonial buildings in farming villages in the Mexic Valley.

13000–9000 BC
Paintings and engravings at Lascaux (France) and Altamira (Spain).

3250–3100 BC
Invention of writing in the Near East (seals and clay tablets bearing pictographic symbols). Cuneiform writing is developed in Mesopotamia.

2600–2100 BC
Egyptian Old Kingdom.

c. 1500 B
The Arya conquer India.

ORIGINS

Humankind is thought to have arrived on the American continent at least 20,000 years ago, when a period of glaciation dried up the Bering Strait and made it possible to

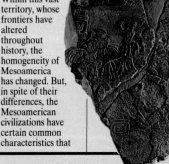

walk from Siberia to Alaska. Compared with the history of the Old World, American history is relatively recent and its cultures have developed in isolation. The reduced or non-existent role of stockbreeding in American societies (apart from the use of llamas and other camelids in the

Andean cultures) helps to explain early forms of nomadism (unrelated to the movement of flocks), reduced mobility and a slower rate of displacement of populations and individuals, because of the absence of horses and practical limitations such as the lack of the wheel. But although it may

be true that transatlantic contacts were not a determining factor, cultural diffusion would appear to be

Until c. 6000 BC the American continen was populated by small bands of hunter-gatherers whose economic activities became increasingly specialized.

the only explanation for the sometimes disconcerting similarities between, for example, Maya art and the art of the civilizations of Southeast Asia. The alternative would be to attribute these resemblances to analogous environments, parallel histories or simply the artistic limitations of the human mind and intellect.

2000 BC

MAYA TERRITORY AND SUBDIVISIONS

GULF OF MEXICO

Yucatán
3

M E X I C O

CARIBBEAN SEA

Chiapas

2

BELIZE

1

GUATEMALA

HONDURAS

PACIFIC OCEAN

EL SALVADOR

To understand the cultural variations within Maya territory, it is important to identify at least three main areas, each characterized by their own specific forms and historical development:

1. The Pacific coast and the highlands of Guatemala and El Salvador;
2. The central and southern lowlands;

3. The northern lowlands.
The history of Mayan civilization has been divided into three main periods, referred to as Preclassic, Classic and Postclassic, which are in turn divided into Early, Middle and Late. These are sometimes subdivided once again to give classes such as Protoclassic, Terminal Classic and Protohistoric.

MESOAMERICA

From 2000 BC the population of Mesoamerica was, generally speaking, sedentary. This is a precondition for the creation of societies sufficiently complex to be called civilizations. The term "Mesoamerica" was first used to refer to an area of civilization that included central and southern Mexico, Guatemala, Belize, El Salvador and parts of Honduras, Nicaragua and Costa Rica. Within this vast territory, whose frontiers have altered throughout history, the homogeneity of Mesoamerica has changed. But, in spite of their differences, the Mesoamerican civilizations have certain common characteristics that

give the region its unity, whether looked at from an economic standpoint (the importance of the maize–squash–bean crops, agricultural techniques, trade networks and markets) or from an artistic, religious or intellectual angle. The Late Preclassical Stele 10 from Kaminaljuyú (below).

1200 BC		600 BC	500 BC	900 AD		
Building of the first Olmec centers in Mexico.		Beginning of the Preclassic Maya civilization.	Start of the Zapotec civilization at Monté Alban.			c. 0 Teotihuacán begun.

1000 BC		800 BC		400 BC		200 BC		100 BC

1200 BC	800 BC	753 BC	336–323 BC	146 BC
Trojan War and collapse of the Hittite empire.	Beginning of the Etruscan civilization.	Foundation of Rome.	Empire of Alexander the Great.	Carthage destroyed by the Romans.

PRECLASSIC AND PROTOCLASSIC (2000 BC–AD 250)

CALENDAR

The Maya are famed for having possessed the most elaborate form of writing in America ● 42 and for having been the only people to measure time using the Long Count (a system starting from an imaginary point corresponding to 3114 BC) ● 44. Paradoxically they do not appear to have invented either but inherited the already complex systems developed by the successors of the Olmecs along the coast of the Gulf of Mexico and in Oaxaca, where calendric and other types of glyphs, as well as numbers represented by bars and dots (all dating from 600–450 BC), have been identified. Stele C at Tres Zapotes, on the Gulf coast, bears a date which uses the same type of numbers but without the period glyphs, and corresponds to 31 BC. On the Pacific coast, dates from the 1st and 2nd centuries AD have been found on the sites of El Baúl (detail of stele, below left, dating from the Late Classic period).

THE OLMECS

San Lorenzo and La Venta (sculpture below) were inhabited by the Olmecs in 1250 and c. 1100 BC respectively. Monumental sculpture (above) played an important role in these centers. Olmec society had a clearly defined hierarchy, highly developed traditional crafts, and an extensive trade network, and its works of art were spread widely across the whole of Mesoamerica by the 1st millennium BC.

THE OLMEC HERITAGE

During the Late Preclassic the sites of Izapa on the Pacific coast and Kaminaljuyú in the highlands demonstrated the sophistication of the calendar and writing system by extending and developing the Olmec heritage. If the Izapa and Kaminaljuyú sculptural styles provide the transition between Olmec and Mayan art of the Early Classic period, it would seem reasonable to suppose that direct contacts existed between the Olmecs and the Maya in other areas. For instance, during their early history the Maya, surprisingly, developed a taste for gigantism, as illustrated by the structures of La Danta and El Mirador which reach heights of 230 feet! In spite of conditions unfavorable to agriculture, important centers developed in the northern lowlands during the Middle and Late Preclassic periods, probably as a result of trade developments. Komchén and Cerros (in Belize) seem to have been staging posts for Yucatec maritime trade.

31

```
c. 250                        250–650
Beginning of the Maya         Golden age of
Classic period.               Teotihuacán.
100        200        300        400        500

                    c. 400–c.    476
            c. 200   1450         Fall of the last
            End of the Han   Byzantine   Western Roman
            Dynasty (China).  empire.     emperor.
```

CLASSIC (250–1000)

A PERIOD OF PROGRESS

In the Classic Maya period, rules of dynastic succession were established and royal power began to manifest itself in art. Both aspects were notably combined in the central lowlands at the end of the 3rd century. The Classic Maya civilization marks the end of a long process of development begun by the latest in the 6th or 5th century BC. The complex societies that built such sites as Nakbé and El Mirador ultimately adopted and then developed the calendar and writing system inherited from the west and south. However, the corbeled vault was a local invention, since it was never used in the highlands. The early steles of Tikal ▲ 324 and Uaxactún ▲ 328 bear an image of the king accompanied by a text which gives, among other things, his name, his date of accession and the name of his city. They provide evidence of the emergence of the state as a system of social and political organization and also of the birth of rival states who would divide up the Maya territory between them. Carved panel (left) at Palenque ▲ 243.

A HIERARCHICAL SOCIETY

Mayan society was divided into classes and professions such as craftsmen and merchants. It was subject to the authority of a centralized government which ruled a territory whose boundaries were clearly defined. The political authority, headed by the king who represented his community, had an army and administration at its disposal. The emblem glyphs appear to designate the state rather than the city, which would explain why several cities used the same emblem. The political map of the Classic Maya territory was a constantly changing mosaic, with the various states acquiring and then losing control of secondary centers which passed into other hands. The Classic Maya civilization was essentially urban. Although they did not look like modern-day towns and cities, Maya centers performed the same function and were responsible for important artistic and intellectual achievements.

DEFINITION
The term "Classic" is used here to define development characterized by the simultaneous appearance of the Mayan corbeled vault in architecture, steles, hieroglyphic writing ● 42 (below) and the calculation of time using the Long Count ● 44.

c. 600	c. 800	c. 900	c. 950
Height of the Zapotec civilization:	Beginning of the decline of the Maya civilization.	End of the Zapotec civilization at Monte Albán.	Arrival of the Toltecs at Tula.

600   **700**   **800**   **900**   **1000**

c. 610	685	800	900–1000
Birth of Islam.	Buddhism becomes the state religion of Japan	Charlemagne crowned emperor in Rome.	Viking expeditions to America.

EARLY CLASSIC (250–600)

he only good xample of the ubdivision of the lassic period is ound in the central owlands. The ighlands, to the outh, passed under he control of eotihuacán and developed along alternative lines characterized by a combination of local Mayan and central Mexican elements. When the great Mexican city fell to the northern barbarians, its trading posts and colonies experienced a degree of difficulty in re-establishing themselves. For example, Kaminaljuyú and the surrounding region suffered a period of decline in spite of the fact that trading links with the lowlands remained intact. Little is known of the Early Classic period in the northern lowlands. Tikal was one of the most important cities of that period. Stele 29 bears the earliest known date on a Mayan monument (corresponding to AD 292), while evidence of the presence and authority of Teotihuacán is apparent on Stele 4 on the same site. The erection of steles at the end of the period is illustrated for the first time at Tikal (Temple 1, right), with the celebration of the end of the eighteenth *katun* of the eighth *baktun* (July 6, 396) ● 44.

The end of the Early Classic is marked by a period of decline which was represented by a worsening in the quality of funeral paraphernalia and an interruption of the custom of periodically erecting steles. This period, referred to as the "hiatus", lasted from 534 until 593 and, at Tikal, until 692. It is presumed that the collapse of Teotihuacán and its empire provoked a serious crisis for the Mayan dynasties. The return to normal, with the resumption of the erection of steles, marks the beginning of the Late Classic period.

LATE CLASSIC (600–800)

ikal's ▲ 322 most mpressive structures ate from this period. t also marked the eight of the glory of alenque ▲ 243, which did not become mportant until the th century and egan to decline from 00 onwards. The olden age of axchilán ▲ 248 egan in c. 630 with ird Jaguar II. Copán ▲ 299, whose valley was occupied from he Middle Preclassic eriod became the nost important city n the eastern rontier of Maya erritory with the oundation of the Yax Kuk Mo dynasty in he 5th century. Quirigua ▲ 306, ounded shortly fterwards, was lominated by its reat neighbor and ival until 737, when it captured nd put to death ighteen Rabbit, he powerful king f Copán. During his period cities in central Yucatán ▲ 190, such as Becán, Xpuhil (bottom right) and Chicanná, reached their apogee. Figurine from Jaina ▲ 230 (below).

TERMINAL CLASSIC (800–1000)

The end of the eighteenth *katun* of the ninth *baktun* (AD 790) was celebrated by the erection of the greatest number of steles known. At this time population density had reached a maximum in the central lowlands. The northern lowlands would soon become famous. With the exception of cities such as Dzibilchaltún ▲ 216, northern Yucatán remained sparsely populated with no majorly important cities.

The situation changed during the 9th century, however, with the development of the Puuc ▲ 220 cities of Uxmal, Labná, Sayil and Kabáh (due to the combined action of foreign Putún and Chontal groups from the Tabasco coast) and of the Chenes and Río Bec centers to the south.

33

c. 1220–1400
Fall of Chichén Itzá and dominance
of Mayapán in Yucatán.

1100	1150	1200	1250	1300

1099
First crusade and
capture of
Jerusalem.

c. 1200
Apogee of the Mongol
empire (conquest of
northern China).

1206
Treaty of Guadalajara
between Castile, Aragon
and Navarre.

c. 1240
Major construction of
cathedrals throughout
Europe

THE BEGINNING OF THE DECLINE

In the 9th century the central lowlands experienced a decline marked by the end of the steles and architectural activity, which represented a breakdown in the organization of traditional political and religious power. Although the population did not disappear, it was significantly reduced during the ensuing period. Centers such as Copán and Palenque ceased to function after 800. By 830 only one tenth of the city of Tikal was occupied. The most recent stele of the central lowlands (AD 909) was found at Toniná ▲ 242. The only exception to this general collapse was Ceibal ▲ 331, which experienced its golden age between 830 and 930. The foreign style of its steles is undoubtedly due to Putún influence. This Mexicanized group from the coast of Tabasco or the north of Yucatán is thought to have reached the Río Pasión by following the Usumacinta upstream. In northern Belize ▲ 340, which escaped the general decline, some major structures were built.

CHICHÉN ITZÁ ▲ 205
This city experienced its golden age during the Postclassic period. The Caracol (above), detail of fresco and a Chacmool (below), and columns from the Temple of the Warriors (right).

CAUSES OF THE DECLINE

In spite of many hypotheses, it is now known that the decline was not so much a sudden collapse or abrupt disappearance as a process of cultural decay which took place over a period of a century. There were a number of contributory factors. Famine was always a risk after a succession of poor crops from the unstable tropical soil. Also the political fragmentation into city-states caused great rivalry as cities tried to surpass their neighbors in magnificence and incurred expenditure which proved ruinous. The final failure of the Maya civilization highlights the fragility of its foundations and its inability to adapt. The first disasters caused the break-up of trade networks, rebellions, wars and invasions, a chain reaction which accelerated the process of disintegration.

POSTCLASSIC (1000–1500)

EARLY POSTCLASSIC (1000–1250)

From AD 1000 Chichén Itzá ▲ 205 became one of the most important sites in the lowlands. During this period the city was characterized by the development of a series of new features which were urban, architectural and iconographic in character and of Mexican origin. Certain of these elements, such as the *tzompantli* (platform carved with human skulls), had already been introduced to the Puuc ▲ 218 by the Putún–Chontal Maya. Others seem to have come direct from Tula, the Toltec capital of the Mexican basin during the Early Postclassic. During the Postclassic period, Chichén Itzá is therefore described as Maya-Toltec (fresco from the Temple of the Jaguars, left). The connection between Tula and Chichén Itzá has still not been clarified. Indeed, the latter is the only Maya–Toltec site in the lowlands, and there is no known staging post between Chichén Itzá and Tula, which are separated by a distance of some 870 miles.

1325	1438	1492	1519–21
Foundation by the Aztecs of the city of Tenochtitlán (future Mexico).	Beginning of Inca expansionism.	Columbus discovers America, which has a population of about 100 million.	Hernán Cortés conquers the Aztec empire and founds Mexico.

1350		1400		1450		1500		1550

1337	1368	1440	1453	1494	1508–15
Beginning of the Hundred Years' War.	Accession of the Chinese Ming dynasty.	Gutenberg invents printing.	Constantinople captured by the Turks.	Treaty of Tortesillas: Portugal and Spain divide up the New World.	Spanish conquest of Cuba and Puerto Rico.

COASTAL AND MOUNTAIN SITES

Apart from Chichén Itzá, there were very few Early Postclassic sites of any importance in the north. In the central Maya territory some Classic cities were inhabited by groups who lived among the ruins without building anything of significance.

along the Yucatecan coast. The changes observed in the highlands at the end of the Classic period were beginning: sites on plains were abandoned in favor of easily defended locations perched on hills or plateaus, a development attributed to new

However, this was not the case in northern Belize ▲ 340, where sites such as Lamanai (remains above), Nohmul, Cerros and Altún Ha were the object of much architectural activity. A few coastal sites constituted other exceptions and suggest the existence of maritime trade

external influences which, by following the natural routes of the Río Usumacinta and Río Motagua, correspond to Chichén Itzá's dominance of Yucatán.

LATE POSTCLASSIC (1250–1525)

After the fall of Chichén Itzá, Mayapán ▲ 212 became the dominant city in Yucatán. The new capital was, once again, the object of Mexican influence but differed considerably from its predecessor, as it did from all the cities of the Classic Maya. The ten thousand or so inhabitants of this walled city were crowded around a political and ceremonial center. The fine masonry of the Puuc sites and Chichén Itzá was replaced by a crude, dry-stone bonding, and the design of the houses changed. So, too, did the form of worship: domestic oratories and sanctuaries were built and huge incense burners, fashioned in terracotta designed to represent the gods (Postclassic censer, right) ● 48. Mayapán was the center of an alliance that dominated Yucatán until the mid 15th century. There seems to have been more

settlement then than during the Early Postclassic period: the eastern coast of the peninsula in particular, with the sites of Xel-Há, Cozumel, Tulum ▲ 177 and Santa Rita, was a maritime trade zone. There were also later sites in the region of Lago Petén Itzá (Topoxté). After the fall of Mayapán, north Yucatán was once again politically fragmented into a series of small "rival states". The highlands witnessed the development of small centers in powerful (rival) regional capitals. At the time of the Spanish conquest Mixco Viejo ▲ 268 was the capital of the Pokomams, Zaculeu ▲ 284 of the Mams, Iximché of the Cakchiquels and Utatlán of the Quichés. The Quichés extended their territory at the expense of their neighbors until the late 15th century, when their king was defeated by the Cakchiquels.

1562
Diego de Landa has a large number
of Mayan manuscripts burned.

1560   1562   1564   1566   1568

1556
Abdication of Charles V
and accession of Philip II
to the Spanish throne.

1561
Madrid
becomes the
capital of Spain.

1562. Beginning
of the Wars of
Religion in
France.

1563. Council of Trent
ends after establishing
principles of the
Counter Reformation.

1565
The Spanish
conquer the
Philippines.

1565
Foundation of t
Portuguese colo
of Rio de Janeir

THE SPANISH CONQUEST (16TH–17TH CENTURIES)

FROM CORDOBA TO CORTÉS

The Spanish conquest of the Americas began with the colonization of Hispaniola (modern Haiti and the Dominican Republic) and Cuba, and continued with forays launched from these islands. In 1517 Hernández de Córdoba (right) led an expedition in search of slaves, gold and new territory. He discovered the Isla Mujeres ▲ 174, near Cozumel, and then sailed along the coast of Yucatán to Champotón ▲ 230, where he suffered heavy losses at the hands of the Maya. The next expedition, led by Juan de Grijalva, took five months to sail round the peninsula as far as the Río Pánuco. Finally

Hernán Cortés (below) set sail on February 18, 1519 with eleven vessels.

He traveled round the peninsula and across the Gulf of Mexico landing at Veracruz, where he burned his boats (the grounded fleet, center). The Aztecs were conquered in a year, but it took another twenty years to conquer Yucatán.

TOWARDS THE HIGHLANDS

In 1523 Cortés asked his lieutenant, Pedro de Alvarado (above, right), to explore the territory now known as Guatemala. The efficient but bloodthirsty Alvarado occupied the province of Soconusco on the Pacific coast and confronted the Quichés, putting them to flight when he killed their chief Tecún Umán (far right). At Utatlán ▲ 288, the Quiché capital, he killed the royal family and successfully attacked Iximché ▲ 276, the capital of the Cakchiquels. His brother Gonzalo occupied Zaculeu ▲ 284, the Mam capital. The Tzutuhils were defeated at Atitlán, and the Pipils at Escuintla. The terrified Maya of the Guatemalan highlands surrendered *en masse*, and Alvarado founded the capital at Santiago de los Caballeros, now Ciudad Vieja ▲ 275. There was continued resistance in Chiapas. Luis Marín attacked but was only partly successful against the Tzotzils and Tzeltals in 1524. Eight years later Mazariegos took them by surprise, but rather than surrender the Indians threw themselves into the Sumidero canyon ▲ 260. In 1528 Mazariegos founded Villa Real, now San Cristóbal da las Casas ▲ 233. Alvarado had founded Comitán, and the two lieutenants, now rivals, divided up the land and the people among their soldiers.

COLONIZATION

The colonial regime was firmly established with Montejo in Yucatán and Alvarado in Guatemala. There were a few short-lived attempts to shake off the Spanish yoke, but a firm hand soon destroyed any hope of autonomy. However, the region inhabited by Chol groups in central Guatemala, to the southwest of modern Belize, remained inaccessible and unconquered. Fray Bartolomé de

GOLPH
MEXI
BAYE

| 1571 | 1572 |
| A tribunal of the Inquisition is established in Mexico. | The Jesuits arrive in Mexico. |

| 1570 | 1572 | 1574 | 1576 | 1578 |

| 1568 | 1570 | 1572 | 1574 | 1576 |
| The Spanish explore Oceania. | The Council of the Indies promulgates a law prohibiting mestizos from holding office as lawyers or caciques. | In Spain, Sister Theresa of Avila writes *The Book of the Foundations*. She is canonized in 1622. | | An epidemic kills 40 percent of the Indians in New Spain |

RESISTANCE

In 1525 Cortés travelled to Honduras to quash a bid by one of his lieutenants for independence. He stopped at Tayasal ▲ *321*, the capital of the Itzás. Almost a century later missionaries from Yucatán paid a second visit to the city without obtaining anything from its king, Canek. A third expedition failed in 1622, and it was not until 1697 that the city fell to the troops of Martín de Ursua, governor of Yucatán. Another expedition left Guatemala for Tayasal, where it was to join up with troops from Yucatán. It occupied Dolores, the center of the unvanquished Lacandons. The Maya territory was finally conquered over two centuries after Columbus had first "discovered" America.

Las Casas and his Dominicans succeeded where all military initiatives had failed. They established their mission there and brought the region, subsequently named Verapaz, peacefully under Spanish rule. However, vast areas of jungle, between the mountains of Guatemala and northern Yucatán, remained unconquered. Maya warrior (right) depicted on a Classic vase.

GUATEMALA AND NEW SPAIN

The function of Captain General of Guatemala was created in 1542 and subsequently incorporated in the *Audiencia de los Confines*, whose jurisdiction covered the whole of Central America down to Costa Rica and included Yucatán. In 1565 the *Audiencia* was moved to Panamá, while Guatemala and Yucatán became part of New Spain (Mexico). Five years later the *Audiencia de Guatemala* was established to cover Chiapas, Honduras, El Salvador, Costa Rica and Nicaragua. Yucatán remained annexed to Mexico.

AUDIENCIA DE LOS CONFINES
The *Audiencia*, a legislative and legal tribunal established in 1543, counter-balanced the powers of the Captain General in Guatemala.

1588
Philip II allows mestizos to become priests provided they are born in wedlock.

1601
Indian cacique rebellion against the Spanish in Mexico.

1585   1610   1635   1660   1685

1584
The British colonize Virginia.

1588
Defeat of the invincible Spanish Armada.

1600
Creation of the British East India Company.

1626
Foundation of New Amsterdam.

1668
Spain recognizes Portuguese independence.

1685
A French color established in Texas.

THE COLONIAL REGIME

THE INDIANS AS ROYAL SUBJECTS

Spanish America formed a vast unit of over six million square miles that was subject to the same legal regime and administered by royal officials. Under Spanish law the Indians were considered subjects of the Spanish crown and slavery was outlawed, which harmed the purses and angered the early conquistadors. They were opposed by jurists, theologians and men of the church including Vitoria, Montesinos and especially Las Casas ▲ 234, who had witnessed the abuse of the Indians during the conquest of Cuba. As Bishop of Chiapas he continued his humanitarian work (Las Casas' book, below). Spanish laws and especially the *Recopilación de las Leyes de Indias*, promulgated in 1681 by Charles II (above), gave the empire a strong legal unity. However, regional variations were taken into account by the Crown and the Council of the Indies. Codicils were added to the general laws to provide solutions to local problems.

AUTOS-DA-FÉ
Indian beliefs persisted in spite of Christianization. At Maní (Yucatán), Landa ● 42 ordered an *auto-da-fé* during which Indians were tortured and executed, and hundreds of idols and more than twenty Mayan codices burnt. *Auto-da-fé* at Solotepec (right).

THE INDIANS UNDER THREAT

As well as being slaughtered during the Conquest itself, the Indians also fell victim to viral infections transmitted by the Spaniards which

decimated the population. The survivors were concentrated in the villages (*reducciones*) and made subject to the Indian nobility, who collected tributes in the name of the Spanish authorities. Spaniards were forbidden to live in Indian villages, and only monks came into contact with the native population. To aid them in their mission, the monks appointed a *maestro cantor* or *fiscal* in each village who taught the catechism and presided over the recitation of prayers. The increase in the power of the *maestros* and the simultaneous re-emergence of ancient beliefs resulted in *autos-da-fé*. These in turn provoked rebellions, including those of Canek (Yucatán) in 1671, Chiapas in 1692, and the Tzeltal rebellion at Cancuc, which was harshly repressed by Cosio in 1713.

RIVALRY WITH BRITAIN

Guatemala and Chiapas, situated far from the pirate-infested coasts and lacking the mineral resources which altered the established agricultural order, lived peacefully through the colonial period. Yucatán, exposed to the plundering of the pirates and too sparsely populated to offer any form of effective resistance, fell victim to the numerous attacks that caused the depopulation of wha is now the coast of Quintana Roo. The British had established themselves near the Laguna de Términos in southern Campeche, and occupied a vast territory where they exploited the mahogany and logwood (used in dyeing) and threatened navigatio in the Gulf of Mexico Driven out by the Spanish in 1716, they established themselves firmly

1731
Rebellion (begun in 1729) by the Natchez Indians of Louisiana, against the French presence, is finally crushed.

1789
Ratification of the American Constitution. George Washington becomes first president of the USA.

| 1700 | 1720 | 1740 | 1760 | 1780 |

1713
The Treaty of Utrecht confirms British maritime supremacy.

1763
The French cede their North American territories to the British.

1776–83
American War of Independence concluded by the Treaty of Paris

long the coast of resent-day Belize, rotected by the fleet nchored off Jamaica. Javal battle (below) etween the British nd Spanish in 1747. n 1763 Spain onceded the erritory of British Honduras to the British. The act was onfirmed by the Treaty of Versailles in 1783, although ownership was not finalized until the British victory of St George's Caye in September 1798. The poor soil and absence of natural resources on the peninsula meant that the province of Yucatán could not become rich. The Indians, subject to the

AFTER INDEPENDENCE

MEXICO AND THE UNITED PROVINCES OF CENTRAL AMERICA

The call for independence issued at Dolores by the Mexican priest Miguel Hidalgo, together with the liberal Constitution of Cadiz proclaimed in Spain in 1812

Yucatán, Chiapas and Guatemala. The representatives of Chiapas demanded reannexation to Mexico, which was accepted in 1822. With the fall of the Mexican emperor Agustín de Iturbide in 1823, Central America parted company with Mexico and Chiapas declared independence. Then in 1824 a plebiscite decided that Chiapas should be part of the Mexican Confederation. The United Provinces of Central America, separated from Mexico, lasted until 1839 but could not withstand the mounting waves of nationalism, and the Spanish colonies became independent countries.

CONSTITUCION política de la MONARQUIA ESPAÑOLA, PROMULGADA EN CÁDIZ

encomienda paid regular tributes to the Spanish in cotton, honey, leather, salt meat and logwood.

(above), reinforced the Creole spirit of independence. The struggle fought in central Mexico was echoed in Yucatán. Mexico declared independence in 1821, followed immediately by

| 1800 | 1820 | 1835
Beginning of hostilities
between Texas and
Mexico. | 1840 | 1860 | 1864–7
Maximilian of Austria
becomes Emperor of
Mexico. | 1880 | 190 |

1810
Rebellions as Spanish colonies fight for independence.

1819
The USA buys Florida from Spain.

1848
Annexation of Mexican territory by the USA.

1861–5
American Civil War.

1898
Spanish–American wa Cuba and the Philippi Annexation of Hawaii

YUCATÁN

After Mexican independence, in a long struggle fuelled by the Mexican government under the dictatorship of Santa Anna,

Federalists were set against Centralists. Yucatán held out against the Mexicans and declared independence from Mexico in 1841, as Texas had in 1836. The so-called "Caste War" ▲ 186 posed a threat to the whites of Yucatán, but after the American invasion Mexico supported the local government against the rebels. Yucatán was reunited with Mexico in 1848, followed by Campeche ▲ 228 in 1857.

HONDURAS AND EL SALVADOR

During the 20th century Honduras and El Salvador have both experienced political instability and relations between them have been difficult. For instance, the "Soccer War" in 1969 was only brought to an end by the intervention of the OAS (Organization of American States). Encouraged by the success of the Sandinista revolution in Nicaragua in 1979, guerrilla movements developed in El Salvador ▲ 314.

During the 1980's the US increased its military presence in Honduras to support the anti-Sandinista Contadora group in El Salvador. With the end of the revolution in Nicaragua in 1990, Honduras and El Salvador enjoyed a return to peace.

> **PEACE ACCORDS**
> Costa Rica, Guatemala, Nicaragua, El Salvador and Honduras signed a series of accords between 1987 and 1989. The civil war in El Salvador ended.

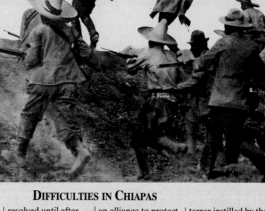

DIFFICULTIES IN CHIAPAS

Chiapas lived through the first years of independence torn between two options for their country: rule by the conservatives (the big landowners, army and high-ranking clergy), who wanted to unite it around a strong, centralized power; or by the reformists (supported by the liberals and republicans), who preferred a federation of free and independent sovereign states. The conflicts were not resolved until after the reformist triumph of 1864. However, new conflicts immediately broke out in an attempt to prevent their re-election. The victor, Miguel Utrilla, established peace in 1879. The liberals took the precaution of transferring the capital from San Cristóbal to Tuxtla Gutiérrez in 1892. The revolution (above) rekindled the old conflict between the conservatives and liberals, who formed an alliance to protect their own land interests at the expense of social achievements. The oil industry currently represents a large proportion of Mexican national production. Disputes between farmers and Indians over land-ownership, the complicity between the oligarchy and the local authorities which was at the root of an absence of laws for the protection of individuals and society as a whole, the terror instilled by the white guard, the lack of accountability, the general corruption and poverty, all culminated in the 1994 rebellion.

1910		1969–80	1987–9	
In Mexico the revolutionaries Francisco Madero and Pancho Villa seize power.		War between El Salvador and Honduras.	Peace accords in Central America (Costa Rica, Guatemala, Nicaragua, El Salvador and Honduras).	
1915	**1930**	**1945**	**1960**	**1975**	**1990**
14–18 orld ar One.	**1917** Russian Revolution.	**1939–45** World War Two.	**1957** Creation of the EEC.	**1993** Signing of ALENA (free trade agreement between the USA, Canada and Mexico).

MEXICO

Mexico adopted an imperial system in 1863 and was governed by Maximilian of Habsburg (receiving the crown of Mexico, above). The liberals subsequently expelled the new emperor, who for a time had the support of French troops sent by Napoleon III. Juárez restored the republic in 1867. A vast plan for reform adopted throughout the country included the construction of railway lines and industrialization projects, while the dictatorship of Díaz (inset, far left) encouraged the creation of vast estates and the modernization of the country. However, the state of serfdom to which the peasants were reduced and the absence of democracy led to the 1910 revolution (left), dominated by the figures of Pancho Villa and Emiliano Zapata. The ensuing period of unrest lasted until the political stability established in the 1930's by the PRI, who are still in power today.

GUERRILLA RESISTANCE
On January 1, 1994, there was a rebellion by Indians in Chiapas (below). The government negotiated.

GUATEMALA

Guatemala came into being as a nation in 1839 and adopted a liberal government, which was overthrown by the conservative Rafael Carrera. Carrera governed from 1844 to 1856 and was succeeded by Justo Rufino Barrios, who came to power following a liberal revolution and implemented many reforms. By the early 20th century, American capital controlled virtually the entire Guatemalan economy. Political unrest brought General Ubico to power, where he remained until 1944. After Arévalo, the land reforms decreed in 1954 by Colonel Jacobo Arbenz Guzman provoked the *coup d'état* led by Colonel Castillo Armas (anti-Arbenz rebel, below), who restored land to the companies. The repressive measures of successive military governments gave rise to the creation of guerrilla resistance from 1963, consolidated by the FAR (Fuerzas Armadas Revolucionarias). The country was caught up in a wave of violence, assassinations and terrorism, followed by repressive measures imposed by the army and paramilitary groups. Thousands of Indians fled to Mexico during the 1980's. The return of constitutional government in 1985 began to change things. Despite pressure from the army, negotiations continued with the guerrillas.

BELIZE

Britain's annexation in 1859 of part of Verapaz (Guatemala) put the two nations on a potential war footing. Maps of Guatemala still included Belize as part of the country. New agreements adopted a *status quo* which was, sooner or later, accepted by both countries. After World War Two the colony of British Honduras suffered a very violent economic crisis which favored the establishment of unions and political parties. Belize finally declared independence on September 21, 1981, and George Price was elected Prime Minister. Generally speaking, Belize is a poor country which lives mainly by agriculture and increasingly tourism, based on its tropical beaches and archeological sites. However, its current poor road network is an obstacle to its development ▲ 335.

● WRITING

About eight hundred different symbols have been recorded Mayan texts. The number is too great for an alphabetic or sylla form of writing but too small for a purely logographic form. somewhat whimsical records (opposite) of Waldeck ●

The Maya are the only civilization on the American continent to have developed a form of writing capable of expressing all types of thought and language through a combination of signs and symbols. As early as the Classic period the Maya had books in the form of long strips of bast paper folded in a "concertina" and covered with a fine layer of lime on which the scribe painted texts and images. There were also carved and painted inscriptions. In recent years considerable progress has been made in deciphering these texts, due to a better understanding of the true nature of the writing, in which certain symbols express concepts while others are a transcription of syllables.

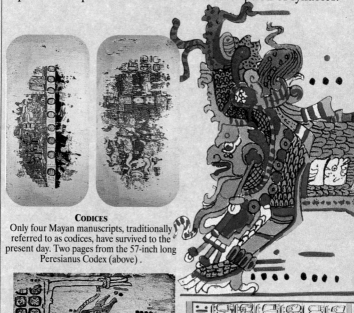

CODICES

Only four Mayan manuscripts, traditionally referred to as codices, have survived to the present day. Two pages from the 57-inch long Peresianus Codex (above).

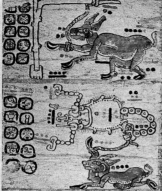

The Dresden Codex (center) is a treatise on divination and astronomy, while the Madrid Codex (above) consists of horoscopes and almanacs to assist priests in their predictions and ceremonies.

READING ORDER

Mayan writing is presented in the form of blocks of glyphs which are arranged either in rows or columns. These glyphic blocks are usually intended to be read from left to right and from top to bottom in pairs of columns. They are made up of various symbols or glyphs: a principal symbol with affixes.

VERB-OBJECT-SUBJECT

In this example taken from the Dresden Codex, each figure is accompanied by a text of four glyphic blocks. The first block, the verb, designates the action: presenting an offering. The second, the object, is the offering itself (the same glyph appears in the hand of each figure). The third names the figure, and the fourth is the omen for this period: good or bad depending on the divinity.

The third block (above) represents the turkey-cock (*cutz*) by using the symbol *cu* and the symbol read as *tzu*.

The dog (*tzul*) is represented in the third block (above) which consists of the glyphs *tzu* and *lu*.

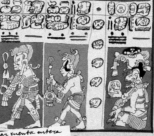

LANDA ALPHABET
In the 16th century the Bishop of Yucatán tried to transcribe the European alphabet into Mayan symbols – an impossible task as Mayan writing is syllabic.

43

● CALCULATION AND CALENDAR

The Maya perfected the discoveries of their post-Olmec predecessors in the fields of positional arithmetic and the calendar, which used independent cycles. The principal cycles were the divinatory cycle or *tzolkin* (260 days), the solar year or *haab* (365 days), and the Great Cycle of 5,200 *tun* (5,200 x 360 days) or Long Count. Their mastery of the calculation of time enabled them to write their history and, above all, to predict the future by means of a cyclical conception of chronological units, as illustrated by their inscriptions.

"KATUN" CALENDAR ROUND

Landa ● 55 reproduced the *katun* cycle on this wheel. The Short Count dates an event in relation to the end of a *katun* (period of 20 *tuns*), while 260 *tuns* (260 x 360 days) elapsed between two *katuns*. Hence the thirteen segments in Landa's wheel.

STELE E AT QUIRIGUA
1. Initial Series
2. 9 *baktuns* and 17 *katuns*
3. 0 *tun* and 0 *uinal*
4. 0 *kin* and 13 *ahau* (260-day calendar)
5. Ninth Lord of the Underworld and Glyph F (undeciphered)
6–8. Supplementary Series

52-YEAR CYCLE. The Long Count can be shortened by indicating the date on the *tzolkin* (260-day) cycle and on the *haab* (365-day) cycle. A combination of two positions from these cycles can only be repeated every 52 years. A cycle of this length is, therefore, exact.

For numerical notations the Maya used a system of bars and dots.
A bar represented 5 and a dot 1.

O	O O	▬	O	O O O O	O O
1	2	5	6	9	12

CALCULATION

To write 1995 (right): 3 bars represent the number of units (15 x 1 = 15), 3 bars (below) and 4 dots represent the number of twenties (19 x 20 = 380), and 4 dots represent the number of four hundreds (4 x 400 = 1,600). Thus 1,600 + 380 + 15 = 1995.

HISTORY AND ASTRONOMY

Although many historical facts specific to each city are recorded in the inscriptions of the Classic period, astronomical observations – such as the solar eclipses described in the 3th-century Dresden Codex ● 42 (fragment above) – are not always represented.

NUMBERS

Unlike the western decimal system which increases in value from right to left, the vigesimal Maya system used two symbols (the dot and the bar) which increased in vertical columns from bottom to top. The lowest value was that of the units (0 to 19), the next was the 20s, then the 400s, the 160,000s and so on.

CALLIGRAPHY AND THE INITIAL SERIES

Another system of calculation used glyphs ● 42, in the form of a complete figure, which mainly symbolized the numbers and periods in certain Initial Series. These appear at the beginning of many inscriptions and indicate the time that has elapsed since the initial date of the Mayan calendar. On Stele E at Quirigua ▲ 306 (detail and general view, left) the numbers are represented by bars and dots, and the periods by a head in profile. On the panel from the "Palacio" at Palenque (right), numbers and periods are represented by a complete figure, while on the panel from Yaxchilán (far left), the numbers are represented by heads and the periods by entire figures.

● HUMAN SACRIFICE AND SELF-SACRIFICE

A jaguar (below left) devours a human heart after
tearing it out. Bas-relief from Chichén Itzá ▲ 205.
Wars between city-states (right) brought
prisoners and sometimes sacrificial victims.

For a long time the Maya have been contrasted
with the bloodthirsty Aztecs. They have
been presented as a non-violent,
intellectual people who were not given to
bloody sacrifices. The most recent
discoveries, however, have shown that,
although the numbers of victims were
much lower than those of their neighbors,
human sacrifice played a major role in
Mayan religion from the very beginning. Iconography and
texts from the Classic period also reveal that the sacrifice of a
victim and self-sacrifice had the same value. Sacrifice was a
payment that had to be made to natural and supernatural
powers to obtain such favors as rain, a good harvest, victory
and universal harmony.

SELF-SACRIFICE

Self-sacrifice, a
characteristic rite of
Mesoamerica, was as
important to the
Maya as the sacrifice
of a victim. The
supplicant would
offer their own
blood, which had
been obtained
through one of
various methods,
some more painful
than others, using
instruments such as
needles, sting-ray
spines and knives.
A rope of thorns
passed through the
tongue of the victim
(below, detail from
a bas-relief at
Yaxchilán
▲ 248).

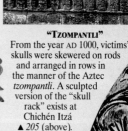

"TZOMPANTLI"
From the year AD 1000, victims'
skulls were skewered on rods
and arranged in rows in
the manner of the Aztec
tzompantli. A sculpted
version of the "skull
rack" exists at
Chichén Itzá
▲ 205 (above).

TEARING OUT
THE HEART
The many
scenes depicting
human sacrifice
by tearing out the
heart date mainly
from the 11th
century AD.
Notable examples
exist at Chichén
Itzá ▲ 205 where
they appear on
repoussé gold
pectoral disks
(right) or painted
on buildings.

> "A VEIL OF AGONY SPREADS ACROSS THE VIRGIN LIDS, AND THE BLOOD THAT SPATTERS THE SACRIFICIAL KNIFE ... HALOES THE HEADS OF THE GODS, SACRED AND INDIFFERENT."
>
> MIGUEL ANGEL ASTURIAS

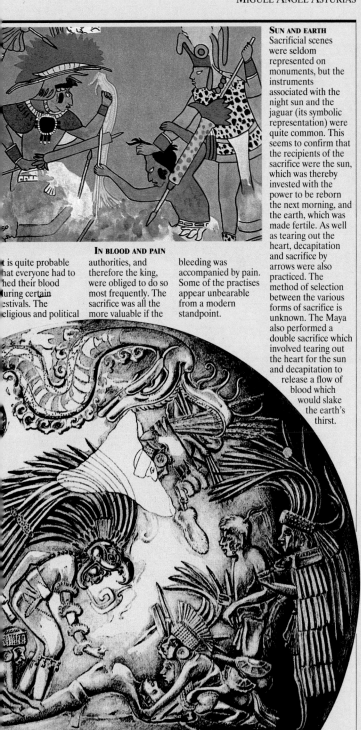

SUN AND EARTH

Sacrificial scenes were seldom represented on monuments, but the instruments associated with the night sun and the jaguar (its symbolic representation) were quite common. This seems to confirm that the recipients of the sacrifice were the sun, which was thereby invested with the power to be reborn the next morning, and the earth, which was made fertile. As well as tearing out the heart, decapitation and sacrifice by arrows were also practiced. The method of selection between the various forms of sacrifice is unknown. The Maya also performed a double sacrifice which involved tearing out the heart for the sun and decapitation to release a flow of blood which would slake the earth's thirst.

IN BLOOD AND PAIN

t is quite probable that everyone had to shed their blood during certain festivals. The religious and political authorities, and therefore the king, were obliged to do so most frequently. The sacrifice was all the more valuable if the bleeding was accompanied by pain. Some of the practises appear unbearable from a modern standpoint.

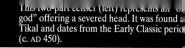

During the Middle Preclassic period the Maya made fairly crude, ceramic figurines. These were mostly solid, with the exception of whistles and hollow rattles, and represented animals and people. After disappearing for almost six centuries, the figurines once again featured on the archeological inventory of the Early Classic period. The new characters and forms were used as intermediaries during communication rituals with the other world. They disappeared during the Postclassic period and were replaced by over-simplified statuettes of the human body.

FIGURINE-WHISTLES
During the Classic period hollow figurines were often used as whistles. This "woman with rabbit" from Campeche (Mexico) is a rare image of a woman.

MOVEMENT
The more elaborate figurines represent moving figures – such as dancers, warriors or ball players.

CENSERS AND ELABORATE DECORATION
It seems that in Mesoamerica censers appeared at the same time as the first ceramics. Copal was burnt in these containers, whose form varied depending on the period and subject. This censer from Teapa (above) has elaborately decorated wings surrounding the central figure (Late Classic).

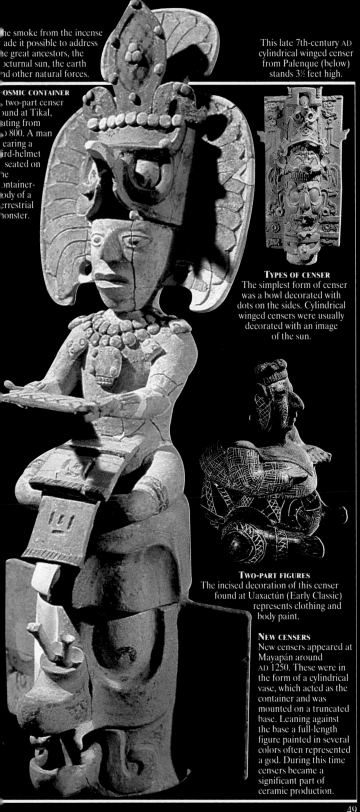

he smoke from the incense
ade it possible to address
e great ancestors, the
octurnal sun, the earth
nd other natural forces.

This late 7th-century AD
cylindrical winged censer
from Palenque (below)
stands 3½ feet high.

OSMIC CONTAINER
 two-part censer
ound at Tikal,
ating from
 800. A man
earing a
ird-helmet
 seated on
e
ontainer-
ody of a
errestrial
nonster.

TYPES OF CENSER
The simplest form of censer
was a bowl decorated with
dots on the sides. Cylindrical
winged censers were usually
decorated with an image
of the sun.

TWO-PART FIGURES
The incised decoration of this censer
found at Uaxactún (Early Classic)
represents clothing and
body paint.

NEW CENSERS
New censers appeared at
Mayapán around
AD 1250. These were in
the form of a cylindrical
vase, which acted as the
container and was
mounted on a truncated
base. Leaning against
the base a full-length
figure painted in several
colors often represented
a god. During this time
censers became a
significant part of
ceramic production.

CLASSICAL COSMOGONY AND THE POSTCLASSICAL PANTHEON

The Mayan religion was developed over the centuries from a fundamental belief in returning power to the world. During the Preclassic and Classic periods natural forces (earth, sky, death, corn, lightning) were represented in the form of hybrid creatures or symbols whose images changed according to what they were actually required to embody. During the Postclassic period these images became fixed; the creatures acquired a personality and became immutable divinities who formed part of a hierarchical pantheon.

ARCHITECTURE
The architecture of the city-states of the Classic period was a joyous representation of all or part of the universe. It created an ideal setting for rituals associated with power and its legitimacy (rites of accession, funeral ceremonies and the worship of dynastic ancestors) and rituals designed to achieve universal order and harmony (the regulation of calendars by means of deambulation, rites performed to feed the earth and the sun, and to make the rain fall).

GOD K
The creature of the Late Classic period traditionally known as God K (Kauil), is represented with a smoking axe embedded in his forehead and symbolized by lightning. He is shown here (above) in both figurative and glyphic form.

Heroes of myths, demons of the underworld, numerous spirits and possibly some gods abound in the scenes painted and engraved on the (mainly funerary) ceramic vases, which tended to be less subject to the official art form. Cosmogonic representation (above) on a vase from Uaxactún, dating from the Late Classic period.

COSMIC MONSTER. This creature from the Classic period is both celestial and subterranean. The world of the natural and supernatural powers is centered around the basic life-death opposition represented by the two heads of the terrestrial monster: the living earth and the skeletal nocturnal sun.

A MULTIPLICITY OF CREATURES
An entire population of creatures associated with humidity, fertility and the fecund earth, with features suggesting reptilian or froglike origins, developed alongside the cosmic monsters. Other types of grotesque figures, with feline features, are represented as solar creatures, the spirits of sacrifice, war and death. They pass from one extreme to the other, just as life ends in death, and death in rebirth.

THE KING RULES
In the monumental art of the city-states the figure of the king represents the center of the universe. Around him are organized the cosmic powers depicted as monsters and grotesque figures who are more spirit-like than god-like. The monstruous appearance of Stele D and its altar at Copán has been accentuated by Frederick Catherwood (lithograph, 1844).

SCULPTURE
The monumental sculpture of the Classic period, usually associated with architecture or in the form of steles, often shows the king in a cosmic setting, with images of the earth and the underworld beneath his feet and the sky above his head. Details (left and right) from the back of an 8th-century AD royal throne.

● CLASSICAL COSMOGONY AND THE POSTCLASSICAL PANTHEON

Carved stone, found at Jonuta (Mexico), showing a kneeling priest making an offering.

CHANGING BELIEFS

The changes in beliefs and rituals that occurred during the Postclassic period were the result of Mexican influences and the weakening of political structures. By the beginning of the Early Postclassic period, monumental art no longer celebrated royal power but two orders of rival warriors. The steles disappeared and worship focused on war and human sacrifice. Gods, especially those of Mexican origin, began to appear. The names of divinities that were not established until the Late Postclassic period were all too readily attributed to images from the Classic, which were probably representations of natural forces. For example, because of their long noses, the masks on the façades of Yucatec sites have been designated as those of the rain god Chac, whereas they are probably masks of the cosmic – and more usually terrestrial – monster.

THE PANTHEON

With the founding of Mayapán in c. 1250 (the combined result of a wave of Mexican influence and a weakening of royal power) there developed a veritable pantheon of gods, all endowed with a physical personality. Places of worship became much more numerous, with oratories and sanctuaries as well as temples. Stele (left) at Yaxchilán showing a high priest holding a scepter which is half-man, half-serpent.

DISCOVERING THE WORLD OF THE MAYAS

After the Spanish Conquest of Central America the already declining Maya civilization became the subject of many investigations, particularly with the rediscovery during the 18th and 19th centuries of cities buried deep in the forest. With a few notable exceptions, such as Diego de Landa, the Spanish conquerors had shown little interest in the region's history. The study of Mayan civilization (or "Mayanism") developed initially as a result of the efforts of European and American travelers and adventurers, and subsequently as professional archeologists gradually began to solve the mysteries of the world of the Mayas

THE EARLY CONQUERORS
The first contact between Europeans and the Maya was an exchange of gifts which took place in 1502 on the Isla Guanaja during one of Columbus' voyages. In 1517 Hernandez de Córdoba found the Maya on the Isla Mujeres ▲ *174* and continued his voyage as far as Champotón ▲ *230*. On February 18, 1519 Cortés set sail with eleven ships and, after stopping at the Isla de Cozumel, landed at Veracruz. It took him less than two years to conquer Mexico but another twenty to bring Yucatán under Spanish control.

FORGOTTEN RUINS
The ruins of ancient cities, which had lain silent and forgotten for centuries, were discovered by missionaries and officials from the colonial administration. However, their reports, both official and private, were rarely acted upon.

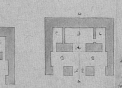

PALENQUE ▲ *243*.
In 1476 the priest from a nearby village was surprised to find "stone houses" in the forest. It took forty-two years for the governor of the province to send an official who requested further investigations. In 1785 Bernasconi drew a plan of the site. In 1786, after visiting Palenque, Captain Antonio del Río concluded that these ruins, like those of Yucatán, pre-dated the Spanish Conquest and were the work of a single "nation".

DIEGO DE LANDA ● *43*
The Spanish Conquest was legitimized by the christianization of the Indians, with the first Franciscans landing in 1535. While persecuting the Maya in the name of the "true faith", Diego de Landa – the future Bishop of Yucatán – was also interested in their history and customs. In his *Relación de las Cosas de Yucatán* (above), found in 1864, he describes ruined cities.

JUAN GALINDO
The son of actors, Juan Galindo (above) left his native Ireland for America at the age of sixteen. By 1827 he was in Guatemala. He was appointed military governor of Petén and went on many voyages of discovery.

It was during one such voyage in 1834 that he discovered Copán ▲ *299*. He remained there for a month, describing and sketching its monuments, drawing plans of the site and region and carrying out excavations.

THE "WINDOWS" OF COPÁN
After the site was abandoned in the 9th century AD, the river flooded the center of the city, leaving only a 100-foot section on which walls, stuccoed floors and tunnels were clearly visible. Galindo mistakenly called the site *Las Ventanas* because he thought it was a wall pierced by windows.

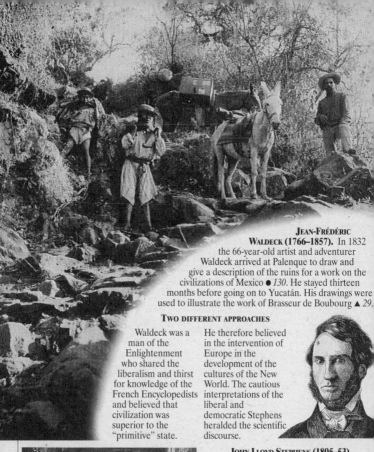

In 1832 the 66-year-old artist and adventurer Waldeck arrived at Palenque to draw and give a description of the ruins for a work on the civilizations of Mexico ● *130*. He stayed thirteen months before going on to Yucatán. His drawings were used to illustrate the work of Brasseur de Boubourg ▲ *29*.

TWO DIFFERENT APPROACHES

Waldeck was a man of the Enlightenment who shared the liberalism and thirst for knowledge of the French Encyclopedists and believed that civilization was superior to the "primitive" state.

He therefore believed in the intervention of Europe in the development of the cultures of the New World. The cautious interpretations of the liberal and democratic Stephens heralded the scientific discourse.

JOHN LLOYD STEPHENS (1805–53)

Although he was far from being the first to visit the Maya sites, Stephens was the first to make them accessible to the general public through his publications. Breaking with the strong "diffusionist" tradition, he declared his support for the independent development of Amerindian civilizations, and the Maya in particular. Born into a wealthy New England family, Stephens studied law before undertaking a series of voyages, accounts of which he later published. In 1836 he met the young English architect Frederick Catherwood who showed him a report by the mineralogist Del Río, illustrated by Waldeck. Captivated by the beauty of its ruins, the two men decided to visit Central America but were initially prevented by a war there. They finally managed to enter the region in 1839 and visited Copán, Quirigua, Toniná and Palenque over the next three years.

TEOBERT MALER
The German archeologist Teobert Maler (right) completed the work of Maudslay by taking some admirable photographs, which are still referred to today.

DÉSIRÉ CHARNAY
Charnay was the first to photograph the Maya sites (right) in 1859. His pictures were used to illustrate *Les Anciennes Villes du Nouveau Monde* published in 1863).

ALFRED MAUDSLAY
The quality of Maudslay's photographs was not only due to improved techniques such as the dry-gelatin negative (invented in 1882), but also to his systematic approach, which was based on the collection of interpretative documents. The four volumes devoted to the archeology of the Maya sites in the collection *Biologia Centrali-Americana* (1889–1902) are a fine example of the genre.

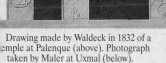

Drawing made by Waldeck in 1832 of a temple at Palenque (above). Photograph taken by Maler at Uxmal (below).

WALDECK FORGOTTEN
Waldeck was a victim of the success of Stephens' work (published 1841–3) and was judged harshly by posterity. Although only eight years separated their visits to Palenque, the two men belonged to different generations of culture and thought.

FREDERICK CATHERWOOD ● 130
The development of new reproduction and photographic techniques made it possible to produce drawings that were much more objective. After the failure of the daguerreotype process, Frederick Catherwood decided to use a *camera lucida*, which enabled him to produce these extremely accurate drawings. View of Sayil (1843) ▲ *221* (right), and views (below left and bottom right) of the ruins of Palenque (1841).

FIRST PROFESSIONAL EXCAVATIONS

The first professional excavations in Maya territory were at Copán ▲ *299* from 1891 to 1895 by Harvard's Peabody Museum. From 1914 to 1958 the Washington Carnegie Institution was in the forefront of Maya archeology with its excavation of the major sites of Chichén Itzá, Copán, Kaminaljuyú and Uaxactún. This last site made it possible to establish the main lines of Maya history and divide them into three periods: Preclassic (2000 BC– AD 250), Classic (250– 1000) and Postclassic (1000–1500). The University of Pennsylvania's Tikal Project (1956–70) was one of the most ambitious in terms of the number of people involved, the length of the project and the diversity of aspects studied.

A series of discoveries in the early 1960's gave Mayan studies a new lease of life. The paintings of Bonampak ▲ *249* and a number of sculptures from other sites demonstrated the importance of war, torture and human and self-sacrifice in the Mayan culture ● *46*.

In 1958 Heinrich Berlin noted the presence in the inscriptions of several major sites of a type of glyph whose main symbol was virtually exclusive to each of these sites. These "glyph-emblems" suggested that Mayan texts might have a historic and local – rather than a calendric – content ● *42*.

THE LATEST DISCOVERIES

It is likely that current research will lead to a better understanding of the origins of the Maya civilization. Evidence suggests that great cities such as El Mirador and Nakbé, with their grand pyramid complexes, were built by the immediate forebears of the Classic Maya, who were most probably direct descendants of the Olmecs ● *31*.

THE LIFE OF KINGS
In the 1960's Tatiana Proskouriakoff noticed that the period covered by each group of steles at Piedras Negras ▲ 332 never exceeded sixty years. This led her to consider the possibility that each group related to the life of a particular king and that the initial date of the group referred to the birth of the king and the second to his accession to the throne. She tested her hypothesis at Piedras Negras and Yaxchilán ▲ 248 by demonstrating that the glyphs associated with the various dates represented the birth, accession and death of the king whose name and titles followed. The inscriptions did not therefore relate solely to religion and the measurement of time.

PROGRESS IN THE STUDY OF MAYAN WRITING ● 42
At the end of the 19th century documents were collected which enabled progress to be made in the study of the Mayan writing system. Its decipherment had been made possible in 1864 when the Abbé Brasseur ▲ 292 discovered Landa's 16th-century text, *Relación de las cosas de Yucatán*, in which Landa describes the calendar and gives the names of the days and months with their respective glyphs, producing what he believed to be an alphabet but which was in fact a syllabary. In 1866 Brasseur noticed that the same symbols appeared in the Madrid Codex and on the sculpted monuments of Yucatán, Petén and Chiapas. In spite of local variations it wa the same system but was different from the symbols observe in the manuscripts o Central Mexico, especially those of th Aztecs. The concept of an independent Mayan civilization was thus born.

In 1950 the Maya were still perceived, through their inscriptions, as a peaceable and religious people, concerned with the passage of time, astrology and prophecies. It was thought that their writing was logographic, in othe words that the textu units represented entire words.

THE MAYA TODAY

Maya territory covers the eastern part of Mesoamerica: southeast Mexico (Yucatán Peninsula and the State of Chiapas), Belize, Guatemala and the west of El Salvador and Honduras. It covers an area of around 125,000 square miles divided into highlands and lowlands – the same area inhabited by the Maya at the time of the Spanish Conquest. Today more than three million people (predominantly Quichés and Yucatecans) speak one of the twenty-eight Mayan dialects, which subdivide into nine large groups.

Most of the Maya are peasants living in villages and tiny rural communities, although they are swelling the urban and suburban populations in increasing numbers. Lacandón Indians from Chiapas ▲ 258 (above) at the turn of the century.

The Indians left their villages in search of work or to escape oppression. Tens of thousands of Guatemalan refugees settled in California, thus contributing to the spread of their languages beyond their traditional borders.

Since the Spanish Conquest and colonization, the Maya have been forced to live alongside mestizos and other ethnic groups.

After a severe decline during the 16th and 17th centuries, the Maya population is slowly increasing.

TENSION AND CONFLICT

he recent increase
the Maya
opulation has led to
screpancies in the
owth of the various
hnic groups (there
e 400 Lacandóns
d 800,000
ucatecan Maya,
hile the Quiché-
akchiquel-Tzutuhil

population exceeds
one million) and their
occupation of land.
This has given rise to
conflict when local
governments have
refused to take it into
account. Lacandón
Indians (right).
Distribution of Maya
groups (below).

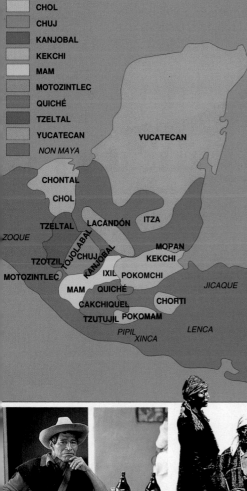

	CHOL
	CHUJ
	KANJOBAL
	KEKCHI
	MAM
	MOTOZINTLEC
	QUICHÉ
	TZELTAL
	YUCATECAN
	NON MAYA

YUCATECAN

CHONTAL
CHOL
TZELTAL   LACANDÓN   ITZA
ZOQUE   TOJOLABAL
TZOTZIL   CHUJ KANJOBAL   MOPAN
                              KEKCHI
MOTOZINTLEC   IXIL POKOMCHI   JICAQUE
        MAM   QUICHÉ
        CAKCHIQUEL   CHORTI
        TZUTUJIL POKOMAM   LENCA
              PIPIL
              XINCA

In the face of the
exploitation,
segregation and
violence of colonial
policies, the Maya
developed
strategies of passive
resistance on a
daily basis. When
this was not enough
they resorted to
open rebellion.

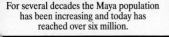

For several decades the Maya population
has been increasing and today has
reached over six million.

63

● COMMUNITY CENTERS

The organization of Indian communities around a village center dates back to the post-Conquest period. It is the result of the *reducciónes* policy conducted by the civil and, more especially, the religious authorities who imposed their own *imago mundi* (influenced, in particular, by the organization of the sacred area of the cloister) on these new settlements. Today these villages still retain the broad outlines of their original appearance and are a focal point for markets, small traders and religious festivals.

COSMIC TREE
The "center of the world and center of the sky" (often a silk cotton tree) spreads its branches above the village square (**1**).
✝ Palín ▲ *269* (above).

COMPOSITION

Village and town squares feature votive chapels (2), associated with various districts and used as stopping-off points during processions. Each village has its own patron and other tutelary saints. There is often a fountain (3), a public wash-house (4) (painting by Samuel Sotz, right), and an ancestral altar (5).

FROM THE SPANISH CONQUEST TO THE PRESENT DAY

After the Conquest, villages where the indigenous population gathered were used as a means of colonial control (through preaching, the collection of tributes, recruitment of labor). Their architecture was based on the neoclassical designs of the Renaissance: perpendicular streets radiating outwards around which the church (6), the priest's residence (7) and the town hall (8) represented the centers of power ● 122.

The Indians live in rural communities, whose size has depended on location and historical period, which are centered around an *ejido* (a square area given over to village buildings) and communal lands. The efforts of the colonial administrators to reduce communities to the smallest possible area were generally unsuccessful. Very early on the Indians abandoned their villages and dispersed to escape the abuses of administrative authority and reoccupied, as far as they could, their former dwellings and places of worship. The Catholic Church responded by building rural chapels and erecting crosses at key points in the landscape: by the roadside, on mountain tops and passes and near springs.

A WORLD IN MINIATURE

Each community is a "world" in miniature, a microcosm of the universe in which the Earth is a flat quadrilateral surrounded by four seas and orientated in relation to the sun's course (the sun's feet or lower parts lie to the East, his head or upper part to the West, while the North and South represent his left and right hands). The mountains (**1**), the ancient pyramids (**2**) and the church (**3**) are steps leading to the heavens, while the grottos, gulfs and sepulchers lead to the underworld.

ARCHEOLOGICAL SITES
Maya territory abounds with archeological sites which bear testament to the distant past. These survivors existed long before the villages which housed the kings and warriors of yesteryear (described in the *Rabinal Achi* ● *148*), figures of authority who were replaced by saints with the arrival of Christianity in the 16th century. Although chapels (**4**) were built on the pyramids (**2**), the sites have always been respected and feared and are often visited by groups offering up prayers to ask for rain or making conciliatory offerings before certain festivals or dance performances.

PATHS, TRACKS AND PASSES. The land is criss-crossed by a vast network of paths, tracks and the more important *caminos reales* (**5**).

MOUNTAIN TOPS

The mountain tops (**6**) mark the limit of the world as well as the frontier with neighboring communities. According to local mythology they often indicate successive stages in the journey of a founding hero, who set up boundary stones to mark the limits of his territory and thus legitimize his claim.

THE FOUR "CORNERS OF THE EARTH"

Around the villages where ancient calendric practices ● 70 are still observed, particularly those in Guatemala, four special sites symbolize the four "corners of the earth". From year to year the *alcaldes del mundo* – the so-called "year bearers" appointed by the communities ● 68 – move between these "corners".

"ALTAR DE COSTUMBRE" OR LOCAL ALTAR

An arrangement of flat stones, blackened with soot and spotted with wax, in an area scattered with shards, withered petals, pine needles and a few feathers, indicates a place of prayer, offering and sacrifice ● 46. Some of these altars (**7**) have stone crosses or even idols in human form. Many show the position of pre-Hispanic places of worship.

SACRED SITES

In the Indian representation of the world all the sacred sites in the community are revered. Their local names reflect their natural characteristics.

RIVERS

Rivers are used for washing and fishing. Fish are caught with nets, poison or dynamite (**8**).

RURAL CHAPEL

Rural chapels (**9**) provide a place of worship for the inhabitants of small villages (*rancherías, aldeas, caseríos*). They are also the venue for the ceremonies held for Santa Cruz (May 3), and the festival of springs, which marks the long-awaited start of the rainy season and the agricultural cycle ■ 22.

"CALVARIO"

The *calvario* or "house of the ancestors" is the counterpart of the church or "house of the saints". It is situated to the west of the village, often on the outskirts, overlooking the cemetery.

CEMETERY

Tombs, consisting of a simple mound marked by a cross or plant, alternate with the cement tombs of the mestizos. Tombs are repainted on All Souls' Day ● 74.

● AUTHORITIES

The family is the basic unit of social organization. It is within the family that most of the productive and domestic tasks are performed. In certain regions the family forms part of a larger group, or lineage, made up of people living in the same village, or immediate vicinity, who often share the same name. One such grouping is the *calpul* (also known as the *chinamit* or *molab*), the remnant of the former *parcialidades*, which consisted of indigenous groups forcibly regrouped into new communities. Another is the *barrio* or district, a grouping created by the colonial administration.

THE MUNICIPALITY
Generally speaking, each community has the status of a municipality (*municipio*) and has a body of officials under the authority of the mayor (*alcalde*). Municipal officials are not elected by the community as a whole, but are appointed by nomination or co-option.

INDIANS, MESTIZOS AND WHITES
The different interests and traditions of the Indians, mestizos and whites in the countries of the Mayan world are often in conflict. In Guatemala, for example, the professionalization of municipal posts since the 19th century has marginalized the indigenous authorities.

COLLECTIVE WORK
Community officials have the right to mobilize an unpaid workforce to carry out work deemed to be in the local interest: for example, repairing a public building or constructing a bridge. This recruiting system is sometimes abused to serve private or external interests (such as the construction of roads and railway lines, or the levying of gangs of seasonal workers for the plantations), reminder of the time when civic duties were an essential part of the colonial system and were used as a means of controlling and exploiting local populations.

The most commonly found symbol of local power is undoubtedly the *vara* (wand of office) carried by holders of high civil office. This is often a silver-knobbed cane decorated with ribbons.

MUNICIPAL COUNCIL

The municipal council is responsible for the day-to-day maintenance, policing, and administrative and financial management of the community. During festivals and on market days a full council sits beneath the gallery of the town hall holding public audiences, recording and judging complaints and requests, and maintaining public order.

DIVISION OF POWER

As in any peasant community where politics and religion are intimately linked and where the destiny of its members is ruled by supernatural forces which control every undertaking, the municipality does not have a monopoly on local power. Religious offices controlled by the priesthood and brotherhood also hold important prerogatives, especially in ritual matters.

Fortune-telling and healing play an important part in the complex ceremonies that are central to the religious life of the Maya. They are practiced by traditional priests whose often ambivalent and ambiguous powers are primarily a product of their own personal talents, revealed in dreams and developed during many years' apprenticeship to their elders. Sometimes these priests are believed to be "sorcerers" (*aj itz*), able to transform themselves into powerful, flesh-eating animals (*nahual*). As "calendar priests" they oversee the use of the 260-day (divinatory) and 365-day (solar) Counts ● *44*.

RITUAL ORATIONS
Mastery of the ritual orations is one of the skills of the healer. These orations are central to the therapeutic process and draw part of their effectiveness from the healer's ability to invoke the aid of supernatural powers in healing the patient.

TOOLS OF THE TRADE AND ROLE OF THE FORTUNE-TELLER
Fortune-tellers use a wide range of objects and accessories to enable them to "see" into the future: translucent stones, quartz crystals and *tz'ite* seeds are always found in the pouches worn over their shoulder or on their belt.

Censers from Amatenango and Chamula (Chiapas).

CONTROLLING
TIME
Fortune-tellers
present the passage of
time in spatial terms.
Each day of the 260-day
divinatory calendar has
its own number and
symbol.

SMALL PLATE FROM CHAMULA ▲ *238*
In 1969 a small wooden plate was discovered, still in use, on which a series of vertical lines marked in charcoal represented the eighteen 20-day months and the five unlucky days.

During seances fortune-tellers answer the questions of those seeking advice by throwing crystals and seeds onto a towel spread on the ground and observing the patterns formed as they fall. Each pattern corresponds to a day on the divinatory calendar and to a specific number–symbol combination whose lucky or unlucky associations predict the success of a particular undertaking, such as marriage, seed sowing or building a house.

A UNIVERSAL APPROACH
Healers master therapeutic techniques such as the use of medicinal herbs, the splinting of fractures and the extraction of venom, all of which are linked to an understanding of the natural world. With their profound knowledge of the balances required by their system of beliefs healers can repair the loss of part of the soul, reestablish the circulation of the vital fluids within the body, identify, locate and expel pathogenic agents sent by a sorcerer, invoke supernatural powers and master the ritual orations. Since all ailments and illnesses are considered to be the result of a disfunction of the component parts of the individual, healing is a matter of performing rituals to reestablish the basic unity between the individual and society, the body and the cosmos, time and space.

● FESTIVALS OF THE BROTHERHOODS

MAXIMÓN BROTHERHOOD
The Santa Cruz brotherhood of Santiago
Atitlán worships the unorthodox Saint
Maximón, a master of the magic arts and
the patron saint of sorcerers ▲ 28

One of the main concerns of Spanish evangelists
was to impose the worship of saints upon the
Maya and to establish brotherhoods within the
communities to serve and preserve this practise.
These brotherhoods (*cofradías*) played an
important role in religious and social life. They
were given land and livestock, and provided part
of the tribute demanded by the Spanish. In the 19th century the
missionary orders were stripped of their wealth and privileges
and expelled by the liberal regimes. The brotherhoods
remained, acting as a melting pot for a syncretic religion, born
of the union of Catholic doctrines and traditional beliefs and
reintroduced a number of practises which, until then, had
remained semi-clandestine.

Each saint has a
votive brotherhood
and an altar-
sanctuary, which
contains their
effigy and
possessions and is
watched over by
brotherhood
officials. The
altar-sanctuary is
for private rituals
and preparations
for ceremonies.
The Tenejapa
brotherhood,
(right), in
ceremonial costume
▲ 238.

> WHILE THE CHILDREN ON THEIR BACKS WERE AMAZED BY THE [CH]ANTING AND THE LIGHTS, THE WOMEN SMILINGLY WATCHED NOT [ON]LY THE IMAGES OF THE SAINTS, BUT ALSO THEIR MEN CARRYING [TH]EM ... INTOXICATED BY THEIR EFFORTS AND THEIR OFFERING."
>
> MICHEL BUTOR

[F]ESTIVAL OF THE [P]ATRON SAINT

[B]rotherhood officials [g]ather on their saint's [fe]stival to perform [ri]tuals which mark [th]e reunion of the [li]ving and the dead [an]d commemorate [th]e mythical passage [fr]om primordial [d]arkness into the [li]ght of day. [P]articipants include [m]embers of other [b]rotherhoods, [m]usicians, dancers [an]d firework-makers, [a]s well as parents and [fr]iends. Next, the [s]aint is worshipped in [p]ublic beneath a [c]anopy of leaves in [th]e court of the [s]anctuary, then in the [c]hurch, and finally in [th]e festal procession [t]he "high day"). [E]ight days later the [s]aint is taken to [a]nother sanctuary [p]repared by the new [b]rotherhood officials.

[T]ransfer of the Saint [b]y the Brotherhood [(l]eft) by the artist [C]havajay.

PROCESSION
The end of the festival, when the saint is borne aloft, is reminiscent of the ancestral inauguration of the sun's course. The ceremonial bearing of these heavy saints' catafalques (the festivals of Cubulco and San Andres Sajcabajá, left) symbolizes the permanent sacrifice of mankind to the service of the universal powers and the binding contract to ensure universal harmony.

The all-pervasive scent of incense and the many flowers distributed on the altars and during the performance of rituals show a desire to please the ancestral spirits, who are believed to like them. The fragrances are supposed to unite the souls of the living and the dead in a single aromatic cloud, as stated in the ritual orations. The explosions of firecrackers and *bombas* let off by the firework-makers, mark the various stages of the rituals. (Smoke from firecrackers on the steps of the church of "Chichi", above.) It is the plumassiers' task to decorate the church doors and the niches containing images of the saints with a profusion of feathers, pieces of cloth and garlands.

73

Procession at Santia
Atitlán ▲ 281: paint
by Martín Ratzan (19

The major Christian festivals, whose prominence depends on the local influence of the Catholic Church, form the third aspect of religious festivals. The cult of the Virgin and the festivals marking the main stages in the life of Christ are often the affair of the official clergy and the Ladinos. Apart from pilgrimages to particular statues of the Virgin or Christ, the religious year is divided into three: the Christmas cycle (Nativity, Epiphany, Candlemas), the Easter cycle (Carnival, Holy Week, Ascension, Whitsun, Corpus Christi), and All Souls' or All Saints' Day.

HOLY WEEK
Although the brotherhoods take part in the celebration of Holy Week, the festival is organized by a committee under the control of the Catholic priest. Each day commemorates an episode in the Passion with a procession. On Easter Day in Antigua the streets are carpeted with flower petals and colored wood-shavings.

ALL SOULS' DAY
All Souls' Day, which is celebrated in the smallest hamlets by Indians and Ladinos alike, is primarily a family festival. Houses are decorated with altars piled high with food and gifts to welcome the returning souls of the dead. During the night of November 1 to November 2 the living go to the cemetery to honor their dead with food, alcohol, various offerings, music and dancing.

FLAGS
Tzeltal Indians during the carniva of Tenejapa (Chiapas).

CARNIVAL

Little is known of the historical process by which Carnival was introduced into Indian culture, but it is a festival that symbolizes the dual heritage of the Mayan religious tradition. It combines certain characteristics of European carnivals (inversion of hierarchies, lack of distinction between the sexes, ritualized rebellion) and elements from local mythology and history.

V Centenario de la Evangelización de América.
III Sínodo Diocesano

Carnivals are at their most spectacular and interesting in Chiapas where "monkeys" and "savages" surround the two villages of Chamula ▲ 238 and Bachajón respectively, transporting them back in time to a previous creation and reinstating the original primordial chaos. It is then up to the civil and religious authorities to ritually re-establish social and cultural order. The Carnival is the modern equivalent of the so-called *uayeb* rites of the ancient Maya and of the ceremonies that accompanied the five-day transition (*ch'ay k'in*) between two solar years. It marks the arrival of the New Year.

THE CHRISTMAS CYCLE

he Nativity, which is arely celebrated in the llages, is primarily n urban, mestizo estival. The vening of ecember 16 arks the start of he Christmas ovena, punctuated y *posadas* (halts of he Virgin). Mary nd Joseph are arried through the streets in search of a house (chosen in advance) that will offer them shelter. Receiving the couple is a great honor. The scene is re-enacted each evening until December 24 when the Holy Family reaches Bethlehem (in this case the church) and joins the nativity scene set up for the occasion.

During the pre-Hispanic period dance, including *palo volador*, war dances and dynastic dramas, was a highly codified form of expression. The Spanish quickly understood that they could capitalize on this form of ritual performance to "colonize" the Indian imagination and spread their ideological message of military and religious conquest among the vanquished nations. Contemporary Spanish dances represented recent Christian victories over the Arabs, a subject which was readily adapted to the new situation and resulted in the *bailes de la Conquista*.

"BAILES DE LA CONQUISTA"
There were different versions of these dances, depending on whether they were presenting Spanish themes (*baile de Moros y Cristianos, Rey Moro, Tamorlan*) or local motifs. In the *baile de Cortés*, the conqueror of Mexico (often on horseback) confronts the Aztec king Moctezuma.

PATZKA
The dancers (below) are dressed in rags, armed with sticks carved with animal motifs (serpents, deer), and wearing goitrous masks. They represent the ancestors of the community of Rabinal ▲ 292 who, in the original dance, carried the patron saint to the high altar, thus triggering the sun's rotation and the first rainfall.

MASKS ● 85
Masks are carved from lightweight wood and painted in bright colors. They represent characters from local myths (jaguars, monkeys, deer, devils and ancestors) and key historical figures (the Spanish, Indian chiefs and kings, princes and princesses of bygone days). Like all effigies, masks are thought of as living beings and, as such, are watched over and fed. In vocal dances the sacred words are spoken by the voices of the masks.

DANCE OF SAN JORGE
This dance, inspired by the biblical episode of Saint George and the Dragon, illustrates the fight between the forces of Good and Evil. The dragon is made of cloth and cardboard.

"PALO VOLADOR"

The *palo volador* originated in central Mexico and was being performed in Guatemala before the Conquest. Two groups of dancers ("monkeys" and "angels") climb, two by two, to the top of a mast fixed firmly in the ground. They then throw themselves from the top, with one foot attached to a rope. As the rope unfurls it causes the *canasta* – a pyramidal structure fixed over a mobile fork set into the point of the mast – to rotate. Another dancer stands on the *canasta*, 50–65 feet above the ground.

COSTUMES AND ACCESSORIES

Spectacular historical dances provide an opportunity to display lavish and brightly colored costumes: velvet jackets and trousers, silk scarves and fringed hats. These *bailes de seda* contrast sharply with the so-called ancestral dances (*Patzkas, Pascares, Viejitos*) performed by dancers dressed in rags with various accessories according to the theme.

"RABINAL ACHI"

Although not particularly spectacular, a performance of the *Rabinal Achi* is still an exceptional event. The text of this pre-Hispanic dance (written in ancient Quiché) has been preserved in its entirety ● *148*. It re-enacts the trial of a Quiché warrior, accused of an incursion into Rabinal territory ▲ *292*, and describes the judicial ritual leading to his sacrifice.

INDIAN DANCES

Some Indian dances are silent, some are vocal and have been passed down by word of mouth, while others have long, recitative dialogues recorded in the *Rabinal Achi* or the *Balam Kej*.

77

Music and song play an important part in Mayan rituals and celebrations. The aerophones of the ancient Maya have been replaced by various kinds of flutes, while percussion instruments, and especially xylophones and drums, have enjoyed greater continuity. As in popular music, where ancient forms co-exist with old Spanish folk tunes, Christian hymns and songs of praise have not completely suppressed Indian recitatives. For example, the *bolonchon* of the Tzotzils, the funerary songs of the Chols and the shamanist incantations of the *h'men* (sorcerers from Yucatán) remain an integral part of traditional rituals and ceremonies.

"MARIMBA"
The national instrument of Guatemala, the *marimba* (right), is extremely popular throughout the region. It is a type of xylophone derived from the African *balafon*, which was introduced to the American continent by black slaves during the 16th century. It consists of strips of rosewood of various lengths, connected to a group of resonators enclosed by a piece of gold-beater's skin or pig-gut membrane. Sound is produced when the wooden strips are struck.

FLUTES AND DRUMS
A flute and large skin-covered drum form the most popular combination of instruments in Indian music. They accompany the central figures in processions and

rituals and punctuate the orations delivered at the entrance to brotherhood sanctuaries. During mass the players stand beneath the porch.

VIOLIN AND "ADUFE"
The Quichés play this pair of instruments (below right) to honor the dead. They are an example of the intermingling and inventiveness of Indian traditions: the rustic violin is made of cypress wood; the sound-post is made from the tail of a rattlesnake and the bow (carved in one piece) is strung with greased horsehair. The square drum consists of two skins stretched over a wooden frame. Its local name, *tupe*, comes from the Spanish *adufe* – in turn derived from the Arabic *duff*, a similar instrument which is its distant ancestor.

"MATRACA"
The *matraca* is a small wooden board to which pieces of metal are loosely attached. These are shaken by rapidly rotating the wrist to produce a rattling noise. It is played only at Easter, to replace the church bells which remain silent for this period of mourning.

The *marimba* is played by at least three people at once who strike it using wooden sticks with hard rubber ends.

VIOLIN, HARP AND GUITAR

Although these are derived from instruments introduced by the Spanish, their rusticity distinguishes them from their ancestors. While the violin and guitar are widespread, the harp is played only by the Tzotzils and Kekchis.

CONCHES AND TURTLE SHELLS

Conches were once used as trumpets to issue rallying or alarm calls. During the Bachajón carnival they are played together with turtle shells struck with corn cobs.

WOODEN DRUMS

The *tun*, the descendant of the drum that the Aztecs called the *teponaztli*, is still heard in the Guatemalan highlands. Its barrel, which varies in size, has two incised tongues of wood.

● FURNITURE AND ACCESSORIES

Yucatecan house ● 126.

Furniture in Indian houses usually consists of a few basic items: one or more beds, depending on the size of the family, consisting of a wooden frame covered with boards or slats – the sleepers lie on a rush mat and wrap themselves in blankets; chests, a few shelves and hanging cords providing storage space; and a ladder, carved out of a tree trunk, giving access to the rafters where tools, baskets and other materials such as ropes and boards, are stored. Tables, chairs, cupboards and even bolsters and mattresses are relatively recent additions. The most frequently used room is still the kitchen, the hub of domestic activity centered around the women and the hearth.

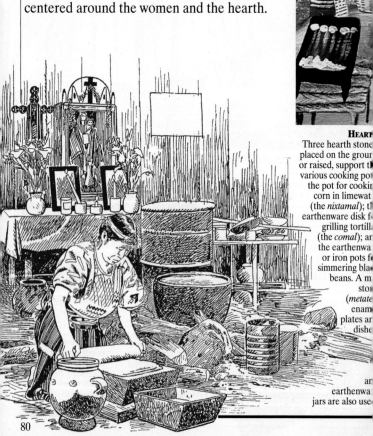

HEART
Three hearth stone placed on the grour or raised, support t various cooking po the pot for cookir corn in limewat (the *nixtamal*); t earthenware disk f grilling tortill (the *comal*); ar the earthenwa or iron pots fe simmering bla beans. A m sto (*metate* enam plates ar dishe

ar earthenwa jars are also use

Gourd spoons ● 85.

DOMESTIC ALTAR

very house has a orner containing a nall domestic altar elow) or *mesa* able) arranged with ligious pictures, ndles, incense and bacco. It is ecorated with wers, fruit and ecial little loaves r the prayer vigils held on occasions such as All Souls' Day (the Day of the Dead) or to commemorate a death (on the seventh and fortieth days, one year and every seventh year after the death). Every day short prayers are said for the souls of the dead, recently lost loved ones and ancestors.

HAMMOCKS

The hammock, which these days is most probably imported from the Caribbean (the close links between Yucatán and the Caribbean are all too often forgotten), is a basic "bedroom" item in Yucatán and the lowlands. It was traditionally made from loosely woven agave fibers (there was once a thriving hammock industry in Yucatán), but today the use of cotton or nylon thread, bought in the nearest town, is on the increase. The weaver incorporates various motifs (*jaspeado, franjas, perritos*) into the warp.

● Markets and Small Traders

In Yucatán and Chiapas markets are essentially an urban phenomenon with a few cities holding the monopoly on this type of trade. In Guatemala, however, the institution is widespread and has given rise to vast trade networks. Markets are held frequently – one or twice a week at each location – throughout Guatemala and attract wholesalers, professional retailers, occasional traders (who come to sell either a small surplus or traditionally made articles), all kinds of street vendors (hawkers, shoe-shiners, ice cream sellers) and, last but not least, preachers.

ASSOCIATED ACTIVITIES
The most important of these activities is the porterage of merchandise. The market also offers people an opportunity to find employment. Some wholesalers act as moneylenders as well as recruiting and transporting labor on behalf of the *fincas*.
Indian borrowers can only repay their debt through a work contract with a plantation of the Pacific coast ▲ *290*.

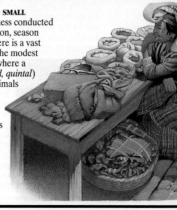

SOUVENIR PHOTOS
Street photographers sometimes provide their customers with an unsophisticated backdrop against which to pose.

MARKETS LARGE AND SMALL
The amount of business conducted varies with the location, season and local events. There is a vast difference between the modest highland markets – where a few measures (*almud, quintal*) of corn and a few animals (cows, mules, pigs, turkeys and chickens) are traded – and the fairs held in conjunction with the saints' festivals or the markets in tourist centers such as Antigua or Chichicastenango.

"MINIFUNDIO"

Divided into tiny, extensively cultivated plots, land is a precious commodity.

ORGANIZATION

The market is divided into specific sections: bread with lime, salt or sugar (*panela*); flowers, incense and spices, including cinnamon, annatto, and fresh and dried chilies; fruit (anona, melons, marmalade plums, papaws, bananas, mangos, oranges); and vegetables (corn, cabbages, beans, carrots, garlic, onions, tomatoes) ◆ *374*.

In another section displays of home-made breads and confectionery (*dulces*) alternate with displays of tortillas and *atole* (corn pancakes and gruel). Some stalls sell cloth, clothes, traditionally made goods (hats, pottery, furniture, mats, saddlery, wool) and manufactured goods (cigarettes, transistor radios, machetes). The cattle market is set apart.

VARIETY OF TRADES
Vendors of fruit and vegetables, hats and other goods sell their wares alongside knife grinders and shoe-shiners.

One of the most striking features of Indian markets is their calm atmosphere. Most market business is carried out in a low voice and is devoid of any form of aggression or street-crying (unlike the sales techniques used by the street vendors who abound in other quarters). Most transactions involve quite small sums of money.

83

The traditional Indian economy is, first and foremost agricultural. Maya (meaning "man of corn") peasants are linked by a quasi-genetic and sacred bond to the land, which is the object of all their attentions. The *milpa* and garden are used to cultivate food crops (corn, beans, marrows and other vegetables) while different plots produce crops for processing (sugar cane and reeds) and sale (onions, garlic and coffee). These crops suffer greatly from the limitations inherent in the *minifundio* system ● *83* – even if the harvest does not fail, it only produces a small surplus and part-time work on coastal or forest plantations is often necessary. For some households the sale of traditional crafts provides only a small income to cover part of the household needs, in others it represents a significant source of supplementary income.

Terracotta bus, wooden horse and pottery from Rabinal.

POTTERY
Mayan potters produce a wide range of items in varying shapes and sizes, from all kinds of functional crockery – baked naturally in the sun or glazed in a kiln – to tiles, animals, human figures and nativity scenes.

WORKING WITH PALMS
Different types of wild palm are plaited to make matting and hats. Hats are manufactured from handmade strips which are sewn together before being pressed into their final shape.

MASKS

Usually made of wood but sometimes of leather, masks are one of the most important elements in the Mayan dances of the highlands ● 76. Tourism has led to an increase in their production and they are now a common sight on market stalls.

LEATHERWORK

The origins of leatherwork lie with the stock-breeders, and it is a craft which tends to be practiced by the Ladinos rather than the Indians. Bags and saddlebags, belts, machete cases, saddlery and harnesses are sold at village markets or in the retail workshops of large towns and cities.

In the 19th century the cultivation of sisal brought prosperity to Yucatán ▲ 196.

ENGRAVED AND PAINTED GOURDS

Decorated gourds are a specialty of one of the districts of Rabinal ▲ 292. They are cut, scooped out and dried before being engraved or painted. The dye for the yellow background used to be obtained by a complicated process which involved extracting the color from a worm (nij), while the red and black pigments used for the animal and flower motifs came from annatto (achiote) and charcoal respectively.

PREPARING TORTII
These corn panca
are always served
with Mayan food.

Black chili sauce is a traditional Yucatecan recipe cooked in tl open air. The Indians grill the long, red chilies on a *comal* (usually the top of an oil drum). They have to be cooked for quite a long time so that they turn from red to black without burning. If they are overcooked they lose their taste, but if the are undercooked they will be too hot and spicy. Tradition has i that if a woman coughs while they are cooking it is a sure sign that she is jealous.

THE SAUCE
INGREDIENTS: 60 red chilies,
6 tomatoes, 4 onions, a pinch of annatto
(red food coloring),

2 lbs cornflour with added lime,
1 cockerel or turkey (6 lbs), salt and peppe

1. Cook the chilies on a wire tray in a partly open oven at gas mark 2, 300°F for about 3½ hours (in a well-ventilated room).

2. Crush the blackened chilies, using your h to obtain a fine powder. Finely chop the tomatoes and onions.

3. Blend the crushed chilies with a paste of cornflour mixed with water until you obtain a *kol* (thick paste).

4. Add the tomatoes, onions, annatto, pepper and salt. The Yucatecans prefer this sauce to be very thin.

Add water until the sauce is thin and will cover the meat during cooking. It can be bought ready made (in Spanish: *recado de chilmole*).

6. Put a quarter of the sauce aside for the stuffing. Place the cockerel in a cooking pot, cover with sauce and cook for about 3 hours.

THE STUFFING

INGREDIENTS: The whites of 15 hard-boiled eggs, 6 to 8 tomatoes, apazote (*chenopodium ambrosiodes*) leaves or, alternatively, oregano or marjoram, 1 lb ground pork, lard.

7. Make a stuffing with the tomatoes, apazote leaves, egg whites cut into fine strips, and pork mince.

Mix the stuffing with the remaining sauce (which may need to be thickened slightly). Fry the mixture gently in a little lard.

9. The Indians usually eat the stuffing separately from the meat and cook it wrapped in a banana leaf. Thicken the stuffing and roll it into a sausage shape. Wrap in foil, making sure it is well sealed, and boil in salted water for about 1 hour.

10. Finally, pour the black chili sauce over the cockerel and serve it either stuffed or with a stuffing sausage.

Young
Garinagus.

Ladino child in
San Salvador.

Mayan history has been deeply affected on many occasions by the arrival of immigrants wh have altered the cultural landscape to a greater or lesser extent. The most significant changes took place with European colonization in the 16th century. Cross-breeding between Spanish settlers and Indians gave rise to the group known as the mestizos, and today they and othe groups with some European origins, known collectively as Ladinos, make up the majority of the population. Other non-Indians live alongside the Maya, in particular Garinagus in Belize and Germans in Guatemala.

Deutsche Schule in Quezaltenang

LADINOS
Ladinos are either white or mixed-race (Indian–European, such as the mestizos) people in Central America. Today they form the majority of the population in each country in the region (with the notable exception of Guatemala) and dominate political and social life. They have adopted a westernized lifestyle both in towns and rural areas. Children from the Ladino bourgeoisie of Mérida (center) in the late 19th century

GERMANS. The Germans settled in Guatemala, and particular in Verapaz ▲ *294* during th 19th century and became integrated into the population while maintaining their own identity. Other ethnic groups in the region include Mennonites Belize and Hindus.

GARINAGUS ▲ *343*. These distant descendants of African slaves have been deeply affected by their extended contact with the Arawakan cultures of the island o St Vincent (Antilles). The Garinagus (belov right) have developed their own extremely rich and complex culture, which combines African and Caribbean traditions.

Mestizo woman from Yucatán, early 20th century.

Ladino from Chiapas (right).

MAYAN TEXTILES

In the following pages t[
letters M and G stand f
Mexico and Guatema

Mayan costume is part of a tradition dating back more than a thousand years and illustrates the fierce attachment of the May to their culture. Textiles provide a link between the pre-Colombian past and the present day, acting as a vehicle for history, legend and myth. For two thousand years production methods have hardly changed and the quality of the weaving has depended on the final use of the clothing and the complexi of the techniques used. Techniques introduced by the Spanish in the 16th century, such as knitting, crochet and the use of the vertical treadle-operated loom, became a male preserve, while weaving with the traditional belt loom remained a female activity.

The "telar de cintura"

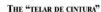

The *telar de cintura*, or belt loom, consists of seven wooden rods. The vertical threads of the warp are held taut between two end-rods. The top rod, fastened at each end by a cord in the form of an inverted Y, is fastened to a tree. The bottom rod is attached to a belt passed behind the back of the kneeling woman to control the tension. Spacer rods separate the two layers of threads: the heddle, or warp rod, which is for controlling the even- and odd-numbered threads; the saber for compressing the weft; the shuttle for passing the threads between the layers; and the "pin spreader", a slender reed rod, for ensuring that the width of the cloth is consistent.

THE "TELAR DE PIE"

is vertical, treadle-operated loom is used to
weave skirts, long lengths of cloth, and
woollen and cotton blankets. This type of
weaving is done by a predominately male
workforce, which is organized in
co-operatives in some villages.

WEAVING TECHNIQUES

The most commonly used of the eleven
official weaving techniques are plain weave,
twill weave, open weave, mottled *ikat* weave
and the "additional weft", which creates a
single- or double-sided brocade effect (the
latter can be used on reversible materials).

▶OMS

▶o types of pre-
▶lombian loom are
▶d: the *telar de
▶tura* (or *de palitos*)
▶, less commonly,
▶ *telar de estacas*.
▶cause they are so
▶ch a part of her
▶, a woman's loom
▶ her finest *huipiles*
▶ buried with her.

"IKAT"

This process consists
of arranging threads
in bundles and
knotting them at
various points before
plunging them into a
dye bath so that only
the exposed
sections are
colored. The
operation is
repeated for each
color. The
different areas of
color are then
arranged on the
warp to create
the design.
Preparing *ikat*
threads at Sololá,
Guatemala
(above).

WOOL

Since the introduction of sheep in the 16th century, the inhabitants of the colder regions have used wool to make clothing. The fibers obtained after shearing are washed and dried in the sun before being carded. This is done using two rectangular wooden combs with handles (above) whose inner surface is covered with tiny metal "teeth". The process involves placing the wool in the center of the combs and drawing it from one comb to the other, teasing out the fibers in the same direction. The wool is then spun in the same way as cotton.

SPINNING

The *malacatl* (or *petet* in the Mayan Tzotzil and Tzeltal dialects) is used for spinning cotton and wool. It consists of a slender wooden rod (between 4 and 15 inches long), filed to a point at both ends, with a clay or stone spindle-whorl inserted into the lower end. The process involves holding the cotton fibers in one hand while using the oth to turn the spindle whose point is placed into a small gourd to keep it stable. With each phase of twisting, the thread is gradually wound onto the spindle (above).

MODERN DEVELOPMENTS

The traditionally dyed and woven material produced by complex techniques have become an established part of modern textil design. Since the 19th century, however, the have tended to be replaced by less expensive, man-made fibers. Today there are an increasing number of projects aimed at reviving ancestral skills.

MOMOSTENANGO

> "WHAT WE INDIANS FIND MOST HURTFUL IS THAT, WHILE THEY
> ⫫D OUR COSTUMES ATTRACTIVE, IT IS AS IF THE PEOPLE WEARING
> THEM DO NOT EXIST."
>
> RIGOBERTA MENCHÚ

THE WHEEL
This more rapid method of spinning involves the use of two wooden wheels, nowadays often replaced by bicycle wheels.

WARPING
This is done prior to weaving. It involves preparing a skein of the same length as the cloth to be woven with the right number of threads for the required width. In order to do this the thread is wound around stakes set in the ground or driven into a plank.

"IXTLE"
Ixtle comes from the agave plant and was utilized to make clothes during the pre-Colombian period. Today it is used for sacking and rope. Preparation and spinning techniques vary according to the region and type of agave (sisal or pita). In Yucatán the leaves are hung over a fire to draw out the sap. When they are soft, they are scraped to remove any excess pulp. The fibers thus obtained are washed, dried and tied in skeins before being spun by the menfolk (tools for spinning *ixtle* are shown above). Near Lake Atitlán, the pulp is crushed with a pestle and the fiber combed, washed and dried in the sun.

COTTON
The more expensive natural white cotton and coffee-colored cotton are used mainly for ceremonial costumes. Once the seeds, leaves and dust have been removed, the cotton is beaten on a leather cushion using two forked sticks to obtain strips for spinning.

93

WOMEN'S COSTUMES

Statuette from the site of Lagartero (Chiapas, Mexico)

The most beautiful examples of weaving are found in the highlands of Chiapas (Mexico) and Guatemala. In other regions, such as the Lacandón Forest, Yucatán, Quintana Roo (Mexico), Belize, Honduras and the lowlands of Guatemala, clothes are more simple. For economic, political and social reasons some ethnic groups have abandoned their traditional costume (to which the women have remained more attached) in favor of a western style of dress. Before the Spanish Conquest this costume consisted of a long *huipil* (a sort of over-blouse) and a skirt. The sophistication of the materials and richness of the jewelry were an indication of the wearer's social status. Traditional costume fulfils the same function today. It consists of a *huipil*, a skirt, a belt, a ribbon for tying the hair, a *tzute* and a *rebozo* (shawl).

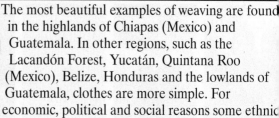

BELTS
Belts of cotton, wool or, more rarely, silk, are decorated with embroidered or brocaded motifs. The colors and the way in which they are worn vary. They are wound round the waist to hold the skirt in place and the ends are only noticeable if they are decorated. The broad belts of Nahuala, Sacatepéquez, Nebaj, Chajul and San Juan (G) are tied at the front or back. In Chichicastenango the threads of the warp are concealed by floral motifs.

The headdresses of the women of Nebaj are of woven cloth, brocaded with colored threads and with large pompons.

In Santiago Atitlán the women wind long red ribbons, brocaded with geometric motifs, around their head.

Women in Palín use long ribbons to make elaborate headdresses, which are twisted, snake-like, above their foreheads.

"TZUTE". The *tzute* consists of one or two rectangular widths of cloth woven on a belt loom then joined together to form a square. Extremely versatile, it can be folded and placed on the head as a protection against the sun, thrown decoratively across the shoulder or opened up and fastened around the neck. It is worn as a cape during festivals.

Belt from Totonicapán (above). Cakchiquel woman (left) from Patzicía (G) wearing a ceremonial *huipil*.

"HUIPIL"
The *huipil* is either square or rectangular in shape. It consists of two or three widths of cloth joined by a seam of vertical stitching which is often embroidered (*randa*), the brocaded section usually forming a cross. The garment is then folded in half and an opening is made in the center for the neck. The stitching at the sides breaks to allow for armholes.

There are two types of *huipil*: tho[se]
worn every day (*huipiles de cocin[a]*
and ceremonial *huipiles*.

**QUICHÉ "HUIPIL"
FROM CHICHICASTENANGO (G)**
The two-headed eagle, the emblem of
Chichicastenango, appears on this *huipil* in
stylized, geometric form. When unfolded, the
design of the Maya cross is visible.

"HUIPIL" FROM RABINAL (G)
The bands of zigzag embroidery on the
shoulders represent lightning. Below these a[re]
dog's paw (possibly symbolizing the
messenger of the Death God), leaf, jar and
flag motifs.

"HUIPIL" FROM SAN JUAN COTZAL (G)
Decorated with alternate bands of animal
and plant motifs.

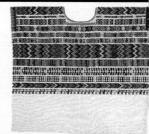

**TZOTZIL "HUIPIL"
FROM SAN ANDRÉS
LARRÁINZAR (M)**
Brocaded with
lozenge motifs in
predominantly red
wool on a white
cotton background.

QUICHÉ "HUIPIL" DE NAHUALÁ (G)
Brocaded with predominantly red animal motifs on a white cotton background.

"HUIPIL" FROM SAN MARTIN JILOTEPEQUE
Characterized by its subtle geometric designs, this *huipil* is decorated with velvet inlays around the neck and armholes.

SKIRT OR "CORTE"
The *corte* is made on a vertical loom and is between 3 and 5 yards long. The ends are sewn together to form a tube. It is worn straight (pulled in at the waist by a belt with the excess material pleated at the front or the back) or gathered at the waist. Costume (left) from San Marcos (G) with a silk *ikat* skirt.

"HUIPIL" FROM SAN MATEO IXTATÁN (G)
Embroidered with concentric motifs.

SPANISH COLLARS
In the Totonicapán region (G), Mayan women wear brightly colored embroidered collars, a legacy from the Spanish. Women from San Cristóbal (left).

● MEN'S COSTUMES

Man from Almolonga (G) wearing traditional costume and holding an *escudo*, the emblem of his brotherhood.

Before the Spanish Conquest basic clothing consisted of a cape (*pati* or *capixay*), a G-string (*maxtatl*) and a long tunic (*xicolli*). On ceremonial occasions the nobility adorned themselves with quetzal-feather headdresses and jewelry. The belt (a remnant of the *maxtatl*) and sandals (*huaraches*) appear on the steles of the Classic period.

The black and wh checked woollen aprons (*ponchitos delantales*), the *tzu* ● 99 and the cape worn by the pre-Colombian Maya still part of the traditional costum

ALMOLONGA
C.L. PETTERSEN.

...e men are gradually abandoning traditional costume, now ...serving it for ceremonial occasions. This is due to their greater ...ntact with the outside world, usually for economic reasons ...uch as seasonal employment – harvesting coffee, picking ...tton, cutting sugarcane – or the need to find work, especially ...the United States) or for political reasons, for example the ...rsecutions of the 1980's.

ZINACANTÁN (M)
The bachelors of this village in Chiapas wear more brightly colored clothes than the married men, and their characteristic pink over-shirts are decorated with larger pompons.

"TZUTE". The square *tzute* is folded in half diagonally, placed on the head and tied at the nape of the neck. On ceremonial occasions it is draped over the shoulder or worn as a bandeau during certain rituals. *Tzute* (above) from Chichicastenango (G).

TODOS SANTOS (G)
Young Mam men wearing shirts with ...rocaded collars and handwoven trousers. ...e black garment worn over the trousers is a remnant of the pre-Hispanic *maxtatl*.

TENEJAPA (CHIAPAS)
A member of the town council in ceremonial dress (below). The straw hat, decorated with multicolored ribbons, is still a common sight in Chiapas (M), especially on ceremonial occasions. Its shape varies, depending on the region.

BELTS
A belt puts the final touch to a costume. Belts are woven on a blue or red ground, sometimes decorated with fine blue stripes. It is brocaded at each end with multicolored motifs and edged with twisted fringes, pompons or macramé work. *Ixil* belt (above) from Chichicastenango.

NAHUALÁ (G)
Man wearing a *tzute*, brocaded with multicolored geometric and zoomorphic motifs, over his shoulder.

99

● THE SYMBOLISM OF CLOTHING

Spinning and weaving are closely associated with the symbolism of childbirth and are placed under the patronage of the Moon goddess. As such they are essential to the reproduction of the mythical universe of the Maya. Each weaver acts as a demiurge and each piece of weaving is a microcosm, a projection of the *imago mundi* and, to some extent, a cosmography whose elements are borrowed from mythology and local history. Thus the composition of the designs of a *huipil* can be read like a text which varies in form and content according to ethnic group, community and lineage. The weaver signs her work with her own particular mark.

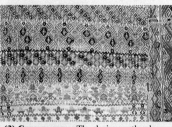

(1) LOZENGES. The rows of brocaded lozenges, or diamonds, on the central motif evoke the cosmos conceived as a cube with three planes: the sky, the earth and the underworld. In the center of each lozenge is the sun (Our Lord Jesus Christ), embodied by Yaxché, the sacred tree of the Maya.

(2) VULTURE AND BEES. The motif below the rows of diamonds represents the vulture and refers to an episode in local mythology. The next row represents bees, the weaver's family motif. The weaver herself signs her work with star motifs.

(3) GERMINATION. The design on the sleeves of this *huipil* describes the complete plant germination cycle. It is also decorated with an inscription of the Mayan calendar (18 months of 20 days, plus 5 unlucky days). Taken as a whole it can be interpreted as a prayer by the weaver to invoke the benevolence of the gods.

ANTHROPOMORPHIC AND ANIMAL SYMBOLS

Just as weaving techniques involve counting the number of threads in the warp and the number of rods, so brocaded designs relate to the measurement of the world. The arrangement of motifs and colors is governed by precise rules. The anthropomorphic and zoomorphic figures symbolize the forces of nature according to local mythology.

Wild animals belong to the dark domain the natural world as opposed to the bright civilized world of Man. The central motif of this *huipil* from San Juan Cotzal (above) consists of bands of geometric motifs and birds.
Flower and deer motifs (left) embroidered on the collar of a Mam *huipil* from San Marcos (G).

**..IPIL" OF THE VIRGIN FROM
..GDALENAS (M).** This shows
..tailed chart of the Maya
..nogony (**1**, **2** and **3**, left).
..y of the pre-Hispanic motifs
.. symbols which appear on
..s, statuettes, codices,
..cos and ceramics
..reproduced on
..ern textiles.

..ntel
..from
..xchilán
..), dating from
..719, depicts
..een Xoc
..aring a *huipil*
..corated with
..e same
..mond motifs
..at appear on
..e modern
..*ipiles* of
..agdalenas (M).

TWO-HEADED ANIMALS. These animals represent the dualistic vision of the world shared by all Mesoamerican cultures. The symbol of the two-headed eagle of Quiché Maya mythology is widely used today on the ceremonial *huipiles* and *tzutes* of Chichicastenango (G).

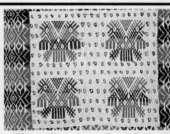

"HUIPILES" AND "TZUTES" FROM PALÍN (G) These *huipiles* and *tzutes* are decorated with two-headed eagles surrounded by zigzag, fly and diamond motifs. The Spanish identified the eagle with the Habsburg eagle but, according to the *Popol Vuh* manuscript, the bird is an ancestor of the Quichés.

"HUIPIL" FROM CHAJUL (G). This *Ixil huipil* is often decorated with a front view of two-headed animals, their heads in profile. These motifs were widely used in pre-Hispanic Mayan iconography. Bird motif (above).

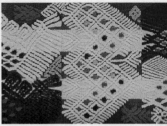

REPTILES. Reptiles wind their way through the designs like a serpent between the earth and sky. The finest examples are found on the *huipiles* of San Juan Sacatepéquez (above), where zoomorphic motifs alternate with a band representing the Feathered Serpent.

PLANTS AND BIRDS. The *huipiles* of Cobán (G) and Venustiano Carranza (M) are characterized by plant and bird motifs. On this *huipil* from Tactic (G) a hummingbird is perched on a clump of tobacco.

TURKEYS. The birds and animals most widely represented are the turkey (above, on a *huipil* from San Pedro Sacatepéquez), peacock, cockerel, deer, squirrel, jaguar, opossum and hummingbird.

FERTILITY
The scorpion, usually associated with flower motifs, is believed to bring rain by causing lightning. These motifs, like the cactus motif (left), decorate the embroidered skirts of the Tzotzils of Venustiano Carranza (M).

BATS
The bat, a common motif on the jackets of Sololá (G), is the symbol of the royal house of Xahilá, whose prince led the Cakchiquels on their legendary journey in search of a permanent home (right).

ZIGZAGS. Zigzags are the symbol of the Lightning god, the dispenser of rain, and re a popular motif on the textiles of many villages. The women of Pantelhó (M) decorate the sleeves of their garments (above) with zigzags and motifs of toads (harbingers of rain).

MONKEYS. Monkeys are associated with disaster and evoke a previous creation. On the *huipiles* of Chenalhó (M) the body of the monkey, represented by three vertical lines, is surrounded by curves representing the arms and legs (above). The motif reminds the Maya of their obligation to worship the gods.

THE COSMIC TREE

The cosmic tree ● 64 also known as *Yaxché* or the Tree of Life, is central to the cosmology of the Maya, who believed that their ancestors came from its roots. It occupies pride of place on the ceremonial *huipiles* of San Pedro Sacatepéquez (left), San Pedro Ayampuc and Chuarrancho (G).

CIRCLES

The tooth-shaped material inlays around the neck of the *huipiles* from Chichicastenango, and the four small circles decorating the front, back and shoulders, are associated with solar worship. Other concentric motifs are embroidered on the "fins" of the trousers of brotherhood members (below).

HUIPIL" FROM SAN JUAN COTZAL. The neck f this *huilpil* (below) is decorated with leaf motifs. The woman who wears it is placed symbolically at the center of the universe, surrounded by four leaves which represent the four points of the compass and correspond to the solstices and equinoxes.

● ACCESSORIES

Pre-Hispanic and contemporary sandals.

Pre-Hispanic iconography attests to a profusion of quetzal-feather headdresses, intricately carved jade jewelry and other finery worn by Mayan dignitaries. Modern accessories have lost this former magnificence and have become much more simple. The women enjoy wearing jewelry, however, and take pride in complementing their clothes with necklaces, rings and earrings. The men make do with sandals and straw hats.

NECKLACE OR "CHACHAL"
The necklace is an important accessory for Mayan women and fine coral necklaces, decorated with silver coins from the colonial period, are a common sight in many villages. Often the women also wear several rows of large glass beads (gold, red or blue, depending on the area) and chains decorated with a heavy cross or, for marriage ceremonies, a huge silver coin.

HEADBAND OR "MECAPAL"
The *mecapal* is indispensable for carrying heavy loads in areas where there are no pack animals. It consists of a flat, leather strip whose ends are joined by a cord. The leather strip is placed on the forehead and the cord used to secure the load.

SANDALS OR "HUARACHES"
In both Mexico and Guatemala *huaraches* are an exclusively male accessory. They have either a leather sole or a rubber one, cut from an old tire, with a single thong which passes between the toes and fastens around the ankle. Some sandals have a heel piece.

BLANKETS
Blankets are an extremely important accessory. As well as providing protection against the cold, they can also be spread on the ground to display produce at market. The smaller, black and white checked *ponchitos* are worn around the waist by the men.

RINGS AND EARRINGS
Mayan women are very fond of rings and earrings. Rings are made of silver or nickel and decorated with a heart, an animal or glass beads. There are long, lightweight, filigree earrings or a heavier variety, made from small coins set off by a stone.

BAG OR "MORRAL"
Although the men do not wear jewelry, they never go anywhere without their *morral* containing seeds, fruit or other items.

ARCHITECTURE

In spite of very serious practical constraints, such as the absence of metals, pack animals and the wheel, the Maya were the first builders in Mesoamerica. From the outset their architecture aimed to impress by its vast size. The effort initially reserved for pyramidal bases, was soon applied to the actual buildings, particularly with the introduction of the arch, which opened the way for the upward development of architecture, a symbol of prestige.

SCULPTED DECORATION
The solidly cemented stones were often decorated with one or several repeating motifs.

WALL BONDING
Originally walls were made of rough-hewn blocks of stone, held together by mortar. However, a new concrete casing technique replaced this type of large-stone construction to some extent. The inner surface of the carefully squared stones, often sculpted on the outside, was left irregular so that it would bond with the concrete.

BASES
The bases consisted of one or several rock-hewn platforms, decreasing in size as they progressed vertically, forming the trunk of a step pyramid. Each step consisted of a rubble and earth bank, retained by a stone wall.

DEVELOPMENT OF THE ARCH
1. Archaic (3rd–8th century), rough-hewn bonding. 2. Classic (9th–16th century), decorative casing.

DIFFERENT TYPES OF CLASSIC ARCH
1. Concave arch.
2. Convex arch.
3. Step arch.
4. Trefoil arch.

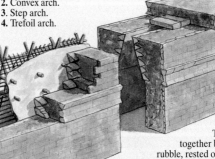

ARCH
The arch, he together by mortar a rubble, rested on two walls gradually increasing thickness. The g was closed by a stone slab. To complete t arch, a wooden framework held each course of sto blocks in place while the concrete was poured on. Apa from its esthetic value, the concrete "veneer" also acted as a casir

LIME KILN

Crushed carbonate (limestone) was tipped into a large pile of logs which served as fuel. A vertical piece of wood was placed in the center during construction. When removed, the chimney thus created was filled with hot coals to set fire to the logs.

CARVED RELIEFS

Each element of a figure in relief was individually carved and painted before being put into place. Gradually building up a relief in this way gave a more natural appearance. Relief (right) on Pillar E of House C at Palenque ▲ 243.

PREPARING A STUCCOED WALL

When a wall had to support a relatively heavy stuccoed relief, a preparation made of small stones and mortar was applied. This acted as a reinforcement or tenon for the relief. Stuccoed mask (left) at the Temple of Kohunlich ▲ 189.

POLYCHROME

The Maya used a fairly wide range of colors to paint walls, pillars and stuccoed reliefs. They were probably obtained locally and included blue, vermilion, yellow and white.

FRESCOS

The walls and arches of many buildings such as Bonampak (▲ 249) were decorated with frescos, often of complex composition. Most surviving frescos are found on internal structures, where they have been protected from the effects of the sun and bad weather.

Mayan architecture of all types was traditionally set on stone bases. Prestigious architecture picks up and accentuates this characteristic feature borrowed from archaic dwellings. The various types of imposing structures (the functions of which are often difficult to determine) all attest to a desire for height: from the temple-pyramids, which symbolize the link between heaven and earth, to the structures defined as "palaces" by the early Spanish conquerors, as well as other buildings of intermediate stature.

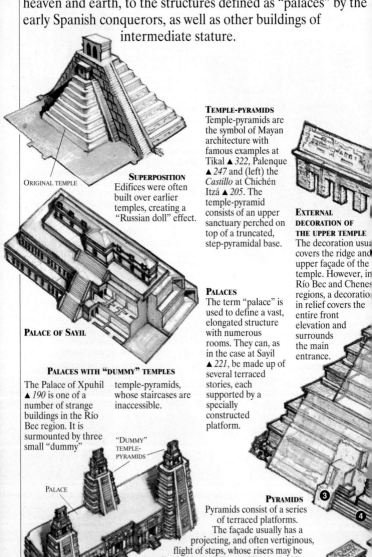

ORIGINAL TEMPLE

SUPERPOSITION
Edifices were often built over earlier temples, creating a "Russian doll" effect.

PALACE OF SAYIL

PALACES WITH "DUMMY" TEMPLES
The Palace of Xpuhil ▲ 190 is one of a number of strange buildings in the Río Bec region. It is surmounted by three small "dummy" temple-pyramids, whose staircases are inaccessible.

PALACE

"DUMMY" TEMPLE-PYRAMIDS

TEMPLE-PYRAMIDS
Temple-pyramids are the symbol of Mayan architecture with famous examples at Tikal ▲ 322, Palenque ▲ 247 and (left) the *Castillo* at Chichén Itzá ▲ 205. The temple-pyramid consists of an upper sanctuary perched on top of a truncated, step-pyramidal base.

PALACES
The term "palace" is used to define a vast, elongated structure with numerous rooms. They can, as in the case at Sayil ▲ 221, be made up of several terraced stories, each supported by a specially constructed platform.

EXTERNAL DECORATION OF THE UPPER TEMPLE
The decoration usua[lly] covers the ridge and upper façade of the temple. However, in Río Bec and Chenes regions, a decoratio[n] in relief covers the entire front elevation and surrounds the main entrance.

PYRAMIDS
Pyramids consist of a series of terraced platforms. The façade usually has a projecting, and often vertiginous, flight of steps, whose risers may be inscribed with glyphic texts (Copán ▲ 299) or the images of conquered enemies (Tamarindito ▲ 332). Where the base of the pyramid is a monumental plinth, it has often been used as a tomb.

❸

❹

❺

PYRA[MID] INSCR[...]

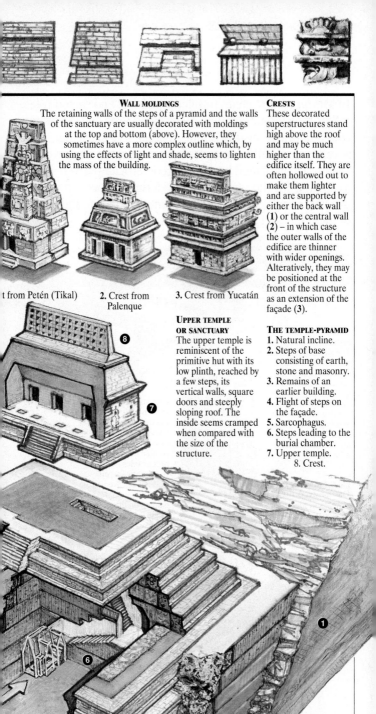

WALL MOLDINGS
The retaining walls of the steps of a pyramid and the walls of the sanctuary are usually decorated with moldings at the top and bottom (above). However, they sometimes have a more complex outline which, by using the effects of light and shade, seems to lighten the mass of the building.

t from Petén (Tikal)

2. Crest from Palenque

3. Crest from Yucatán

CRESTS
These decorated superstructures stand high above the roof and may be much higher than the edifice itself. They are often hollowed out to make them lighter and are supported by either the back wall (**1**) or the central wall (**2**) – in which case the outer walls of the edifice are thinner with wider openings. Alteratively, they may be positioned at the front of the structure as an extension of the façade (**3**).

UPPER TEMPLE OR SANCTUARY
The upper temple is reminiscent of the primitive hut with its low plinth, reached by a few steps, its vertical walls, square doors and steeply sloping roof. The inside seems cramped when compared with the size of the structure.

THE TEMPLE-PYRAMID
1. Natural incline.
2. Steps of base consisting of earth, stone and masonry.
3. Remains of an earlier building.
4. Flight of steps on the façade.
5. Sarcophagus.
6. Steps leading to the burial chamber.
7. Upper temple.
   8. Crest.

CHOOSING A SITE
The best site was a natural incline because it enabled the pyramidal base to be built against the slope. This natural foundation limited the size of the structure to be built.

QUE

109

Part of the altar associated
with Stele 22 at Tikal.

In Mayan culture steles fulfilled a political and sacred role
rather than a funerary one. Their dated texts and decorations
commemorated historic events relating to a particular
sovereign, as well as episodes from mythology. They were
usually accompanied by a huge, geometrically carved stone used
as an altar for the sacrifices and offerings associated with
dynastic rituals. The stele-altar combination is found at the foot
of pyramids and in certain holy places.

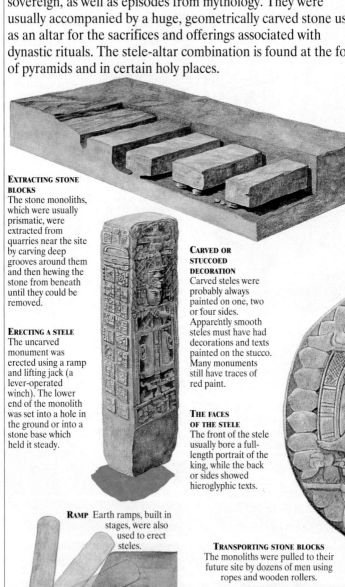

EXTRACTING STONE BLOCKS
The stone monoliths, which were usually prismatic, were extracted from quarries near the site by carving deep grooves around them and then hewing the stone from beneath until they could be removed.

ERECTING A STELE
The uncarved monument was erected using a ramp and lifting jack (a lever-operated winch). The lower end of the monolith was set into a hole in the ground or into a stone base which held it steady.

CARVED OR STUCCOED DECORATION
Carved steles were probably always painted on one, two or four sides. Apparently smooth steles must have had decorations and texts painted on the stucco. Many monuments still have traces of red paint.

THE FACES OF THE STELE
The front of the stele usually bore a full-length portrait of the king, while the back or sides showed hieroglyphic texts.

RAMP Earth ramps, built in stages, were also used to erect steles.

TRANSPORTING STONE BLOCKS
The monoliths were pulled to their future site by dozens of men using ropes and wooden rollers.

"…OOMORPHIC" ROCK

…variation to the usual …le-altar combination … be found at …irigua ▲ 306, …ere a …oomorphic" …k is paired with …at, irregularly …ped stone, used … an altar.

SCALE

… stele usually stands …etween 6½ and 13 …eet high, but much …rger examples have …een found. Stele E …Quirigua is over 38 feet high.

ICONOGRAPHY OF A STELE

Stele 22 at Tikal ▲ *324* is a fine example of the political and religious symbolism of this type of monument. It commemorates the performance by King C of one of the rites celebrating the end of the *katun* ● *44.* The date is scrupulously recorded and corresponds to AD 771.

…RM AND ICONOGRAPHY OF AN ALTAR

…is altar, associated with Stele 22 at …kal, is in the fairly common form of a …v cylinder. The carved surface (above) …ows a captive about to be sacrificed. …ound the edge a plaited motif (a royal …ribute) is repeated at intervals and …ere is another image of a bound …soner.

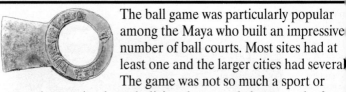

The ball game was particularly popular among the Maya who built an impressive number of ball courts. Most sites had at least one and the larger cities had several. The game was not so much a sport or spectacle as a ritual, symbolizing the struggle between the forces of life and death. It was sometimes associated with a divine judgement and may have been used to settle a conflict. After the game, victims (most probably the losers or their representatives) were decapitated.

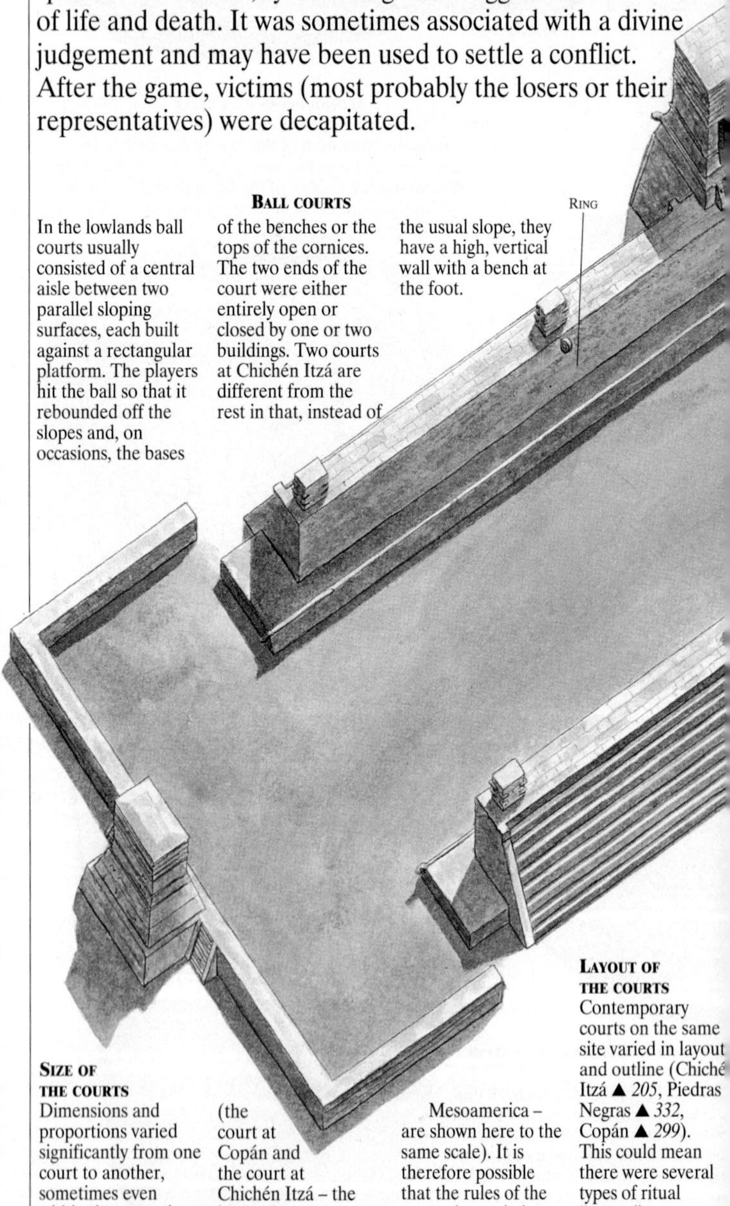

BALL COURTS

In the lowlands ball courts usually consisted of a central aisle between two parallel sloping surfaces, each built against a rectangular platform. The players hit the ball so that it rebounded off the slopes and, on occasions, the bases of the benches or the tops of the cornices. The two ends of the court were either entirely open or closed by one or two buildings. Two courts at Chichén Itzá are different from the rest in that, instead of the usual slope, they have a high, vertical wall with a bench at the foot.

RING

SIZE OF THE COURTS
Dimensions and proportions varied significantly from one court to another, sometimes even within the same site (the court at Copán and the court at Chichén Itzá – the largest in Mesoamerica – are shown here to the same scale). It is therefore possible that the rules of the game also varied.

LAYOUT OF THE COURTS
Contemporary courts on the same site varied in layout and outline (Chichén Itzá ▲ 205, Piedras Negras ▲ 332, Copán ▲ 299). This could mean there were several types of ritual "games".

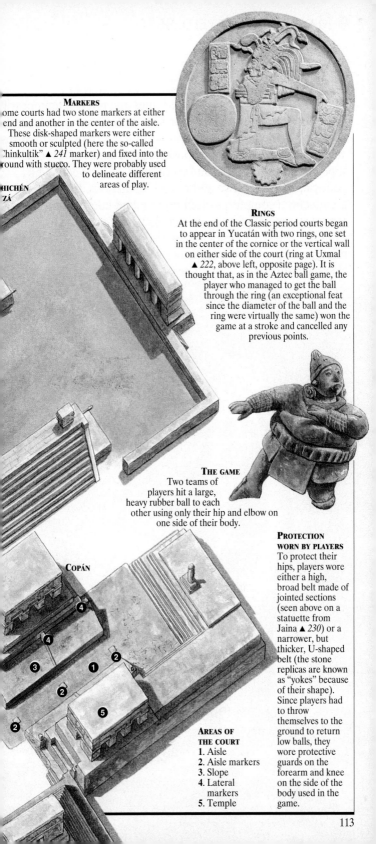

MARKERS

Some courts had two stone markers at either end and another in the center of the aisle. These disk-shaped markers were either smooth or sculpted (here the so-called "Chinkultik" ▲ 241 marker) and fixed into the ground with stucco. They were probably used to delineate different areas of play.

CHICHÉN
ZÁ

RINGS

At the end of the Classic period courts began to appear in Yucatán with two rings, one set in the center of the cornice or the vertical wall on either side of the court (ring at Uxmal ▲ 222, above left, opposite page). It is thought that, as in the Aztec ball game, the player who managed to get the ball through the ring (an exceptional feat since the diameter of the ball and the ring were virtually the same) won the game at a stroke and cancelled any previous points.

THE GAME

Two teams of players hit a large, heavy rubber ball to each other using only their hip and elbow on one side of their body.

COPÁN

AREAS OF THE COURT
1. Aisle
2. Aisle markers
3. Slope
4. Lateral markers
5. Temple

PROTECTION
WORN BY PLAYERS
To protect their hips, players wore either a high, broad belt made of jointed sections (seen above on a statuette from Jaina ▲ 230) or a narrower, but thicker, U-shaped belt (the stone replicas are known as "yokes" because of their shape). Since players had to throw themselves to the ground to return low balls, they wore protective guards on the forearm and knee on the side of the body used in the game.

● MAYAN URBAN DEVELOPMENT

The major Mayan sites were true cities and not just temporarily inhabited ceremonial centers. In spite of their fairly loose-knit network of dwellings, apparently scattered groups of structures and an urban environment consisting of a series of superpositions, the cities in fact fulfilled definite economic, political, administrative and religious functions. Edifices and architectural complexes often represented microcosms and served as a setting for rituals that may have involved movement from one area to another. These various areas had to observe relations of proximity or distance which gave the city its characteristic, open appearance.

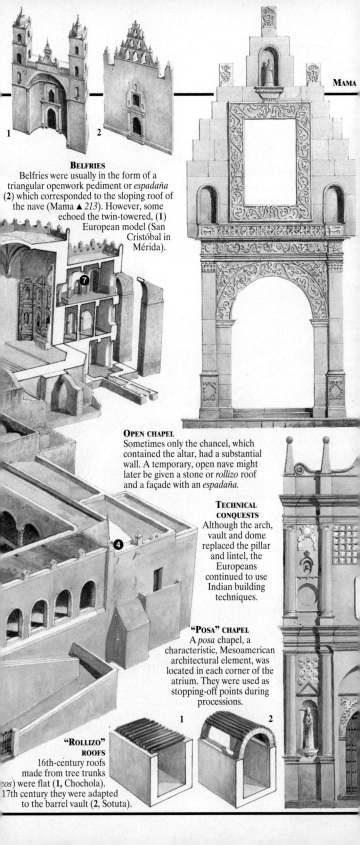

BELFRIES
Belfries were usually in the form of a triangular openwork pediment or *espadaña* (2) which corresponded to the sloping roof of the nave (Mama ▲ *213*). However, some echoed the twin-towered, (1) European model (San Cristóbal in Mérida).

OPEN CHAPEL
Sometimes only the chancel, which contained the altar, had a substantial wall. A temporary, open nave might later be given a stone or *rollizo* roof and a façade with an *espadaña*.

TECHNICAL CONQUESTS
Although the arch, vault and dome replaced the pillar and lintel, the Europeans continued to use Indian building techniques.

"POSA" CHAPEL
A *posa* chapel, a characteristic, Mesoamerican architectural element, was located in each corner of the atrium. They were used as stopping-off points during processions.

"ROLLIZO" ROOFS
16th-century roofs made from tree trunks (*zos*) were flat (**1**, Chochola). 17th century they were adapted to the barrel vault (**2**, Sotuta).

URBAN LAYOUT: DWELLINGS AND CEREMONIAL CENTER

ever the ation density of habited regions, mmunity et, village or as not built on layout and its

streets were not lined with buildings. As a general rule dwellings were scattered and situated on high ground. The layout of the center varied: at

Copán and Quirigua, the Acropolis and Great Plaza form the nucleus, while the center of Becán ▲ 191 (below) is less compact.

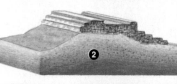

SCULPTED DECORATION OF A GATEWAY
LAB

TEMPLE-PYRAMID

DITCH

a

After the 16th-century Spanish Conquest Christian
architecture spread across traditional Maya territory.
Religious complexes were built along similar lines to their
European counterparts. A monastery with cloister, cells,
refectory, kitchen and hospital was linked to a single-nave
church. The priest's residence, complete with ribbed vault,
was adjacent to the church. Architectural elements
specific to the colonial mission included an atrium with
monumental entrances, chapels to the Virgin, open
chapels and *posas* chapels.

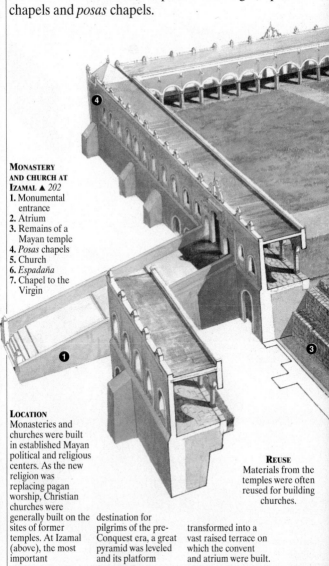

**MONASTERY
AND CHURCH AT
IZAMAL ▲** *202*
1. Monumental
   entrance
2. Atrium
3. Remains of a
   Mayan temple
4. *Posas* chapels
5. Church
6. *Espadaña*
7. Chapel to the
   Virgin

LOCATION
Monasteries and
churches were built
in established Mayan
political and religious
centers. As the new
religion was
replacing pagan
worship, Christian
churches were
generally built on the
sites of former
temples. At Izamal
(above), the most
important

destination for
pilgrims of the pre-
Conquest era, a great
pyramid was leveled
and its platform

REUSE
Materials from the
temples were often
reused for building
churches.

transformed into a
vast raised terrace on
which the convent
and atrium were built.

WATER SUPPLY
Different towns and cities solved the problem in different ways:
river (Copán), *chultunes* (Labná ▲ *220*),
reservoirs (Tikal), and *cenotes*
(Chichén Itzá ▲ *205*).

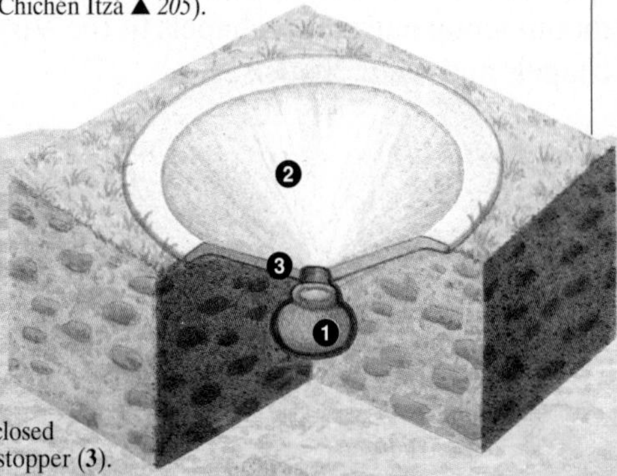

"CHULTUN"
The *chultun* was a
small, pear-shaped
cistern (**1**) dug in
the ground. It was
filled with water by
means of a steeply
sloping, funnel-
shaped chamber
(**2**) whose "feed
hole" was closed
with a stopper (**3**).

RESERVOIR
This former clay
quarry was used to
collect rainwater. The
excavation of the
retaining walls
revealed a clay lining
which ensured that
the reservoir was
watertight.

"CENOTE"
In Yucatán, the *cenote*
is a large, natural well
which connects with
the watertable via a
network of drains in the
limestone ■ *16*. Offerings were
thrown into some *cenotes* ▲ *209*.

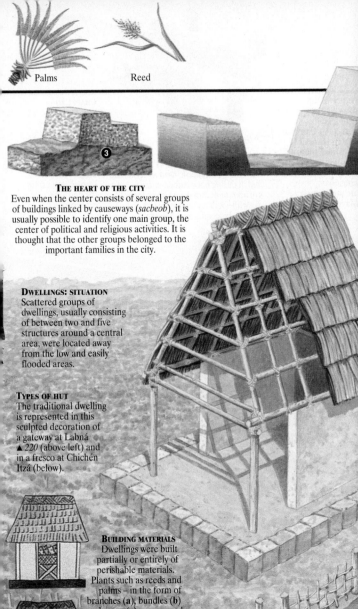

Palms   Reed

③

THE HEART OF THE CITY
Even when the center consists of several groups
of buildings linked by causeways (*sacbeob*), it is
usually possible to identify one main group, the
center of political and religious activities. It is
thought that the other groups belonged to the
important families in the city.

DWELLINGS: SITUATION
Scattered groups of
dwellings, usually consisting
of between two and five
structures around a central
area, were located away
from the low and easily
flooded areas.

TYPES OF HUT
The traditional dwelling
is represented in this
sculpted decoration of
a gateway at Labná
▲ *220* (above left) and
in a fresco at Chichén
Itzá (below).

BUILDING MATERIALS
Dwellings were built
partially or entirely of
perishable materials.
Plants such as reeds and
palms – in the form of
branches (**a**), bundles (**b**)
or sheaves (**c**) – were used
for roofs: wattling and
mudbrick were used for
walls, wood for palisades
and stone for
foundations.

b   **c**

WALLS AND
ENCLOSURES
Walls and enclosures were made from
vertical stakes interwoven with branches

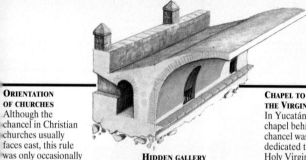

ORIENTATION OF CHURCHES
Although the chancel in Christian churches usually faces east, this rule was only occasionally observed in colonial religious architecture on Maya territory.

HIDDEN GALLERY
This strange invention, used to aerate the church during hot weather, consisted of a corridor built into the width of the wall, with windows on the outside and balconies on the inside.

CHAPEL TO THE VIRGIN
In Yucatán, the chapel behind the chancel was dedicated to the Holy Virgin. The oldest example, at Izamal, dates from the mid 17th century.

(rollo
In the

'DÉJAR STYLE
e first urban
ous monuments
ed, with slight
tions, the strict
etric planes of
ish decoration.
age churches
d this influence
r a long time
afterward.

LATERESQUE
ECORATION
 Spanish-style
tion, influenced
e Renaissance,
spired by (and
after) the art of
e silversmith
). The entrance
church of Mama
osite) and the
çade of the
ral of Mérida
8 (right).

BAROQUE STYLE
From the late 17th century the Baroque style
exerted its influence on the façades (cathedral
of San Cristóbal de las Casas ▲ 233) and
interior decoration of Ladino architecture.
Statues, paintings and the painted wood,
silver-gilt or gilt columns of retables were
combined with pre-Hispanic motifs to
produce a superficially Baroque style.

121

ARCH. Arch of Santa Catalina Mártir, Antigua Guatemala.

During the Conquest Hispanic towns were created on empty or abandoned land, where their layout was plotted in straight lines. The pretexts used to justify the colonization of Maya territory were "civilization" and "evangelization". Both concepts were embodied in the new towns which initially provided a base for European settlers and subsequently became a showcase both for the West and for the Catholic Church. At the same time the towns were used to control a vast hinterland through strategic concentrations of the Indian population.

FIRST GENERATION TOWNS
The design and development of towns such as San Cristóbal de las Casas ▲ 233 (founded in 1528) reflected the desire to avoid possible Maya rebellions.

OUTLYING INDIAN DISTRICTS
The colonial town's principal means of combating rebellion was to create an urban population. Groups of the conquered people were moved into a series of outlying Indian districts (*barrios*) encircling the Spanish center (*recinto*).

MEANS OF PROTECTION
Natural protection and human shields separated the *recinto* of San Cristóbal from those Indians living in the mountains:
1. Prairies.
2. Rivers.
3. Cultivated plots of the *barrios*.
4. Perimeter patrols of the six Indian *barrios*.
5. Open areas between the *barrios* and the *recinto*.
6. Monasteries.
7. Marshland replacing a defensive moat.

SITE
The site of San Cristóbal lies in a valley surrounded by mountains rising to more than 6,500 feet. It is depicted here as it was a century after it was founded.

MONASTERIES. The monastery lay between the Spanish center of the town and the outlying Indian *barrios*. It acted as an embassy for the Maya and an intermediary in this segregated community. One such example is the monastery of Santo Domingo de San Cristóbal ▲ 235.

**SECOND
GENERATION TOWNS**

In towns such as
Mérida ▲ 198
(founded in 1542)
and Antigua ▲ 270
(founded in 1543) the
barrios were absorbed
into the recinto. From
this point onwards,
towns focused on the
management of a new
mestizo society. They
became the
headquarters of
religious and civic
organizations. Urban
architects determined
their layout,
coordinated the
major buildings and
used the site to the
best advantage.

CENTRAL SQUARE
The central square (zócalo) was
occupied by the cathedral, the
governor's palace, the conquistador's palace
and the municipal buildings. This
type of square (Mérida, above)
united and gave structure to
the checkerboard layout of
the towns in colonized
Maya territory.

NEOCLASSICISM
With independence,
the influence of
neoclassicism – the
architectural showcase
of republican and
secular ideals – was
seen in a number of
civic buildings. It
replaced the Baroque
style, perceived as a
humiliating reminder
of colonial
rule.

**URBAN
LAYOUT**
Towns were designed
with obvious foresight and
included undeveloped areas to
allow for expansion. Modern San
Cristóbal and Mérida have been able to
develop around the framework of roads and plots
of land established when they were first founded.

**CONTROL OF THE
HINTERLAND**
In the hinterland the
Indian population
was grouped in
strategically placed
villages known as
reducciones – smaller
scale replicas of the
regional town ● 64.

123

Urban dwellings were based on, and as complex as, the design of monasteries. They were organized around the *casa grande* (reception area and domestic altar) and the *casa chica* (bedroom area). The two *casas* were linked by a patio surrounded by a gallery, a replica of the cloister, used as a living area. Built along similar lines, the hacienda – the country residence of a landowner – was more spacious.

WINDOWS
Windows and their grilles show all the successive decorative styles of colonial towns: from the Plateresque, through the geometric Mudéjar and exuberant Baroque (window in San Cristóbal, above), to the neoclassicism of Independence (window in San Cristóbal, below).

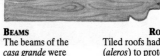

BEAMS
The beams of the *casa grande* were carved with the characteristic *pecho de paloma* (pigeon breast) decoration.

ROOFS
Tiled roofs had very wide eaves (*aleros*) to protect the walls from the heavy seasonal rains.

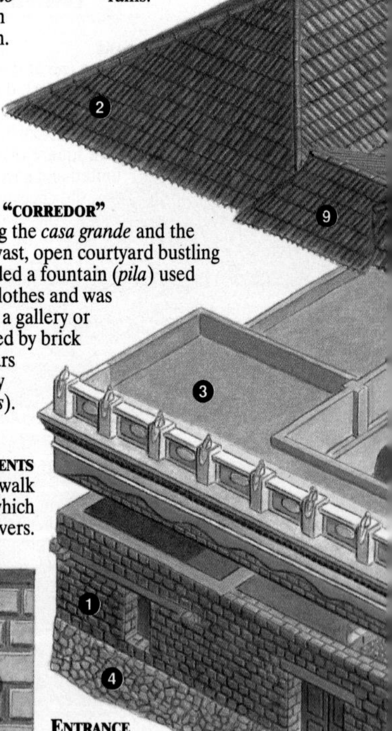

2

9

PATIO AND "CORREDOR"
The patio linking the *casa grande* and the *casa chica* was a vast, open courtyard bustling with life. It included a fountain (*pila*) used for washing clothes and was surrounded by a gallery or *corredor*, supported by brick or wood pillars surmounted by capitals (*zapatas*).

3

PAVEMENTS
High pavements enabled pedestrians to walk dry-footed after the heavy rains which transformed the streets into rivers.

1

4

ENTRANCE
Early entrances echoed the Plateresque ● *121* Renaissance style: flat surfaces with a sculpted, almost incised, decoration whose abundance sometimes suggests a prefiguration of the Baroque. Entrance to the *casa de la Sirena*, San Cristóbal ▲ *233* (left).

HACIENDA AT CHUNCHUCMIL, MEXICO.

COUNTRY RESIDENCES

he hacienda (**A**), also known as a *finca* or *rancho*, echoed the basic ayout of the urban dwelling but was characterized by the inclusion of a chapel (**B**). It was here that the peons gathered to receive their otted tasks for the day. The patio was replaced by a vast courtyard, shaded by the branches of a guardian tree (● *64*, ● *103*).

RAW MATERIALS
Hispanic builders ignored the limestone rock resource of the Maya, preferring the better insulating properties of clay. This was used in its raw state for walls (*adobe*) and fired to make bricks, tiles and decorative ceramics.

ANGLE JOINTS AND LACING
Frameworks were not nailed together but tied with leather lacing.

CLAMPING
The walls had to be able to withstand earthquakes and were clamped using a concealed wooden brace or *alma*.

URBAN DWELLING

1. Adobe	11. Covered gallery
2. Half-round tiles	12. Pillar surmounted
3. Roof terrace	by capitals
4. Stone wall	13. Tiled roof
5. Chalk coating	14. Wooden brace
6. Cladding to protect	15. Window with grille
against damp	16. Pavement
7. *Casa grande*	17. Workshop, stable
8. *Casa chica*	or farmyard
9. Porch	18. Workshop
10. Patio	entrance

125

A far cry from the temples and palaces of bygone days, Indian houses are essentially crude and rustic. The two main types of construction are distinguished by whether the roof is supported by load-bearing walls or stakes set in the ground. Today traditional building materials are being replaced by modern materials which, although more expensive and less conducive to comfort, extend the life of the building and make it more likely to withstand bad weather and earthquakes.

"ADOBE"
Adobe bricks are made of raw clay and straw.

TROPICAL LOWLANDS
In these forest regions, houses are often only a basic hut with fence-like walls made of planks and branches. The roof is covered with palm fronds.

NEW ROOFING MATERIALS
1. Gutter tiles.
2. Corrugated iron.
3. Corrugated cardboard coated with tar.

HIGHLANDS OF GUATEMALA
The most common form of highland dwelling is a solid structure with *adobe* brick walls supporting a heavy tiled roof. The living area contains a corn loft, hives and sometimes a steam-bath (*tenazcal*).

CHIAPAS
The very elaborate framework of thatched or palm-leaf roofs is supported by pillars. The mud walls (*bajareques*) are built afterwards. Mud is flattened and smoothed by hand onto horizontal slats before sometimes being whitewashed. Stone bases are used less systematically than in the past
● 116.

126

THE ROUTE OF THE MAYAS
AS SEEN BY ARTISTS

The spectacular development of Mayan pictorial art during the Late Classic period (AD 600–800) both illustrated and accompanied a religious and esthetic ideology which liberated the various forms of Mayan representations from the power of authority and death. The mediums used were various: codices (manuscripts written in hieroglyphics and illustrated with drawings), wall paintings and polychrome vases. The codex was a manuscript consisting of a strip of bast paper several yards long, covered with a fine layer of lime and folded in a "concertina". On this page of the Madrid Codex (1) ● 42 the Death God strikes the celestial serpent with his axe to make rain fall. Glyphs representing days on the divinatory calendar are arranged in four rows across the center of the image. Reproductions, made in 1947 by the artist Antonio Tejeda Fonseca, of the frescos of Bonampak ▲ 249 are on display at the Mexican National Museum of Anthropology. In this scene (2) showing Chan Muan surrounded by his generals, the captive at the king's feet symbolizes Death and thus confirms the ruler's omnipotence. The drama of the scene is heightened by the brilliantly colored figures. The subject of this polychrome vase (3) reiterates the theme of human sacrifice ● 46 with its depiction of a captive being led away. It is one of several Late Classic vases, discovered at Altamira, in the State of Campeche (Mexico). One of the vases found at Altar de los Sacrificios ▲ 333 dates from AD 754 and shows a dancer representing the Bird Jaguar (previous page).

1	2
3	

Even before Independence Guatemala had already produced some extremely talented artists One notable example was José Casildo España, who depicted the descendants of the Maya in a pure neoclassical style. His *Guatemala-Kiché* (1818, below) represents, for the first time in the colonial history of Guatemala, the very real presence of the Maya population. In 1832 the artist and adventurer, Jean-Frédéric Waldeck (1766–1857) ● *56*, discovered the world of the Maya and embarked upon an exploration of the temple of Palenque in Chiapas ▲ *244*. He produced over one hundred drawings and watercolors of a clearly academic nature. In *Façade orientale du palais de Palenque* (**1**) he drew on the Western Classical repertoire (the nude in the foreground and the posing figures) to present Europe with an idealized perception of the world of the Maya. *Incidents of Travel in Central America, Chiapas and Yucatán* (1841), a work by two cultured and resolutely "modern" travelers, combined the talented writings of John Stephens (1805–52) ● *56, 153*, with the remarkable engravings of Frederick Catherwood ● *58*. It was an immediate bestseller and exercised a decisive influence over generations of Mayanist scholars. Catherwood's quasi-photographic reproductions give a much more realistic impression of Mayan architecture as, for example, in his *View of a temple to the south of the Castillo of Tulum* ▲ *177* which shows *macheteros* clearing land for cultivation (**2**).

1

2

"E BEAUTY OF THE SCULPTURE . . . , THE DESOLATION OF THE CITY ND THE AIR OF MYSTERY THAT ENVELOPED IT INSPIRED IN ME A E OF EXCITEMENT MORE ACUTE THAN ANY I HAD EXPERIENCED ONG THE RUINS OF THE OLD WORLD." JOHN LLOYD STEPHENS

RECIBIÓ COFRADIA QUE E...
LANDO EN EL MEDIO Y LO...
ESTAN SENTADO EN LA CA...
RON ADEJAR HECHO POR...

Andrés Curruchich (1891–1969), a member of the Cakchiquel community in Comalapa ▲ 276, was one of the founders of 20th-century Guatemalan Indian painting. This self-taught artist drew his inspiration from everyday life and traditions. With paintings like *Transfer of the Saint by the Brotherhood* (**2**) he produced a visual record of the work and daily life of a peasant community where the spiritual and supernatural were all-important. These themes were reiterated and developed by his descendants and by the many popular artists, from Comalapa to Santiago Atitlán ▲ 281, who celebrated the peaceful world to which they aspired. None of these more recent works, although painted at a time of extreme violence, depicts the contemporary massacres or the burning of houses and cornfields. Rather they focus on everyday life (cooking and harvest), festivals (processions, libations and dances) and rituals (healing, marriage and funeral services) revealing an overwhelming interest in the cycle of life and its continuity. José Eladio Mux Curruchich (1955–91) established himself as the champion of this domain, so vital for the development of community values. *Panorama of my Village* (**3**) consists of a series of "snapshots" (detail below) of an active society where everyone has their place and function, but not always enough money for a proper marriage ceremony, with the result that young men are sometimes forced into *Kidnapping a Fiancée* (**1**), under the conspiratorial eye of the young artist Filiberto Chali (b. 1967). Whether in the dark of night or the light of day, the main theme is to survive and celebrate every aspect of life, from the mundane to the supernatural; to reinvent the most basic gestures with their original meaning and provide a reminder of the collective responsibility to re-assert and perpetuate myths and traditions.

Roban a una muchacha. Comalapa. Filiberto Chali.

1

2	3

Rodolfo Galeotti Torres (1912–88), a mestizo of Italian origin, drew his inspiration from the oral traditions and history of the still unfamiliar world of the Maya, enobling these elements in his sculptures and paintings. His series of portraits of the *Mayan Priest* (**4**) combines artistic quality with ethnographic detail. At the same time, a certain paternalism makes the Indian simply a visual object as in *The Wedding* (**3**) by Alfredo Gálvez Suárez (1946–88), the most outstanding member of the neo-Impressionist school. Some contemporary Guatemalan artists have opened up rich new horizons where ancient symbols are invested with new meaning. The *Gucumatz* (**1**) – the chimeric part-serpent part-quetzal, represented as a transpierced victim – resists aggression with an unbelievable strength forged by centuries of passion and courage. It appears in the work of Rolando Aguilar (b. 1957), an active member of the Indian community, as the root and ideological foundation of the Maya. In the work of Zipacná de León (b. 1948), the *Tree of Ixquic* (**2**), mother of the divine twins

Hunahpu and Xbalanque (mythical figures from the *Popol Vuh* manuscript), conveys a new message – that of a generation of highly creative artists fiercely proud of their cultural heritage.

1		
2		4
3		

The work of Carlos Mérida (1891–1984) celebrates traditional craft techniques. *The Mestizo Race*, a mosaic installed in the town hall of Guatemala City in 1957, shows the dual influences Cubism and traditional weaving.

THE ROUTE OF THE MAYAS
AS SEEN BY WRITERS

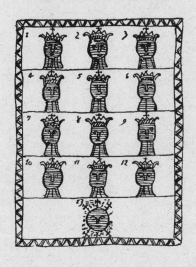

ANCIENT WISDOM

CURATIVES

*Francisco Cervantes de Salazar (c. 1500–75) prepared a book
dialogues about life in ancient Mexico which he used in his teaching
Latin.*

❝AL. Those Indian men and women sitting there – what wares a
they selling? Most of them seem cheap and of very little worth.

ZUAZO. What the earth brings forth: ají [chili], beans, Persian pears, guavas,
mameyes, zapotes, camotes, gícamas, cacomites, mesquites, tunas, gilotes, xocote
and other fruits of this nature.

AL. I have never heard of such names or seen such fruits! What drinks are those i
the large earthenware jars?

ZUAZO. Atole, chía, zotol, made of certain ground seeds.

AL. Outlandish names!

ZA. As ours to them.

AL. What is that dark liquid with which their limbs are smeared, as with pitch, so
that they are made blacker than the Ethiopians? And also that filthy, clay-like stu
with which their heads are daubed and incrusted? Explain why they do this.

ZUAZO. The Indians call the liquid *ogitl*, and they use it as a protection against co
and the itch. In their tongue, the clay is called either *zoquitl* or *quahtepuztli*. It is
useful for dyeing hair very black, as well as for killing lice.

AL. Medicaments indeed unknown to Hippocrates, Avicena, Dioscorides, and
Galen. I notice, too, quite a large supply of worms for sale. For what purpose? I a
moved to laughter.

ZA. They are aquatic and are brought from the marsh. The Indians call them
oquilín, and they themselves eat them and feed them to their little sparrows.

AL. Strange things you tell. Who would ever believe that worms are food for men
since men, when dead, are food for worms?❞

FRANCISCO CERVANTES DE SALAZA
LIFE IN THE IMPERIAL AND LOYAL CITY OF MEXICO IN NEW SPA.
TRANS. MINNIE LEE BARRETT SHEPAR
PUB. UNIV. OF TEXAS PRE
AUSTIN, 19

TARAHUMARA HERBS

...xican poet Alfonso Reyes (1889–1959) wrote of the Indians who live in the ...huahua region and adjacent parts of northern Mexico.

    ❝The Tarahumara Indians have come down,
sign of a bad year
and a poor harvest in the mountains.

Naked and tanned,
hard in their daubed lustrous skins,
blackened with wind and sun, they enliven
the streets of Chihuahua,
slow and suspicious,
all the springs of fear coiled,
like meek panthers.

Naked and tanned,
wild denizens of the snow,
they – for they thee and thou –
always answer thus the inevitable question:
"And is thy face not cold?"

A bad year in the mountains
when the heavy thaw of the peaks
drains down to the villages the drove
of human beasts, their bundles on their backs.

The people, seeing them, experience
that so magnanimous antipathy
for beauty unlike that to which they are used.

Into Catholics
by the New Spain missionaries they were turned
– these lion-hearted lambs.
And, without bread or wine,
they celebrate the Christian ceremony
with their chicha beer and their pinole
which is a powder of universal flavour.

They drink spirits of maize and peyotl,
herb of portents,
symphony of positive esthetics
whereby into colours forms are changed;
and ample metaphysical ebriety
consoles them for their having to tread the earth,
which is, all said and done,
the common affliction of all humankind.
The finest Marathon runners in the world,
nourished on the bitter flesh of deer,
they will be first with the triumphant news
the day we leap the wall
of the five senses.❞

ALFONSO REYES,
ANTHOLOGY OF MEXICAN POETRY,
SELECTED BY OCTAVIO PAZ,
TRANS. SAMUEL BECKETT
PUB. CALDER & BOYARS,
LONDON 1970

SPIDER SPELLS

Is there a logical explanation for the effects of spider spells? Mig
Angel Asturias (1899–1974) ponders the question.

❝He stopped in front of a desk once varnished black, now as
like his hair, to take out from a locked drawer his nursery of notes
he called a diary he kept in folio form...

Earlier he had written, and now reread, 'Little is known of "spid
spell" bites – bites being the popular term – but they cause gr
suffering in my parish, such is the way of things here, and the same may be s
with respect to fabrications about "naguals", or animal protectors, who, throu
the lies and fictions of the devil, these ignorant people believe to be not only th
protectors but their other selves, so much so that it is thought they can change th
human form for that of the animal which is their 'nagual', a tale as old as i
foolish. Little is known about, but much suffering is caused by, the stings of th
"spider-spells", as was noted above, for there are frequent cases of women who
taken with ambulatory madness and escape from their houses, never to be hear
again, thereby swelling the number of "tecunas", as they are called, a name wh
derives from the legend of an unfortunate woman named María Tecún who, i
said, took a pinole powder which had been crawled through by spiders as a resul
some mischief done to her, some evil of witchcraft, and set out to wander the ro
like a madwoman, followed by her husband, who is depicted as being blind l
Cupid. He follows her everywhere and finds her nowhere. Finally, after search
heaven and earth, after a thousand trials, he hears her speak in the m
inhospitable place in all Creation. And such is the commotion undergone by
mental faculties that he regains his vision, only to see – unhappy creature –
object of his wanderings turn to stone in the place that henceforth is known
María Tecún Ridge.'

'Personally,' Father Valentín read swiftly over his burgeoning crop of notes w
two small buzzard's eyes, common to all the Urdáñez family, 'personally, on f

sten yan in vol yn viloe, velijier
vob teeh. lic vaya kal tintane, lic vo

ing charge of the parish of San Miguel Acatán, I visited María
ún Ridge, and I can testify to what is suffered for various reasons
those who venture there. The altitude fatigues the heart and the
rnal cold which reigns at midday and at all hours makes one's flesh
bones ache. Morally, the spirit of the most valiant wilts in the silence, two
ables of a word which here, as at the Pole, takes on all its grandeur: silence due
he altitude, "far from the madding crowd", and above all to the fact that in the
stant, swirling mist, no bird ventures, and so saturated is the vegetation that it
ms mute, ghostly, swathed always in a cloak of frost or migrating rains. Yet this
pression of a dead world due to the silence is accompanied by another no less
naying. The low clouds and thick mist blot out the surrounding landscape and
n it is that a man feels he is going blind himself, so much so that when he moves
arms he can scarcely see his hands, and there are moments when, looking for
feet, he cannot see them, as though he were already in a cloud, changed to a
ged being. The close proximity of the abyss completes the picture. If, elsewhere,
an who penetrates deep into the forest goes in fear of wild beasts and senses
ir presence even before they become flesh before his terrified gaze, here it is the
gs of the earth which assail him, the earth transformed into a wild beast, like a
nale jaguar whose cubs have been taken from her. The precipices cannot be
n, for they are covered over with fluffy quilts of white cloud, but so evident is
ir threat that the hours seem like years on a visit to the famous María Tecún
lge. Inspired by the Holy Virgin, Our Lady, though without formal authorization
m my hierarchical superiors, I carried there with me what was necessary to bless
rock, and I must here record under oath that as I completed the blessing, and
no apparent reason, our horses kicked out at one another and whinnied, with
ir eyes staring from their sockets, as though they had seen the devil himself. **99**

MIGUEL ANGEL ASTURIAS,
MEN OF MAIZE,
TRANS. GERALD MARTIN,
PUB. VERSO, LONDON, 1988

HUNTING MONKEYS

Alexander O. Exquemelin (c. 1645–1705) describes the sights [encountered while sailing along the coast of Costa Rica.

66We came to a large bay known as Bleeckveldt Bay, after a buccanee who used to put in there very often, to repair his ship. This was a excellent place for careening, and we set to work as quickly as possible. While son of our men were busy on the ship, the others went hunting in the forest. In thes woods are wild pigs which have their navels on their backs, and are called nav pigs on this account; there are also badgers, but not many. We met with few wi boar or badgers, so most of our hunting consisted of shooting monkeys an pheasants for our daily food – mostly monkeys, which are found in great numbers. Although we were in a wretched state for want of fresh food, we did not take muc pleasure in shooting the monkeys, for out of every fifteen or sixteen that we hit, w scarcely got three or four. Unless they were shot stone dead it was impossible to g hold of them, for they would cling by the tail to the tips of thin branches until the died, and even then, hang there until they rotted. The females carry their young o their back like the Negro women carry their babies. If the mother was shot dea and the young monkey remained alive, it would not leave its mother, whether sl fell or not, but stay clinging tight to her back.

When anyone passes under a tree full of monkeys, they will spatter him wi excrement and break off branches and throw them at his head. When a troop monkeys has been fired on and one of them is hit, the others immediately gathe round and sniff the wound. If there is much blood spurting out, some of the squeeze the wound to check the blood, others get moss from the trees and stick in the place, while still others fetch certain herbs, which they chew and then press the wound. I have often observed with great wonder the way these animals stand b each other in time of need and endeavour to help their fellows, though in peril their lives.

These monkeys are tasty and very nourishing; every day we boiled and roasted much monkey-flesh we became used to it, and to us it tasted better tha pheasant.99

ALEXANDER O. EXQUEMELIN, *THE BUCCANEERS OF AMERIC*
TRANS. ALEXIS BROWN, PUB. PENGUIN BOOKS, 19

BEING A HUNTER

In "Journey to Ixtlan", Carlos Castaneda (b. 1931) explains the teachings of don Juan Matus, a Yaqui Indian sorcerer to whom he was apprenticed.

66'Your hunter's spirit has returned to you,' don Juan said suddenly and with a serious face. 'Now you're hooked.'
'I beg your pardon?'
I wanted him to elaborate on his statement that I was hooked, but he only laughed and repeated it.
'How am I hooked?' I insisted.
'Hunters will always hunt,' he said.
'I am a hunter myself.'
'Do you mean you hunt for a living?'
'I hunt in order to live. I can live off the land, anywhere.'
He indicated the total surroundings with his hand.
'To be a hunter means that one knows a great deal,' he

nt on. 'It means that one can see the world in
ferent ways. In order to be a hunter one must be in
rfect balance with everything else, otherwise
nting would become a meaningless chore. For
tance, today we took a little snake. I had to
ologize to her for cutting her life off so
ddenly and so definitely; I did what I did
owing that my own life will also be cut off
meday in very much the same fashion,
ddenly and definitely. So, all in all, we and
e snakes are on a par. One of them fed us
Jay.'

had never conceived a balance of that kind
en I used to hunt,' I said.

nat's not true. You didn't just kill animals. You
d your family all ate the game.'

s statements carried the conviction of
meone who had been there. He was, of course,
ht. There had been times when I had provided
e incidental wild meat for my family.

ter a moment's hesitation I asked, 'How did
u know that?'

nere are certain things that I just know,' he
d. 'I can't tell you how though.'**99**

CARLOS CASTANEDA, *JOURNEY TO IXTLAN –*
THE LESSONS OF DON JUAN,
PUB. SIMON & SCHUSTER, NEW YORK, 1973

THE TWO VOLCANOS

glish traveler Thomas Gage (1600–56)
dertook a survey of the West Indies in 1648, in
ich he describes Guatemala City.

The chiefest mountains which straighten in
s city and valley are two, called volcanoes,
e one being a volcano of water, and the
her a volcano or mountain of fire, termed
so by the Spaniards, though very
improperly a volcano may
be said to contain water, it
taking its name from the heathenish God Vulcan,
whose profession and employment chiefly was in
fire. These two famous mountains stand almost
the one over against the other, on each side of
the valley; that of water hanging on the south
side almost perpendicularly over the city, the
other of fire standing lower from it, more
opposite to the old city. That of water is higher
than the other, and yields a goodly prospect to
the sight, being almost all the year green, and
full of Indian *milpas*, which are plantations of
Indian wheat; and in the small and petty
towns which lie some half way up it,
some at the foot of it, there are roses,
lilies, and other flowers all the year long
in the gardens, besides plantains, apricots
and many sorts of sweet and delicate
fruits. It is called by the Spaniards, *el*

volcán del agua, or the volcano of water, because on the other side of it from Guatemala it springs with many brooks towards a town called Saint Christopher, and especially is thought to preserve and nourish on that side also a great lake of fresh water, by the towns called Amatitlan and Petapa. But on the side of it towards Guatemala and the valley it yields also so many springs of sweet and fresh water as have cause[d] and made a river which runneth along the valley close by the city, an[d] is that which drives the water-mills spoken of before in Xocotenang[o]

This river was not known when first the Spaniards conquered th[e] country; but since (according to their constant tradition) the city of Guatema[la] standing higher and nearer to the volcano in that place and town which to this da[y] is called *la Ciudad Vieja*, or the Old City, there lived in it then about the year 1534 [a] gentlewoman called Donna Maria de Castilla, who having lost her husband in th[e] wars, and that same year buried also all her children, grew so impatient under the[se] her crosses and afflictions, that impiously she defied God, saying: 'What can Go[d] do more unto me now than he hath done? He hath done his worst without it be [to] take away my life also, which I now regard not.' Upon these words there gushed o[ut] of this volcano such a flood of water as carried away this woman with the strea[m,] ruined many of the houses, and caused the inhabitants to remove to the plac[e] where now standeth Guatemala. **99**

THOMAS GAGE, *THOMAS GAGE'S TRAVELS IN THE NEW WORL[D]*
ED. A.P. NEWTON, PUB. GEORGE ROUTLEDGE & SONS, LONDON, 192[?]

MONTEZUMA

THE LEGENDARY RULER

William Carlos Williams (1883–1963) describes the importance [of] Montezuma to his people.

66Surely no other prince has lived, or will ever live, in such state as did th[e] American cacique. The whole waking aspirations of his people, opposed to an[d] completing their religious sense, seemed to come off in him and in him alone: th[e] drive upward, toward the sun and the stars. He was the very person of their orna[te] dreams, so delicate, so prismatically colorful, so full of tinkling sounds and rhythm[s], so tireless of invention. Never was such a surface lifted above the isolate blackne[ss] of such profound savagery. It is delightful to know that Montezuma changed h[is] clothes four times a day, donning four different suits, entirely new, which he nev[er] wore again; that at meals he was served in a great clean-swept chamber on ma[ts] upon the floor, his food being kept warm in chafing dishes containing live coal[s]; that at meals he sat upon a small cushion 'curiously wrought of leather'. B[ut] nowhere in his state was the stark power of beauty, the refined and the barbaric, s[o] exquisitely expressed as in his smaller palaces and places of amusement. 'What ca[n] be more wonderful than that a barbarous monarch, as he is, should have eve[ry] object in his domain imitated in gold, silver, precious stones and feathers; the go[ld] and silver being wrought so naturally as not to be surpassed by any smith in th[e] world; the stonework executed with such perfection that it is difficult to conceiv[e] what instruments could have been used, and the feather work superior to the fine[st] production in wax and embroidery.' 'There is one palace inferior to the res[t,] attached to which is a beautiful garden with balconies extending over it supporte[d] by marble columns and having a floor formed of jasper elegantly inlaid. Belongin[g] to it are ten pools, in which are kept the different species of water birds found [in] the country, all domesticated: for the sea birds there are pools of salt water and f[or]

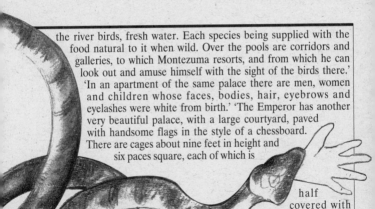

the river birds, fresh water. Each species being supplied with the food natural to it when wild. Over the pools are corridors and galleries, to which Montezuma resorts, and from which he can look out and amuse himself with the sight of the birds there.' 'In an apartment of the same palace there are men, women and children whose faces, bodies, hair, eyebrows and eyelashes were white from birth.' 'The Emperor has another very beautiful palace, with a large courtyard, paved with handsome flags in the style of a chessboard. There are cages about nine feet in height and six paces square, each of which is

half covered with a roof of tiles, and the other half has over it a wooden grate, skilfully made. Every cage contains a bird of prey, of all species.' 'In the same palace there are several large halls on the ground floor, filled with immense cages built of heavy pieces of timber, well put together, in which are kept lions, wolves, foxes and a great variety of other animals of the cat kind.' 'The care of these animals and birds is assigned to three hundred men.' Daily the Emperor's wine cellar and larder were open to all who wished to eat and drink. His meals were served by three or four hundred youths who brought on an infinite variety of dishes; indeed, whenever he dined or supped, the table was loaded with every kind of fish, flesh, fruits and vegetables which the country afforded. Both at the beginning and end of every meal they furnished water for the hands, and the napkins used on these occasions were never employed a second time. 99
  – WILLIAM CARLOS WILLIAMS, *IN THE AMERICAN GRAIN*,
  PUB. NEW DIRECTIONS, 1956

A ROYAL WELCOME
Spanish Conquistador Bemal Diaz de Castillo (c. 1492–1581) joined Cortés on his 1519 expedition to Mexico and was invited to dinner by Montezuma.

6His cooks had upwards of thirty different ways of dressing meats and they had earthen vessels so contrived as to keep them always hot. For the table of Montezuma himself, above three hundred dishes were dressed, and for his guards, above a thousand. Before dinner, Montezuma would sometimes go out and inspect the preparations, and his officers would point out to him which were the best and explained of what birds and flesh they were composed; and of those he would eat. But this was more for amusement than anything else. It is said that at times the flesh of young children was dressed for him; but the ordinary meats were, domestic fowls, pheasants, geese, partridges, quails, venison, Indian hogs, pigeons, hares and rabbits, with many other animals and birds peculiar to the country. This is certain; that after Cortes had spoken to him relative to the dressing human flesh, it was not practised in his palace. At his meals, in the cold weather, a number of torches of the bark of a wood which makes no smoke and has an aromatic smell, were lighted, and, that they should not throw too much heat, screens, ornamented with gold, and painted with figures of idols, were placed before them. Montezuma was seated on a low throne, or chair, at a table proportioned to the height of his seat. The table was covered with white cloths and napkins, and four beautiful women presented him with water for his hands, in vessels which they call Xicales, with other vessels under them like plates, to catch the water; they also presented him with towels. . . . Fruit of all the kinds that the country produced was laid before him; he ate very little, but from time to time, a liquor prepared from cocoa, and of a stimulative, or

corroborative quality, as we were told, was prepared to him in golden cups. \
could not at that time see if he drank it or not, but I observed a number of ja
above fifty, brought in, filled with foaming chocolate, of which he took some, whi
the women presented to him. At different intervals during the time of dinner, the
entered certain Indians, humpbacked, very deformed, and ugly, who played tric
of buffoonery, and others who they said were jesters. There was also a company
singers and dancers, who afforded Montezuma much entertainment. To these I
ordered the vases of chocolate to be distributed. The four female attendants the
took away the cloths, and again with much respect presented him with water
wash his hands, during which time Montezuma conversed with the four o
noblemen formerly mentioned, after which they took their leave with ma
ceremonies. One thing I forgot, and no wonder, to mention in its place, and that
that during the time Montezuma was at dinner, two very beautiful women we
busily employed making small cakes with eggs and other things mixed therei
These were delicately white, and when made they presented them to him on plat
covered with napkins. Also another kind of bread was brought to him in lo
loaves, and plates of cakes resembling wafers. After he had dined, they presente
to him three little canes highly ornamented, containing liquid amber, mixed with a
herb they call tobacco; and when he had sufficiently viewed and heard the singer
dancers, and buffoons, he took a little of the smoke of one of these canes, and the
laid himself down to sleep; and thus his principal meal concluded. **99**

BERNAL DIAZ DEL CASTILL
THE TRUE HISTORY OF THE CONQUEST OF NEW SPAI
TRANS. M. KEATINGE, PUB. LONDON, 19

A BLOODY HISTORY

FIRST IMPRESSIONS

*Hernán Cortés (1485–1554) wrote to the king and queen of Spain in 1519, describir
the land and the people he encountered.*

66The people who inhabit this land, from the island of Cozumel and the cape
Yucatán to the place where we are now, are of medium height and of wel
proportioned bodies and features, save that in each province their customs ar
different; some pierce their ears and put very large and ugly objects into them
others pierce their nostrils down to the lip and put in them large round ston
which look like mirrors; and others still split their lower lips as far as the gums an
hang there some large stones or gold ornaments so heavy that they drag the lip
down, giving a most deformed appearance. The clothes they wear are like larg
highly colored yashmaks; the men cover their shameful parts, and on the top half of
their bodies wear thin mantles which are decorated in a Moorish fashion. Th
common women wear highly colored mantles from the waist to the feet, and other
which cover their breasts, leaving the rest uncovered. The women of rank wea
skirts of very thin cotton, which are very loose-fitting and decorated and cut in th
manner of a rochet.

The food they eat is maize and some chili peppers, as on the other islands, an
patata yuca, just the same as is eaten in Cuba, and they eat it roast, for they no
make bread of it; and they both hunt and fish and breed many chickens such a
those found on *Tierra Firme*, which are as big as peacocks. . . .

They have their shrines and temples with raised walks which run all around the
outside and are very wide: there they keep the idols which they worship, some of
stone, some of clay and some of wood, which they honor and serve with suc
customs and so many ceremonies that many sheets of paper would not suffice t
give Your Royal Highnesses a true and detailed account of them all. And th
temples where they are kept are the largest and the best and the finest built of a
the buildings found in the towns; and they are much adorned with rich hangin
cloths and featherwork and other fineries.

Each day before beginning any sort of work they burn incense in these temples an

ometimes sacrifice their own persons, some cutting their tongues, others their
ars, while there are some who stab their bodies with knives. All the blood which
ows from them they offer to those idols, sprinkling it in all parts of the temple, or
ometimes throwing it into the air or performing many other ceremonies, so that
othing is begun without sacrifice having first been made. They have a most horrid
nd abominable custom which truly ought to be punished and which until now we
ave seen in no other part, and this is that, whenever they wish to ask something of
e idols, in order that their plea may find more acceptance, they take many girls
nd boys and even adults, and in the presence of the idols they open their chests
hile they are still alive and take out their hearts and entrails and burn them before
e idols, offering the smoke as sacrifice. Some of us have seen this, and they say it
the most terrible and frightful thing they have ever witnessed. **"**

HERNÁN CORTÉS, *LETTERS FROM MEXICO*,
TRANS. AND ED. A.R. PAGDEN, PUB. OXFORD UNIVERSITY PRESS, LONDON, 1972

THE INQUISITION

*ailor Miles Philips was abandoned in the West Indies, attacked by Indians and then
aptured by the Spanish. Here Richard Hakluyt (1551/2–1616) describes his ordeal.*

"We were all soon apprehended in all places, and all our goods seized and taken
or the Inquisitors' use, and so from all parts of the country we were conveyed and
nt as prisoners to the city of Mexico, and there committed to prison in sundry
ark dungeons, where we could not see but by candle light, and were never past
vo together in one place, so that we saw not one another, neither could one of us
ll what was become of another. Thus we remained close imprisoned for the space
f a year and a half. We were often called before the Inquisitors alone, and there
everely examined our faith, and commanded to say the Paternoster, the Ave
Iaria, and the Creed in Latin, which God knoweth a great number of us could not
ay, otherwise than in the English tongue. . . . Yet all this would not serve; for still
om time to time we were called upon to confess, and about the space of three
nonths before they proceeded to their severe judgement, we were all racked, and
ome enforced to utter that against themselves, which afterwards cost them their
ves. And thus having gotten from our own mouths matter sufficient for them to
roceed in judgement against us, they caused a large scaffold to be made in the
idst of the market place in Mexico right over against the head church, and 14 or
5 days before the day of judgement, with the sound of a trumpet, they did
ssemble the people in all parts of the city: before whom it was then solemnly
roclaimed, that whosoever would upon such a day repair to the market place, they
hould hear the sentence of the Holy Inquisition against the English heretics. The

night before they came to the prison where we were, bringing with them certai
fool's coats which they had prepared for us, being called in their languag
sanbenitos, which coats were made of yellow cotton and red crosses upon them
they were so busied in putting on their coats about us, and bringing us out into
large yard, and placing and pointing us in what order we should go to the scaffol
or place of judgement upon the morrow, that they did not once suffer us to slee
all that night long. The next morning being come, there was given to every one o
us for our breakfast a cup of wine, and a slice of bread fried in honey, and so abou
eight of the clock in the morning, we set forth of the prison, every man alone in hi
yellow coat, and a rope about his neck, and a great green wax candle in his han
unlighted, having a Spaniard appointed to go upon either side of every one of us
and so marching in this order and manner toward the scaffold in the market place
which was a bowshoot distant or thereabouts, we found a great assembly of peopl
all the ways and so coming to the scaffold we went up by a pair of stairs and foun
seats ready prepared for us to sit down on, every man in order as he should b
called to receive his judgement. Presently the Inquisitors came up another pair c
stairs, and the Viceroy and all the chief justices with them. When they were se
down, then came up also a great number of friars, white, black and grey, about th
number of three hundred persons. Then was silence commanded, and the
presently began their severe and cruel judgement.**99**

RICHARD HAKLUYT, *VOYAGES AND DISCOVERIES*
EDITED, ABRIDGED AND INTRODUCED BY JACK BEECHING
PUB. PENGUIN BOOKS, 197

CANNIBALS

Suspicion was rife on both sides. English sailor John Chilton (fl. 1561–85
describes how he was nearly eaten by cannibals in New Spain (Mexico) i
1569.

66The next day in the morning we passed over the river in a canoa; and being o
the other side, I went my selfe before alone: and by reason there met many waye
traled by the wilde beasts, I lost my way, and so travelled thorow a great woo
about two leagues: and at length fell into the hands of certaine wilde Indians, which
were there in certaine cottages made of straw; who seeing me, came out to th
number of twenty of them, with their bowes and arrowes, and spake to mee in thei
language, which I understood not: and so I made signs unto them to helpe me
from my horse; which they did b
commandement of their lord, which wa
there with them. They caried me under on
of their cottages, and layed me upon a ma
on the ground: and perceiving that I could no
understand them, they brought unto mee a littl
Indian wench of Mexico, of fifteene or sixteen
yeeres of age, whom they commanded to aske me i
her language from whence I came, and for what I wa
come among them: for (sayth she) doest thou not know
Christian, how that these people will kill and eat thee? T
whom I answered, let them doe with me what they will
heere now I am. She replied, saying thou mayest thanke
God thou art leane; for they feare thou hast the pocks
otherwise they would eate thee
So I presented to the king a littl
wine which I had with me in a bottle
which he esteemed above any treasure
for for wine they will sell their wives an
children. Afterwards the wench asked me
what I would have, and whether I would ea
any thing. I answered that I desired a little wate

drinke, for that the countrey is very hote. . . . Having now bene conversant with
[the]m about three or foure houres, they bid her ask me if I would goe my way. I
[an]wered that I desired nothing els. **99**

JOHN CHILTON, FROM HAKLUYT'S *PRINCIPAL VOYAGES*,
EXTRACT FROM ERIC NEWBY'S *TRAVELLERS' TALES*, PUB. COLLINS, LONDON, 1985

MEXICO

*[The] dust of history rests in the present land. Robert Lowell (1917–77) questions the
[nat]ure of history in his poem entitled 'Mexico'.*

[T]he lizard rusty as a leaf rubbed rough
[eat]s nothing for days but puff his throat
[for] oxygen, and tongue up passing flies,
[his] only similar rusty lizards pant:
[se]ems worthy this lord of the universe –
[eac]h thing he does generic, and not the best.
[Ho]w fragrantly our cold hands warm to the live coal!
[We] sit on the cliff like curs, chins pressed to thumbs,
[the] Toltec temples changing to dust in the dusk –
[eye] of the vulture, white brow of the moon: this too dust...
[Ou]t of time, two clocks set back to the Toltec Eden,
[as i]f we still wished to pull teeth with firetongs –
[whe]n they took a city, they too murdered everything:
[ma]n, woman and child, down to the pigs and dogs. **99**

ROBERT LOWELL, FROM *NOTEBOOK*,
PUB. FABER & FABER, LONDON 1970

SALVADOR

*[Wh]en mass murder becomes commonplace, after a while the evidence is taken for
[gra]nted. Joan Didion (b. 1934) describes a body dump in El Salvador.*

[I] drove up to Puerta del Diablo one morning in June of 1982, past the Casa
[Pre]sidencial and the camouflaged watch towers and heavy concentrations of troops
[and] arms south of town, on up a narrow road narrowed further by landslides and
[dee]p crevices in the roadbed, a drive so insistently premonitory that after a while I
[beg]an to hope that I would pass Puerta del Diablo without knowing it, just miss it,
[writ]e it off, turn around and go back. There was however no way of missing it.
[Pue]rta del Diablo is a 'view site' in an older and distinctly literary tradition, nature
[as l]esson, an immense cleft rock through which half of El Salvador seems framed, a

site so romantic and 'mystical', so theatrically sacrificial in aspect, that it might be a cosmic parody of nineteenth-century landscape painting. The place presents itself as pathetic fallacy: the sky 'broods', the stones 'weep', a constant seepage of water weighting the ferns and moss. The foliage is thick and slick with moisture. The only sound is a steady buzz, I believe of cicadas.

Body dumps are seen in El Salvador as a kind of visitors' must-do, difficult but worth the detour. 'Of course you have seen El Playón,' an aide to President Alvaro Magaña said to me one day, and proceeded to discuss the site geologically, as evidence of the country's geothermal resources. He made no mention of the bodies. I was unsure if he was sounding me out or simply found the geothermal aspect of overriding interest. . . .

'Nothing fresh today, I hear,' an embassy officer said when I mentioned that I had visited Puerta del Diablo. 'Were there any on top?' someone else asked. 'There were supposed to have been three on top yesterday.' The point about whether or not there had been any on top was that usually it was necessary to go down to see bodies. The way down is hard. Slabs of stone, slippery with moss, are set into the vertiginous cliff, and it is down this cliff that one begins the descent to the bodies, or what is left of the bodies, pecked and maggoty masses of flesh, bone, hair. On some days there have been helicopters circling, tracking those making the descent. Other days there have been militia at the top, in the clearing where the road seems to run out, but on the morning I was there the only people on top were a man and a woman and three small children, who played in the wet grass while the woman started and stopped a Toyota pickup. She appeared to be learning how to drive. She drove forward and then back toward the edge, apparently following the man's signals, over and over again.

We did not speak, and it was only later, down the mountain and back in the land of the provisionally living, that it occurred to me that there was a definite question about why a man and a woman might choose a well-known body dump for a driving lesson. This was one of a number of occasions, during the two weeks my husband and I spent in El Salvador, on which I came to understand, in a way I had not understood before, the exact mechanism of terror. **99**

JOAN DIDION, *SALVADOR*,
PUB. CHATTO & WINDUS, LONDON, 1983

GUADALUPAN

*e development of a new Mexican culture incorporating elements of Indian and
anish styles is described here by Octavio Paz (b. 1914).*

The curiosity which the Indian past excites should not always be regarded as a
ere thirst for the exotic. During the seventeenth century many minds were
cupied with the problem of how a colonial order could assimilate the native
orld. The ancient history of the Indians, their myths, their dances, and their crafts,
en their religion, formed a secret and inaccessible universe. At the same time, the
d beliefs were mingling with the new, and the remnants of the native culture
sed questions to which there was no answer. The Virgin of Guadalupe was also
onantzin, the coming of the Spaniards was confused with the return of
uetzalcoatl, and the ancient native rituals revealed disturbing analogies with
ose of the Catholic Church. If certain presages of the coming of Christ were to be
und in the pagan faith of the Mediterranean, why should they not be
countered also in the history of ancient Mexico? The Conquest was no longer
garded as an event brought about by the will of Spain alone, but as an occurrence
r which the Indians had been waiting, and which had been prophesied by their
ngs and priests. By dint of such interpretations a supernatural link was
tablished between the ancient religions and Catholicism. The Virgin of
uadalupe, ancient goddess of fertility, on whom so many ideas and psychic forces
ere focused, became the meeting place of the two worlds and the center of
exican religious life. Her image embodied the reconciliation of the two
nflicting worlds, and at the same time expressed the originality of the nation that
as coming to birth. Through the Virgin of Guadalupe, Mexico claims to be heir to
o traditions. Baroque colonial art exploited this situation, mixed the Indian with
the Spanish tradition, and produced a new form of exoticism. A
peculiar form of baroque, which might be labeled 'guadalupan,'
was to become the pre-eminent style of New Spain.**"**

FROM *ANTHOLOGY OF MEXICAN POETRY*,
COMPILED BY OCTAVIO PAZ, TRANS. SAMUEL BECKETT,
PUB. CALDER & BOYARS, LONDON, 1970

GOLDSMITHS

Thomas Gage was fascinated by the intricate craftsmanship.

66The art, or science, of goldsmiths among them was the most curious, a
very good workmanship engraven with tools made of flint or in mou
They will cast a platter in mould with eight corners, and every corner of seve
metal, the one of gold, and the other of silver, without any kind of solder. They w
also found or cast a little cauldron with loose handles hanging thereat, as we use
cast a bell; they will also cast in mould a fish of metal, with one scale of silver on
back, and another of gold; they will make a parrot or popinjay of metal that
tongue shall shake and his head move and
his wings flutter; they will cast an ape in
mould, that both hands and feet shall stir,
and hold a spindle in his hand seeming to
spin, yea and an apple in his hand as
though he would eat it.99

THOMAS GAGE, *THOMAS GAGE'S TRAVELS
IN THE NEW WORLD*, ED. A.P. NEWTON,
PUB. GEORGE ROUTLEDGE & SONS,
LONDON, 1928

ANCIENT ARTS

In his history of the Conquest, William Prescott (1796–1859) admired the rich col
and ornate designs of ceramics and fabrics.

66The ancient Mexicans made utensils of earthenware for the ordinary purposes
domestic life, numerous specimens of which still exist. They made cups and vases
a lackered or painted wood, impervious to wet, and gaudily coloured. Their dy
were obtained from both mineral and vegetable substances. Among them was
rich crimson of the cochineal, the modern rival of the famed Tyrian purple. It w
introduced into Europe from Mexico, where the curious little insect was nourish
with great care on plantations of cactus, since fallen into neglect. The natives we
thus enabled to give a brilliant colouring to the webs which were manufactured,
every degree of fineness, from the cotton raised in abundance throughout
warmer regions of the country. They had the art, also, of interweaving with the
the delicate hair of rabbits and other animals, which made a cloth of great warm
as well as beauty, of a kind altogether original; and on this they often laid a r
embroidery, of birds, flowers, or some other fanciful devic
But the art in which they most delighted was their *plume*
or featherwork. With this they could produce all the eff
of a beautiful mosaic. The gorgeous plumage of t
tropical birds, especially of the parrot tribe, afforded ev
variety of colour; and the fine down of the hummingb
which revelled in swarms among the honeysuc
bowers of Mexico, supplied them with soft ae
tints that gave an exquisite finish to the pictu
The feathers, pasted on a fine cotton web, we
wrought into dresses for the wealthy, hangi
for apartments, and ornaments for the temp
No one of the American fabrics excited su
admiration in Europe, whither numero
specimens were sent by the Conquerors. It is to
regretted that so graceful an art should have be
suffered to fall into decay.99

WILLIAM HICKLING PRESCO
HISTORY OF THE CONQUEST OF MEXI
PUB. GEORGE ALLEN & UNWIN LT
LONDON 1

SCULPTURE

...tish sculptor Henry Moore (1898–?) was much influenced by Mexican art.

66 ...Mexican sculpture, as soon as I found it seemed to me true and right, perhaps ...cause I at once hit on similarities in it with some eleventh-century carvings I had ...n as a boy on Yorkshire churches. Its 'stoniness', by which I mean its truth to ...terial, its tremendous power without loss of sensitiveness, its astonishing variety ...d fertility of form-invention, and its approach to a full three-dimensional ...nception of form, make it unsurpassed in my opinion by any other period of ...ne sculpture.**99**

JOHN RUSSEL, *HENRY MOORE*,
PUB. PENGUIN BOOKS, LONDON, 1973

...IE NATURAL WORLD

A MUDDY ASCENT

...n Lloyd Stephens (1805–1852) climbed the Volcan de Agua near the city of Copán ... Honduras.

At half past ten we were above the region of forest and came out upon the open ...e of the volcano. There was still a scattering of trees, long grass, and a great ...riety of curious plants and flowers, furnishing rich materials for the botanist. ...nong them was a plant with a red flower, called the *mano del mico*, or hand-...nt, but more like a monkey's paw, growing to a height of thirty or forty feet, the ...ide a light vermilion color, and the outside vermilion with stripes of yellow. My ...mpanion, tired with the toil of ascending even with the aid of the rope, at length ...ounted an Indian's shoulders. I was obliged to stop every two or three minutes, ...d my rests were about equal to the actual time of walking. The great difficulty ...s on account of the wet and mud, which, in ascending, made us lose part of every ...p. It was so slippery that, even with the staff and the assistance of branches of ...es and bushes, it was difficult to keep from falling. About half an hour before

reaching the top, and perhaps one thousand or fifteen hundred feet from it, th
trees became scarce and seemed blazed by lightning or withered by cold. Tl
clouds gathered thicker than before, and I lost all hope of a clear day.

At half an hour before twelve we reached the top and descended into the crater.
whirlwind of cloud and vapor was sweeping around it. We were in a perspiratio
our clothes were saturated with rain and mud, and in a few moments the co
penetrated our very bones. We attempted to build a fire, but the sticks and leave
were wet and would not burn. For a few moments we raised a feeble flame and a
crouched around it, but a sprinkling of rain came down, just enough to put it ou
We could see nothing, and the shivering Indians begged me to return. On roc
near us were inscriptions, one of which bore the date of 1548, and on a cut stor
were the words:

> ALEXANDRO LDVERT
> DE SAN PETERSBURGO;
> EDVARDO LEGH PAGE,
> DE INGLATERRA;
> *JOSE CROSKEY,*
> *DE FYLADELFYE,*
> BIBYMOS AQUI UNAS BOTEAS
> DE CHAMPANA, EL DIA 26
> DE AGOSTO DE 1834.

It seemed strange that three men from such distant and different parts of the worl
– St. Petersburg, England, and *Philadelphia* – had met to drink champagne on the
top of this volcano. **99**

> JOHN LLOYD STEPHENS, *INCIDENTS OF TRAVEL IN CENTRA*
> *AMERICA, CHIAPAS, AND YUCATAN*, ED. RICHARD L. PREDMOR
> PUB. RUTGERS UNIVERSITY PRESS, NEW BRUNSWICK, 194

THE MOUNTAINS

D.H. Lawrence (1885–1930) traveled throughout Mexico between 1922 an
1928. Here he describes a walk to Huayapa.

66The morning is perfect; in a moment we are clear out of the town. Most towns i
Mexico, saving the capital, end in themselves, at once. As if they had been lowere
from heaven in a napkin, and deposited, rather foreign, upon the wild plain. So w
walk round the wall of the church and the huge old monastery enclosure that i
now barracks for the scrap-heap soldiery, and at once there are the hills.

will lift up my eyes until the hills, whence cometh my strength.' At least one can ways do *that*, in Mexico. In a stride, the town passes away. Before us lies the flaming, pinkish-ochre of the valley flat, wild and exalted with sunshine. On the ?, quite near, bank the stiffly pleated mountains, all the foot-hills, that press annah-coloured into the savannah of the valley. The mountains are clothed okily with pine, *ocote*, and, like a woman in a gauze *rebozo*, they rear in a rich e fume that is almost cornflower-blue in the clefts. It is their characteristic, that ?y are darkest-blue at the top. Like some splendid lizard with a wavering, royal ie crest down the ridge of his back, and pale belly, and soft, pinky-fawn claws, on ? plain.

tween the pallor of the claws, a dark spot of trees, and white dots of a church h twin towers. Further away, along the foot-hills, a few scattered trees, white dot d stroke of a *hacienda*, and a green, green square of sugar-cane. Further off still, the mouth of a cleft of a canyon, a dense little green patch of trees, and two ots of proud church. **99**

D.H. LAWRENCE, *MORNINGS IN MEXICO*,
PUB. MARTIN SECKER, LONDON, 1930

NIGHT

"Under the Volcano", Malcolm Lowry (1909–57) uses the Mexican landscape to nforce his theme of self-destructiveness.

The jungle closed over them and the volcanoes were blotted out. Yet it was still t dark. From the stream racing along beside them a radiance was cast. Big yellow wers, resembling chrysanthemums, shining like stars through the gloom, grew on her side of the water. Wild bougainvillea, brick-red in the half-light, occasionally ush with white handbells, tongue downwards, started out at them, every little while a notice nailed to a tree, a whittled, weather-beaten arrow pointing, with the words hardly visible: *a la Cascada* –

Farther on worn-out ploughshares and the rusted and twisted chassis of abandoned American cars bridged the stream which they kept always to their left.

e sound of the falls behind was now lost in that of the cascade ahead. The air s full of spray and moisture. But for the tumult one might almost have heard ings growing as the torrent rushed through the wet heavy foliage that sprang up erywhere around them from the alluvial soil.

at once, above them, they saw the sky again. The clouds, no longer red, had come a peculiar luminous blue-white, drifts and depths of them, as though mined by moon rather than sunlight, between which roared still the deep homeless cobalt of afternoon.

Birds were sailing up there, ascending higher and higher. Infernal bird of Prometheus! They were vultures, that on earth so jealously contend with one another, defiling themselves with blood and filth, but who were yet capable of rising, like this, above the storms, to heights shared only by the condor, above the summit of the Andes –
Down the south-west stood the moon itself, preparing to follow the sun below the horizon. On their left, through the trees beyond the stream appeared low hills, like those at the foot of the Calle Nicaragua; they were purple and sad. At their foot, so near Yvonne made out a faint rustling, cattle moved on the sloping fields among gold cornstalks and striped mysterious tents.
Before them, Popacatepetl and Ixtaccihuatl

continued to dominate the north-east, the Sleeping Woman now perhaps the mo[st]
beautiful of the two, with jagged angles of blood-red snow on its summit, fading [as]
they watched, whipped with darker rock shadows, the summit itself seemi[ng]
suspended in mid-air, floating among the curdling ever mounting black clouds. **"**

MALCOLM LOWRY, *UNDER THE VOLCAN[O]*
PUB. JONATHAN CAP[E]
LONDON, 19[4-]

BIRDS
The cacophony of the thousands of birds is one of the lasting memories [of]
Tzinzuntzan for writer Lesley Blanch.

"No one told me about the birds. Every province has its own special birds, li[ke]
its fruit or flowers, a thousand different fluttering, shimmering creatures, fluti[ng]
cawing, shrieking. At Purapechas, by the end of the lake, there is a whole world, [a]
concentration of humming-birds, where these beetle-sized little beauties zoom a[nd]
dart about the honied trails of vine, 'cup-of-gold', or a plant called *izgujochitl* – 't[he]
flower of the raven'. Pelicans and cormorants in Yucatan. Gaudy macaws a[nd]
parakeets flashing through the tropic groves round Orizaba. Under the toweri[ng]
ash trees at Tzinzuntzan I heard the nightingale at noon; but it turned out to be [a]
yellow-feathered bird, and I recalled that the Emperor Maximilian importe[d]
two thousand nightingales from Germany: where they, perhaps, then crossed wi[th]
canaries? Everywhere, in the mountains, in the valleys, I see those long-taile[d]
black magpie-like birds, so impudently friendly, which seem to address on[e]
personally, as they flutter close to perch on the spear-tip of a cactus or on [a]
window-sill. The Mexicans call them 'ouraki'; in Mayan, they are 'toh'. Their so[ng]
has the heart-piercing sweetness of a blackbird's trill, with something melancho[ly]
added, something which epitomises all Mexico at dusk.**"**

LESLEY BLANCH, *UNDER A LILAC-BLEEDING STA[R]*
PUB. JOHN MURRAY,
LONDON, 1963

A JOURNEY BY COACH

Scottish-born traveler Madame Calderon de la Barca (1804–82) spent two years in Mexico and described her experiences in vivid letters which were later published as a book.

We climbed into the coach, which was so crowded that we could but just turn our heads to groan an adieu to our friends. The coach rattled off through the streets, dashed through the Alameda, and gradually we began to shake down, and, by a little arrangement of cloaks and serapes, to be less crowded. A *padre* with a very Indian complexion sat between K– and me, and a horrible, long, lean bird-like female, with immense red goggle-eyes, coal-black teeth, fingers like claws, a great goitre, and drinking brandy at intervals, sat opposite to us. There were also various men buried in their serapes. Satisfied with a cursory inspection of our companions, I addressed myself to *Blackwood's Magazine*, but the road which leads towards the Desierto, and which we before passed on horseback, is dreadful, and the mules could scarcely drag the loaded coach up the steep hills. We were thrown into ruts, horribly jolted, and sometimes obliged to get out, which would not have been disagreeable but for the necessity of getting in again. The day and the country were beautiful, but impossible to enjoy either in a shut coach. We were rather thankful when the wheels, sticking in a deep rut, we were forced to descend, and walk forwards for some time. We had before seen the view from these heights, but the effect never was more striking than at this moment. The old city with her towers, lakes, and volcanoes, lay bathed in the bright sunshine. Not a cloud was in the sky – not an exhalation rose from the lake – not a shadow was on the mountains. All was bright and glittering, and flooded in the morning light; while in contrast rose to the left the dark, pine-covered crags, behind which the Desierto lies. At Santa Fé we changed horses, and found there an escort which had been ordered for us by General Tornel; a necessary precaution in these robber-haunted roads. We stopped to breakfast at *Quamalpa*, where the inn is kept by a Frenchman, who is said to be making a large fortune, which he deserves for the good breakfast he had prepared for us. . . . After leaving this inn, situated in a country formed of heaps of lava and volcanic rocks, the landscape becomes more beautiful and wooded. It is, however,

dangerous, on account of the shelter which the wooded mountains afford to th
knights of the road, and to whose predilection for these wild solitudes, the numb
of crosses bore witness. In a wooded defile there is a small clear space called 'L
Cruces', where several wooden crosses point out the site of the famous batt
between the curate Hidalgo and the Spanish General Truxillo. An object really i
keeping with the wild scenery, was the head of the celebrated robber *Maldonad*
nailed to the pine-tree beneath which he committed his last murder. It is now qui
black, and grins there, a warning to his comrades and an encouragement t
travellers. From the age of ten to that of fifty, he followed the honourabl
profession of free-trader, when he expiated his crimes. The padre who was in th
coach with us, told us that he heard his last confession. That grinning skull wa
once the head of a man, and an ugly one too, they say; but stranger still it is t
think, that that man was once a baby, and sat on his mother's knee, and that h
mother may have been pleased to see him cut his *first tooth*. If she could but see h
teeth now! **99**

MADAME CALDERON DE LAS BARCAS, *LIFE IN MEXIC*
PUB. CHAPMAN & HALL, LONDON, 184

SANITATION

Aldous Huxley (1894–63) observed the basics of human life in his journ
around the Bay of Mexico. The first extract describes a hotel in Belize; th
second a market in Guatemala city.

66Walking through the streets, one saw but little traces of the great calamity
1930, when a hurricane blew the sea in a huge wall of water right across the tow
A heap of bricks, it is true, was all that was left of the principal house of God; b
Mammon, Caesar and the Penates had risen fresh and shining from the ruin
Almost all the private residences and all the government offices, all the shops ar
warehouses, had been rebuilt or repaired. The town as a whole looked remarkab
neat and tidy. Even a tidal wave may have something to be sa
for it. It does at least clear away the slums. Our governmen
and municipalities are less brutal; but they are also, alas,
good deal less effective.

The sanitary arrangements at the new hotel were all tha
could be desired; but the proprietor, who was a Spanis
American, was evidently unacquainted, not only with

nglish spelling, but also (which was worse) with our English euphemisms. At the p of the stairs I found myself confronted by a door, on which were written, in very rge black letters, the words: FOR URIN.

hy not, after all? Nevertheless, I was a little startled. We are all like Pavlov's dogs so conditioned that, when the scatological bell rings, we automatically egin to frown or blush. It is absurd, it is even, if you like to think yourself as a rational being, rather humiliating. But ere it is; that is how the machine happens to work.**

Outside in an overflow market we saw an old Indian oman selling iguanas. They were cheap; you could buy a iniature dragon with three feet of ship-lash tail, all alive, r twenty or thirty cents. Flayed and gutted, the dried rcasses of several more lay in a neat row on the pavement, a le meat crusty with flies. Near them stood an enormous bowl, ll of iguana eggs. Curiosity wrestled with prejudice and was at st defeated; we moved away, leaving the eggs untasted. That ening we happened to pass again along the same street. usiness in lizards had evidently been slack; the old woman's tch was still crawling with monsters. While we were looking, e began to pack up her wares for the night. One by one, she ok up the animals and dumped them into a circular basket. e tails projected, writhing. Angrily she shoved them back into ace; but while one was being folded away, another would ring out, and then another. It was like a battle with the hydra. e abhorred tails were finally confined under a net. Then, hoisting the lizards on her head, and with the bowl of their eggs under her arm, the old woman arched away, muttering as she went heaven knows what imprecations against all ptiles, and probably, since she shot a furious look in our direction, all foreigners well.**

ALDOUS HUXLEY, *BEYOND THE MEXIQUE WAY*, PUB. CHATTO & WINDUS, LONDON 1934

BY TRAIN

American poet Elizabeth Bishop (1911–79) described a train journey in a letter to Marianne Moore.

Oaxaca is very nice – I like it next best to Mérida, I think. We came from ebla by *narrow-gauge Pullman*, the tiniest train I have ever seen. It ran all day rough a narrow mountain gorge filled with cactus, beside a raging torrent of mud, d it kept coming off the tracks and bumping along on the ties. Then the engineer d the conductor would hop off and somehow boost it back on again – and set up miniature broadcasting station beside the track to let the day train behind us ow where we were so they wouldn't bump into us. We were ten hours late, but parently that wasn't bad – sometimes it gets stuck for days, and the company riously suggests that you bring some groceries along.

ELIZABETH BISHOP, *LETTERS*, SELECTED AND EDITED BY ROBERT GIROUX, PUB. CHATTO & WINDUS, LONDON 1994

MEXICANS

The travel writing of Graham Greene (1904–9) reflects his preoccupations with religion and moral dilemmas. The first of these extracts describes Huichapan station; the second, the nightlife of El Retiro.

**The whole long platform was given up to beggars – not the friendly Indian men bearing tortillas and legs of chicken, preserved fruits dried in the dusty sun, d strange pieces of meat, who pass at every station down the train, not even the d of resigned beggars who usually sit in church porches waiting dumbly and tiently for alms – but get-rich-quick beggars, scrambling and whining and

snarling with impatience, children and old men and women, fighting their wa
along the train, pushing each other to one side, lifting the stump of a hand,
crutch, a rotting nose, or in the children's case a mere bony undernourished hand
A middle-aged paralytic worked himself down the platform on his hands – thre
feet high, with bearded bandit face and little pink baby feet twisted the wrong way
Someone threw him a coin and a child of six or seven leapt on his back and after a
obscene and horrifying struggle got it from him. The man made no complaint
shovelling himself further along: human beings here obeyed the jungle law, eac
for himself with tooth and nail. They came up around the train on both sides of th
track like mangy animals in a neglected zoo."

"El Retiro is the swagger cabaret of Socialist Mexico, all red and gold and littl
balloons filled with gas, and Chicken à la King. A film star at one table and
famous singer, and rich men everywhere. American couples moved sedately acros
the tiny dance floor while the music wailed, the women with exquisite hair an
gentle indifference, and the middle-aged American business men like overgrow
schoolboys a hundred years younger than their young women. Then the cabare
began – a Mexican dancer with great bold thighs, and the American women lost
little of their remote superiority. They were being beaten at the sexual game
somebody who wasn't beautiful and remote was drawing the attention of their men
They got vivacious and talked a little shrilly and powdered their faces, and suddenl
appeared very young and inexperienced and unconfident, as the great thigh
moved. But their turn came when the famous tenor sang. The American men l
their pipes and talked all through the song and then clapped heartily to show tha
they didn't care, and the women closed their compacts and listened – avidly.
wasn't poetry they were listening to or music (the honeyed words about roses an
love, the sweet dim nostalgic melody), but the great emotional orgasm in th
throat. They called out for a favourite song and the rich plump potent voice waile
on – interminably, a whole night of love. This was not popular art, nor intellectu
art – it was, I suppose, capitalist art. And this, too, was Socialist Mexico."

GRAHAM GREENE, *THE LAWLESS ROADS – A MEXICAN JOURNE*
PUB. LONGMANS, GREEN & Cc
LONDON, 193

TRAVELING AROUND THE ROUTE OF THE MAYAS

▲ "Castillo" at Tulum (Mexico)   ▼ Temples at Palenque (Mexico)

▼ Mayan edifices and causeway at Labná (Mexico)

"Caracol" at Chichén Itzá (Mexico)   ▼ Temple 1 at Tikal (Guatemala)

Nunnery quadrangle at Uxmal (Mexico)

▲ Lake Atitlán (Guatemala) ▼ Field at Quetzaltenango (Guatemala)

▼ Pool in the Lacandón Forest (Mexico)

Livingston Beach (Guatemala)

▼ Agua Azul Falls (Mexico)

Panamerican road in the highlands (Guatemala)

▲ Tzotzil Indians at Zinacantán (Mexico)

▲ San Antonio Palopó (Guatemala)　　▼ Market at Almolonga (Guatemala

Dzibalchen (Mexico)

▼ "Garifunas" in Belize City (Belize)

Santa Lucía Cotzumalguapa (Guatemala)

▲ Church in Yucatán (Mexico)　　　　▼ San Cristóbal de Las Casas (Mexico)

▼ Bolonchen (Mexico)

EASTERN YUCATÁN

QUINTANA ROO
The state of Quintana Roo occupies the eastern half of the Yucatán Peninsula. It covers an area of 19,387 square miles and has a population of 500,000. From 1902 it was governed as federal territory by the military and it only became a state in 1974.

This long, rocky, forested coastal strip is bordered to the north and east by the Caribbean. The coast is protected by the coral reef (yellow coral, above) ■ *18* and has some of the finest beaches in America. In recent years, with the development of Cancún, the tourist trade has become increasingly important.

Detail from wall painting, Cancún, showing the 1910 Mexican revolution.

Before the Spanish Conquest the coastal region of Eastern Yucatán, bordered by the Caribbean, underwent an extraordinary period of development equalled only by the modern tourist boom. The so-called "East" or "East Coast" lay on the long-distance trade routes between Central America, Honduras and Guatemala, on the one hand, and the northern Maya region of Yucatán and the Gulf of Mexico, on the other.

AN UNSETTLED PERIOD. During the Classic period (3rd–9th centuries AD) the major urban centers were concentrated in the forests of Petén ▲ *317*, in Guatemala, and along the Motágua ▲ *296* and Usumacinta ▲ *248* rivers. Northern Yucatán was less developed at this time and did not flourish until the Terminal Classic and, more especially, the Postclassic periods, following the collapse of the great cities. In the eastern region, Cobá ▲ *182* was the only important trading center,

sending salt, shells, honey, wax and cotton to the coasts of Belize and Honduras.

TERRITORIAL AND ECONOMIC RE-ORGANIZATION. When these consumer centers disappeared, large-scale population migration altered the cultural, economic and demographic balance of the entire region. Other major centers developed in the highlands of Guatemala ▲ *261*, northern Yucatán and along the coast of Tabasco. It was from here that navigators organized new (maritime and river) trade routes and controlled the cocoa-producing regions of Guatemala, Honduras and the coast of Belize, establishing trading posts along the Caribbean coast. Many new towns (such as Tulum ▲ *177* and Cozumel ▲ *174*) developed, along with small sanctuaries (providing shelter for some and acting as trading posts for others) where goods could be exchanged or sent inland.

1. ~~CANCÚN~~
2. ISLA MUJERES
3. PUERTO MORELOS
4. PLAYA DEL CARMEN
5. COZUMEL
6. TULUM
7. COBÁ
8. VALLADOLID
9. FELIPE CARRILLO PUERTO
10. POLYUC
11. PETO
12. CHETUMAL
13. KOHUNLICH
14. RÍO BEC
15. XPUHIL
16. BECÁN
17. CONHUAS

⏱ Four days

CARIBBEAN SEA

THE EUROPEAN CONQUEST. Having dispossessed the Indians
of their commercial activities, the Spanish proceeded to
decimate the population with imported epidemics. Although
the villages of Polé (Xcaret), Cozumel and Zama (Tulum)
survived for a some time, they were abandoned after being
plundered by pirates, and the east coast remained virtually
deserted for almost two centuries. Only the English went
there to cut wood and replenish their freshwater supplies.
THE CASTE WAR ▲ 186. When the Maya rebelled in 1847, the
new inhabitants of the coastal region sought refuge on the
Isla Mujeres and the Isla de Cozumel. The Maya,
driven back from the regions of central Yucatán,
built their sacred capital, Chan Santa Cruz ▲ 184
in the eastern forests. The capital was finally
seized by the Mexicans in 1901.

FISHING FOR
PLEASURE
The Caribbean coast
is an ideal place to
fish for *sábalo* (shad),
corvina, macabi or
robalo (sea bass),
barracuda, sailfish,
marlin and groupers
(below).

171

MAGNIFICENT BEACHES

Cancún's beaches are remarkable both for the color of the sea, which is transparent to a depth of up to 130 feet and ranges from emerald green to sapphire blue, and for their fine, white sand. The sand contains

microscopic fossilized plankton, known as "discoaster", which ensure it always remains cool, even under the blazing sun. Currents and sudden changes in the wind can make these beaches dangerous for bathing. Summer temperatures remain around 104°F with humidity levels of between 70 and 80 percent. The best time to visit Cancún, and indeed the rest of Maya territory, is in the winter, between December and March.

CANCÚN

Since the 19th century the Yucatán Peninsula has been a popular destination for travelers with an interest in archeology. The absence of roads and any kind of tourist infrastructure put the dedication of these intrepid early travelers to the test. The final port of call on these archeological journeys was invariably Chichén Itzá ▲ 205. T Caribbean coast, so naturally beautiful and so rich in beache and archeological remains, was inaccessible until the early 20th century because of the insurgent Indians of Chan Santa Cruz ▲ 184.

A MODERN RESORT. During the 1970's a vast project was conceived to use this deserted coastline, trapped between the jungle and the sea, to create a series of tourist centers which could compete wit the internationally renowned resort of Acapulco, which was already at saturation point. So the tiny island of Cancún, south of the Isla Mujeres ▲ 17 was joined up with the mainland and a vast tourist complex was created. Today with 300,000 inhabitants, Cancún is one of the most visited tourist resorts in the world.

TWO MAIN AVENUES. The city is crossed two main avenues. One, the Avenida Tulum, joins the Mérida–Chichén Itzá road at Puerto Juárez to the north, and crosses the city from north to south, in the direction of the airport and Tulum ▲ 177. The other, the Avenida Kukulcán, opens onto the Avenida Tulum in the cit center, continues east for 5 miles towards the hotel zone and then south along the seafront where it services a further 8 miles of hotels. Finally it turns west towards the airport and Tulum.

THE LAGOON. The vast lagoon between the island and the mainland has been divided into sections: Laguna de Nichpu Bojórquez, Laguna del Amor and Río Inglés. It is bordered by mangroves ■ 20 and linked to the sea by the Nizuc canal i the south and the Nichputé canal to the north. The lagoon (6 miles long by 3 miles wide) is an ideal place to go fishing, water skiing and diving. There are also boat trips round the lagoon, to the mangroves and archeological sites.

MAYAN REMAINS. The island of Cancún was inhabited by the Maya before the Spanish Conquest. In the center of the isla lie the remains of two Mayan sites: SAN MIGUELITO (Xlab-Multun) which overlooks the sea and EL REY (Kin ich Ahau Bonil) which overlooks the lagoon. The site of El Rey consis of a central plaza surrounded by three platforms, a pyramid, two small temples and a vaulted structure. A second plaza ha two platforms and a vaulted building with a small oratory in the center. Near the Sheraton Hotel a small structure and a statue of the *Chacmool* are all that remains of the site of YAMIL LU'UM, while the remains of POK-TA-POK can be seen 4 miles away near a golf course of the same name. These Postclassic structures are in the same style as those found along the coast of Quintana Roo.

The beaches of Quintana Roo extend over 100 miles along the shores of the Caribbean.

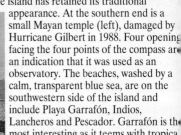

ISLA MUJERES

HACIENDA MUNDACA
A 19th-century smuggler, Fermin Mundaca, made his base on the Isla Mujeres. He was in love with a beautiful Spanish woman and built her a palace and a fort to protect it. But the object of his affections married another man and the pirate died of a

broken heart. The ruined fort and gardens are due to be restored.

The ranch of Miguel Molas at Cozumel (drawing by Frederick Catherwood).

The Isla Mujeres (Island of Women), situated a few miles north of Cancún, was probably discovered in 1517 by Francisco Hernández de Córdoba ● *36* who was visiting one of the temples when he noticed several female idols. The island is 4 miles long, between 330 and 875 yards wide and lies just over 4 miles from the quay at Puerto Juárez. The tiny fishing village (1,400 inhabitants) at the northern end of the island has retained its traditional appearance. At the southern end is a small Mayan temple (left), damaged by Hurricane Gilbert in 1988. Four openings facing the four points of the compass are an indication that it was used as an observatory. The beaches, washed by a calm, transparent blue sea, are on the southwestern side of the island and include Playa Garrafón, Indios, Lancheros and Pescador. Garrafón is the most interesting as it teems with tropical fish and is an ideal spot for divers, although care should be taken near the coral reef. To the north of Garrafón, the Playa Cocoteros or Los Cocos (also known as North Beach), with its fine sand and transparent waters, is popular among the local population.

A PIRATES' HAVEN. For centuries the Isla Mujeres was used as a base by pirates and smugglers. In 1821 Jean Lafitte was mortally wounded here by the Spanish. Although he died at sea and was buried at Dzilam ▲ *216* in north Yucatán, Lafitte has become a legendary figure in the region.

COZUMEL ★

The Isla de Cozumel is the largest of the Mexican islands. It is 33 miles long, 8 miles wide and has a population of fifty

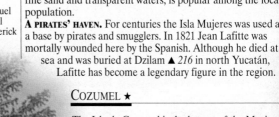

…usand. Its Mayan name, Cuzamil, means "island of …allows". It was occupied by the Maya for two thousand …rs and still boasts a number of archeological remains.

…N GERVASIO. Inhabited up to the time of the Conquest, this …portant site included the sanctuary of the goddess Ixchel, …elary divinity of pregnant women, medicine and the fertility …the moon. Her oracle attracted many Mayan pilgrims who …ded at Xamancab, modern San Miguel.

…RADING HISTORY. The important trade network between …atemala, Honduras, the Gulf of Mexico and northern …catán ended at Cozumel which was protected by the sea. …e intermediate ports were open to attack and, like Tulum …177, had defensive walls. Among the thirty-five Mayan …es known on Cozumel is the temple of Cedral, used …a prison during the 19th century.

…RIVAL OF THE EUROPEANS. In 1518 Juan de …ijalva was the first Spaniard to visit the …and where Hernán Cortés ● 36 would later …ke a long halt before embarking on his …nquest of Mexico. The Spanish occupation …Yucatán destroyed the Mayan trade …twork and the ruined Caribbean ports …re gradually abandoned. In the 16th …ntury French pirates plundered the …maining villages and during the 17th …ntury Cozumel was used as a base by …glish pirates who exploited the …ecious tropical hardwoods. The …and was subsequently abandoned …til the Indian uprising of 1847 ▲ 186. …e coastal fisherman used to take …fuge there, but the population …ver exceeded five hundred.

…CREASING PROSPERITY. …e chewing-gum boom …330 transformed Cozumel into …rading port. During World War Two it became the site of an …nerican military airport and was then forgotten until …cques-Yves Cousteau explored the Palancar Reef and …ought the beauty of the site to the attention of the world. In …ite of tourism and an international airport, Cozumel has …tained all the charm of a traditional Mexican village. A road …w makes it possible to tour the island.

…ACHES. About 5 miles to the south of the town is the …rque Chankanaab, a botanical garden built around a …agoon and a favorite site with locals and tourists alike. However, the Playa San Francisco and Playa Palancar, both about 9 miles south of the town, are the most beautiful beaches and a true paradise for divers, snorkelers and bathers. The lighthouse on Punta Celarán, to the south, offers a magnificent view of the island and mainland. The coastal landscapes are famed for their beauty, but the water can be dangerous for bathers. The northern part of the island has no roads and is inaccessible to tourists.

Village of Punta Molas, at the northern end of the Isla de Cozumel.

THE TOWN OF COZUMEL
The town, with its grid of streets, is pleasant and quiet. A museum overlooking the beach offers a complete history of the island and its wildlife. Of particular note are the reconstructions of underwater scenes ■ 18.

ISLA CONTOY
About 15 miles north of the Isla Mujeres lies the Isla Contoy, a bird sanctuary made famous by Jacques Cousteau. It attracts large numbers of birdwatchers and divers hoping to photograph the birds, see the tropical fish (above) and sample the seafood. As there is no hotel on the island, visitors sleep on the beach near a camp fire to keep mosquitos at bay.

175

Detail of decoration in the north passage of the Temple of the Frescos (plan opposite).

PUERTO MORELOS
The Alfredo-Barrera-Marín Botanical Gardens have a wide variety of regional plants and archeological remains (below) which can also be seen

elsewhere in the village. The Palancar Aquarium, about a mile away, presents every aspect of marine life, including the coral reef, *cenotes* (sinkholes), lagoons and mangroves. The nearby crocodile farm, *Croco'Cun* (top right), is open to the public.

PUERTO MORELOS

There is a ferry service, which takes two hours, between Cozumel and Puerto Morales ◆ *354*. Opposite the port of this fishing village a vast reef harbors a wide variety of corals and tropical fish living in the transparent blue waters.

PUNTA BETE. A very poor dirt track leads through the jungle for about 3 miles to the beaches of Punta Bete, whose placid waters are protected from the open sea by a coral reef. The beaches are equipped with restaurants, chalets, a campsite and *palapas*: open-sided, wooden structures with palm roofs.

PLAYA DEL CARMEN

Among the palm trees of the residential district of this small town (which is fast becoming an important tourist center), the remains of small temples bear silent witness to the presence of the Maya who once sailed along these coasts from Honduras in dugout canoes. The port of Xaman-Há (Playa del Carmen) was in fact one of the boarding points for pilgrims on their way to Cozumel to hear the oracle of the goddess Ixchel ▲ *175*.

COASTAL REGION

BEACHES ★. XCARET (Polé), on the road to Tulum, is a tourist center with beaches and underground rivers offering safe bathing, *cenotes*, and a dolphin aquarium. PUERTO AVENTURAS has a marina, luxury hotels, a golf course, shops and a museum. At KANTENAH, to the south, you can hang your hammock among the palm trees on the edge of the beach and eat fried fish under a *palapa*.
PAAMUL, a small, quiet beach where giant turtles come to lay their eggs in spring, has cabins and a campsite.

AKUMAL. Situated about 60 miles south of Cancún, Akumal was made famous by the discovery of the Spanish galleon, *Nuestra Señora de los Milagros*, which sank off the reef in 1741. The objects recovered are on display in the local museum and the village now houses the headquarters of CEDAM (the Mexican underwater exploration and water sports club), responsible for gathering information on ships which were wrecked in the region. Akumal was one of the first beaches to

ve diving and surfing facilities. The blue-green waters of its
y bay and its reef make it a favorite spot for tourists and
ers. In summer giant turtles lay their eggs on the beach.
EMUYIL AND XCACEL. Chemuyil and its beautiful beach
ovide an ideal setting from which to go diving or simply
ax. On Sundays giant iguanas look on as the beaches are
aded by bathers. Xcacel is another forgotten corner of
radise waiting to be explored. Visitors can view a *cenote* and
e to a sunken wreck.
NKAH. The region was converted into a plantation which
ew coconut palms and later produced *chicle* during the first
lf of the 20th century. Its beach does not have tourist
:ilities, but the offshore reef is extremely beautiful. The
:heological remains are an extension of the Tulum complex
niles away.

JLUM ★

Jum, about 80 miles south of Cancún, is the most important
:heological site on the Caribbean coast. The cliffs on which
stands form a natural protection. Like Mayapán ▲ *212*, the
e was originally surrounded by walled defenses including a
mpart walk and parapet. The fortifications protected the
rt and sanctuary against attack, while a small beach
rrounded by rocks created a natural safe haven where
ding could take place all year round. Causeways fashioned
om stone and known as *sacbeob* ("white roads" in Maya) led
o the forest towards the interior of Yucatán. The city was
ll occupied when the Spanish landed in 1518.

XEL-HA NATIONAL PARK
Tropical forest surrounds the lagoon, a beautiful natural aquarium fed by the sea and the fresh water of the sinkholes. A restored archeological site prepares tourists for their visit to Tulum.

TULUM
1. Castillo
2. Great Palace
3. Temple of the Frescos
4. Temple of the Diving God
5. Enclosure wall

CARIBBEAN SEA

Tulum, famed for its remarkable position on the shores of the Caribbean and its wall paintings (similar to those found in Mexican manuscripts) was an important city and port in the century before the Conquest. With the neighboring sites of Tancah and Xel-Há, Tulum offers some of the finest examples of monumental paintings and strictly religious architecture in Maya territory.

HISTORY

Tulum was founded in c. 1200 as a commercial port on the east coast of Yucatán. In close contact with Mayapán ▲ 212, it overtook that city in importance in c. 1400. Most of the ruins that can be seen today date from this period.

RESEARCH

Frederick Catherwood and John Lloyd Stephens ● 56, ▲ 130 visited the site in 1841. The first excavations were carried out in the 1920's by American and Mexican researchers who drew a plan of the site and studied its ceramics and architecture. Emphasis was given to preserving paintings and establishing the dates of the various styles. The center of the site, with buildings grouped round a plaza, is clearly Mayan. Other structures, built along a street running to the northeast, suggest Mexican influence, since this orientation is commonly found in Mexico, notably at Teotihuacán. The columned edifices date from the Middle Postclassic, while most of the other buildings date from the Late Postclassic.

THE "CASTILLO"

he largest edifice on the site overlooks the
'aribbean to the east and, on the landward
ide, looks onto a courtyard surrounded by
mall buildings. The *Castillo* today (above)
and in 1841 (below, by Catherwood).

CORNER MASK

Stucco mask (above) decorating one of the
corners of the Temple of the Frescos.
Stephens and Catherwood (who made the
drawing) measuring the façade of a temple to
the south of the *Castillo* (top).

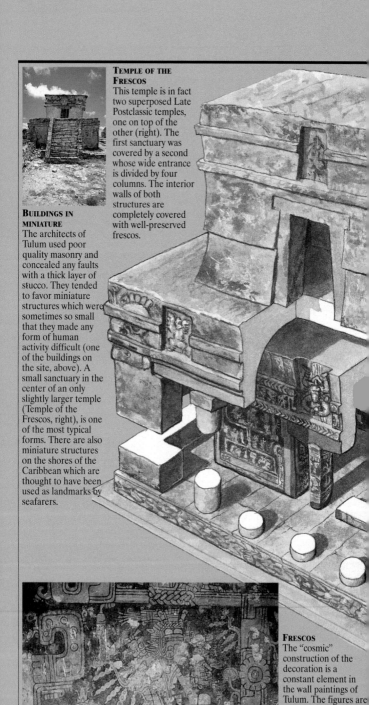

BUILDINGS IN MINIATURE

The architects of Tulum used poor quality masonry and concealed any faults with a thick layer of stucco. They tended to favor miniature structures which were sometimes so small that they made any form of human activity difficult (one of the buildings on the site, above). A small sanctuary in the center of an only slightly larger temple (Temple of the Frescos, right), is one of the most typical forms. There are also miniature structures on the shores of the Caribbean which are thought to have been used as landmarks by seafarers.

TEMPLE OF THE FRESCOS

This temple is in fact two superposed Late Postclassic temples, one on top of the other (right). The first sanctuary was covered by a second whose wide entrance is divided by four columns. The interior walls of both structures are completely covered with well-preserved frescos.

FRESCOS

The "cosmic" construction of the decoration is a constant element in the wall paintings of Tulum. The figures are represented with the sky above their heads and the underworld beneath their feet, while the scenes are divided into panels by coiled serpents.

In the inner sanctuary of the Temple of the Frescos, the central iconographic theme is corn. The divinities represented are all connected with this cereal crop. The so-called "Diving God" has two plants in his headdress; in the upper register a kneeling goddess is grinding corn, while above her and to the right, the seated God K (Kauil) ● *50* is presenting a small Maize God to a standing goddess.

THE "DIVING GOD"

Although he is usually interpreted as the image of a specific divinity (the planet Venus or the Bee God), the variations noted in the representations tend to suggest that there are several "Diving Gods". His posture most probably illustrates the theme of the god descending from the heavens to receive the offerings of men.

The Temple of the Frescos, by Frederick Catherwood.

back
l of the
mple of the
iving God", the
estial frieze includes one
he sun's rays and (possibly) a
mbol for Venus. It is surmounted by

a band terminated at either end by the top half of a creature, probably an image of the sky in the form of a two-headed serpent. The earth is also represented as a two-headed serpent, the counterpart of the celestial monster. Below the earth a central panel depicts the aquatic underworld. The terrestrial scene includes two groups of figures in which a woman is presenting an object to a man, probably a divinity.

HOLBOX
Holbox is reached via
the road from Cobá
to Nuevo Xcan which
crosses the Cancún-
Mérida road. At El
Ideal, a road runs
north to Kantunil Kin
and Chiquila. The
village of Holbox, an
ancient port used by
shark fishermen, is
reached by boat.
After sharks (tiger
shark, opposite),
lobsters are the most
highly prized catch.

PUNTA ALLEN
This tiny fishing
village is at the end
of a sandbar looking
across the Bahia de
la Ascensión. The
fishermen of the
village catch lobsters
in the bay with their
bare hands.

COBÁ

This virtually unexplored archeological region, about 30 mil
from Tulum, covers an area of 20 square miles. Cobá was
founded at the beginning of the 7th century and was occupie
with a few interruptions, until the 15th century. Its
architecture is reminiscent of that of Tikal ▲ *322*. In fact the
two cities flourished at the same time – between the 7th and
10th centuries – when Cobá was the most important city in
northeast Yucatán. This is evidenced by the many steles and
the impressive network of raised causeways (*sacbeob*) leadin
to the city. An alliance between Cobá and Tikal made the tw
cities important trading centers with products, especially sal
being delivered there from the coast before being sent on to
Petén.

RECENT EXCAVATIONS. The site (above), initially explored by
Washington's Carnegie Institution, has recently been
excavated and restored by the Mexico National Institute of
Anthropology and History. To the northeast of the main
group, Structure 1 (also known as the "Tallest Pyramid" or
Nohoc Mul) reflects the city's long occupation. A Late
Postclassic structure, similar to those at Tulum, was built on
top of the 78-foot high Late Classic pyramid. At its foot Stel
20 was discovered, one of the best preserved on the site,
dating from AD 684. From the top of the pyramid of the
Castillo, there is a magnificent view across the forest and the
five lakes (including Lake Macanxoc, opposite page)
surrounding the site.

RAISED CAUSEWAYS. *Sacbeob*
leading in five directions link the
central group to the other
architectural groups on the site. These
roads (sixteen have been recorded) are
between 1 and 8 feet above the ground and
about 14 feet wide. Their sides are rough stone
walls, filled with rubble and covered with *sascab*, a
natural limestone cement which sets when wet and

Black-headed gulls and turnstones are a common sight on the coasts of Yucatán.

...der pressure. *Sacbeob* also linked Cobá to other sites: Ixil, ...out 12 miles to the southwest, and Yaxuná, 62 miles to the ...st. The Cobá–Yaxuná causeway, most probably constructed ...ring the Late Classic period, is perfectly straight, except for ... first 20 miles when it must have had to skirt around small ...mmunities. It is the longest Maya road discovered to date. ...3-foot limestone cylinder was found on the causeway, ...ighing around 5 tonnes. It was probably used as a roller for ...mpressing the surface.

...WARD PUNTA ALLEN

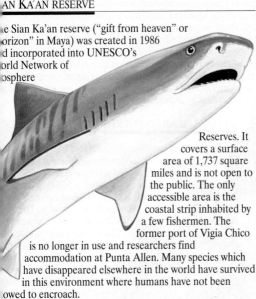

...sandy track runs from Tulum to Punta ...len, a distance of some 35 miles. At ...ca Paila there are chalets for visitors ...m Cozumel and Cancún who come for ... deep-sea fishing. The road runs ...tween the sea and the Laguna de ...unyaxché, winding between palm trees and ...pical plants, and crosses a wooden bridge with a ...arby camping facility. The lagoon is situated in a nature ...serve and is a sanctuary for migratory birds such as ...mingos, herons and egrets. There are over three hundred ...ecies of birds in the reserve, while two species of tropical ...ocodile (*Crocodylus moreletti* and *Crocodyluus acatus*) ...abit the lagoon.

...AN KA'AN RESERVE

...e Sian Ka'an reserve ("gift from heaven" or ...orizon" in Maya) was created in 1986 ...d incorporated into UNESCO's ...orld Network of ...osphere

Reserves. It covers a surface area of 1,737 square miles and is not open to the public. The only accessible area is the coastal strip inhabited by a few fishermen. The former port of Vigia Chico is no longer in use and researchers find accommodation at Punta Allen. Many species which have disappeared elsewhere in the world have survived in this environment where humans have not been ...owed to encroach.

...HALES. Several species can be seen around the Yucatán ...ninsula. Cuvier's whale or *picuda* (*Ziphius cavirostris*) tends ... live only in warm waters. In the past, the most widely ...nted species was the sperm whale (*Physeter macrocephalus*), ...ized for its meat and blubber, but also for its spermaceti, a ...ite waxy substance obtained from oil in the whale's head ...d used to make cosmetics and candles. Ambergris, an

SEA BIRDS
Birds such as sandpipers and curlews live on the beaches and in the mangroves where they find their food. Wilson's snipes, sandpipers and turnstones frequent the damp areas of the peninsula. The more commonly found seabirds in the Caribbean are the black-headed gull, with its dark head and orange-red beak; the herring gull, white with a yellow beak; the brown (*pontoh*) and white (*sac pontoh*) pelican; the frigate bird (*chimay* in Maya); the brown booby (*alcatraz*), with its white underbelly; and the blue-footed booby; the scissor-bill (*rayador*) which skims along the surface of the water with its beak open; the cormorant (*mach* in Maya); the *anhinga*, a strange animal known as the serpent-bird because of its long neck and beak; and, finally, Cabot's tern, and the royal and common terns.

183

On the road from Chetumal to Xpuhil.

DOLPHINS
There are five species of dolphin in the Caribbean: the *bufeo* or *tonina* that can be seen in aquariums (at Xcaret, for example); the manchado (*Stenella frontalis*) which travels the open sea in bands of up to a thousand individuals; *Stenella attenuata* and the *giradora* dolphin (*Stenella longirostris*), well-known to fishermen; and, living alongside the above species, the smaller and much rarer *Steno bredanensis*.

Fruit sellers in Yucatán at the end of the 19th century.

intestinal secretion used as a fixative fo scents in perfumes is also in demand. T rorqual or fin-back whale (*Balaenoptera physalus*) is the largest species (80 feet long) found in the Caribbean, while the orca or killer whale (*Orcinus orca*) is the most common. The best known species Yucatán is the *ah k'anxoc* or pilot whale (*Globicephala macrochynchus*), so calle because it is thought that bands of fifty sixty individuals often follow one male, who acts as their guide. This is the species that is most frequently found beached and in 1985 there was a mass "suicide" at Xpet Há northern Yucatán. The fishermen of Holbox were experts at hunting this whale.

MUYIL

From Tulum a road heads south towards Chan Santa Cruz, modern Felipe Carrillo Puerto, the former capital of the insurgent Indians of the Caste War ▲ 186. For over 60 miles the road runs through what was, up to twenty years ago, thic jungle. Today it is an uninteresting expanse of vast, deforest areas and *ranchos*. About 15 miles south of Tulum, on the road to Chetumal, the ruins of Muyil (also known as Chunyaxché) appear on a rocky promontory on the Laguna de Chunyaxché. The first surveys indicated that the site had been occupied continuously from the 1st century AD to the time of the Spanish Conquest. A *sacbé* (raised causeway) linked the ceremonial center with the lagoon 3 miles away. S edifices are still standing along the *sacbé*, at intervals of 130 yards. With the exception of the edifice furthest from the lagoon, they all face west. The *Castillo*, situated mid-way along the causeway, and almost 70 feet above the level of th lagoon, supports a circular tower which is the only one of i kind in Mayan archeology.

FELIPE CARRILLO PUERTO

During the Caste War the insurgent Maya (*cruzob*), driven back by the federal troops of Yucatán in 184 regrouped around a *cenote* in the jungle. An then a miracle occurred: a "Talking Cross" appeared at Kampocolché and promised th Maya a decisive victory. The "little sacred cross" became "Chan Santa Cruz" and its sanctuary the center of a ne power. A huge church, the Balam Na, was built in its honor and surrounded by vast complex of residenc barracks and training grounds. It was here that the *Tatich* or patron of the Cross – the supreme chief – resided, as did his aid de-camp, the *Tata*

Fresco from Chichén Itzá ▲ 205 representing life in a Yucatecan village during the pre-Hispanic era.

ohuch Zul or chief of spies (who infiltrated the enemy camp prepare the attacks), and the *Tata Polin*, the interpreter of Cross. The rest of the town's population was made up of rvants of the Cross, garrison soldiers who came regularly m the surrounding villages to do their turn on guard duty, d European and Indian slaves used for the building work.

ACES OF WORSHIP. The *cenote* (left) where the cross peared and the tiny sanctuary built to commemorate the ent can still be seen at the intersection of streets 69 and 58. veral sanctuaries were built, including the sanctuary of Tumul where a woman called Maria Huicab officiated. The great Balam Na became a Catholic church and the barracks behind it were converted into schools. The tiny chapel at the side of the church was built by the Mayan general Francisco May. In 1901 when the town was occupied by federal troops, several villages vied for the honor of hiding the Talking Cross, and the modest churches of the Indian villages continued to preach cult. Today on May 3 (Santa Cruz) the Maya still visit the all *cenote* of Carrillo Puerto where the Cross first spoke to m, and they still believe that the tower of the Balam Na l not be finished until they once more have control over ir own destiny.

ACALAR LAGOON

e lagoon (right), known as the Laguna de Siete Colores, is ked to the Bahia de Chetumal (Chetumal Bay). About 20 les before Chetumal, a turning leads to the *Cenote Azul* ich, with a depth of 295 feet, is one of the most impressive kholes after Chichén Itzá ▲ 205. The road continues along lake to the village of Bacalar. This once densely populated gion declined rapidly after the Spanish Conquest. The age of Salamanca de Bacalar, founded in 1544 by Gaspar checo, was abandoned after an Indian uprising. The village s rebuilt during the 17th century, but remained under nstant threat from marauding pirates who plundered it veral times, and was eventually abandoned once again. ring the first quarter of the 18th century, the governor, tonio Figueroa, built a fort (now a museum) there to

XCALAK
Mid-way between Carrillo Puerto and Chetumal, a road leads to the peninsula of Xcalak. After Majahual a track follows the coast north to Punta Herrero and south to Xcalak. This region has a number of unexplored archeological sites. Although the existence of the coastal sites has been recorded, nothing is known of the interior. During the colonial era the region served as a refuge for the Maya fleeing Spanish

domination. In 1900 the army built a lighthouse and station at Xcalak and a lighthouse at Punta Herrero.

▲ Caste War

In 1901 Porfirio Díaz (below) sent federal troops to quell the Yucatecan insurrection.

Group of soldie[...]
and civilians [...]
Chan Santa Cru[...]

During the second half of the 19th century the Yucatán Peninsula was shaken by a violent conflict between the Maya and Europeans. The Indians, heavily taxed by the government, saw their ancestral lands being taken from them. Their chiefs, whose privileges were threatened by liberal laws and the European abuses of power, launched a violent campaign which intensified from 1847 onward. The insurgents held a large territory until the end of the 19th century, but were eventually defeated.

BEGINNING OF THE INSURRECTION

In July 1847 the public execution of one of the Indian rebels and the burning of the Maya village of Tepich and its inhabitants provoked a full-scale insurrection by the Maya in eastern Yucatán. The Indians gave free rein to their hatred of the Europeans, attacking villages, burning, massacring and destroying anything that reminded them of their oppressors.

RECONQUERING THE MAYA

The Maya, armed by English settlers in Belize, regained 90 percent of their ancestral lands and established outposts 5 miles from Campeche and 15 miles from Mérida. But when panic was at its height the Maya inexplicably withdrew to their villages. The Europeans regrouped and, with the end of the war between the United States and Mexico in 1848, were able to procure arms and reinforcements. The Maya were driven back and regrouped around Chan Santa Cruz where they founded the cult of the Talking Cross. Inspired by the oracle that promised them victory, they resisted vigorously for several years.

At the end of the 19th century the Indians, weakened by disease and deprived of weapons, fell easy prey to federal troops who, in 1901, occupied Chan Santa Cruz, (right) following a Mayan withdrawal. Thus, after fifty years of independence, their ancestral lands became federal territory under military control.

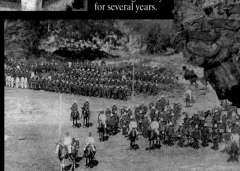

186

Stucco
mask from
Kohunlich.

observe the English who were in the
process of moving into Belize ▲ 335. In
1859, during the Caste War, the village
was captured by the Maya who
massacred the population. It was not
recaptured until 1901.

CHETUMAL

Chetumal was founded in 1898
following the signing of the Spencer-
Mariscal treaty, in accordance with
which Mexico recognized the border
of British Honduras (now Belize). A
pontoon built in New Orleans was
anchored in the bay opposite the
village of Payo Obispo from where
watch could be kept on the
illegal trade in arms and
tropical hardwoods which
were being brought down the
Río Hondo. Soon the
refugees from the Caste War
returned from Belize and the
village of Payo Obispo began to
develop. The name Chetumal probably
means "place of red wood" (*chacté*). In
1915 the regional government was
transferred from Chan Santa Cruz to
Chetumal which became the capital.
Situated in a hurricane zone, it was
destroyed several times – first in 1916,
then in 1942 and, most violently, in 1945
by Hurricane Janet. With a population
of 120,000, Chetumal (left) is a modern
city and an important trading center for
the neighboring villages of Quintana
Roo and Belize. As yet Chetumal does not have a well-
developed tourist industry.

RÍO HONDO. The Río Hondo forms the natural border
between Mexico and Belize. From Chetumal you can travel
up the river by boat as far as the village of Subteniente López.
Alternatively you can take a boat along the coast to the
Laguna Milagros and the town of Calderitas where you can
sample the local seafood by the water's edge. The few
archeological sites in this region are either unexplored or, like
Ichpaatún, have been destroyed.

AROUND CHETUMAL. A road runs west from Chetumal to
Ucum, 15 miles away, where it forks south to Belize, crossing
the border at La Unión 53 miles away. The other fork leads
west to Francisco Escárcega
180 miles away, passing
through Kohunlich and the
various sites of central
Yucatán (Río Bec) ▲ 190.
Beyond Francisco Escárcega,
it is possible to continue
all the way to Palenque
▲ 243 and Campeche ▲ 228.

"When Francisco
Hernandez de
Córdoba reached this
land and
disembarked at a
place that he called
Cabo Catoche, he
came across some
Indian fishermen and
asked them what
their land was called.
They replied:
'Catoche', meaning
'our houses' .... He
then asked, by means
of signs, what their
land was like to which
they replied:
'Ciuthan' meaning
'so they say'. The
Spanish made this
into Yucatán."

Diego de Landa
*Relación de las cosas
de Yucatán*

HUNLICH

ut 43 miles west of Chetumal, on the main Escárcega
d, a track leads south for about 5 miles to the ruins of
hunlich, a site occupied from the Preclassic to the
stclassic periods. Excavations and restoration work
gun in the late 1970's were resumed on a more
ensive scale in 1992.

Cattle breeding is one of the traditional economic resources of the Yucatán Peninsula.

AZA MAYOR. Three smooth steles stand on the entrance
ps to this great Late Classic plaza. Below them lies a stone
ar. At right angles to the entrance is a long platform, lined
various buildings whose doors are flanked by twin columns.
MPLE OF THE MASKS. The Temple of the Masks stands at
far end of Kohunlich, beyond numerous structures,
luding a large ball court ● 112. Painted stucco masks
posite page) decorate the four steps of this Early Classic
amid, on either side of the staircase. They have been
tected from the elements and vandals by the construction
a later pyramid over the first. This second pyramid still
ers the base of the first. The masks on Steps 2 and 3 have
man faces, the symbol *kin* (sun) in their eyes and incisors
ved in the form of a T.
ey are seen inside the
vs of a serpent,
st probably
resenting the
, formed by
vertical jaws
ned by a
estial band
e symbol
nat, star, can be
n below the
-hand mask of
third step).
ch face is
med by two
sks, one on its
ad and the other
der its chin. The ear
naments are surmounted by a
h mask and extended below by a
pent's mask. On the fourth step the human
e is replaced by that of a jaguar beneath a
ge *kin* symbol. The masks of this pyramid
resent the ceremonial aspects of the sun –
star itself and the king with whom it was
ociated.

**THE SILK COTTON
TREE** ■ 28
The silk cotton tree,
the Cosmic Tree of
the Maya, towers
above the villages of
Yucatán and is
sometimes seen by
the roadside (drawing
by P. Langlois, late
19th century).

IBANCHÉ. The ruins of Dzibanché lie about
miles north of Kohunlich, in a region which
s clearly well-populated during the
-Columbian era and where a great deal of
heological work is being carried out.
e ruins have been intensively excavated since
12. Some remarkable tombs have been
covered in the large pyramids forming
rt of the main group. Further results of
excavations are awaited with great
icipation.

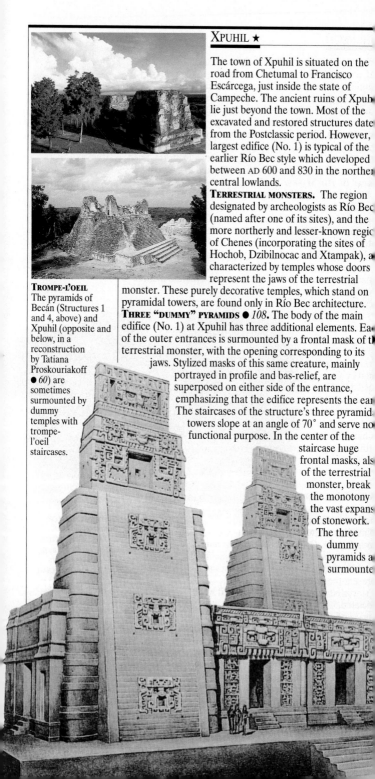

XPUHIL ★

The town of Xpuhil is situated on the road from Chetumal to Francisco Escárcega, just inside the state of Campeche. The ancient ruins of Xpuhil lie just beyond the town. Most of the excavated and restored structures date from the Postclassic period. However, largest edifice (No. 1) is typical of the earlier Río Bec style which developed between AD 600 and 830 in the northern central lowlands.

TERRESTRIAL MONSTERS. The region designated by archeologists as Río Bec (named after one of its sites), and the more northerly and lesser-known region of Chenes (incorporating the sites of Hochob, Dzibilnocac and Xtampak), are characterized by temples whose doors represent the jaws of the terrestrial monster. These purely decorative temples, which stand on pyramidal towers, are found only in Río Bec architecture.

THREE "DUMMY" PYRAMIDS ● 108. The body of the main edifice (No. 1) at Xpuhil has three additional elements. Each of the outer entrances is surmounted by a frontal mask of the terrestrial monster, with the opening corresponding to its jaws. Stylized masks of this same creature, mainly portrayed in profile and bas-relief, are superposed on either side of the entrance, emphasizing that the edifice represents the ear. The staircases of the structure's three pyramid towers slope at an angle of 70° and serve no functional purpose. In the center of the staircase huge frontal masks, also of the terrestrial monster, break the monotony the vast expanse of stonework. The three dummy pyramids a surmounte

TROMPE-L'OEIL
The pyramids of Becán (Structures 1 and 4, above) and Xpuhil (opposite and below, in a reconstruction by Tatiana Proskouriakoff ● 60) are sometimes surmounted by dummy temples with trompe-l'oeil staircases.

> THE PROVINCE OF RÍO BEC, MADE PROSPEROUS BY INTENSIVE AGRICULTURE, IS CHARACTERIZED BY A REGIONAL STYLE, AS UNUSUAL AS IT IS WIDESPREAD."
>
> PAUL GENDROP

HORMIGUERO

Hormiguero, which can only be reached with a guide and a four-wheel-drive vehicle, is indisputably the strangest and most excessive of the Río Bec sites. Structure 2 is the best example of this distinctive style. Masks in relief – a late addition – are superposed on the corners of Structure 5, a small temple entirely covered in sculptures. The masks have very pronounced elongated, sinuous or hooked muzzles.

...dummy temples whose central doorways also represent the ...rrestrial monster's jaws. Here, too, the false doors are ...rmounted by a frontal mask and flanked by two masks in ...ofile. Each of the dummy temples is further extended by a decorative crest.

BECÁN ★ ● 114

Becán is the largest and best-known of the Río Bec sites. It lies just off the main road, a few miles beyond Xpuhil. The city center is surrounded by a moat, originally 16 feet deep by 52 feet wide. Although this moat has been dated to the Preclassic period, the earliest recorded buildings at Becán date from the end of the Early Classic period. Río Bec is the oldest architectural style which has been identified at the site.

MONUMENTS. The considerable architectural activity that took place during the five or six centuries when Becán was a living center is revealed in the numerous additions, superpositions and modifications made up to and

CENTRAL YUCATÁN

The Río Bec region is situated in the center of Maya territory, a few miles north of what is now Guatemala and midway between Chetumal ▲ 188, in the east, and Francisco Escárcega, in the west. The only road linking the two towns, Mexico 186, also gives access to the region's archeological sites. While most are easily accessible, getting to the groups at Río Bec, Hormiguero and, further south, Calakmul, involves more of an expedition.

Insects of Central America:
species found throughout Yucatán.

RÍO BEC

Río Bec is less easily accessible than Xpuhil or Chicanná. The site gave its name to the Mayan architectural style in the region. There are various groups at Río Bec, of which the best preserved is group B. Here, the central section, pierced by a single entrance, is set back in relation to two pyramidal towers on either side. Inside, the walls have retained some interesting graffiti. Although very badly damaged, Group 2 has some beautiful remains which have been invaded by creepers and flowering trees. It is one of the most romantic ruined sites in Central America.

"From Río Bec to the hills of the Puuc region, the further you travel towards the northwest of the peninsula, the more the rounded and sensual exuberance of the ornamentation is replaced by an eminently architectural form of art in which geometric carvings are subordinated to the demands of a rigorous composition dominated by clearly defined outlines and well-contrasted dimensions.**"**
Paul Gendrop,
The Maya

during the Early Postclassic period. The decorative repertoire of the Río Bec style is well illustrated in this regional capital where small, engaged columns, "checker boards", crosses and a profusion of superposed masks are scattered liberally across the façades. Structure 4, however, is something of an enigma. Nine interconnecting rooms, some as high as 26 feet, were discovered within the main body of the pyramid. The rooms were completely dark, with the only means of access being a narrow passageway connecting them with the outside. One theory proposed by archeologists is that the complex may have been used for ritual ambulations in an environment designed to represent the underworld.

CHICANNÁ

Easily accessible from the road which runs across the Yucatán Peninsula, Chicanná has several well-preserved and restored edifices. The façade of Structure 2 (above right) consists of three sections: a central building with two additional wings. The cornices above the lateral entrances are in the form of simple peasant dwellings with

tched roofs, whose empty niches once contained statues.
low the cornices, the smooth walls were covered with
cco and painted with glyphs, a few of which are still visible
day.

NT MONSTER-MASK. In contrast to the soberness of the
ngs, the façade of the central building is heavily sculpted
ound the entrance (below). Above the entrance the main
otif is the frontal mask of a terrestrial monster whose lower
is represented by the projecting platform of the threshold.
e upper jaw is drawn back to reveal a row of impressive-
oking teeth in relief, with two T-shaped incisors in the
ddle. The eyes have hook-shaped pupils. The two spirals
erging from the corners of the mouth probably represent
e breath of life. The rectangular ear ornaments are each
rmounted by another spiral

nbolizing plant growth, and extended
a bone, the symbol of death. A
shaped cavity on the forehead
oresents access to the underworld and
e statue that it once contained was
obably an image of the king. The
trance is also flanked by two identical
ofiles of the same terrestrial monster.
e teeth of both jaws are clearly visible.
ove the eyes the broad forehead is

General view of
Structure 2 at
Chicanná. In the
center is a doorway in
the form of a
terrestrial monster.

LATER EXCAVATIONS
For a long time the
Maya sites of Central
Yucatán remained
undiscovered by
explorers and
archeologists. John
Lloyd Stephens,
Frederick
Catherwood, Désiré
Charnay and Alfred
Maudslay did not
explore the region
● 56. It was the
Frenchman, Maurice
de Périgny, who first
visited central
Yucatán in 1907. The
Carnegie Institution
organized several
expeditions during
the 1930's and Xpuhil,
Chicanná and Río
Bec were excavated
and restored during
the 1970's. It is highly
likely that other sites
in the region contain
secrets yet to be
revealed, as was the
case at Balamkú
▲ 194.

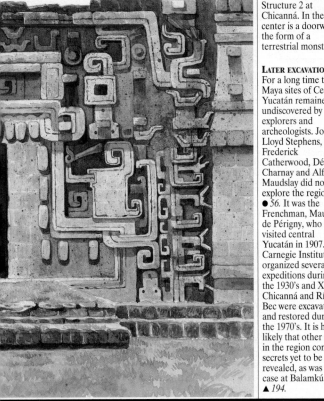

indented at the top and decorated with spirals. The nos
is extended by a jade tube which, like those emerging
from the mouth, probably symbolizes the breath of
life. Behind the great profile masks are two sculpted
panels of superposed, stylized, terrestrial masks. The
massive two-headed serpent arching above the
frontal mask probably represents the sky.

BALAMKU

About 37 miles from Xpuhil, in the
direction of Francisco Escárcega, the
first track on the right after the village
of CONHUAS runs through the trees for
about a mile to the site of Balamkú.
Discovered by chance as recently as
1990, it is today famous for its HOUSE
OF THE FOUR KINGS. The façade of th
edifice dates from the Early Classic
period and bears a 55-foot-long stucco
frieze. The decoration is extended
upward by four masonry blocks added onto the roof. The
edge of the roof is incorporated into the decoration to
represent the level of the earth's surface which
separates the
underworld from the world of
the living. Four scenes of
emergence alternate with three
jaguars, in either seated or
kneeling positions and heavily bound
in the manner of sacrificial victims.

CELEBRATION OF ROYALTY.
Below the scenes of emergence on
the frieze a terrestrial-monster
mask is depicted. The mask is
surmounted by a toad (above
left) and a crocodile (above
right), both of which have
their heads thrown back.
From their open jaws the
king emerges, seated on a
jaguar-skin cushion and
wearing his "chin" and
"headdress" masks. This
decoration is a celebration
of royalty which stresses its
intimate relationship with
the cosmos. It represents the
accession to the throne of the
sovereign from the bowels of
the earth, a process regarded
as symbolizing rebirth and
associating the king with
the sun and corn. This complex
representation also serves to
proclaim the sovereign as the
guarantor of the prosperity of
the kingdom throughout the
four corners of the earth.

**TRADE IN THE
YUCATÁN**
The Yucatán does
not feature the
traditional Indian
markets found in the
highlands of
Guatemala ● 82,
♦ 374. Since the pre-
Hispanic era, trade
has been an activity
linked with sorcery.
Today commercial
activity is conducted
through local
merchants who buy
their supplies in the
cities. Trade is
nevertheless highly
developed in
Yucatán and corn,
for example, is
grown as a
commercial as well
as a subsistence
crop. The large
urban centers of the
region in fact act as
markets which
attract trade.
Chetumal ▲ 188, on
the border of Belize,
is an important
smuggling center
where many
industrial products
can be bought.

Yucatecan peasant
woman (right), early
20th century.

WESTERN YUCATÁN

▲ WESTERN YUCATÁN

CRUCERO GANADO

1. MÉRIDA
2. IZAMAL
3. PISTÉ
4. CHICHÉN ITZÁ
5. VALLADOLID
6. MAYAPÁN
7. TEABO
8. M

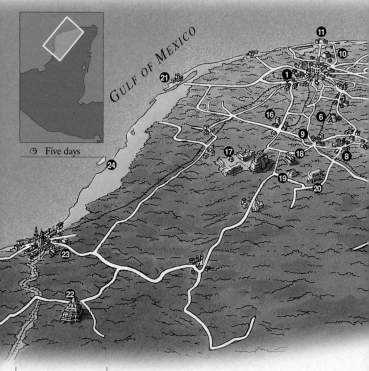

GULF OF MEXICO

🕐 Five days

The characteristically high windows, protected by wrought-iron grilles, of the houses of the aristocracy in the center of Mérida.

The modern state of Yucatán is the result of the successive divisions, begun in the 19th century, of a territory which once covered the entire Yucatán Peninsula. Today it covers a triangular area of 15,425 square miles bordered by the Gulf of Mexico to the north, the state of Campeche to the south, and Quintana Roo to the east. Most of the state's 1,365,000 inhabitants are of Maya origin. The climate is warm and wet virtually all year. From November to March, breezes from the north bring cooler evening temperatures, while from April to September, the streets of the capital, Mérida, are flooded by tropical rains. The rainwater is absorbed by the chalky soil and collects beneath the layer of surface rock and in the *cenotes* (*dzono* in Maya) ■ *16*. Yucatán is the home of sisal (*Agave sisalana*), grown during the pre-Hispanic period for its fiber. During the 19th century it brought prosperity to the region, but the dispersion of the crop (now grown in Brazil and Tanzania) and competition from artificial fibers, soon put an end to the sisal "boom". The only evidence of this short-lived period of prosperity are the palatial French-style residences in the center of Mérida and the former haciendas – now mostly abandoned – whose distinctive, tall, brick chimneys can be seen from the roads.

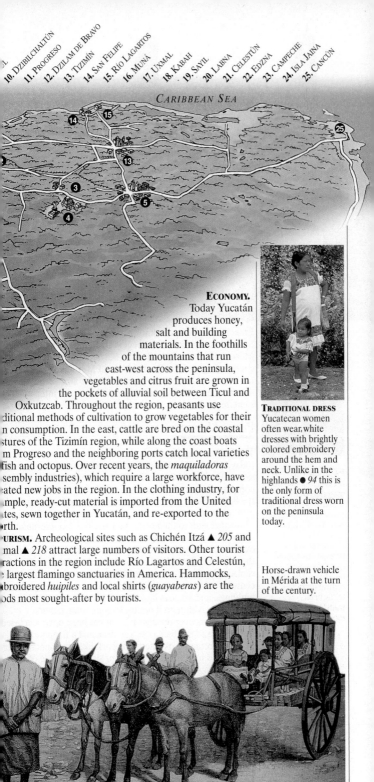

CARIBBEAN SEA

ECONOMY.
Today Yucatán
produces honey,
salt and building
materials. In the foothills
of the mountains that run
east-west across the peninsula,
vegetables and citrus fruit are grown in
the pockets of alluvial soil between Ticul and
Oxkutzcab. Throughout the region, peasants use
traditional methods of cultivation to grow vegetables for their
own consumption. In the east, cattle are bred on the coastal
pastures of the Tizimín region, while along the coast boats
from Progreso and the neighboring ports catch local varieties
of fish and octopus. Over recent years, the *maquiladoras*
(assembly industries), which require a large workforce, have
created new jobs in the region. In the clothing industry, for
example, ready-cut material is imported from the United
States, sewn together in Yucatán, and re-exported to the
North.

TOURISM. Archeological sites such as Chichén Itzá ▲ *205* and
Uxmal ▲ *218* attract large numbers of visitors. Other tourist
attractions in the region include Río Lagartos and Celestún,
the largest flamingo sanctuaries in America. Hammocks,
embroidered *huipiles* and local shirts (*guayaberas*) are the
goods most sought-after by tourists.

TRADITIONAL DRESS
Yucatecan women
often wear white
dresses with brightly
colored embroidery
around the hem and
neck. Unlike in the
highlands ● *94* this is
the only form of
traditional dress worn
on the peninsula
today.

Horse-drawn vehicle
in Mérida at the turn
of the century.

197

Ancient Tiho, or Ichcanzih was one of the principal towns in the Maya province o Chacán. On January 6, 1542

Francisco de Montejo, known as El Mozo, confirmed the Spanish occupation of the region by founding the town of Mérida on the ancient site (the Mayan ruins reminded the conquistadors of the Roman ruins of Mérida in Spain). The town's layout is the same as that used for all colonial towns America: a central square with parallel streets intersecting right angles ● *123*.

PLAZA MAYOR

"The town of Mérida, built with the materials of the Indian city, is, like all Spanish towns in the New World, little more than a vast checkerboard of straight streets and perfectly square buildings. The large central plaza has today been transformed into a modern square."
Désiré Charnay
Voyage au Yucatán et au pays des Lacandons (1882)

The Cathedral (pictured in the 19th century, above, and today, left) and the bishop's residence were built on the eas side of the Plaza Mayor. The Palacio Montejo, built for the conquistador, originally occupied the entire south side, but the building was subsequently divided up and is today flank by a number of other buildings. To the west is the Palacio Municipal and, to the north, the Palacio del Gobierno and other official residences. These buildings have been modifie over the years, with the bishop's residence being replaced b the offices of the federal authorities, which have in turn bee replaced by the MUSEUM OF MODERN ART. Other late 19th-century "modernizations" have replaced some of the older buildings, and arcades have been built along the north side the square. Although it has undergone some major modifications over the centuries (it has been open, enclose by grilles, and has had a central kiosk and a flagpole) the Plaza has retained its essentially park-like atmosphere wher visitors and inhabitants can walk or sit in the shade of the Weeping Figs (*Ficus benjamina*).

CASA DE MONTEJO. Built between 1543 and 1551, the Casa de Montejo is one o the oldest residences in Mérida. All tha remains of the original structure is the sculpted Plateresque façade (19th century, far left, and today, left). Its entrance depicts the Montejo coat of arms flanked by two armed conquistado with their feet standing on grimacing heads (the symbol of the Conquest). Th scene is completed by several other

res and motifs. Today the residence has been transformed
a bank.

HEDRAL. The cathedral, built between 1562 and 1598, was
first to be completed on the American continent. It was
ed on a basilican layout, with three naves and twelve
ars, and its distinctive dome is the oldest in Mexico. In the
ter of the austere façade, with its two Renaissance-style
ers and three entrances, a huge blazon bore the Spanish
t of arms. This was replaced, after Independence, by the
xican eagle. Its layout and decoration were partly modified
result of the damage sustained in 1915 during the
olution ● 40. The two side chapels on the south side were
troyed, while venerated sculptures such as the *Christ of the
ters*, the altar, the organ and other works of art and
nishings were burnt. The Cathedral houses important
hives and a collection of ancient paintings.

ACIO MUNICIPAL. The palace (below) stands on the site of
ancient pyramid from which materials were used to
struct the Cathedral, the Casa de Montejo and other
dings in the town. The original 17th-century structure has
ergone several transformations, including the addition of
wer completely out of harmony with the architectural style
he town.

ACIO DEL GOBIERNO. The present Palacio del Gobierno –
vo-story building with a central courtyard, built on the site
he former "royal residences" – was opened in 1892. It is
ous for the paintings (which trace the region's history)
orating its corridors and a so-called "history" room.
ey are the work of one of the last great
xican mural artists, Fernando Castro
heco.

NASTERIES

ring the colonial era the town was
ded into "ethnic" districts. The
nish occupied the town center while
barrios (outlying districts) were
abited by the Maya, Blacks and
xicans (Atzcapotzalco Indians who
ompanied the Spanish troops). The
ginal layout was gradually modified
l by the 17th century the town
upied a vast square area delimited by
ne arches, three of which still exist
rcos de los Dragones, del Puente, de
Juan). Several monasteries were built
he town.

NASTERY OF SAN FRANCISCO. The
ge Monastery of San Francisco was

lt on the ruins of an ancient pyramid. The site was chosen
construct a fortification which would protect the town
inst attack by marauding pirates. A defensive wall
losed the monastery, but it was not strong enough: it was
ndoned and plundered in 1820 when its archives were
stroyed.

NASTERY OF LA MEJADORA. This beautiful 17th-century
nplex (Calles 59 and 50) today is occupied by a church, an
hitectural college and the MUSEO DE ARTES POPULARES.

THE STREETS OF MÉRIDA
The streets of Mérida
are all numbered.
With the exception of
a few squares, none
of the city center's
main thoroughfares
has a name. The
streets running
north–south have
even numbers, while
those running
east–west have odd
numbers. The
residential districts
to the north of the
town, with their
shady avenues and
brightly colored
Delonix regia and
cascades of golden
Cassia fistula flowers
are a great
advertisement for life
in the tropics. In spite
of its city-center
traffic jams and the
deafening noise of
traffic, Mérida is a
delightful town which
still bears the marks
of its secular history.

THE MUNICIPAL MARKET
The central market
(above) was built on
the site of the ruined
monastery of San
Francisco. Calles 65
and 67, opposite
Calle 56, are reserved
for local crafts.

MONASTERY OF NUESTRA SEÑORA DE L CONSOLACIÓN. The monastery, known today as Las Monjas, was founded in 1633 as a residence for the Sisters of th Immaculate Conception. It has a distinctive arcaded tower. The church i still open to the public although the monastery is occupied by a workshop a CULTURAL CENTER.

CHURCHES

Although many of the original building in Mérida were subsequently converted the churches (each *barrio* had its own church and square) tended to be preserved.

Iglesia de Jésus and its square in the 19th century and today.

HERMITAGE OF SANTA ISABEL. The Hermitage of Santa Isabel (19th centur and today, opposite) is situated on the outskirts of Mérida, on the old Campeche road. This elegan but modest, single-nave structure, which stands alone in its garden (a converted square), is today a refuge for walkers. Many churches are reminders of the colonial era: the Iglesia de Jésus (left), built by the Jesuits in the 17th-century; the 18th-century Iglesia de San Cristóbal; Santa Lucia, which stands opposite a tiny arcaded square where public musical evenings are held every Thursday; Santa Ana, Itzimná, San Sebastián, La Candelaria, Santiago and, finally, San Juan Bautista, where the first liberals met on the eve of Independence to develop a political system more favorable the Indians.

UNIVERSITY OF YUCATÁN

The Colegio de San Pedro de la Real y Pontificia Universid de San Francisco Javier, founded by the Jesuits in 1624, use to occupy the land between the Iglesia de Jésus and the present site of the Teatro Peón Contreras (opposite). In 171 the seminary of San Pedro was founded on the site of the present university. The university closed long before the Jesuits were expelled in 1767. After Independence in 1824, the seminary buildings were occupied by the Literary University until it was closed in 1861.

It reopened in 1864 as the Real Universidad Literaria and became a Literary Institute in 1867. It lost its university status in 1869, but had it restored in 1922 by decree of the governor Felipe Carrillo Puerto. In 1984, it became the autonomous University of Yucatán. The old Jesuit building was transformed by the addition of an upper story and the entrance porch on the corner of Calles 60 and 57.

> **"**Yucatán... is covered by a vast underwood... you can try climbing to the top of the pyramids, but you will still see the same continuous, unbroken, desolate horizon. But Yucatán is favored by travelers, for it is a land rich in memories: extraordinary monuments, beautiful women, picturesque costumes... things that leave a lasting impression. It appeals

to the heart, soul, imagination and mind. Anyone who can leave Yucatán with indifference, has never been an artist and will never be a scholar.**"**
>
> Désiré Charnay
> *Un Voyage au Yucatán*
> (1860)

D CORN EXCHANGE. The old corn exchange (Calles 65 and ..., built beneath the arcades which today are occupied by all businesses, has retained all the atmosphere of the old onial markets.

RBAN DEVELOPMENT

SEO DE MONTEJO. The town expanded rapidly and, from early 20th century, the main avenue – the Paseo de ontejo – was enhanced by palatial residences such as the one which today houses the MUSEO DE ARQUEOLOGIA (on the corner of Calle 43), built by General Francisco Cantón, the then governor of the state. A number of these beautiful edifices were subsequently replaced by modern buildings of somewhat dubious taste. At the end of the Paseo de Montejo, a monument by the Colombian sculptor Romulo Rosso gives an account of the country's history in bas-relief.

ENIDA ITZÁ. During the same period, a number of buildings re erected at the western end of the town along the enida Itzá which today leads to the airport. They included e Benito Juárez prison complex and the hospital. Some of se buildings have been converted into e CULTURAL INSTITUTE. Opposite the stitute is the EL CENTENARIO ZOO AND RK, created to mark the centenary ebrations of Independence.

RKS AND SERVICES. After the 1910 volution the town underwent further velopment, this time in the field of blic services and parks. The Parque de Américas has many fountains and an en-air theater, built in a neo-Mayan le typical of the 1940's and 1950's.

STUCCO MASK
This lithograph by Frederick Catherwood depicts a stucco mask on a pyramid at Izamal, with an imaginary jaguar hunt in the foreground. Today, unfortunately, jaguars are rarely seen in northern Yucatán.

IZAMAL ★

Izamal (above and right), the most beautiful colonial town in Yucatán, lies about 12 miles north of Kantunil (on the Mérida-Cancún road). Before the Conquest it was a prosperous, ancient city which had been occupied from the Preclassic period onwards and had the largest pyramids in Yucatán. The temples were dedicated to the worship of Itzamná – "Lizard House", patron of learning and the sciences and inventor of writing – and to Kinich Kakmo, the Sun God. Several pyramids survive today and are currently being restored, including the small pyramid behind the arcaded plaza built by the Spanish (above), and the pyramid dedicated to the Sun.

BUILDING THE MONASTERY. Until the Spanish occupied the region, Izamal was a place of pilgrimage for the Maya. The friars saw it as their religious duty to convert the Indians to Christianity. Diego de Landa ● 55 demolished one of their temples – the Popolchac, dedicated to the rain gods – so that a monastery could be built on its vast platform (570 yards long by 470 yards wide and 40 feet high).

Work on the monastery began in 1553 under the direction of the Franciscan architect, Juan de Mérida, who designed and built the most important monasteries in the region. The monastery, church and atrium were completed by 1561, while the additional buildings and arcades were not finished until the first half of the 17th century.

AN IMPRESSIVE COMPLEX. The Izamal complex is the largest of its kind in America. Three ramps on the sides of the atrium give access to the complex. The principal ramp was

surmounted by a magnificent triumphal arch. The arch opened on either side onto the arcades surrounding the atrium where a chapel with a pyramidal roof was built in each of the four corners. In 1880 a small, rather unprepossessing tower was added to the simple but robust original façade of the church, while the former open chapel was converted into the chapel of La Tercera. The venerated statue of the Virgin of Izamal (left) – the patron saint of Mérida and Yucatán – still stands behind the chancel. The statue, as well as a copy, were commissioned in Guatemala and destined for Mérida and Valladolid, but on leaving Izamal the porters felt that the statue was growing heavier and heavier the further they got from the town. Instead of proceeding to their destinations, they returned to Izamal with the statue and installed it in the sanctuary which soon became a place of pilgrimage. The original statue, destroyed by fire in 1829, was replaced by a copy.

"The third pyramid, to the east, supported a temple dedicated to Ytzamat-ul, Itzamna or Zamna, described as the founder of Izamal. According to the 17th-century writer, Lizana 'This king or false god was represented by the Indians in the form of a hand ... and they say that the sick and the dead were brought to him and that the god cured them by touching them with his hand; and that is why the temple is called Kab-ul, which means the industrious hand, the miraculous hand.' The temple, where so many miracles were performed, was the object of numerous pilgrimages..."
        Désiré Charnay
        Voyage au Yucatán et au pays des Lacandons

▲ WESTERN YUCATÁN
MÉRIDA TO VALLADOLID

"CENOTES" ■ 16
● 114
The *cenote* of Zaci
(above), at
Valladolid, lies in a
garden. Its vaulted
depths and dark
waters are extremely
impressive. The
cenote of Dzitnup
(top), one of the most
beautiful in Yucatán,
lies about 3 miles
from Valladolid, in
the direction of
Chichén Itzá.

Plaza Principal in
Valladolid. The twin
towers of the church
were a common
feature of colonial
religious architecture.

BALANKANCHÉ CAVES

The Maya venerated all caves and these
dark and mysterious places are still the
sites for secret acts of worship today. Th
Balankanché Caves, about 10 miles from
Valladolid, were discovered in 1959. A
rocky passageway leads to the
underground chambers where objects
from the Toltec period, presented as
offerings, can still be seen as they were
left. At the end of the passage is a pool,
lost in the darkness. There is a botanica
garden near the entrance.

VALLADOLID

After Mérida, Valladolid is the most
important town in Yucatán. It was
founded in 1543 by Montejo ▲ 198 on th
ruins of ancient Zaci (pronounced Zaki) and, with Mérida,
Campeche and Bacalar, was one of the four main Spanish
towns on the Yucatán peninsula. Valladolid was badly
damaged by fire during the Caste War ▲ 186 and will never
recover its former splendor.

SISAL CONVENT. When the Spanish occupied ancient Zaci,
they built a church and convent on the outskirts of the town,
in the neighborhood of Sisal, in order to preach the Gospel t
the Indians. The convent was deconsecrated in 1755 and
gradually abandoned until restoration work began in the
1970's. Sisal is a distortion of the Maya word *sis-ha* meaning
"cold water" and the convent was so called because it was
built near a *cenote*. The convent, church and open chapel,
designed by the architect Juan de Mérida, were completed
in 1560. Strangely, the open chapel was built onto the
side of the church rather than the façade of the
convent. Its palm-leaf roof still existed at the
beginning of the 19th century. It is now known as
the chapel of San Marco.

CONVENT CHURCH OF SAN BERNADINO
This single-nave church is 50 yards
long by 11½ yards wide, and has
a vaulted apse, decorated
with Gothic-type ribs. The
cloister is 22 yards square, the
largest in Yucatán after that
of Izamal (23 yards square).
Of the seven surviving
retables, that of San Antonio
is one of the most beautiful
examples of the early 18th
century. The chancel retable
is still attached to the wall
with reeds dating from the
18th century. The church had
a statue of the Virgin of
Guadalupe and was the first in
Yucatán to worship the
Mexican Virgin.

CHICHÉN ITZÁ ★

● 34, 112

Valladolid (above) and the Christ of San Bernadino (below), whose church dates from the 17th century.

HISTORY. Chichén Itzá is one of the most famous and spectacular of the Mayan sites. At the end of the Classic period it was a small town, possibly even then called Itzá, which was soon subjected to Putún influence or occupation. The term "Putún" (or "Chontal") is used to designate various "Mexicanized" Maya groups of merchants and warriors who had settled along the coast of the Gulf of Mexico and who, at various points throughout history, introduced "Mexican" characteristics to Yucatán. These are already noticeable in the Puuc ▲ 220 architecture of Chichén Itzá. The strength of Puuc influence varied across the north and center of the Yucatán Peninsula and was very noticeable in the Uxmal region. In the 10th century a group of Putún Maya, almost certainly with the assistance of Toltec warriors, established a new capital at Chichén Itzá. Their chief bore the Mexican title of Quetzalcoatl, the Feathered Serpent, translated into Mayan by Kukulcán. This Putún occupation lasted for more than two centuries, confining itself to Chichén Itzá and demanding tributes and allegiance from other Mayan provinces.

DECLINE. According to Mayan chronicles of the colonial period, the circumstances surrounding the abandonment of Chichén Itzá were never fully understood. It is probable that Toltec domination ended as a result of the repeated attacks of a group of Mexicanized Maya from Tabasco who belonged to

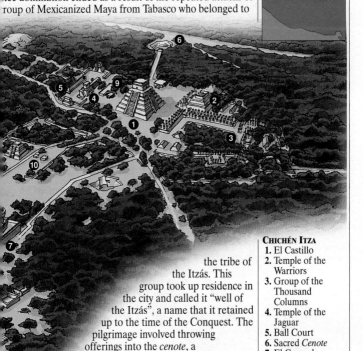

the tribe of the Itzás. This group took up residence in the city and called it "well of the Itzás", a name that it retained up to the time of the Conquest. The pilgrimage involved throwing offerings into the *cenote*, a manifestation of the Rain God. This ritual continued to exist after the Toltecs left and the cult was secretly maintained throughout the colonial period.

CHICHÉN ITZA
1. El Castillo
2. Temple of the Warriors
3. Group of the Thousand Columns
4. Temple of the Jaguar
5. Ball Court
6. Sacred *Cenote*
7. El Caracol
8. Nunnery
9. Tzompantli
10. Tomb of the High Priest

205

▲ CHICHÉN ITZÁ

Chichén Itzá, mid-way between Mérida and Cancún, is undoubtedly the best-known of the Mayan sites. It was originally a small Puuc town which, as a result of direct Putún and indirect Toltec influence from the 11th to the 13th centuries, became the most important city in Maya territory and the "Mecca" of Mayan pilgrimages. Unlike other Mayan cities, which remained forgotten for centuries, Chichén Itzá was quickly discovered by the Spanish during the Conquest.

NUNNERY
On the Puuc-style entrance to the Nunnery, the jaws of the terrestrial monster are represented by a row of teeth above the lintel. Higher up, in the recess of the monster's forehead, is an image of a seated sovereign. The rest of the façade is covered in frontal masks.

PUUC STYLE ▲ 220
Chichén Itzá's Puuc-style edifices, attributed to the Terminal Classic period, are found in the southern section of the site, while the Early Postclassic structures, with their characteristic "Mexican" additions, are located in the northern section.

ARCHEOLOGY
The site has always been well known. In the 16th century its *cenote* ● *117* made it a place of pilgrimage and Diego de Landa described it in his *Relación de las Cosas de Yucatán*. The first archeological research, undertaken in 1841–2 by Stephens and Catherwood ● *56*, was continued in the late 19th century by Maler, Maudslay and Holmes. In c. 1900 Edward Thompson, the United-States consul in Yucatán, bought and took up residence in the Chichén hacienda from where he carried out excavations and dragged part of the *cenote* on behalf of

the Peabody Museum. Large-scale excavations were begun in 1924 by the Carnegie Institute team, under the direction of Sylvanus Morley, but although the larger edifices were excavated and restored the cultural chronology of the site still had to be compiled, since various structures could not be dated precisely.

[TE]MPLE OF THE [JA]GUAR

[Be]hind the huge ball
[cou]rt, this low
[tem]ple, decorated
[wit]h warriors in bas-
[reli]ef, was partially
[cov]ered by the
[pyr]amid of the upper
[tem]ple.

[Th]e temple's façade
[is d]ecorated with
[Azt]ec-inspired
[frie]zes, showing a
[pr]ocession of jaguars
[an]d shields.

EL CASTILLO ● *108*

El Castillo stands in
the center of the great,
square plaza, in the
northern section of the
site. It consists of two
superposed temple-
pyramids dating from
the Early Postclassic
period. The first,
consisting of nine,
sloping terraces and a
single staircase, was
surmounted by a two-
roomed temple with
vertical walls and no
serpent-columns
▲ *210*, and a single
entrance to the north.
The Mexican
decorative elements
were interspersed with
a procession of
jaguars, round fringed
shields and a
chacmool ▲ *211*. The
second pyramid also
had nine sloping
terraces with
rectangles in relief,
becoming increasingly
thin towards the top to
emphasize the overall
effect of height, and
four staircases, each of
91 steps, with
handrails in the form
of serpents. The 364
steps, added to the
step of the temple
entrance, symbolize
the 365 days of
the solar year.

At the top is a temple with four
entrances. The main entrance, to
the north, is flanked by serpent-
columns. The central
sanctuary is preceded by
a vestibule and
surrounded by a
passageway.

BALL COURT

The ball court (180 yards long by 75 yar[ds] wide) is not only the largest of the thirte[en] courts ● *112* discovered at Chich[én] but also the largest [of] the whole of Mesoamerica. It ha[s] markers on the vertical walls on eit[her] side of the central

aisle. At the foot of the walls a sloping bench is covered wi[th] bas-reliefs representing two teams witnessing th[e] decapitation of the captain of the losing team. Certain elements of the ball game, which dated from the Postclassic period, were the res[ult] of Central Mexican (walls and rings) an[d] Gulf coast (bas-relie[f] of Tajín) influence.

CASA COLORADA

This reconstruction (below) by Tatiana Proskouriakoff ● *60* shows the *Casa Colorada* ("Red House"), a rather austere, Puuc-style edifice, on which all the decoration appears above roof level on the façade and on the projecting ridge. Beyond the house, to the right, is El Caracol. Tatiana Proskouriakoff imagined the site as it must have been when it was occupied, with a few inhabitants and priests officiating at an imagined ritual.

El Caracol

circular
ture, which
ds on two
rposed,
angular platforms,
built during
rent periods: the
col itself is more
nt than its
forms. Round
ces, which
eared in Yucatán
re is one at Uxmal
79) during the
ninal Classic, were
orted" from
ral Mexico where
are traditionally
associated with
Quetzalcoatl in the
form of the Wind
God. In the center a
spiral staircase
(*caracol* is the Spanish
word for "snail") leads
to a small room
pierced with square
openings, whose
directions appear to
have some
astronomical
significance. El
Caracol (below) in the
19th century and in its
present, restored
state.

Human sacrifice

ccording to the chroniclers, victims were
rown into the *cenote* at daybreak. If they
re still alive at noon, they were pulled out
and asked to make predictions for the
forthcoming year ● 46.

Sacred "cenote"

The *cenote* is reached
along a 300-yard-long
specially built
causeway or *sacbé*.
Archeological
excavations have
confirmed the account
of Diego de Landa
concerning the human
sacrifices and offerings
of precious objects
thrown into the *cenote*
at the north end of the
site, where some fifty
skulls and numerous
long bones have been
discovered. Contrary
to the persistent
legend that the Maya
threw only maidens
into these sinkholes,
bones from skeletons
of both sexes and all
ages have been
retrieved. Rustic pots
were also found which
still contained incense,
but the most beautiful
objects were in copper
and gold: disks with
repoussé decorations,
necklaces, masks,
pendants, rings, ear
ornaments, bells and
beads. While most
came from central
America, Oaxaca and
the Mexican Valley,
the repoussé disks

were made locally and
illustrate scenes of
battle and sacrifice.
Fragments of burnt
cloth, jade beads,
sacrificial knives and
bone and shell
ornaments were also
found.

T. Proskouriak

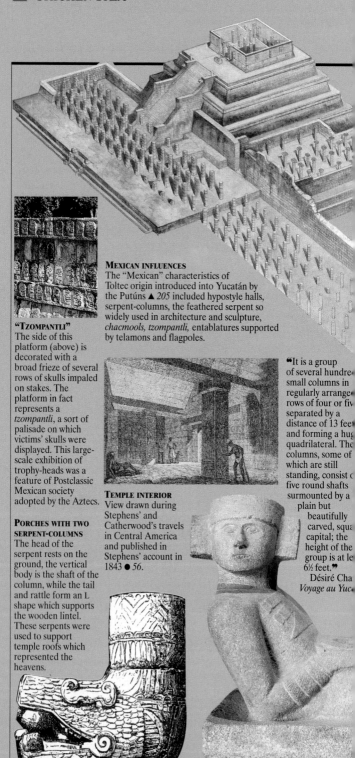

MEXICAN INFLUENCES
The "Mexican" characteristics of
Toltec origin introduced into Yucatán by
the Putúns ▲ *205* included hypostyle halls,
serpent-columns, the feathered serpent so
widely used in architecture and sculpture,
chacmools, tzompantli, entablatures supported
by telamons and flagpoles.

"TZOMPANTLI"
The side of this
platform (above) is
decorated with a
broad frieze of several
rows of skulls impaled
on stakes. The
platform in fact
represents a
tzompantli, a sort of
palisade on which
victims' skulls were
displayed. This large-
scale exhibition of
trophy-heads was a
feature of Postclassic
Mexican society
adopted by the Aztecs.

**PORCHES WITH TWO
SERPENT-COLUMNS**
The head of the
serpent rests on the
ground, the vertical
body is the shaft of the
column, while the tail
and rattle form an L
shape which supports
the wooden lintel.
These serpents were
used to support
temple roofs which
represented the
heavens.

TEMPLE INTERIOR
View drawn during
Stephens' and
Catherwood's travels
in Central America
and published in
Stephens' account in
1843 ● *56.*

❝It is a group
of several hundre[d]
small columns in
regularly arrange[d]
rows of four or fiv[e]
separated by a
distance of 13 fee[t]
and forming a hug[e]
quadrilateral. The[se]
columns, some of
which are still
standing, consist o[f]
five round shafts
surmounted by a
plain but
beautifully
carved, squa[re]
capital; the
height of the
group is at le[ast]
6½ feet.❞
        Désiré Cha[rnay]
        Voyage au Yuc[atán]

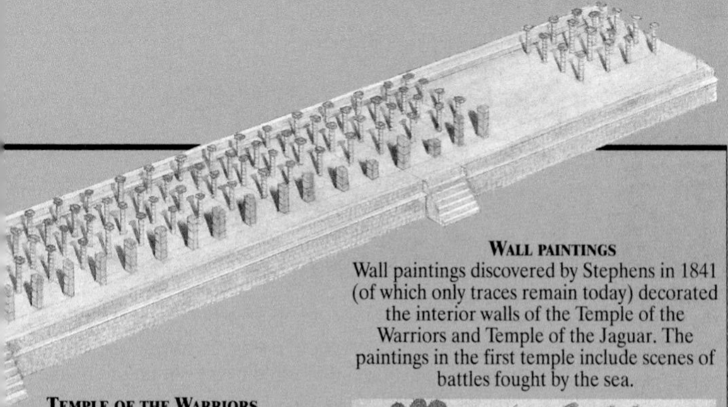

WALL PAINTINGS

Wall paintings discovered by Stephens in 1841 (of which only traces remain today) decorated the interior walls of the Temple of the Warriors and Temple of the Jaguar. The paintings in the first temple include scenes of battles fought by the sea.

TEMPLE OF THE WARRIORS AND GROUP OF THE THOUSAND COLUMNS

Temple of the
riors, whose
ut is very
ously inspired by
cture B at Tula
, is named after
sculptures of
ec warriors on the
lars of the front
portico and
those
supporting

the temple roof. The Thousand Columns are the remains of a series of vast hypostyle meeting halls. The bonded columns have square or round drums and are often sculpted in bas-relief. The exact nature of the roof they supported is not known. It was probably flat and made of beams covered with mortar or thatch, or a corbeled vault.

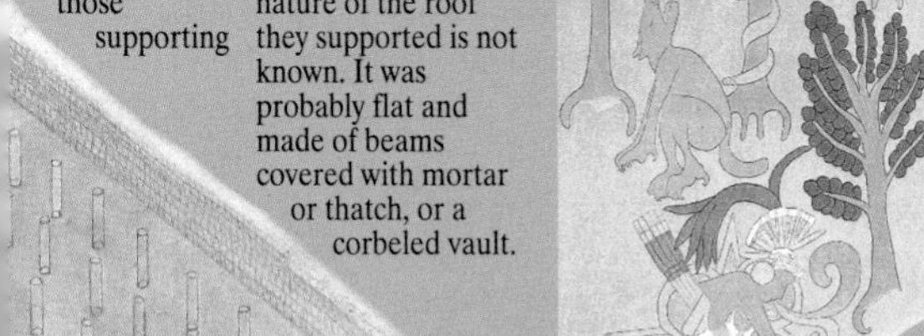

The frescos in the Temple of the Jaguar show crowded battle scenes dominated by two chiefs. One has the solar disk as his emblem, while the other has the feathered serpent. There is also a village on the edge of the forest populated with animals (reproduced, above, and re-touched by Maudslay ● 56 at the end of the 19th century).

"ACMOOL"

chacmool is a
pture
esenting a
ining man,
ling an offerings
el or tray.

Warrior sculpted in bas-relief on a column (below) and Quetzalcoatl, the Feathered Serpent, in the guise of Venus, the Morning Star (Temple of the Warriors).

▲ WESTERN YUCATÁN
THE MONASTERY ROUTE

TECOH
The village of Tecoh
has a 16th-century
Franciscan monastery
and an 18th-century
church (detail of the
remains of a window
gable, right). The
single nave is flanked
by side chapels. The
baptismal fonts are
16th century, while
the three gilt and
polychrome retables
are 18th century.

MAYAN CITIES
Mayapán was
surrounded by a wall
and had a population
of fifteen thousand.
The city's dwellings
were constructed
partly in stone and
preferably on high
ground.
Thoroughfares were
the result of the fairly
arbitrary arrangement
of the houses and
were not based on the
grid system used in
the towns of the
Mexican Valley.

RELIGIOUS STELES
The (thirteen
sculpted and twenty-
five smooth) steles of
Mayapán represent
divinities and not, as
was the general rule
● *110*, political
figures.

ACANCEH

Acanceh means "the cry of a stag" in Maya. The church in
center of the village, dedicated to the Virgin of Guadalupe
was built in the 16th century and subsequently modified. T
17th-century façade has an entrance with twisted columns a
an entablature at the dividing point between the two parts.
Above the entrance, the chancel window is surmounted by
curved pediment. Next to the church are the ruins of a
pyramid with four tiers and a central staircase (above) and,
about 300 yards further on, the ruins of another, monumer
pyramid. The façade of the so-called "Stucco Palace" is
decorated with an extremely rare, Late Classic cosmologica
composition whose main figures are symbolic animals.
TIMUCUY HACIENDA. About 6 miles from Acanceh is the
Timucuy hacienda with its central porticoed residence,
machine room, chapel and outbuildings. The hacienda is o
to the public.

MAYAPÁN ● 35

This important archeological
site (Mayapán was one of the
Maya capitals) has still not been restored although the
Carnegie Institution of Washington have been researching
for five years.
HISTORY. The Mayapán chieftains belonged to the Cocom
lineage, descended from a certain Hunac Ceel who capture
and destroyed Chichén Itzá ▲ *205* at the beginning of the
13th century. With the decline of Chichén Itzá, Mayapán's
importance increased and the city underwent significant
changes (due to a new wave of Mexican influence) in the
fields of structural and decorative architecture, as well as th
birth of a new religion. Just before 1450, one of the noble
houses of Mayapán – the Xiú – rebelled against the Cocom
Shortly afterward Mayapán was plundered and abandoned,
leaving the way open for a number of "warring kingdoms" i
state of permanent conflict.
REMAINS. Mayapán has a temple comparable to El Castillo
Chichén Itzá, complete with serpent-columns, serpent
handrails, flagpoles and small telamons. But the *chacmools*
ball courts, *tzompantli* and evidence of the worship of jagua
and eagles have all disappeared. The monster-masks a
the two- and three-part moldings inherited from the
Puuc tradition ▲ *220* can still be seen on a few façade
RELIGIOUS BUILDINGS. There are two types of
ceremonial complex found in Mayapán.
One type has a hypostyle hall, a
sanctuary and an oratory, wh
the other has a right-ar
temple with a hypost
hall, an oratory on t
vertical side of the
temple, a sanctua

osite the oratory
, between the
a platform for
ues. It is difficult
scertain the exact
tion of these edifices since
decorations, usually
ted or stucco, have
ppeared. However, the
e number of associated
rs, caches, sepulchers,
ossuaries for sacrificial
ms suggest that
y had a religious
tion. The
plexes
ubtedly
esponded to different
ages, consisting of several
lies, who practiced a private
n of worship alongside the
cial and collective form. The
dential complexes also have a
tuary or domestic altar which
ts to the existence of private
ns of worship.

SERS ● 48. The new
ortance of religion was
represented by the
e numbers of censers
ceramic effigy vases which
the images of actual
s rather than cosmic
bols. A columned hall was

overed containing 38,000 fragments of these censers
ch appear to have been particularly prolific between 1300
1450. The censers bore identifiable images of Mexican
s as well as the Mayan gods who appear in the wall
tings of Tulum ▲ 177 and in the pictographic
uscripts of the Madrid and Dresden Codices ● 42. The
n of a religious pantheon and the development of a
entralized form of worship, which was addressed to
onal deities, corresponded to a weakening of centralized
tical power ● 50.

ABO

RCH OF SAN PEDRO AND SAN PABLO. This 17th-century
lican church was built along similar lines to the churches
xkutzcab and Tekax ▲ 215. The nave, built between 1650
1695, is 60 yards long and 22 yards wide. The retable in
of the lateral naves is thought to be the work of the artist
produced the San Antonio de Maní retable. Frescos
ntly discovered in the sacristy are clearly of European
iration and are among the most beautiful found anywhere
ucatán. The cloister, which like most Yucatecan colonial
dings is ruined, was part of a complicated network of
sive structures. Fragments of frescos on these structures
survived the eroding effects of the weather.

Ceramic censer from
Mayapán,
representing the god
Chac and dating from
the Late Postclassic
period. It can be seen
in the Mexico
National Museum of
Anthropology ▲ 376.

MAMA
The name of the
village of Mama
means "no, no". The
17th-century church,
dedicated to the
Assumption of the
Virgin, has a sober
façade but an
extremely elaborate
entrance carved by
Mayan sculptors. The
church is crowned by
a bell tower.

CHUMAYEL
The *Chilam Balam* of
Chumayel, the sacred
book of the Maya
● 140, discovered in
the 19th century,
came from this tiny
village near Teabo.

Well and building at Sabacché, drawn by Frederick Catherwood.

MANÍ

The province of Maní, meaning "all is past" in Maya, was the first to form an allegiance with the Spanish. A treaty establishing Indian borders was signed here in 1557. Maní was also the first province to welcome Franciscan friars who, having established their first mission in Oxkutzcab, transferred here shortly afterward.

CONSTRUCTION OF THE MONASTERY. In 1550 Fray Juan de Mérida assumed responsibility for the construction of the monastery. Six thousand Indians worked on it for seven years. The complex comprised the monastery, the church, the great atrium, the school and the hospital. Fray Juan de Herrera, accompanied by the French monk, Jacobo (Jacques) de Testera, who invented a writing system which enabled him to give religious instruction to the Indians, took charge of the school, which became famous throughout Yucatán. Herrera also had a great open chapel built, the first of its kind on the Peninsula, probably to make the Indians feel more comfortable with this new imposed religion. However, any dreams of religious coexistence were shattered with the *auto-da-fé* of 1562, when many images and codices were destroyed by the monastery walls. This, combined with the large numbers of dead ● *38*, terrified the Maya and disturbed Spanish conscience.

RETABLE OF MANÍ
The magnificent, giltwood retable (opposite) in the lateral nave was dedicated to San Antonio and dated c. 1700. It served as a model for the retable of Teabo ▲ *213*.

YAXCOPOIL HACIENDA
This 17th-century hacienda, situated between Muná and Umán, was converted for the production of sisal at the end of the 19th century. Now restored, it is a fine example of the famous haciendas (like Xcanchakán, above) which made the fortune of Yucatán before 1920.

VISITING THE MONASTERY. The sheer bulk of the monastery and church is impressive. The stones used to construct the complex – built on a pre-Hispanic platform – came from ancient Mayan temples. During the 18th century, the original façade of the church was demolished, the nave extended forward and a new façade built (below). Only one of the chapels still exists. Some very beautiful frescos decorated the sanctuary and the date 1580 is still legible in a cartouche. The two-story, cloistered monastery is supported by pillars almost 10 feet square. The walls of the cloister were also covered with frescos. Maní began to decline in importance from the 17th century. The larger, more prosperous villages near the hills built bigger, more elegant and better lit churches and the dark and massive church of Maní was gradually abandoned, as was the village. The former Casa Real, next to the monastery, still has its magnificent 16th-century façade.

XKUTZCAB

CHURCH OF SAN FRANCISCO DE ASIS. The town of Oxkutzcab (land of three tobaccos") in Maya has an important, early th-century, basilican church (below right). The church's rk façade is pierced by a portal with lateral pilasters pporting a classic pediment.

ENVIRONS OF OXKUTZCAB. Small archeological sites in the ea include Sabacché, Xul and Kiwic. The road to Peto (and Chetumal) passes through Tekax, an important agricultural center. The monastery of San Juan Bautista was begun here in 1564 and completed in 1609. The complex consists of a church with three barrel naves and a façade bearing the characteristic bell towers of Yucatán; a vast square with angle chapels; and a monastery which is falling in disrepair. Near Tekax are the ruins of Chacmultún.

TICUL

cul, which lies 73 miles southeast of Mérida, is known for its rracotta crafts and is an important agricultural center. The th-century church of San Antonio has a sober façade and entrance decorated with two double columns, niches for ulptures and a Franciscan coat of arms. The church was ce part of a monastery of which only a few elements have rvived. The chapels of San Enrique and La Mejadora were ilt in the 19th century.

MUNÁ

uná is a small wn on the road om Mérida to the uuc sites (Uxmal s a few miles to e south) ▲ 219. he 16th-century onastery, edicated to the ssumption of the Virgin, stands in a large plaza and, like ost Yucatecan monasteries, is partly preserved. The church uare has been transformed into a public square. The onastery and church were extended in the 17th century and her elements added subsequently. The furniture and altars ere destroyed in 1915.

MÁN

he monastery of San Francisco de Asís was demolished, cept for the annexes and the church, which was rebuilt in e 18th century. Unusually for Yucatán the nave has a ansept, while the dome, visible from some distance away, oks incongruous in the Yucatecan landscape. The th-century open chapel (now dedicated to San Pedro and n Pablo) is joined to the church and monastery.

> **"**Ticul, situated near the chain of hills that runs across the peninsula from northwest to southeast, is a real town, prosperous and attractive, with beautiful houses and large shops. All traces of the Indian war seem to have disappeared: everything seems new, except the church and great cloister, the home of Abbé Carillo – whose praises were sung by Stephens – and which is now falling into ruins. This is where the new priest lives, in one of the few rooms that is still habitable. He is cheerful, charming, talkative, and a brother of the *padrecito* mentioned so often by the American traveler.**"**
> Désiré Charnay
> *Voyage au Yucatán et au pays des Lacandons* (1882)

Paying homage to the flag in front of the church in Oxkutzcab (above left).

LOLTUN CAVES
About 4 miles south of Oxkutzcab are the Loltún ("stone flower" in Maya) Caves, a stone fairyland of vast, underground chambers. Bones found in the caves provided the earliest evidence of human habitation in Yucatán.

CELESTÚN ★
Celestún (above), a fishing port situated about 57 miles west of Mérida, is home to another of Yucatán's world famous nature reserves. Although the beach is unremarkable, the marshes are well worth a visit, with their flocks of flamingos, herons, anhingas,

ibises, pelicans and frigate birds. Returning to Mérida via Halachó offers a chance to visit Uayalceh Chunchucmil, and other haciendas in a quiet and little-known area of Yucatán.

NATURE RESERVES
Few tourists visit the northern coast of Yucatán, a region unique for the beauty of its landscapes and abundance of its fauna. The nature reserves of San Felipe and Río Lagartos are natural sanctuaries for migratory birds, in particular the thousands of flamingos that ~~on~~ ~~look fo~~ the shallow waters of the coastal marshes.

TOWARD RÍO LAGARTOS

MOTUL. The road from Mérida to Conkal (famous for its magnificent Monastery of San Francisco de Asís) passes through Motul, once the center of sisal production. Its 16th-century monastery, dedicated to San Juan Bautista, still has its covered chapel, its *posas* chapels and its two-story cloister. A small museum honors the memory of Felipe Carrillo Puerto, the socialist governor assassinated in 1924.

DZIDZANTÚN. At Cansahcab, the road forks north toward Dzidzantún which has one of the most majestic convents in Yucatán, built in the 16th century by Fray Francisco de Gadea. The church, whose single nave (85 yards by 12 yards) is the largest in Yucatán, was completed just before 1588. Deliberately damaged and badly restored, its remaining frescos are pale reflections of their former glory.

DZILAM DE BRAVO. The mangroves and freshwater canals fed by *cenotes* attract thousands of flamingos, while beautiful, fine white sandy beaches make this an ideal place to relax. Boats take visitors to Bocas de Dzilam.

RÍO LAGARTOS. Returning to Cansahcab, another road leads to Tizimín (linked directly to Valladolid ▲ *204*) and then turns north to Río Lagartos, a small fishing port hidden in the jungle. Boats take visitors along the coast to San Felipe or Las Coloradas. This uninhabited and protected strip of coast is the site of America's largest sanctuary for migratory birds. The reserve, which extends beyond El Cuyo (59 miles from Tizimín), attracts large numbers of visitors.

DZIBILCHALTÚN

HISTORY. The Maya city of Dzibilchaltún, 7½ miles north of Mérida, was founded in 600 BC. For a long time Dzibilchaltún remained a small village, dominated by the more northern community of Komchén, but by c. AD 200 it had grown into a city of almost a thousand houses in an area of less than one square mile, with three great platforms (26 feet high) and a *sacbé*. The population declined significantly toward the end of the Preclassic period and the site was ~~...~~ ~~...~~ ~~...~~ ~~...~~, probab ~~...~~ and in c. 800 had a population of ~~...~~,000. After 1000 the rate of occupation declined rapidly and building ceased altogether. There was a modest revival in c. 1200 and the site was intermittently inhabited during the Late Postclassic period when the existing buildings were re-used.

GOLDEN AGE. In the 9th century Dzibilchaltún's town center covered an area of ½ square mile and included about a hundred stone buildings, some of which had arched roofs and were supported by step pyramids. A total of eight thousand houses was recorded in the vicinity, over an area of 7 square miles. Most of these were huts but two thousand had part-masonry walls, although the roofs were thatched. The center of the site, which included the Xlacah *cenote,* was linked by *sacbeob* (causeways) to the other groups of dwellings. The first excavations were carried out by members of Tulane University between 1956 and 1966. The (165 feet deep) Xlacah *cenote* revealed thirty thousand Mayan objects from various periods. A museum is being built on the site.

TEMPLE OF THE SEVEN DOLLS. Built in c. 700, the Temple of the Seven Dolls (below) is one of the earliest structures in Dzibilchaltún. It is perched on top of a pyramidal base with four staircases and has four doors which open onto a corridor surrounding a central room. The room is surmounted by a vault in four sections which appears to be a sort of tower dominating the rest of the building. The upper sections of the walls were decorated with an aquatic frieze celebrating underground water, the source of the Earth's fertility. At the end of the Classic period the temple was covered by another, larger pyramid. Centuries later, during the Late Postclassic period, a passage was opened into the temple and an altar was built. The temple was named after an offering of seven clay dolls was found in front of the altar.

PROGRESO

The port of Progreso was founded in the mid-19th century, about 22 miles north of Mérida, to replace the port of Sisal which had been used since the Conquest. The new port was better protected from the winds and currents, and was equipped to handle exports of sisal and imports including paving stones from England and tiles from Marseilles, still used today in Mérida and the neighboring villages.

Beyond Umán and south of Mérida, the road passes through Calcehtok (pronounced "calketok"), where a track leads north to the caves of the same name. Another track leads south to the recently restored ruins of Oxkintok. The museum at Hecelchakan houses Mayan objects from the Isla Jaina ▲ 230 and other sites in the Campeche region. About 29 miles further on, the road rejoins the route from Hoplchén and continues towards Campeche ▲ 228.

PUUC REGION

The Puuc region, to the south of Mérida, had its center at Uxmal (right). Its influence spread to the north of the peninsula, reaching Chichén Itzá, Tiho and modern Mérida. The Puuc style ▲ 220 represented a transition from the Classic to the Postclassic period (during which Chichén Itzá ▲ 205 was built) in Yucatán. It flourished during the Late Classic and into the 11th century, well after the equivalent cities in the central region had been abandoned. In this karstic region, where there is no surface water, the Maya survived by building underground cisterns known as *chultúns* ● 117 to collect rainwater. They also obtained water from the region's natural sinkholes or *cenotes* ■ 17 ● 117. About a mile from Bolonchén, to the south of the Puuc sites, the Xtacumbilxunán Caves have the largest *cenote* on the peninsula (drawn by Frederick Catherwood ● 58, 130 in 1842, above).

UXMAL AND THE PUUC SITES ★

RUTA PUUC". The inland road to the region's capital, Campeche, is marked "via ruinas". The excavated and restored sites form a circuit known as the *Ruta Puuc* (Puuc route) which covers the finest examples of Puuc architecture: Uxmal, Kabáh, Sayil and Labná (the four most important), as well as Kiuic, Xlabpak, Oxkintok, Xul, Chamultún and Bakná. These sites, today largely restored, experienced their golden age between AD 800 and 1000. They are characterized by large, elongated structures with sculpted decoration. The Puuc cities collapsed with the arrival of the Toltecs in Yucatán, particularly at Chichén Itzá ▲ *205*. Further south, on Route 261, the Puuc-style ruins of Itzimté lie near the road just before Bolonchén.

HOCHOB AND DZIBILNOCAC. These two accessible and virtually unexplored sites near Hopolchén are fine examples of the splendor of the Chenes style. At Hochob, (the better restored of the two) the façade of the temple, to the right of the plaza, represents the terrestrial monster. Most of the ruins in this vast site are as yet unexcavated and still keep the secrets of the people who lived there. After Dzibilchén and Vicente Guerrero, a track leads to the site of Dzibilnocac. Here the first two temples are disappointing, but the delicacy of the architecture, and the fineness of the frescos and sculptures of the third pyramid make the journey worthwhile. From the top of the temple there is a spectacular view of the surrounding ruins. At Cayal, about 25 miles from Hopolchén, a road leads to Edzná, the most important Maya site in Campeche. Rejoin the road at Cayal and continue to Campeche (32 miles).

Detail of the decoration on the arch of Labná.

UXMAL
1. Nunnery Quadrangle
2. Pyramid of the Magician
3. Ball Court
4. Cemetery Group
5. Palace of the Governor
6. The Turtle House
7. The Pigeon House
8. Great Pyramid

The *Codz pop* of Kabáh.

The Puuc style takes its name from the range of hills running northwest-southeast across the north of the Yucatán peninsula, but its influence extends much further. It made its appearance in the 8th century and reached its height during the second half of the 9th century. The style is distinguished by decorative techniques, which include stone veneering and the inclusion of mosaics in relief on the upper portion of façades.

ORIGINS

Many of the characteristics of central Yucatán ▲ *190* began to emerge from 770 onwards. These elements included basal moldings decorated with groups of small drums, beveled moldings and small engaged columns (first single and then attached). Terrestrial monster masks, adopted from the Chenes tradition, formed doors and ran riot over façades.

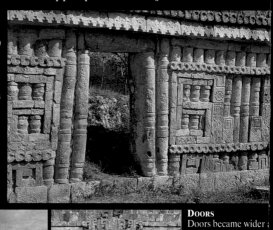

DOORS

Doors became wider a columns with capitals were used to support the lintel. Labná (above) and Sayil (right).

DEVELOPMENT OF THE PUUC STYLE

Early monumental columns enabled doors to become wider, and had a simple lower molding. Then engaged columns with masks appeared (above, at Kabáh). Finally, after 870, mosaic decorations triumphed over a limited area combining engaged columns with openwork and fret motifs.

MOSAIC DECORATIONS

The Puuc style often used sculpted stone mosaics composed of prefabricated elements. The decoration consisted of openwork, multiple (keyed or non-keyed) columns, step-and-fret motifs and frontal masks on façades or superposed on the corners of buildings, all geometrically arranged and repeated. The mosaic decoration in relief on the upper part of the façade of the Nunnery Quadrangle at Uxmal (above), illustrates this very distinctive style. The lower parts of buildings are smooth and stucco is very rarely used. The mosaic is bordered by a broad molding below and a cornice above.

VAULT

While the vault retained its corbeled shape, the stones which formed it did not support anything and were purely a veneer.

ARCH OF KABÁH

The arch, in the Early Puuc style, stands at the south en of the causeway linkin Kabáh to Uxmal.

ARCH OF LABNÁ

PALACE OF SAYIL

The palace has three terraced stories, each resting on a stone base, with a broad central staircase (above). The first story is also the oldest. Pillars have been used to widen the doorways and the decoration is limited to a single frieze. The numerous openings on the second story alternate with panels of small, engaged, keyed columns (detail above), while the

...like the arch of ...báh, the arch of ...bná (today, below, ...d drawn by ...therwood, bottom) ...not a monumental ...triumphal arch but ...e vaulted ...ssageway of a

quadrangle; a square or rectangular courtyard surrounded by buildings and closed off, apart from a gateway. On the courtyard side, the principal decoration consists of miniature

thatched huts, forming niches that originally contained statues. On the outside the frieze, bordered by the same moldings decorated with broken, zigzag lines and step motifs, comprises two step-and-fret motifs joined edgewise against a background of small, engaged columns. The motif represents the jaws of the terrestrial monster, the symbolic access to the underworld. Monster masks (above).

frieze on the upper part of the wall has masks of the terrestrial monster. The third story, in late Puuc style, was decorated much more soberly with a full-length stucco figure of a man

(strengthened by stone tenons) standing above each door.

Uxmal is one of the best-known and most frequently visited of the Mayan sites due to its relatively good state of preservation (a number of structures are still standing) and the quality of its Puuc-style stone mosaic decorations. Little is known of the origins and development of this important political and economic center which was at its height between AD 800 and 1000. Uxmal's many (mostly undated) steles have revealed the existence of Lord Chac who probably reigned in the early 10th century. The city is characterized by its quadrangles in which large, elongated, multi-roomed edifices form a closed complex around a rectangular or square courtyard.

1836 Waldeck
blished the first,
ef description of
e site, visited a few
ars previously.
though extensive
-storation work was
gun in 1928 and
ain in 1938, the site
s never been
stematically
cavated.

PALACE OF THE GOVERNOR

The Late-Puuc palace (9th-10th century) comprises a main building and two wings. It is almost 110 yards long by 13 yards wide, and 28 feet high. Thirteen doors give access to twenty rooms. It has been estimated that the stone mosaic decoration of the façade has some twenty thousand sculpted parts. The two largest rooms, aligned in the central building, are 22 yards long and are connected to the outside by three doors.

DECORATION

The main entrance to the Palace of the Governor is surmounted by an image of the king seated on his throne against a background of two-headed serpents, decorated with celestial symbols (like those on the east building in the Nunnery Quadrangle). Other dignitaries are represented emerging from the open jaws of the terrestrial monster. The decoration is completed by step-and -fret motifs and frontal masks against a background of lattice work (top of page). The main figure represented in the heavens is probably the founder of the dynasty. (Top to bottom and left to right): general view of Uxmal; jaguar throne and Palace of the Governor; two details of façades; and two views of the Palace of the Governor, drawn by the architect Frederick Catherwood ● 58, 130 during his travels with Stephens.

NUNNERY QUADRANGLE

The name of the quadrangle was coined by ancient travelers who compared the closed complex to that of a monastery (above). The courtyard is surrounded by buildings, each with a double row of rooms. The building on the north side of the courtyard (top) appears to be the most important. The eleven-doored façade is decorated with superposed masks of the terrestrial monster and pseudo-Tlaloc masks which alternate with images of huts surmounted by two-headed serpents (detail below). The decoration on the east building consists of several groups of rigid, two-headed serpents which

decrease in length towards the base. On the south façade, huts are surmounted by a mask of the terrestrial monster. The decoration becomes more complex on the west side: as well as the usual superposed masks, there are enthroned figures beneath a dais and warriors in relief, the whole encircled by plumed serpents. Detail of the west façade (below) by Catherwood.

THE PIGEON HOUSE

This residential palace (above) was built between AD 700 and 800 in a style which pre-dates that of the Nunnery Quadrangle. In spite of its rather poor state of preservation it is known that the exterior walls were once lavishly covered in stucco elements and ornaments. It was named after the long, elaborate roofcomb reminiscent of European dovecotes.

e visible temples
resent the two
l stages in the
struction of the
amid. On the west
e is a Chenes-style
ple, an imitation
n earlier, Puuc-
e structure. The
st recent temple
built at the top of
pyramid. The
lpture (right) is
m the first stage of
struction of the
ple and shows a
n's head emerging
m a serpent.

A king of
Uxmal's
head
emerging from
the jaws of a
serpent; Pyramid of
the Magician.

THE TURTLE HOUSE
The Turtle House is remarkable for its
proportions and simplicity. The frieze consists
of an uninterrupted decoration of small,
engaged columns between two
characteristically Puuc-style dovetail
moldings with a central cordon. On the upper
cordon is a row of realistically carved,
regularly spaced turtles (above). In Maya
culture the turtle is one of the creatures that
symbolizes the Earth.

MONUMENTS
As well as its
quadrangles and the
Pyramid of the
Magician, Uxmal also
has the Great
Pyramid, a small ball
court and various
temples, some of
which are still hidden
in the undergrowth.

225

TWO GROUPS
The ancient structures of Edzná form two groups, linked by a *sacbé* (causeway). The eastern Group of the Ceremonial Center consists of buildings overlooked by the Great Acropolis. The unrestored, western group is dominated by a large structure called La Vieja.

EDZNÁ ★

URBAN CENTER. Edzná is a fine example of the organization Mayan society. In 600 BC a group of Maya settled in the valley, isolated from other population centers, where they lived continuously until the 10th century. In the 3rd century AD an urban center developed, which provided a focal point for the region's surplus agricultural products. Trade links we established with the region of Petén, in Guatemala ▲ *317*, a the influence of that area can be seen in the period rituals, crafts and art of Edzná. The local aristocracy controled the valley's rural population ordering them to find and build magnificent temples and palaces.
After the 6th century other neighboring provinces (R Bec ▲ *190*, Chenes and Puuc) developed to the east and north, opening up new commercial possibilities. These may have included a community of merchants from the Puuc region acting as a trading post in Edzná.

The Puuc-style site of Iturbide, to the north of Edzná, drawn by Catherwood.

NEITHER PUUC NOR CHENES. Edzn sometimes included in the Chenes and sometimes the Puuc region, appears to have retained a certain autonomy and individuality. Although it was not altogether impervious to t influence of its powerful neighbors, it remained a tiny, independent kingdom amidst all the cultural changes affecting the region. Lubná is the only other site of any importance recorded in the valley. After the collapse of the great Maya civilization in the 9th century, Edzná declined ir importance and was abandoned like all the other such town and cities. The peasants retreated, probably in the interests safety, to the foothills of the valley where they built the villages of Tixmucuy, Nohyaxché, Hontún and Bolonchencahuich which still exist today. It is believed that Lubná may have been another of these villages.

ANNEX OF THE KNIVES
The partially excavated annex consists of a central plaza (44 yards square), surrounded by structures dating from different periods. An arch links the plaza to a *sacbé*. Southwest of the annex the great structure known as the Nohol Na, with its 394-foot wide façade, has not yet been restored.

GROUP OF THE CEREMONIAL CENTER. The group around the vast Plaza Mayor is largely dominated by the partly restored Great Acropolis to the east, the Nohol Na to the west, the Annex of the Knives (Cuchillos) to the north and the Templ of the House of the South (Casa del Sur) to the south. A *sacbé* leads from the Great Acropolis toward a group of dwellings, situated between the Annex of the Knives and the Nohol Na, and surrounded by other structures. This complex is based on those of Petén and Tikal ▲ *322*.

SMALL ACROPOLIS
A small acropolis, to the south of the Great Acropolis, consists of a 246-foot square platform on which four structures surround a central courtyard. At the foot of a ruined temple on the west side of the courtyard, steles dating from 672 to 810 were discovered on the platform.

PLAZA MAYOR. The rectangular (185 yards by 105 yards) Plaza Mayor, formerly covered in stucco, slopes slightly downward to the south to allow any rainwater to drain into the canal.

GREAT ACROPOLIS. The impressive Great Acropolis (its overall height is 100 feet)

> "REGARDLESS OF THE CIRCUMSTANCES THAT CONTRIBUTED TO THIS CLASSIC [PERIOD] BLAZE OF GLORY, NOTHING SO REFINED OR SO VARIED WAS EVER PRODUCED DURING THE PRE-COLUMBIAN ERA."
>
> PAUL GENDROP

...nds on a platform (175 yards by 162 ...rds and 20 feet high) on the east side of ...e Plaza Mayor. Each of the four ...5 foot high) pyramidal tiers of this ...ve-story building consists of rows of ...lls, while the temple on the top is ...rmounted by a 20-foot-high crest. ...path links the plaza to a courtyard, in ...nt of the temple-pyramid, which used ...contain an altar. From here a central ...aircase (some of the steps bear glyphs) ...ads up to the temple. At the entrance to ...e seven first-story rooms (one beneath ...e staircase) are the remains of Río Bec-...yle, cemented stone pillars, while the ...onolithic columns on the fourth story ...e in the Puuc style ▲ 220.

...he five-story temple-pyramid partly ...overs an older, Petén-style temple. ...the south of the courtyard a temple, ...ached via a 57-foot wide staircase, ...ands on a platform measuring 44 yards ... 33 yards. This edifice also covers an ...der structure. At the southwest corner ...its platform stands a temple influenced ... the Petén style and a later annex which ...rtly blocks the central staircase. ...similar structure existed at the other ...d of the staircase, leaving only a ...rrow access into the courtyard. ...ther structures on the Great Acropolis ...clude the Temazcal (steam bath), ...e northwest temple, the Puuc ...atform and the north platform.

EXCAVATION
It will take many more years to explore, excavate and restore Edzná, and discover the carefully guarded secrets that lie beneath its stones.

PLUNDER
Yucatán was constantly exposed to attack by pirates, buccaneers, corsairs and enemy warships which sought refuge along its coast and plundered villages to replenish their supplies. Campeche, the only port on the peninsula, was plundered by French pirates in 1559.

Campeche, founded in 1540 by Francisco de Montejo, alias El Mozo ▲ 198, 204 is the oldest Spanish town on the Yucatán Peninsula and the only import and export point for the region's products. Situated on a flat coastline, with no natural land or sea defenses, it was an easy target for pirates. Accordingly, a 26-foot-high enclosure wall was built around the town, with protective bastions and coastal batteries. The wall was opened up toward the end of the 19th century to allow the town to expand more freely. Today, vast areas of land have been reclaimed outside the old wall and modern buildings have totally altered the landscape of Campeche's golden age.

CAMPETIE

Maya terracotta figurine from the Isla Jaina ▲ 230, Mexico National Museum of Anthropology.

FORTIFICATIONS

The fortification of the port began in the 16th century (a tower was built and equipped with a small artillery) and was completed in the 19th century. The defenses were slowly modified, demolished and rebuilt. Despite being captured and burned by pirates on several occasions during the 17th century, Campeche remained without any effective defense until the fortifications proper were built in the 18th century.

VAUBAN IN AMERICA. Following the sack of the port in 1685, Martín de la Torre's idea of building a wall around the city, like those of Havana and Santo Domingo, was accepted by the Spanish king and work was begun during the early 18th century under the direction of the German, Johannes Franck. The peace signed between France and Spain at Ryswick made collaboration between the two nations possible and the French engineer, Louis Bouchard de Bécour, suggested certain modifications as well as additional protective measures. In this way the Vauban-style fortress was introduced to America. Minor modifications and additions were made up to the early 19th century without the fortifications being significantly altered. They formed an irregular hexagon, with a bastion (*baluarte*) at each corner, another in the center of the rampart overlooking the sea, and another in the center of the landward-facing rampart. The wall, which was over a mile long, became

Maya statuette from the Campeche region.

superfluous and was gradually demolished from the 19th century onward. Today, only the *baluartes* remain and have been converted into museums.

MUSEUMS AND GARDEN. The Puerta del Mar, overlooking the sea, was protected by the Baluarte Soledad, which is now an archeological museum containing Mayan steles. To the west the Baluarte de San Carlos, now the town museum, was used to protect the town against attacks from the sea. On the landward side the Baluartes de Santa Rosa (now the tourist office) and San Juan (center for traditional dance) protected against attack from the south, as did the Baluartes de San ancisco, near the Puerta de Tierra (*son et lumière*), and San dro (center for regional handicrafts). The northern luarte de San José, was demolished, while the partly ruined luarte de Santiago is now occupied by the Xmuch Haltún tanical garden. The marshes to the northeast of the town d not provide sufficient protection and several forts were ilt to watch for intruders from the Isla Jaina including San atías, situated on the hills above the beach, and San José El to, overlooking the coast and the sea.

LAZA MAYOR DISTRICT ★

ATHEDRAL. The Catedral de la Concepción, the oldest urch on the Yucatán Peninsula, was built between 1540 and '05. One of its towers is known as the Spanish tower while e other, completed after Independence, is known as the ampeche tower.

OLONIAL RESIDENCES. Behind the cathedral, the Mansión arbajal (bottom) which has been converted into an office d craft shop, is a fine example of a wealthy colonial sidence with its marble floor, columns and Mozarabic ches. The exteriors of other colonial uses can be seen on Calles 55, 57 and .

EGIONAL MUSEUM. Another interesting lonial residence, that of the king's utenant, has been converted into a gional museum where Mayan objects e on display.

ONASTERY OF SAN JOSÉ. Like all lonial towns Campeche had a onastery: San José, built by the Jesuits 1700. The monastery's beautiful aroque church, used as a barracks ring the town's turbulent history, is w a craft center.

THER CHURCHES. There are two other cient churches of interest to visitors: at of the demolished monastery of San ancisco, founded in 1546, which still s its magnificent open chapel, and San omán, built in 1565 to the south of the

BASTIONS
All the ports on the peninsula were fortified during the 18th century and remains of forts can still be seen at El

Carmen, Champotón, Lerma, Sisal, Mérida and Bacalar, the last having also been converted into a museum. To the south of the town, the battery of San Luís (above, foreground), with its guns pointing out to sea, was protected by the fort of San Miguel (above, background).

CATHEDRAL
The cathedral (below) dominates the town's central plaza where a band plays on Sundays.

229

Cemetery of
Champotón.

Fort of Champotón
(below) and Ciudad
del Carmen (bottom).

city walls in the Indian districts, where a black Christ, sculpt
in Guatemala, is worshipped. The fair of San Román is held
from September 14 to September 28. The Church of San
Roque, built in 1654, has five beautiful wooden retables.

ENVIRONS OF CAMPECHE

ISLA JAINA. The island, famous for its ancient cemetery datin
from the Classic period, was originally a coral reef. The May
raised its surface by transporting limestone (*sascab*) to the
island as a base for their architectural structures. Jaina was
described in 1886 by Désiré Charnay ● *57*. The island (just
over ½ mile long and 820 yards wide) lies about 18 miles nor
of Campeche and is separated from the mainland by a narro
channel between 88 and 109 yards wide. Among the treasure
found there are the wonderful polychrome statuettes, often
referred to as "American Tanagras," for which the island is
famous. They represent various types of figures, clothed and

"Our water ran out.
We had to go ashore
near the town; it was
Sunday, St Lazarus'
Day, so that is what
we called the place,
although we later
found out that the
Indians called it
Campeche. In order
that we could all go

armed, and provide direct information
the costumes and ritual objects of the
Classic period. A group of these Jaina
statuettes is on display at the
Hecelchakán museum ▲ *218*. Two partl
restored complexes are open to the
public, but visitors must obtain a permit
from the Tourist Office in the Plaza
Cohuo in Campeche.
CHAMPOTÓN. The road runs south from
Campeche along the coast to
Champotón, a small colonial village
which still has its fort, El Moro, and a
17th-century church. Two roads run sou
to the state of Tabasco. The inland road
passes through Escárcega where it joins
the road from Chetumal ▲ *188*.

SILVITUK. About 18 miles east of
Escárcega, the ruined complex of Silvitu
– where two Classic steles were
discovered – lies near Lake Noh. To the

together, we decided
to take our smallest
ship and the three
rowing boats, keeping
a good lookout.... We
left our ships at
anchor a good league
from the shore and
landed near the town
by a freshwater
course that the
natives used for
drinking water.**
Bernal Díaz
del Castillo
The True History
of the Conquest
of New Spain

south of the road, which leads to Chicanná, Becán,
Hormiguero, Xpuhil and Río Bec ▲ *190*, the thick jungle
conceals largely unexplored Mayan ruins such as the vast
complex of Calakmul. This site covers an area of several mil
and is one of the largest of the Mayan sites. Currently being
excavated it has already revealed some wonderful structures
and extraordinary items. From Escárcega the road runs sout
direct to Palenque ▲ *243* and Villahermosa.
CIUDAD DEL CARMEN. From Champotón a scenic coastal rou
runs south to Ciudad del Carmen, an island at the entrance
the Laguna de Términos and linked to the mainland by the
2-mile-long Puente de la Unidad. Today Ciudad del Carmen
is a commercial center and fishing port, but its economy
depends mainly on oil. The fort of San Felipe is the only
reminder of the colonial period and the struggle to resist the
English occupation ● *38*. Across from the island the
Xicalango peninsula marked the western limit of Maya
territory and several small sites have been excavated in the
region, yielding interesting objects. The road continues
westwards into the state of Tabasco.

CHIAPAS

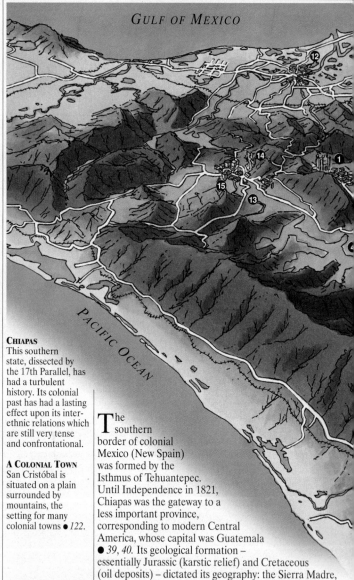

GULF OF MEXICO

PACIFIC OCEAN

CHIAPAS
This southern
state, dissected by
the 17th Parallel, has
had a turbulent
history. Its colonial
past has had a lasting
effect upon its inter-
ethnic relations which
are still very tense
and confrontational.

A COLONIAL TOWN
San Cristóbal is
situated on a plain
surrounded by
mountains, the
setting for many
colonial towns ● 122.

The
southern
border of colonial
Mexico (New Spain)
was formed by the
Isthmus of Tehuantepec.
Until Independence in 1821,
Chiapas was the gateway to a
less important province,
corresponding to modern Central
America, whose capital was Guatemala
● 39, 40. Its geological formation –
essentially Jurassic (karstic relief) and Cretaceous
(oil deposits) – dictated its geography: the Sierra Madre,
which reaches its highest point with the
Tacaná volcano (13,450 feet), marks the
beginning of the long volcanic chain
running along the Pacific coast; the
highlands, with their highest point at
Tzontehuiz (9,840 feet), extend into the
Cuchumatanes ▲ 284, whose foothills are
formed by the great arc of middle-range
mountains in the north and east. The
Lacandón Forest ▲ 258 marks the
beginning of the great tropical forest of

1. CRISTÓBAL LAS CASAS
2. AMATENANGO DEL VALLE
3. COMITÁN DE DOMÍNGUEZ
4. PRESA DE LA ANGOSTURA
5. OCOSINGO
6. TONINÁ
7. PALENQUE
8. YAXCHILÁN
9. BONAMPAK
10. USUMACINTA
11. LACANDÓN FOREST
12. VILLAHERMOSA
13. CHIAPA DE CORZO
14. CAÑÓN DE SUMIDERO
15. TUXTLA GUTIÉRREZ

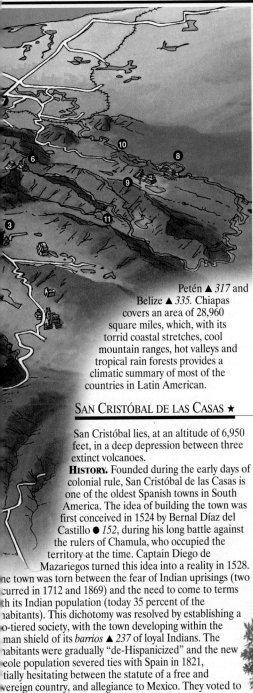

🕓 Four days

A MOUNTAIN CLIMATE
Mornings and evenings are cool. In winter (December–January) early morning mists or ground frosts are the best guarantee of a cloudless blue sky.

TEREBINTH
The terebinth (*ocote*) tree is widely found in Chiapas above 2,600 feet and has given its name to several villages in the state, for example Ocosingo. Its wood is used to make much of the furniture and many of the retables in Chiapas and Guatemala. Its needles are scattered on the ground to form a scented carpet during festivals. An ink used for the codices ● *42* was made from this conifer.

Petén ▲ *317* and Belize ▲ *335*. Chiapas covers an area of 28,960 square miles, which, with its torrid coastal stretches, cool mountain ranges, hot valleys and tropical rain forests provides a climatic summary of most of the countries in Latin American.

SAN CRISTÓBAL DE LAS CASAS ★

San Cristóbal lies, at an altitude of 6,950 feet, in a deep depression between three extinct volcanoes.

HISTORY. Founded during the early days of colonial rule, San Cristóbal de las Casas is one of the oldest Spanish towns in South America. The idea of building the town was first conceived in 1524 by Bernal Díaz del Castillo ● *152*, during his long battle against the rulers of Chamula, who occupied the territory at the time. Captain Diego de Mazariegos turned this idea into a reality in 1528. The town was torn between the fear of Indian uprisings (two occurred in 1712 and 1869) and the need to come to terms with its Indian population (today 35 percent of the inhabitants). This dichotomy was resolved by establishing a two-tiered society, with the town developing within the human shield of its *barrios* ▲ *237* of loyal Indians. The inhabitants were gradually "de-Hispanicized" and the new creole population severed ties with Spain in 1821, initially hesitating between the statute of a free and sovereign country, and allegiance to Mexico. They voted to join Mexico in 1824, but later had to fight frequent battles to maintain their federal status.

233

▲ CHIAPAS
SAN CRISTÓBAL DE LAS CASAS

The town was named after Bartolomé de las Casas, protector of the Indians (painting by Félix Paira, 1875).

Chiapas has fought constantly for its identity with the Mexican Constitution. Under the leadership of Joaquín Miguel Gutiérrez until 1838, and then Angel Albino Corzo (1854–64), it struggled to resist the centralism advocated by the Conservatives and the Emperor Maximilian. Later, under Miguel Utrilla pressed for free and open elections (1866–76). In each case, armed struggle was involved. The choice of San Cristóbal by the AZLN – Zapata's National Liberation Army – as the seat of the uprising of January 1, 1994, was partly in line with this tradition of insurgence. The social influence of the town's stockbreeders and landowners, who had blocked the 1910 Revolution, caused the marginalization of San Cristóbal, with the majority of the population reaping no benefit from the wealth generated by the area's agriculture, oil, hydroelectric dams, coffee or tourism. The anarchists built new towns to the north and south, in the shadow of the historic town. Between 1982 and 1992 the population of San Cristóbal de las Casas doubled and today stands at almost 100,000.

LAYOUT OF THE TOWN
● 122
San Cristóbal is built along a north-south axis and is dominated by three architectural complexes: the monumental complex of Santo Domingo in the north, the *zócalo* in the center, and El Carmen in the south. The former Calle Hidalgo links all three together. The secondary centers which developed around this axis were interspersed with beautiful residences. Beyond these lie the *barrios* (former Indian districts).

"ZÓCALO"

CATHEDRAL ★. The cathedral, which dominates the central plaza (*zócalo*), has been renovated many times. In the 16th century, it was a large chapel whose entrance (to the south) opened onto the present square. Still surviving are two huge gargoyles, adorning the west side, and the square Mudejar bell tower whose height has been reduced by several earthquakes and which was originally separate from the main structure. The west façade was completed in 1696. The restoration (in 1993) of its original colors (produced using natural colorings, lime, salt and cactus sap) have recreated the effect of an architectural *huipil*: the dominant colors – yellow ocher from the soil of Chamula and red ocher from Cuxtitali – provide the "cloth", while the white "embroidery" is rendered by the stucco (lime, sand and egg-white moldings) and highlighted by two black panels and columns (Chamula wool).

CHURCH OF SAN NICOLÁS. San Nicolás has served as the church of the town's Negro slaves (when the Indian population was in decline due to epidemics), a canonical church (chapter

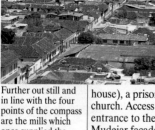

Further out still and in line with the four points of the compass are the mills which once supplied the town.

house), a prison during the Reform wars and finally a parish church. Access is via a Baroque porch, which was formerly the entrance to the bishop's palace gardens. It has a typically Mudejar façade.

"PORTALES". According to Thomas Gage, during the 17th century idlers would pass the time under the *portales* (arches on the east side of the *zócalo*, rebuilt after the conflict of 18

Detail of a retable in the cathedral, which represents a dark-skinned "Indian" cherub. The angel has a blond wig and a pre-hispanic pectoral as well as quetzal-feather wings.

0. An 18th-century manuscript tells how messengers from haciendas came to conduct business. They would sing : "How much for a black slave, how much for each of my nkeys, my mares or my plots of land."

SIDENCES. The east façade of the hotel Santa Clara, a 17th-ntury residence, has Plateresque motifs; the hotel Ciudad al is neoclassic in style; the Bancomer bank, with its nch-style façade, is reminiscent of the Diaz period. ● *41*.

ACIO MUNICIPAL. Built as the governor's palace by Carlos res, a local engineer, the Palacio Municipal was intended amiliarize masons with the designs and proportions of the oclassic style. In 1895 the building was completed after ich its Doric and Ionic windows, denticles, cornices and liments were frequently reproduced as part of a new urban ign trend.

NTO DOMINGO DISTRICT

is historic church and monastery complex in the northern t of the town dispersed its monuments in the gardens of La meda when, in 1863, it was used as part of the tifications during the Reform wars ● *40*. The two-headed, strian Habsburg eagle on the façade of Santo Domingo couraged supporters of Maximilian ● *41* to seek refuge in e church.

NASTERY. The monastery was established in 1546 by the nks of Las Casas who made it into an "Indian house".

CATHEDRAL
The Baroque interior has cedar retables, made and assembled at the time of the Indian bishop Moctezuma (1754–66). The two pine retables, at the top of the side aisles, and the pulpit supported by a Mexican eagle (1708) were brought from the Jesuit church. The carved wood ceiling has been restored, but without the gold which made the cathedral famous in the 17th century.

CHURCH OF SANTO DOMINGO
The damaged statues are a reminder of the days of conflict, when General Utrilla opened fire on the Imperialists from the Calle Real de Mexicanos.

most famous prior was Fray Matías de rdoba, author of the "cry" of dependence (1821). Remodeled before 2, the monastery houses a museum of gional history and a cloister.

URCH OF SANTO DOMINGO ★. The nstruction of the church, adjoining the nastery, began with the façade at the d of the 17th century. The interior was l being built in 1735.

The market in San Cristóbal.

CHURCH OF SANTO DOMINGO

In the 18th century the church was literally lined with gold, silver and the paintings of its thirteen retables. Today it has eight intact retables. To create an effect of uninterrupted continuity, the retables in the nave are set between vertical carved giltwood panels whose motif repeats to create an overall effect of rhythm and unity (above).

TEMPLO DE LA CARIDAD. On the lower south terrace the Templo de la Caridad (Charity), built in 1714, is the memori to the repression of the Indian rebellion of Cancuc (1712) ● *38* when the Tzeltals' patron saint, Our Lady of the Rosar was defeated by the Spanish equivalent, Our Lady of Charity (or the Presentation). After the victory of San Cristóbal on November 21 (the festival of the Presentation), Our Lady of Charity was proclaimed "general" (after 1747 a field-marshal's baton was added to her statue) and protectress of the town. The church's façade is a more sober but equally animated expression of colonial Baroque architecture.

CHAPEL OF THE SOTANO. Adjoining the Templo de la Caridad the Chapel of the Sótano (Christ in the Dungeon) was built between 1831 and 1839 by local Indians in response to the

construction of the rebellion memorial. Th masons working on the chapel had restore the cathedral in 1815 and imitated its gargoyles and neoclassic south entrance.

KIOSK WITH NEOCLASSIC DOME. The kiosk was built by the government of General Miguel Utrilla (1879–83), the first peace-time government of the 19th century, to glorify the federalist liberal constitution of the Reform in 1857.

EL CARMEN DISTRICT

CHURCH OF EL CARMEN. El Carmen, damaged by a fire in 1993 when its retables and ancient paintings were destroyed, has retained its double, right-angled façade (1744 and 1764) Currently being restored, the edifice is a fine example of vernacular, polychrome Baroque. Nearby is the ruined nunnery of the Franciscan Sisters of the Incarnation, who played an important part in the life of the town's female population during the colonial period, and subsequently during the struggle for Independence, when they supported the rebels.

TOWER-PORCH. An anarchistic restoration of the roof of El Carme mistakenly attached the church to the tower-porch of 1677, obscurin the latter's west façade. The tower-porch's former status as a city gate and its style of geometric Mudejar, stucco arabesques and naive polychrom beneath the arch combine are a valuable remind of the early urbanization of Sa Cristóbal.

...ABLE IN THE CHURCH OF
...O DOMINGO
...il of a retable in the Chapel
...e Rosary, representing a
...que figure.

CULTURAL CENTER. The cultural center is housed in the former farm (*casa de labor*) which supplied the convent. The 17th-century building, with its extensive gardens and broad *corredor* is a particularly fine example of the local style of living.

GRAND RESIDENCES ★

...TEL MAZARIEGOS. This 18th-century residence stands one ...ck north of the *zócalo*. The building has a broad, wood ...redor while an annex on the other side of the street has ...cco moldings and friezes. This was the residence of Bishop ...ctezuma (1754–66), a descendant of the last Aztec king.

...ZA REAL. Built at the end of the 18th century, this stands ...f a block east of the *zócalo*. In the 19th century it housed ... offices of the local representatives. Today it is a busy ...opping arcade.

...SAJE MAZARIEGOS. The Pasaje Mazariegos, next to the ...za Real, is lined with patioed shops and a café.

...TEL FRAY BARTOLOMÉ. In the 19th century the Hotel Fray ...rtolomé housed the bishop's court. It has an attractive ...tio surrounded by a beautiful *corredor*.

...ENSEÑANZA. This residence, on the corners of Calles ...lisario Domínguez and Adelina Flores, is an experiment in ...eoclassic adobe" by Carlos Flores, the town's architect ...ween 1880 and 1920.

...TEL CASA MEXICANA. The former residence of the fathers ...San-Juan-de-Dios, who ran the hospital, has been ...nverted into a luxury hotel. The patio has a bronze ...lpture by Zuñiga.

...SA NA BOLOM. This late 19th-century residence with its ...ological garden, library, museum and neoclassical chapel ...003), stands at the top of Calles Chiapa de Corzo and ...mitán. It was owned by the anthropologist, Frans Blom.

...E "BARRIOS"

...e adobe town is best appreciated in the old Indian districts: ...exicanos; Cerrillo; San Antonio with its hill; Cerrito, the ...rador of the town and its valley, and Cuxtitali with its ...onial toll bridge (tiled roof and benches), *El Peje de Oro* ...d "Miguel Utrilla" mill. The districts were identified by ...nic origin (Aztec, Tzotzil, Zapotec, Quiché), the religious ...ler responsible (Dominicans, Franciscans) and traditional ...ecialties, such as wood, wrought iron, fire-crackers, cloth ...d wool dyeing and cooked meats. The streets often have no ...ndows as the traditional houses usually only open onto a ...tio. They are very different from the streets of the ...lightened" town center where neoclassic modernization ...rced impressive windows with adobe edicules. To the south ...the valley, the Hotel de la Alborada offers a splendid view ...the mill, the town and its natural setting. Footpaths lead to ...other mills. In the forest to the east, about 3 miles beyond ...e so-called "la Garita" district, is the natural arch of the ...co Tete. It is possible to continue with a guide as far as the ...intana de los Obispos, a small, 18th-century Baroque ...lding which was the bishops' country residence and the ...farm hospital.

"GALERÍA"
Built for the town's founder in 1528, this is San Cristóbal's oldest ... residence. Situated in the Calle Hidalgo (no. 7), it is now used by businesses.

Other churches (below) are open to the public including: Santa-Lucia, San-Felipe Ecatepec, San Francisco and El Carmen.

RANCHO NUEVO

The site became a battlefield in January 1994 during the
Zapatista rebellion ● *40* and is now closed to the public.
However, about 50 acres of the forest are still open to hikers
(access is about 6 miles from San Cristóbal, on the right in the
direction of Comitán). The only river in this high valley (7,500
feet) is a dry channel. During the rainy season (June–
September) this becomes a torrent which "disappears" into
the caves which run into the hollow mountain range (*Cerro
hueco*) closing the San Cristóbal valley to the south.
Approximately the first 500 yards of the caves are lit and are
open for public viewing.
A NATURAL SITE. This limestone site, characteristic of the
region's Jurassic landscapes, is scattered with karstic
landslides, covered with conifers and pierced by small, funnel-
shaped water sinks which "feed" the water table that in turn
waters the forest. The forest is populated by ibex and other
rare species of deer, badgers (*zorrilla*), armadillos, squirrels,
green woodpeckers and snakes.

TZOTZIL VILLAGES ★

Chamula and Zinacantán, in the
vicinity of San Cristóbal de las
two of the most visited Tzotzil
authorities have introduced
in an attempt to limit tourism,
to churches, and
additional charges
to photograph certain
ceremonies. The ceremonies for
which a small charge is made
Year, the festivals of San Juan,
Domingo, and the Carnival
As well as being occasions for
important rituals,
strengthen ties
the parent

immediate
Casas, are
villages. The local
severe measures
such as entrance fees
permits and special

are those for the New
San Lorenzo and San
(*k'in tajimoltik*) ● *74*.
the performance of
they also serve to
between members of
community and its
migrants (settlers in the
Lacandón Forest), who
today constitute an

portant diaspora. These villages are still the scene of bitter
nflicts between Catholics and Protestants (especially in the
lage of Chamula, where large numbers of Protestants have
d to leave for the new shanty towns around San Cristóbal).
e communities have developed amidst conflict, either as
e innocent victims of regional or national politics, or
cause the religious and administrative pressures exerted by
e colonial authorities became an unbearable assault upon
eir very existence.

The church of
Chamula as it is
today.

DIAN REBELLIONS ● 38. These same communities were the
at of the great, early 18th-century rebellions, a reaction
ainst the extortionate tributes exacted by the conquerers
d the efforts of the Spanish clergy (especially Bishop
ancisco Nuñez de la Vega) to eradicate idolatry and destroy
e power of sorcerer-priests (or shamans) who perpetuated
ditional Indian religious practices. With their idols
ndemned and destroyed by the priests, the Indians turned
to the Catholic Christs, Virgins and Saints to
represent their claims and defend their concept of a
more just and equitable alternative society. The
appearance of a Saviour-Virgin at Zinacantán in 1708,
and then at Santa Marta in 1711, were the early signs
of the great 1712–13 uprising, which spread across a
large part of Chiapas from Cancuc. A total of thirty-
three Tzotzil, Tzeltal and Chol communities
rebelled and swelled the ranks of the
"soldiers of the Virgin", but they were
soon subjected to the most terrible
repression, followed by years of
poverty and famine. Hopes of an alternative society
were not entirely destroyed; they merely took on
other less spectacular means of expression. In 1994
they re-emerged in a well-organized form and for the
first time in history, they attracted international
attention.

San Juan Chamula in
the early 20th
century.
The
crosses
and grazing
land have been
replaced by a
square,
surrounded by
buildings,
where the
local market
is held.

CARNIVAL OF CHAMULA. The carnival period
corresponds to the five transitional days of the
ancient Mayan calendar and involves the ritual
presentation of a series of historical events involving
invaders and enemies whose intrusion represents
the disorder of the world and the threat to Mayan
society (opposite above).

"CHINKULTIC" DISK
The so-called
"Chinkultic" disk is in
fact one of the aisle
markers ● *112* from
the ball court of a
minor site in the
Chinkultic region. It
is in sculpted
limestone and dates
from AD 590.

**A WALK THROUGH THE
RAIN FOREST**
In the region of the
Montebello Lakes, at
altitudes of between
650 and 2,300 feet,

the early morning
jungle mists lift as the
sun rises and fall
again during the
afternoon as the air
temperature cools.
The eastern exposure
of the site and its
altitude (4,600 feet)
form a barrier against
the trade winds and
create the conditions
necessary for a high-
altitude rain forest.
The most commonly
found species of trees
are sweet-smelling
conifers, oaks (with
epiphytic bromeliads
and orchids) and
sweet gums (with
their maple-like sap
and leaves). They
grow above a dense
undergrowth of
flowers, aromatic
plants, giant ferns and
shrubs.

TEOPISCA

In 1626, the size of this church-
cemetery and the sound of its
constant music had already
attracted the attention of the
English traveler Thomas Gage.
In an attempt to control the
Mayan funeral rites that were
still being practiced in the 17th
century, the nave of the church
was designed for receiving the
dead rather than for worshippers.
During services, the parishioners
gathered in the chancel. Of the ten
Baroque retables which once decorated
the church, only three remain. Two of
these, transferred in the 19th century, came
from the Jesuit church of San Cristóbal ▲ *233*.
Behind the recently restored giltwood retable in
the chancel (1706), the polychrome remains of another
retable installed in 1688 were discovered.

TENAM PUENTE

About 6 miles beyond Comitán, a track on the right leads fo
3 miles to the site of Tenam Puente. Current excavation wo
has revealed a large Late Classic site on one of the hills
bordering the plateau of Comitán (which offers a magnifice
view extending from the range of the Tzontehuitz to the
Cuchumatanes ▲ *284*). This Mayan city is built on three
levels, each with a ball court and several pyramids, often
arranged around a sunken patio. Its architecture, which is
sometimes superposed, represents two successive stages of
the Late Classic period. With the exception of one dated st
in bas-relief (on display at the museum of Tuxtla Gutiérrez
▲ *260*), the steles discovered on the site were smooth.

MONTEBELLO LAKES

About 9 miles south of Comitán, take the left fork just befo
La Trinitaría and follow the road for about 18 miles. At an
average altitude of 4,900 feet, the road crosses a long platea
sloping gently toward the lakes. This plateau is bordered on
the right by the central mountains of Chiapas and, on the le
by the hills running along its southern edge before the land
plunges down into the jungle and the central depression. A
the tracks along this road lead to
historical *fincas* (today mostly communal
land) which initially belonged to the first
inhabitants of San Cristóbal, and these
then passed in some cases to the
Dominicans before finally, in the 19th
century, they were embraced by Comitán.
They are situated in a key area: on the
edge of Lacandón territory, which was
unsubjugated during colonial rule ▲ *258*,
and on the border of Guatemala, which
was a refuge for the fighters of the civil

wars of the Reform
(1855–64) ● 40. Several of
these estates were the
scene of battles, either to
occupy a strategic
position or replenish
supplies of corn, beans,
livestock and dairy
products.

THE SITE ★. The lakes
form overflow "sinks" for
the rivers of the valley of
Comitán. Their color varies
according to the composition
of the lake floor – sand (blue-
green) or rocks (chalky) – and
their orientation – shadow (deep
blue-black) or sun (opal-blue). A
series of pools begins about 12 miles
before the lakes. The water pours into the
river basins and then plunges into the jungle
which begins at La Cañada (in the foothills of the
[..]uchumatanes) about 12 miles to the east. For those traveling
[..] road, the fork about half a mile before the first lake leads
[..] several other lakes, including the lake at the border village
[..] Tziscao. Don't go too close as its shores are quicksand.

[..]HINKULTIC

[..] reach the site of Chinkultic (above), take a left turn about
[..] miles before the Montebello Lakes. A track (about half a
[..]ile) leads to the ruins. The site covers a long period of
[..]story as there is evidence of a connection with Toniná ▲ 242
[..]or which the last known date is AD 909), while colonial
[..]anuscripts refer to its occupation in the 16th century. The
[..]ost interesting sculptures, although in a poor state of repair
[..]e to long neglect, are near the ball court. They bear the
[..]ayan symbols for war and death. Higher up the mountain,
[..]n the other side of the stream, is a monumental complex
[..]th two small platforms: one at the foot of the pyramid, and
[..]e other on the edge of a deep *cenote* which, when explored,
[..]vealed several cavities containing mortuary offerings. The
[..]p of the pyramid offers a panoramic view of the series of
[..]kes (Lake Chinkultic, left) and the valley's dense vegetation
[..]d orchids.

"FINCA SANTA MARIA"
This former *finca*,
situated about 12
miles from La
Trinitaría, has been
converted into a
hotel: the *Posada
Museo Santa Maria*. It
consists of a main
building (*casa grande*
and restaurant), a
restored chapel,
stables (with horses
for hire), a large
courtyard, a vegetable
garden (where guests
can choose their own
salads) and an
orchard. The rooms
are authentically
furnished with 18th-
and 19th-century
furniture, paintings,
sculptures and
chandeliers.

CONETA ★
About 25 miles from
Comitán, near the
Maya site of Tenam
Rosario (closed to the
public), a track on the
left leads to Coneta.
This Dominican
foundation (below)
has existed since the
16th century,
although the village
disappeared in the
mid-19th century.
The ruins of the 17th-
century church stand
in the fields. Its
atypical façade is
sculpted with pre-
Hispanic motifs,
while the lower
section has five
arcades whose niches
are painted with
saints. The
polychrome porch
represents a field
of corn.

The Mayan site of Toniná is still b
excavated by the Mexico National Institu
Anthropology and His

The first part of the route runs through the
Ocosingo fault which separates two tectonic
plates: the Central American plate (highlands) to
south and the North American plate (northern
mountains) to the north ■ *16*. These plates move
about three-quarters of an inch every year. Bene.
the fertile pastures of the valley floor are the
alluvial deposits of the fossil meanders of a river
whose course is often altered by earth tremors.

OXCHUC

This Tzeltal village is the focal point of an
agricultural pilgrimage held on the festival
Santo Tomás (December 21), which is also
attended by the Tojolabals ● *63*. Its church is on
of the few whose atrium still has three of its four
capillas posas (repository chapels) where traces
paintings can still be seen. In the chancel (south
window) a sculpture with a pre-Hispanic motif
was discovered embedded in the wall. It represe
three shells, the distinctive symbols of both the
name of the village in Tzeltal and of Quetzalcoa
In 1687 Bishop Nuñez de la Vega confiscated a
Mayan calendars and codices and demanded
that all worshippers should repeat the *cred*
Today Oxchuc is still a seat of Maya
resistance.

TONINÁ ★

Toniná, at an altitude of 2,950 feet, lies on the
border of the Mayan highlands and lowlands, b
belongs to the lowland tradition.

HISTORY. Although the Ocosingo Valley and th
site were occupied from the Late Preclassic,
Toniná experienced its golden age during the
Late Classic period. This border town probably resisted the

STATUARY OF TONINA
Life-size (or smaller)
statues in the round
have a vertical tenon
which was set into a
socket in the wall.
The altars of Toniná
are thin disks, usually
sculpted with
inscriptions.
Sovereigns are
depicted wearing a
long cloak and either
holding a ceremonial
staff or with their
hands resting on their
belts. Their
headdresses consist of
superposed masks.

collapse of the Maya civilization ● *34* better than most
because of its geographical position. It was here that the m
recent stele was erected (AD 909). Although its statues and
inscriptions were destroyed during the Early Postclassic, the
ruined city was inhabited intermittently and its Classic tomb
re-used. The center of Toniná, built on the side of a hill in
seven terraces, produced the overall form of a pyramid. The
site was briefly described and some of its statues illustrated
by an expedition from the University of Tulane in the
1920's but it was only during the 1970's that the French
researchers, Pierre Becquelin, Claude-François
Baudez and Eric Taladoire devoted several
campaigns to the excavation of Toniná.

SCULPTURES. A naked and decapitated captive in
relief, a colossal trophy-head and numerous
panels of scenes depicting capture and sacrifice
decorated the temples and pyramids. The sculptures
on the stucco-work structures were also based on the
themes of war and sacrifice. A huge relief, discovered
at the foot of the sixth terrace, presented one of the
most terrifying images in the Mayan culture. It depicted

enes of a hellish underworld, scattered with
ulls, and severed heads and fearsome
ythical creatures.

HOL TERRITORY

efore the Spanish Conquest the Chol
oups ● 63 occupied the vast territory of
e lowlands between the Usumacinta ▲ 333
d Lake Izabal ▲ 313. In the 16th century they
ere deported to the highlands where they were decimated by
ld and disease and assimilated into other groups. Other
embers of this linguistic group are found in Tila, Tumbalá
d several villages near Palenque, where they settled as a
sult of tradition or coercion during the Conquest.

AGUA AZUL
Before Palenque, a
road leads to the
Agua Azul Cascades.
The color of the
water varies with the
season.

ALENQUE ★

lenque is built at the foot and on the sides of a specially
prepared hillside site. It has three levels
– the plain at sea level, an intermediate
level (about 330 feet) and an upper
level (390-490 feet) – and covers an
area of 6 square miles. Only the center
(or Principal Group), which covers an
area of 37 acres, has been cleared and is
accessible to visitors. Excavations in the
past, mainly carried out by Mexican
archeologists, have been completed by
researchers of various nationalities who
have analyzed the images, carved
scriptions and natural relief of the site.

PALENQUE
1. Palace
2. Temple of the
Inscriptions
3. North Temple
4. Temple of the Cross
5. Temple of the Sun
6. Temple of the
Foliated Cross
7. Ball Court

▲ PALENQUE

HISTO
Although the site was occupied in 100 ▸
the city did not expand until the ?
century. By the end of the 9th century
golden age was over, and no new buildi▸
or inscriptions were commission▸

Palenque was one of the earliest Mayan sites to be discovered.
is also one of the best preserved and has a remarkable royal
sepulcher. The city not only had access to the most famous and
imaginative architects in the Mayan civilization, but also the
best scribes. It consequently has some of the most beautiful
calligraphy.

WALDECK
In 1784 the governor of Guatemala ordered several people to carry out an on-the-spot enquiry into the truth of the rumors circulating about "stone houses" buried deep in the forest. In 1832 the neoclassical artist, Jean-Frédéric Waldeck ● 56, 130 (a naturalized Frenchman born in Austria), spent over a year among the ruins of Palenque where he studied the architecture, made drawings of the sculptures and carried out a few excavations. His works included this *View of the Temple of the Cross*. The results of his research were not circulated for another thirty years and it was Stephens ● 56 who published the first description of Palenque in 1841. Since then vast numbers of artists, scientists and tourists have visited the site.

The first sovereign of the Palenque dynasty, Chaacal I, acceded to the throne in 501 and the last, Kuk, ended his reign after 784. The most recent inscriptions date from the very end of the 8th century.

GROUP OF THE CROSS

The references to mythical creatures are clearly expressed. The so-called Group of the Cross consists of three pyramid-temples built around a square open to the south. The Temple of the Cross is the largest and highest placed (top left); the Temple of the Sun (center left) occupies the lowest position on a four-story pyramid; the third is the Temple of the Foliated Cross (bottom left). They were built during the reign of the sovereign Chan Bahlum, between 683 (date of the death of his father, Pacal, whose jade funeral mask is shown above) and 692, and represent a three-stage cosmic journey, each defined by a specific orientation and environment. The Temple of the Cross represents the first stage and symboliz the place of origin the supernatural ar the world of Man. The next stage of th journey is the underworld, throu whic

the nocturnal sun (embodied by the jaguar) has to pass. The final stage, in t sanctuary of the Foliated Cross, involves rebirth via the fertility of the upper layers of the earth. The richness the symbolism of th Group of the Cross lies in their differen orientations and the relationship betwee the different stages.

"EL PALACIO"

The so-called Palace of Palenque is in fact a platform (82 yards long by 60 yards wide and about 33 feet high) supporting fifteen or so structures (usually referred to as "houses" and designated by a letter of the alphabet) arranged around three courtyards. The complex is the result of almost two centuries of architectural activity which covers at least six reigns. The first structures were built in the early 7th century by Pacal (AD 615–83). In spite of its name, the Palace was not a royal residence but a religious complex reserved for the king and his elected priests, in which the various buildings are dedicated to different ritual ceremonies.

HOUSE D

This ancient reproduction of one of the stuc bas-reliefs decorating the pillars of House I shows a figure presenting a thunder-and-lightning serpent to the sovereign. House D associated with agrarian rites.

Head from the Late Classic period, found in the tomb.

TEMPLE OF THE INSCRIPTIONS ● 108

This structure is in fact the funerary monument of Pacal, the first great sovereign of Palenque. The tomb, which lies beneath the temple, at the foot of a long staircase, was discovered in 1952. Prior to this it was thought that the pyramids were merely foundations for temples. Also discovered in the pyramid were three panels carved with glyphs which constitute one of the longest known Mayan inscriptions (617 glyphic blocks).

THE SARCOPHAGUS
The sarcophagus contained the royal remains, surrounded by a rich collection of jewelry and jade. It was covered with a huge, sculpted slab (right) showing the dead sovereign falling into the fleshless jaws of the terrestrial monster. On the mask representing the "underworld" is one of the sacred trees from the four corners of the world. The two-headed serpent represents the sky, while the quetzal bird at the top of the tree symbolizes the zenith of the diurnal Sun. The ten half-figures emerging from the earth, sculpted on the sides of the sarcophagus, represented some of Pacal's royal ancestors.

YAXCHILÁN ★

HISTORY. The region surrounding the river Usumacinta and its tributaries became increasingly important during the early 6th century with the development of Yaxchilán, its principal center. The site, nestling in a bend of the river, experienced its golden age during the Late Classic period, with the Jaguar dynasty, whose reigns and conquests appear on many of the site's sculpted monuments: steles, altars and lintels. The latest inscriptions date from the early 9th century.

MONUMENTS. Some of the structures are built on a terrace bordering the left bank of the river, while others occupy the slopes above. The majority are gathered together in two acropolises reached via long staircases (below). They are predominantly elongated, rectangular edifices with single or double rows of rooms and three entrances in the façade. Their foundations are relatively low and the large, openwork crests to their roofs are less massive than those of Petén.

SCULPTURES. The upper section of the façades is often elaborately decorated with stone mosaics as well as three-dimensional sculptures and stucco motifs. For example, the frieze of Structure 33 included statues of dignitaries seated on monster masks or appearing at inverted T-shaped window openings, while the center of the roof crest was occupied by the colossal statue of a seated sovereign. The lintels of the three doors were entirely sculpted, and a stele and altar stood before the central door. The sculptural style of the Usumacinta region, and of Yaxchilán in particular, is justly famed for its freedom of expression. The architectural sculpture and exterior monuments – steles and altars – are damaged, whereas most of the detail on the lintels

MAYAN PROFILE
The Mexico National Museum of Anthropology ▲ 376 has some fine examples of lintels from Yaxchilán. Lintel 26, dating from 719, with a detail of a face (above), offers a good impression of the typically Mayan profile of pre-Columbian sculptures and paintings. The characteristically flattened forehead was obtained by compressing the skull of newly born babies between two planks of wood, held in place for several days.

248

been preserved. The iconography highlights the
s performed by the sovereign and a member of
immediate entourage: wife, mother, sons or
tenant. Scenes of self-sacrifice, such as a woman
sing a cord of thorns through her tongue, are
licitly depicted ● 46. Sometimes the ritual is
ked by its result, represented by a basket of
rificial instruments (stingray spines, sharp
ves and cords of thorns) and accompanied
strips of bast paper on which the victim's
od was offered to the beneficiaries of the
ifice. The sculptures also show
eral scenes of capture in which the
es of the victor and vanquished
inscribed, sometimes on their
h. Other rituals involve objects
ch are rare or unknown in other
ions. Apart from the famous
rine, depicting a high-priest
ding a sceptre which is half-man,
f-serpent ● 52, the sovereigns of
chilán and their entourage are shown
ding scepters in the form of a directional
e surmounted by a bird, torches, long rods
ended by a wickerwork structure, and others which are
er and decorated with partly mobile crosses, jaguar paws
sacred packages.

**WARRIOR AND
CAPTIVE**
This detail from Stele
15 (AD 680) at
Yaxchilán shows a
warrior seizing his
prisoner by the hair.

NAMPAK ★   ● 128

highly probable that the interior walls of the more
stigious edifices on all Mayan sites were covered with
ntings which complemented the carved or sculpted
oration of the exterior. The damp, tropical climate has
ant that most of these paintings have not survived to the
sent day.

NUMENTS. When it was constructed, Bonampak
a site of average importance, but today its
nprehensive collection of Mayan painting
vides historians with vital information.
covered in 1946, it is situated a few
es south of the Usumacinta and
chilán Rivers, on the edge of the
candón Forest ▲ 258. The center of the
e consists of an Acropolis (a terraced hill
h several small temples) overlooking a
are bordered by structures on three sides.
e stone sculpture, in the form of steles and lintels, is very
l preserved. The edifice containing the paintings
ructure 1) and the three steles dates from the reign of
aan-Muan, who acceded to the throne in 776 and was still
ower in 790.

NTINGS ▲ 250. Structure 1, on the first terrace of the
ropolis, comprises three non-connecting rooms whose walls
vaulted ceilings have retained most of their paintings.
e lintels of the three doors depict scenes of capture in
ich a sovereign seizes his fallen enemy by the hair. The
ntings in the three rooms illustrate three stages of the
e story: before, during and after a battle.

**.ACROPOLIS OF
BONAMPAK**
In the foreground is
the first terrace of the
Acropolis and a stele
protected against the
weather. Beyond and
to the right, Structure
1 still has its famous
paintings.

The first room depicts dignitaries standing inside a edifice (shown by a red background), at the foot of the royal throne. The sovereign, pictured above the door, is dressed for a dance being performed in the lower register (blue background) in the open air. To the left of the dancers is a procession of musicians and masked figures and to the right a crowd of dignitaries watching the ceremony. Opposite the entrance to the second room another fresco depicts a battle in which the armed and richly dressed warriors of Bonampak triumph over their unarmed and almost naked adversaries. The judgement and torture of the prisoners is described on the lintel of the door. The principal scene in the third room is a dance, accompanied by music, performed at th op and foot of a pyramid. The vaulted ceilings in Rooms 1 and 3 are decorated with images of the celestial cosmic monster, while those in Room 2 are decorated with captives and the symbols of constellations.

FERTILITY DANCE

A group of six dancers, wearing masks and costumes and flanked by musicians (playing trumpets, turtle shells and rattles) and fan bearers, prepare to perform. One of the dancers is dressed as a crab and raises his claws. There is also a seated crocodile. The other figures, apart from one, are wearing the masks of imaginary reptilian creatures. The dancers probably represent spirits associated with water and vegetation and are about to perform a fertility dance.

"This art is inspired by a spirit which sweeps aside all theocratic and aristocratic artistic convention. It is not afraid to depict brutality, the cruelty of scenes of war, but also likes to portray scenes of everyday life, clothing and finery."

Jacques Soustelle

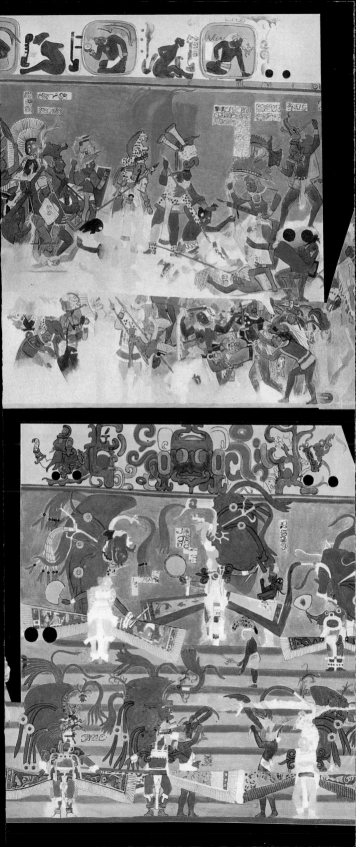

Details of the vaulted ceiling in Room 2.

THE SOVEREIGN AND HIS ENTOURAGE
The sovereign Chaan-Muan is seated on his throne and surrounded by members of his entourage, including several women. He seems to be speaking to the man seated at the foot of the royal throne. Further to the left another man, holding a child in his arms, is turning to the king. The generally accepted interpretation of this scene is the presentation of the royal heir to the court. It is thought to be the principal theme of Room 1, and perhaps even the entire edifice. But this theory is thrown into question if one takes into account the air of total indifference displayed by the dignitaries gathered at the foot of the platform.

ROOM 1

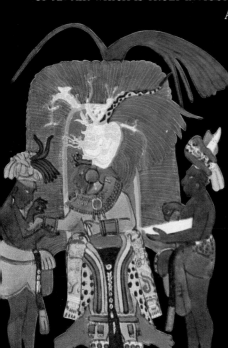

DANCE PREPARATIONS
The three principle dancers are preparing to perform (they can be seen in action in the lower register against the blue background). The tallest of the three, standing on the right (below) is thought to represent the king. In the detail (left) he appears in the center and is wearing a jaguar skin, jaguar-skin sandals and a necklace decorated with pearls. The central image of his impressive headdress is a water lily being nibbled by a fish, the symbol of fertility. A framework of feathers is attached to the dancer's back. While one servant fastens a bracelet, another offers him jewelry.

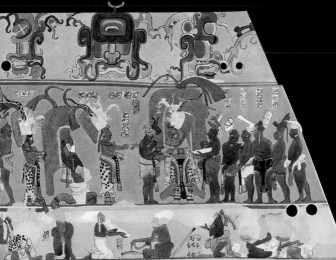

"Bonampak occupies a unique position in the history of Mayan art, both in terms of the documentary value and beauty of its wall paintings in which clarity and firmness of line are combined with a highly developed sense of composition and an extraordinarily rich use of color. The dying "captive" is truly inspired, not to mention the many subtle ways in which the master of Bonampak brought his scenes to life in a manner that far excels the stiffness and conventionality of so much Mayan monumental art."
Paul Gendrop, *Les Mayas*

ROOM 2

ROOM

PROTAGONISTS OF THE BATTLE
Parasol bearers and musicians can be seen among the victorious warriors who wear various headdresses. The trumpet player, in the angle between two walls, is wearing a necklace of severed heads.

COLLECTIVE SELF-SACRIFICE ● 46.
The battle is followed by the capture and torture of prisoners and the story painted on the walls of Structure 1 ends with a great dance. The sovereign and two of his entourage take part at the top of the pyramid while other dignitaries gather at its foot. But the sacrifice is still to come. The king and his entourage, seated on the bench which serves as a throne, offer their blood (and their pain) by passing a cord through their tongue. Their self-sacrifice automatically complements the sacrifice of the prisoners.

HE FRESCOS OF BONAMPAK COMPEL US TO REVISE THE GENERAL ACCEPTED IDEA THAT THE MAYAN CIVILIZATION OF THE FIRST MILLENNIUM WAS OF A MORE OR LESS PERMANENTLY PEACEABLE NATURE." JACQUES SOUSTELLE

THREE ROOMS
ture 1 at Bonampak consists of three s, each with a single door. In each room ssic vault ● *106* bears most of the ation. The triangular partition are also painted.

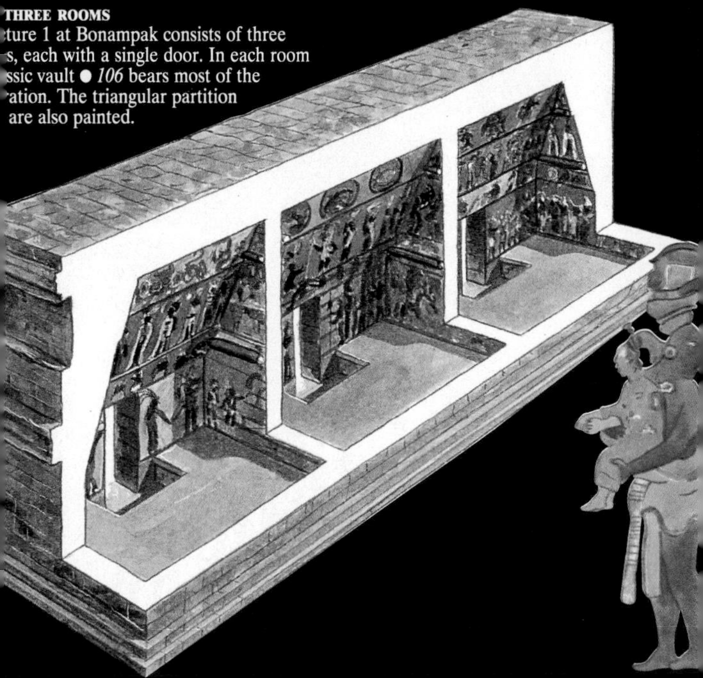

COSMIC MONSTER
The vaulted ceiling of Room 1, like that of Room 3 (see reverse side of gatefold) is decorated with images of the celestial cosmic monster which can be seen in the upper, blue band.

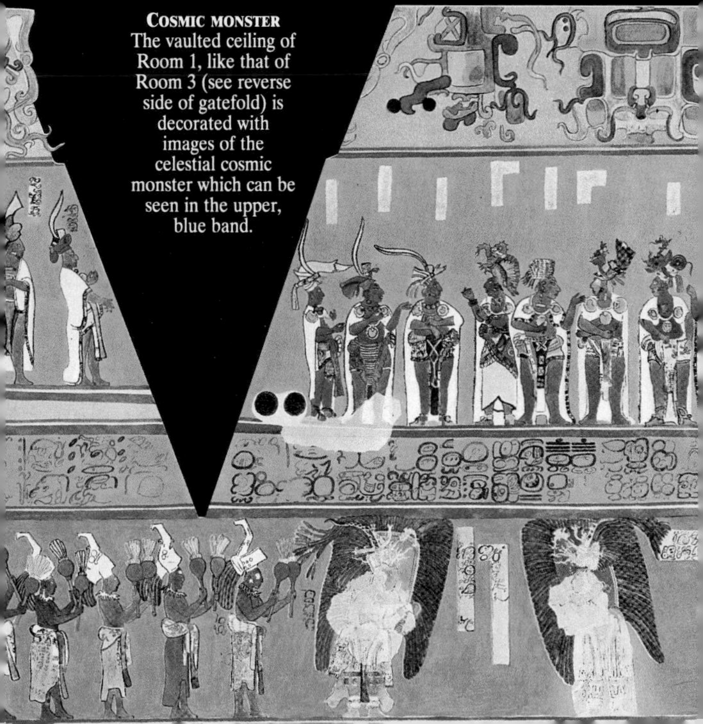

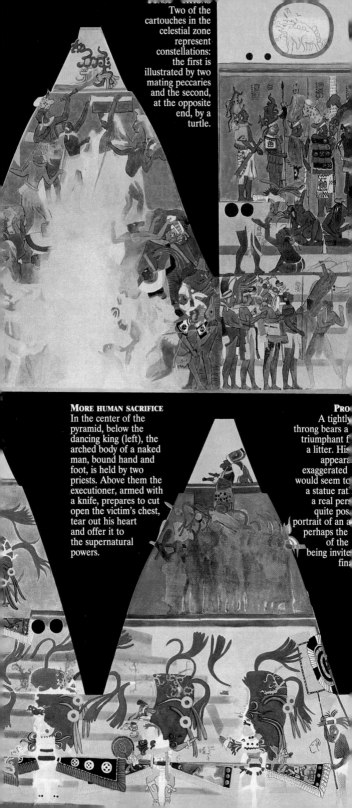

Two of the cartouches in the celestial zone represent constellations: the first is illustrated by two mating peccaries and the second, at the opposite end, by a turtle.

MORE HUMAN SACRIFICE

In the center of the pyramid, below the dancing king (left), the arched body of a naked man, bound hand and foot, is held by two priests. Above them the executioner, armed with a knife, prepares to cut open the victim's chest, tear out his heart and offer it to the supernatural powers.

PRO

A tightly throng bears a triumphant f a litter. His appear exaggerated would seem to a statue rat a real pers quite pos portrait of an a perhaps the of the being invite fin

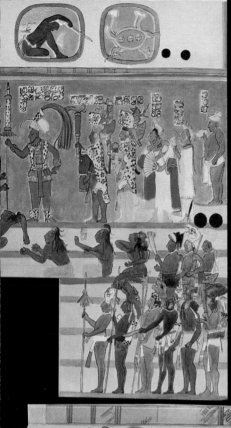

JUDGEMENT OF THE PRISONERS ● 128

The battle ends with the defeat of the enemy, their judgement and torture. Chaan-Muan appears in the center of the composition, at the top of the pyramid, accompanied by dignitaries, captains, courtiers and women of the court. The conquered enemy have been stripped of their jewelry and clothes (except for a loincloth) and their hair is loose. A dead prisoner lies at the king's feet. Everywhere tortured prisoners awaiting execution hold out bloodstained hands. On the far left an executioner holds his victim by the wrist. A severed head rests on a bed of leaves. Other warriors watch the scene at the foot of the pyramid.

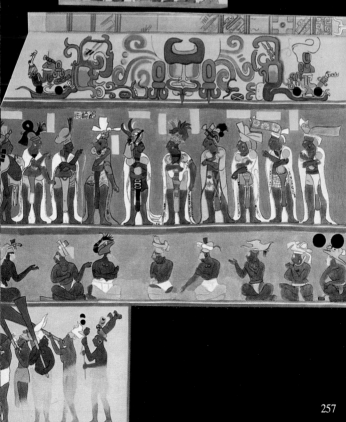

LACANDÓN FOREST
The Lacandón Forest (Selva Lacandona) lies in east Chiapas, in the part of Mexico which on the map seems to project into Guatemala. It covers an area of around 1,900 square miles to the south of Yaxchilán and Bonampak. The region, classified as the Montes Azules Biosphere Reserve, has only recently been protected against the aggressive policies of land development companies who have been exploiting the forest's valuable mahogany reserves since the 19th century.

Lacandón village (right) photographed in the early 20th century.

THE LACANDÓNS

The four hundred or so surviving Lacandóns who live in the forests of Chiapas have found themselves, unwittingly, at the center of a scientific controversy which has not yet been entirely resolved. For a long time they have been thought to be the direct

descendants of the Maya of the Classic period, heirs of the architects of Yaxchilán ▲ 248 and the artists of the temple frescos of Bonampak ▲ 250. Ethnologic and historical studies have shown that the Lacandóns of today are in fact descended from populations who migrated from the south of the Yucatán Peninsula and Petén during the 18th century. Although they refer to themselves as *Hach Winik* ("the True Men"), they are also referred to somewhat pejoratively as *Caribes* (cannibals) and *Lacandones*.

The term *Lacandones* is probably derived from Acam Tun, the name of an island in Lake Miramar applied, during the 16th century, to the whole of the forested region of East Chiapas, then inhabited by groups who remained unsubjugated by Spanish authority and were feared by the Christianized Indians of the highlands.

TOWARD OBLIVION? Whole areas of Lacandón mythology and ceremonial practices have been forgotten and only a few fragments of a complex pantheon dominated by Hachakyum the Creator, of the worship of censers, of the ritual use of *balché* (a fermented drink), and of the complex skills linked to hunting and fishing have survived. These people are mere shadows of their ancestors, caricatures of the last of the "noble savages". They are still exploited, nowadays by a lucrative tourist trade. In only a few years the fervor of evangelical pastors, the greed of hardwood extraction companies, and the brutal colonization of the Lacandón Forest by thousands of landless peasants have got the better of this original culture. In the words of Didier

ANIMAL SPIRITS
The little terracotta figurines made by the Lacandóns represent the animal spirits of the forest. They are both worshipped and feared, like the forest itself which is a source of life and danger for those who live there.

remanse: "[The *Hach Winik*] are the survivors of a lost world, an age that has disappeared for ever during which [they] lived free and at one with nature, lost and forgotten in the depths of the virgin forest. Their way of life may indeed have been harsh, and even cruel; but the tropical forest is kinder to Man than industrial civilization. And if one had to compare their past life with the life they lead at present and are likely to lead in the future, it would not be an exaggeration to say that the 'True Men' have been driven out of Paradise." (*Contes et mythologie des Indiens Lacandons*, 1986).

CENSERS. Only the Nahá Lacandóns still practise this form of worship. The clay censers bear the modeled effigy of a god and are arranged in a sanctuary separate from the people's dwellings. They are considered to be the permanent representatives of the gods among Man. During ceremonies they are placed in a row on a mat of palm fronds and offerings of incense and *balché* are made in support of a request or repay a beneficent act on the part of the gods concerning agriculture, health or a birth.

THE "BALCHÉ" RITUAL. *Balché*, prepared in a dugout canoe, is fermented from the sap of sugar cane or honey diluted in water in which strips of bark are left soaking for twenty-four hours. It is prepared and drunk for a number of different reasons and not on specific occasions. The *balché* ritual is performed to entreat or thank the gods, individually or collectively, and as such provides frequent opportunities for the men in the *paribal* (Lacandón community) to get together without their womenfolk and talk, drink and sing all day long. This propitiatory and communal ceremony is also seen as a test for those who may have transgressed certain common rules or codes of ethics. Vomiting as a result of drinking too much is not only thought of as an indication of guilt, but also is believed to be a process of purification.

"They all wore the same garment; a sort of wide tunic with short sleeves made of a very coarse but supple cotton cloth, spun and woven by the women. These tunics were marked with red stains which I took to be mud; but they had been made deliberately as a form of decoration, using the berries from a bush whose name I do not know."

Désiré Charnay
Voyage au Yucatán et au pays des Lacandons, 1882

An Olmec engravir
dating from 36 BC v
found on this site,
which was occupied
c. 1000 by the
Chiapanecs and, at
the beginning of th
16th century, by the
Aztecs. Chiapa de

FOUNTAIN OF CHIAPA DE CORZO
The fountain was the result of the extensive hydraulic work carried out during the colonial period. The monumental Mudejar fountain with its diamond-shaped bricks was built in 1562 by the Dominican friar, Fray Rodrigo de León. Today it is more of a kiosk than a fountain.

Corzo was the first town in the region to be conquered by t Spanish and remained the most important town in the province until the 18th century. The former agricultural wealth (sugar cane, livestock, tropical fruits) produced by t *fincas* has been replaced by intensive industrial activity.

DOMINICAN MONASTERY. The monastery's two cloisters represent two successive structures. On the first floor, a stucco mural (Dominican shields and pairs of hounds) evok the order of the brotherhood (the so-called "hounds of God"), protectors of the faith and Indian rights.

CHURCH OF SANTO DOMINGO. This huge edifice was origina the monastery chapel. The 16th-century church was serious damaged by natural catastrophes and badly restored during the 1960's.

CHURCH OF SAN SEBASTIAN. The remains of the church, abandoned during the 19th century, can be seen on the hill Atalaya. Its adobe colonnades and walls were flattened by a tornado in 1989.

TUXTLA GUTIÉRREZ

CAÑÓN DE SUMIDERO
Leave Tuxtla via the north bypass in the direction of Sumidero. The road winds steeply through the shanty town of La Granja and then on up the mountainside. It comes to a dead-end at 4,265 feet. The second route (25 miles) from Tuxtla follows the north bypass west as far as a summerhouse and then turns off right towards Chacona, San Fernando and Chicoasen. Beyond the tunnel the road overlooks the dam.

Originally Olmec territory and then an Aztec garrison ● 37 this colonial town was relatively unimportant until 1892 wh it became the capital of Chiapas ● 40. A regional museum traces the region's pre-Columbian history. Joaquín Miguel Gutiérrez (1796–1838), the son of a Spanish immigrant, bor in Tuxtla, who became a militant of the federalist cause and was a representative, governor and then *guerillero*, made the town into a liberal center and a "mapache" alternative duri the Revolution ● 41. With its 300,000 inhabitants, Tuxtla is the only town in Chiapas with modern urban developments parks, bypasses and 20th-century monuments built by famo contemporary Mexican architects. The Zoological Gardens with characteristic lowland vegetation contains fauna from Chiapas.

CAÑÓN DE SUMIDERO ★ ● 36. The canyon, situated to the north of Tuxtla Gutiérrez, can be visited by road from Tuxtl or by boat from Chiapa de Corzo or Cahuaré. Its rocky wal rise to a height of 4,900 feet. Three huge hydroelectric dams have been built to control the Grijalva, Mexico's second largest river, which used to constantly change its course.

Highlands
of Guatemala

▲ HIGHLANDS OF GUATEMALA

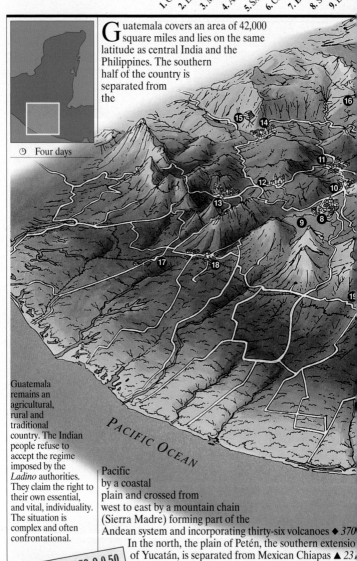

Guatemala covers an area of 42,000 square miles and lies on the same latitude as central India and the Philippines. The southern half of the country is separated from the

⏱ Four days

Guatemala remains an agricultural, rural and traditional country. The Indian people refuse to accept the regime imposed by the *Ladino* authorities. They claim the right to their own essential, and vital, individuality. The situation is complex and often confrontational.

PACIFIC OCEAN

Pacific by a coastal plain and crossed from west to east by a mountain chain (Sierra Madre) forming part of the Andean system and incorporating thirty-six volcanoes ◆ *370*

In the north, the plain of Petén, the southern extensio of Yucatán, is separated from Mexican Chiapas ▲ *23* by the great Usumacinta river. Guatemala lies on the point of convergence of three tectonic plates – the Pacific, North American and Caribbean plates – whose movement causes regular earthquakes.

CLIMATE. Guatemala has a hot, wet climate in the lowland areas and a more temperate climate in the highlands where its major towns and cities are located.

POPULATION. The population of Guatemala currently stands at ten million and is increasing a a rate of 2.9 percent per year. Its very unequal distribution – a sort of ethnic "mosaic" – is the legacy of the country's history. The Indian half the population, concentrated mainly in the

GUATEMALA AEREO Q.0.50

TRAJE TÍPICO DE COBÁN, ALTA VERAPAZ
FESTIVAL FOLKLORICO
NACIONAL
Cobán, Alta Verapaz
TALLER NAC · GRABADOS EN ACERO · GUATEMALA

hlands, consists of twenty-two ethnic groups
2. The other half is made up of mestizos or
dinos, either people of mixed race or
ultured Indians who have left their
ive communities for the capital, the
ge towns or the settlement areas of
rapaz ▲ *292* and Petén ▲ *317.* The
ites (3 percent) are directly descended
m Spanish and European stock.
ONOMY. Guatemala has a predominately
icultural economy based on coffee, sugar cane,
nanas, cotton and livestock. Remaining exports consist of
ustrial products sold to the countries of Central America.
her important resources, such as a wide range of semi-
cious stones, lead and marble, are still relatively
explored and unexploited. The only resource which is
rently being exploited is oil. It has been extracted in
rapaz and Petén since 1978.

After
centuries of colonial
domination, the
Indians are still a long
way from achieving
full citizenship in a
country dominated by
a form of
"apartheid".

263

The coat of arms of Guatemala City: three volcanos and a horseman.

The plaques showing the old Spanish street names are still there, but the names have been replaced with numbers ◆ *361* (right).

PALACIO NACIONAL
On the façade the national coat of arms shows a quetzal bird perched on the top of a parchment bearing the date of Independence (September 15, 1821). The parchment is framed by olive branches and rifles, the respective symbols of peace and national defence. The building is designed in composite style, but the interior patios are of Andalusian inspiration – their fountains and faience tiles add a touch of lightness to the stately grandeur of the palace.

Mosaic on a public bench.

The official name of Guatemala's relatively new capital Guatemala-de-la-Asunción, but is more often referred to as "the capital", "Guate" or "Guatemala-Ciudad" (Guatemala City). As it does not have any major attraction of its own, it is best incorporated into another visit, such as an excursion to Petén ▲ *317* or, better still, seen just before leaving Guatemala when its museums will complement earlier visits to the archeological sites.

HISTORY

FOUNDATION. The city was officially founded during a mass held on January 2, 1776 and placed under the patronage of the Virgin. While adopting the traditional layout of colonial towns ● *122*, it retained a neoclassic architectural style which broke with that tradition. After the 1871 Revolution, the French architectural style dominated but was largely erased by the earthquakes of December 1917 and January 1918.
MAJOR CONSTRUCTION WORK. The Belle Epoque style of which the Museo Nacional de Historia, the offices of the Banco Agricola Mercantil and the Hotel Fénix are fine examples, lasted for some time before it, too, was swept aside. A wave of major construction work produced public building which can still be seen today: the Palacio Nacional, the Central Post Office, Police Headquarters, the State Museum in Aurora Park ▲ *267* and, next to the museums, the more austere buildings of the General Directorate of Highways an Ministry of Communications. There are also examples of Ar Deco influence, for example the Lux cinema (6 Avenida), th

building of the Directorate of Public Health (9 Avenida) and the official presidential residence, behind the Palacio Nacional.
HAPHAZARD DEVELOPMENT. The type of building that predominates today is fairly uninteresting. The urban structure maintained during the 18th century – a plateau surrounded by ravines, which create a natural barrier against earth tremors – has burst wide open. One fifth of the city's estimated population of two and a half million, lives in the shanty towns built on the side of the ravines (*barrancos*).

PARQUE CENTRAL

PALACIO NACIONAL. The Palacio Nacional (president's palace), built between 1938 and 1943, stands on the north si of the central square. Today it houses the presidential office and several ministerial offices. On the second floor the reception rooms are decorated with stained-glass windows and the parquet floor is made from some of the most resista tropical hardwoods. The huge crystal chandelier is surmounted by bronze quetzals indicating the four points of the compass. The banqueting hall overlooking the central square has Mudejar-style paneled ceilings, two tapestries depicting the arrival of the Spanish and stained-glass windows celebrating the four cardinal virtues.
CATHEDRAL. The Baroque-style cathedral, built between 1782 and 1865, stands on the east side of th

> "A COLONIAL TOWN. IN ITS SANDY STREETS, THE VOICES OF CLERICS MUTTER AVE MARIAS, WHILE THE VOICES OF HORSEMEN AND CAPTAINS ARE RAISED IN ANGER, CALLING GOD AS THEIR WITNESS."
>
> MIGUEL ANGEL ASTURIAS

Mercado en dia de Corpus, Guatemala, C. A.

MERCADO CENTRAL
The Mercado Central lies below the central square. Its three levels include a craft section, a fruit and vegetable section and an underground section which sells traditionally made objects for everyday use and is well worth a visit. Early 20th-century views of the capital (left, top to bottom): the open-air market, the entrance to the covered market, the Calle Oriente and the Palacio del Centenario.

PRESIDENT BARRIOS
The Torre del Reformador (tower of the reformer) is a 245-foot iron tower, inspired by the Eiffel Tower in Paris, which straddles the 7 Avenida in Zona 9. It was built in 1935 in honor of General Barrios who undertook numerous reforms at the end of the 19th century.

PRINCIPAL THOROUGHFARES
Today, the parallel avenues, 6 and 7 Avenida, cross the city from one end to the other. The Pasaje Rubio, between the shopping arcade and 6 Avenida, was built at the end of the 19th century and based on the Parisian "galeries".

RELIEF MAP ★
This huge, open-air model of Guatemala and Belize, built in 1905, stands on a stone base and covers an area of 2,150 square yards. Its orientation exactly matches that of the country. The relief has been reproduced using 13 tonnes of cement and all the 550 yard contour lines have been marked. The railway lines are in nickel-plated lead and the water for the rivers comes from a reservoir below the peak of Xemal, the highest point in the Cuchumatanes range.

The central square of Guatemala City has been dominated by the cathedral since the 19th century. It stands opposite the Palacio Nacional.

central square. It was damaged by the earthquakes of 1917 and 1976. As well as sculptures and altars decorated with gold leaf, it also has a statue of the Virgin, Our Lady of Mercy, the oldest statue made in Guatemala. To the left of the entrance is a replica of the black Christ of Esquipulas ▲ *298*.

CITY CENTER

CHURCH OF SAN FRANCISCO. The church is built in a neoclassic, Italianate style, with a domed glass roof. It has a small museum with paintings of various martyrs. A black wo statue of Saint Benoît of Messina is the object of popular worship.

FORMER UNIVERSITY OF SAN CARLOS. The present neoclassi structure, opposite the Congreso de los Diputados (House Commons) on 7 Avenida, is the result of several major building phases (in 1810, 1850 and 1870 and repairs betwee 1918 and 1925). Although it was built as a university, the buildings were appropriated between 1823 and 1831 by the National Assembly of the United Provinces of Central America ● *39* and then by the Cámara de Representantes (House of Representatives) of the Republic of Guatemala. The National University was subsequently divided into seve independent faculties and the building was occupied by the Faculty of Law and in the 1960's the University moved to a campus south of the city.

MUSEO NACIONAL DE HISTORIA. This modest museum, hous in a period building in the city center, has an old-fashioned, provincial charm. It is the only museum provide general information, presented anecdotally, on events that the Guatemalans consider the high points of their history. There are objects and furniture from the colonial period and reminders of Independence (1821).

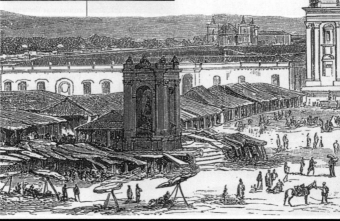

There is no shortage of public transport in the capital. "Recycled" school buses ◆ 354 from America are a common sight in Guatemala.

UTHERN DISTRICT

LYTECHNIC. The buildings formerly occupied by the War ice, with their medieval-style crenellations, date from the d of the 19th century. On the same side of the street, past intersection, the residence of the Minister of Defence is a ilar blend of neo-medieval, neo-Renaissance architecture. **SEO IXCHEL ● 89.** The Museo Ixchel, named after the yan goddess of weaving, opened its new building in early 4. Only part of its collection is on display as its spacious v accommodation is still being completed. Exhibitions vide a valuable complement to the rich overview of ditional Guatemalan textiles. Also on play are paintings of Mayan clothes textiles by Carmen Petersen. **SEO POPOL VUH ★.** The museum, ned after the sacred book of the ichés ● 146, has an exceptional ection of painted Mayan funerary s from Nebaj ▲ 289 and a fine ection of ceramic pieces. There are sections on ethnological and colonial igious art.

AURORA DISTRICT

SEO NACIONAL DE ARQUEOLOGÍA Y ETNOLOGIA ★. The seum is housed in a 1930's, neo-colonial style building. o of the museum's three wings have collections of the most utiful pieces from the country's different archeological es, while the third presents ethnological collections, ticularly textiles. An attractive, central patio contains Classic steles from Petén.
MUSEO NACIONAL DE ART MODERNO. With only a few exceptions the best examples of modern art are found in private galleries.

CENTRO CÍVICO
Built in the 1960s, the Centro Cívico houses various government ministries, the tourist office (INGUAT), the central bank and the national building society, as well as the fairly unprepossessing city hall.

TEATRO NACIONAL
The Miguel Angel Asturias cultural complex (above) was the last large-scale building project to be completed (1978) in the capital.

PINULA AQUEDUCT
The aqueduct was built by the Spanish towards the end of the 18th century to bring water to the new capital. Remains can still be seen in the La Aurora district, to the south of the city.

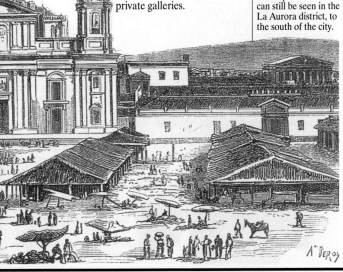

▲ HIGHLANDS OF GUATEMALA
AROUND GUATEMALA CITY

PLACE NAMES
Place names in
Guatemala are
usually composite,
with the name of a
saint (imposed by the
Spanish) preceding
the Indian name. A
commonly found
suffix is -tenango
which means "the
place of" or "the
place where ...
abounds". Names
therefore tend to be
long and difficult to
remember and there
is a tendency to
abbreviate them. So
the city of Guatemala
becomes "Guate" or
"la ciudad" (the city)
or "capital".
Chichicastenango is
shortened to "Chichi",
Panajachel to "Pana"
and Totonicapán to
"Toto". The Indian
place names are used
by the various
ethnic groups.

KAMINALJUYÚ

The valley of Guatemala City lies on the traditional route
from the north and has experienced a series of occupations.
The remains of Kaminaljuyú, now covered by the city's
northern suburbs, are evidence of the importance of the site
during the Preclassic period. Kaminaljuyú was at its height at
the same time as Teotihuacán ● 33 during the early centuries
AD, when it served as a staging post between the great
civilizations of central Mexico and the lowlands of Petén
▲ 317. The few surviving remains of this period have been
covered by haphazard urban development. Here and there a
mound, the ruins of an ancient pyramid, rises incongruously
between the houses, while an abandoned public garden can
offer an opportunity to explore what was once a great Maya
city. On the outskirts of the modern city (30 Avenida, Zone
7), the area around the largest of these mounds is now geared
toward tourists. Many objects found at Kaminaljuyú,
including this 5th-century vase (below), are on display in the
Museo Nacional de Arqueología ▲ 267.

MIXCO VIEJO

SAN PEDRO AND SAN JUAN SACATEPÉQUEZ. The
Sacatepéquez region has become an important
flower-producing area, growing roses,
carnations, chrysanthemums and
gladioli for export. The road
winds between greenhouses
covered with black plastic.
The inhabitants of
these villages, the most
"Indian" near the capital,
also weave baskets and
make pottery and
wooden furniture.
San Juan has a daily market
and is a hive of commercial
activity.
MIXCO VIEJO ★ ● 117.
Mixco Viejo dates from the
Late Postclassic period (also
known as the Protohistoric)
and was the Pokomam
capital at the time of the
Conquest ● 36. This
defensive site comprises at
least twelve groups of
structures built on leveled
hilltops or on rocky spurs
surrounded by deep ravines.
The village population lived
on the slopes and withdrew to
the hilltops during times of
emergency. The site consists of
edifices arranged around large
well-paved squares with a central
altar; elongated, rectangular
structures with several

268

> "OUR PEOPLE WILL NEVER BE DISPERSED. THEIR DESTINY WILL TRIUMPH OVER THE DISASTROUS DAYS THAT WILL OCCUR AT AN NOWN POINT IN THEIR HISTORY. THERE WILL ALWAYS BE A SPECIAL PLACE ON THIS EARTH THAT WE HAVE OCCUPIED." POPOL VUH

oms; twin temples built on top of the same pyramidal base d reached via a broad staircase flanked by large balustrades d divided by a central, sloping ramp which becomes vertical st before the summit; and platforms designed to support veral temples, which stood side by side and were reached a a number of staircases. Large earthenware storage jars re found buried beneath the floors of the houses. The komams cremated their dead and the ashes were placed in ge, triple-handled, polychrome (white decoration on a red ound) or monochrome earthenware jars.

HINAUTLA

is Pokomam village, to the north of the capital, produces a be of low-fired, unpainted, red or cream pottery decorated th lozenges and inlaid work. Articles include large and all plant-pot holders in the form of birds and the Nativity enes popular in Guatemala.

SCUINTLA

MATITLÁN. The "place of the Amates" (fig trees) is the name both the town and the lake. The lake (5 square miles) is the arest to Guatemala City and has for a long time been a pular resort for relaxation with the city's inhabitants. spite of an alarmingly high level of pollution (sewage works not exist in Guatemala), on Sundays its beach and expensive restaurants are completely engulfed by crowds of ople from the capital. To the north and west, the altitude ,260 feet) and climate favor the cultivation of ffee, tobacco and sugar cane (processed in e nearby refineries).

OLCAN PACAYA ★ ◆ *370*. Several of the ung cones in this complex volcanic nge are still active, particularly the 530-foot cone to the southwest. though Volcan Pacaya is easily reached two hours of fairly unstrenuous walking om the village of San Francisco de Sales, tential visitors to the volcano should always ercise extreme caution. Sudden resurgences of lcanic activity often lead to the frequent evacuation of e surrounding villages and the release of toxic gases is gularly recorded.

ALIN ★. The Pokomam village of Palín is famous for its vast d beautiful silk-cotton tree ● *64*, dating from the early days colonial rule. Its spectacular branches provide shade for e market held in the square.

ESCUINTLA
Escuintla lies on the Pacific plain ▲ *290*, at the foot of the mountains (above). Its status as a leading commercial center is reinforced by its position at the intersection of the Pacific Highway (running to Mexico and El Salvador) and the main road linking the capital to the ports of San José and Puerto Quetzal. Escuintla is also an important railway junction, with one branch running westwards and the other south to service the ports. To the south of the town is the country's only mineral oil refinery (Texaco), while several other refineries in the vicinity produce cotton seed oil.

MIXCO VIEJO
A marker with a horizontal tenon was found in one of the I-shaped ball courts ● *112*, of Mixco Viejo. Part of the marker was sculpted with a human head in the open jaws of a serpent.

STREET SCENES
Indians selling their
wares, the paved
streets, the
monuments and the
colors of the houses
all contribute to
creating the special
atmosphere of
Antigua.

Antigua Guatemala stands in the center of the Panchoy valley, at an altitude of 5,000 feet, surrounded by mountains and volcanos: Agua (12,300 feet), Acatenango (12,990 feet) and Fuego (12,470 feet). This former capital of the Captaincy General is a fine example of colonial urban architecture, a little too artificial for some tastes. Once the seat of the colonial metropolitan, religious and civil authorities, today Antigua is a city of some 25,000 inhabitant and, although quiet during the week, is a popular place for weekend visits. Originally called Santiago de los Caballeros, Antigua Guatemala was founded in 1543 and remained the capital of Guatemala for 232 years, until the transfer of powe to Guatemala City following the 1773 earthquake ▲ 264.

HISTORY

ADMINISTRATIVE CAPITAL.
The administrative district
that lay between the vice-
royalties of New Spain
(Nueva España) in the

north (now Mexico), and New Granada (Nueva Granada) in the south (modern Colombia), was known variously as the kingdom of Guatemala (Reyno de Guatemala) or the Captaincy General. It was administered by a Captain General, a governor whose powers were equivalent to those of a viceroy, but which were tempered by two influences. One was the presence of a royal tribunal, the Audiencia de los Confines ● 37, a legislative and judicial body created in 1543 the other was the local power of the *criollos* – white Guatemalans of Spanish stock.

RELIGIOUS POWER. The bishops played a key role in the political, economic, social and cultural life of the colony. There was no shortage of religious orders in Antigua: Franciscans, Dominicans, Mercedarians and Jesuits, as well a Carmelites, Franciscan nuns, nuns of the order of St Clare (Clarisses) and Capuchins. In 1773, there was a total of thirty eight monasteries and convents, fifteen chapels and oratories and several hermitages. The University of San-Carlos-Borromeo (1676) was the third to be founded on the continent after those of Mexico and Lima. By 1773, the population had reached sixty thousand (*intra muros*) with thirty thousand in the surrounding villages.

ARCHITECTURE ★

The city's architectural development can only be understood when put in context with the earthquakes that shake it periodically. The effects of those which followed its

undation between 1590 and 1650 meant that little building
was done during this period. Designs and techniques were
always based on the need for solidity. In view of its turbulent
story, it is extremely difficult to establish an exact
chronology of the construction, destruction, renovation and
reconstruction of the city's monuments. Paradoxically, the
earthquake of 1773 and subsequent transfer of power
probably helped to save the city from a development that
could have totally destroyed its character.

PLAZA MAYOR

In 1543 the Italian architect Antonelli designed the city's
checkerboard layout around the Plaza Mayor. Although its
gardens were redesigned in 1993, the so-called Fountain of
the Sirens (1739) still stands in the center.

CITY HALL. The City Hall, officially opened in 1743, has a
freestone façade and a double arcature. There is a splendid
view from the balcony.

MUSEO DE SANTIAGO. The museum, situated on the first floor
of the City Hall around a central patio and fountain, has
exhibits from the colonial period, paintings, and weapons,
some of which were used during the 1871 Revolution, while
others are from the Castillo of San Felipe ▲ *312*.

MUSEO DEL LIBRO ANTIGUO. This building once housed
Central America's first printing press, imported by Bishop
Payo Enríquez de Riviera in 1660. The museum has a replica
press and printing examples from the 16th to 19th centuries.

ARCHBISHOP'S PALACE. All that has survived of this two-story
palace (access via the cathedral), built between 1706 and
1711, are the remains of the cloister and a few columns. The
see was made an archiepiscopacy by Benoît XIV in 1743. A
restored room on the façade houses the cultural center.

CATHEDRAL. The cathedral, consecrated in c. 1565, was badly
damaged by several earthquakes. After the 1773 earthquake,
only the façade (restored in 1986–7), with its carved spandrel
and numerous saints' niches, and the first three bays could be
saved. Today it is used as a parish church.

PALACE OF THE CAPTAINS GENERAL. The residence and offices
of the Captain General also housed the royal tribunal, the
Mint, the offices of the military authorities, the dragoons'
quarters, the royal chapel and prisons. Built from 1549
onward, it was renovated and extended several times. The
buildings, restored in the mid-19th century, today serve as the
tourist office, the police headquarters and the administrative
offices for the region of Sacatepéquez, of which Antigua
is the capital.

MERCHANTS' AND BAKERS' GALLERY. The gallery, on
the west side of the square, once symbolized the
prosperity of the
merchants of
Antigua.

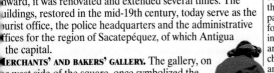

OTHER MONUMENTS

MUSEO DE ARTE COLONIAL ★
Antigua prided itself on havi[ng]
the third university founded i[n]
Spanish America: San Carlos
(1676). Initially it occupied t[he]
Colegio de Santo Tomás
Aquino before this building
was completed in 1763.
Although the earthquakes of
1773 did not really affect its
thick walls, it had to move in
1776. Four galleries surround[
single, central courtyard who[se]
composite arches are
reminiscent of the Mudejar
style. The Museo de Arte
Colonial took up residence i[n]
1936 and has a collection of
Guatemalan paintings and
polychrome sculptures from
the city's churches.

CONVENT OF SANTA CATALINA
Founded in 1613, the conven[t]
was the smallest of the eleven religious complexes existing a[t]
the time, and the second convent for women. In 1694 an arc[h]
was built across the street to link it with newly acquired land
on the other side. The church was completed in 1647.

CHURCH OF LA MERCED. The Mercedarian order were the
first to build a monastery after the Conquest. They settled
initially in Ciudad Vieja ▲ 275, remaining there for two
hundred years before their monastery was built in Antigua.
Having observed the effects of the 1751 earthquake, the
architect constructed a squat building, with particularly thick
walls and small, high-placed windows. Inaugurated in 1767, s[ix]
years later it was badly damaged by earthquakes. Today the
restored church is flanked by two low towers and has a
lavishly decorated, stuccoed façade. All that remains of the
monastery is a huge pool and fragments of walls.

MONASTERY OF SAN JERONIMO (ROYAL CUSTOMS HOUSE).
Because it had not been granted prior royal authorization, th[e]
vast two-story college, built by the Mercedarians between
1739 and 1745, was confiscated in 1761 and
converted into a customs house, then a barracks.

CONVENT OF LA MONASTERY. All that remains of
this monastery, restored in 1978, is a kitchen,
fountain and refectory. It may have been
used as an infirmary or orphanage.

JESUIT MONASTERY. This included an entire
block of houses inhabited, among others, by
Bernal Díaz del Castillo. Beyond the square,
cluttered with stands displaying traditional
crafts, the façade still bears traces of painted
floral and geometric motifs.

MONASTERY OF SAN AGUSTIN. This church
and monastery was founded in 1657,
destroyed by an earthquake and rebuilt
in 1735.

HOLY WEEK
Holy Week
celebrations are
particularly
spectacular in the
colonial setting of
Antigua. As well as
the Antigueños, they
also attract crowds of
visitors ● 74.
Magnificent carpets
of colored sawdust
and flower petals
cover the ground
along the route of the
processions ▲ 271,
which advance to the
sound of funeral
marches. Palm
Sunday is celebrated
amidst a forest of
palm branches. The
processions begin on
Maundy Thursday.

**CROSS AND FOUNTAIN
OF LA MERCED**
The cross stands
opposite the church
of La Merced and
bears two dates: 1688,
inscribed in a heart-
shaped escutcheon,
and 1765, on the
base. A fountain
(probably 17th
century) to the right
of the façade used to
belong to the
Franciscan cloister.

PEDRO DE BETANCOURT

...ro de Betancourt (1626–67), buried in the transept of the ...rch of San Francisco, is one of the most revered religious figures in Central America. He led an exemplary life of ...votion and charity and was beatified in 1981. The votive ...ferings around his former sepulcher are evidence of the degree to which he is venerated.

N JOSÉ EL VIEJO. This hermitage, ...mpleted in 1761, is a fine example of ...thquake-resistant architecture. Its low ...lls are strengthened by small, low ...vers incorporated into the façade.

...ONASTERY OF SANTA CLARA. The ...nastery was begun in 1700 and ...mpleted in 1715. The then Captain ...neral provided the funds for the ...urch which was consecrated in 1734 ...d, unusually, opens onto the monastery ...ther than onto the street.

...nfortunately there is not enough room ... stand back and admire its sculpted ...ade as an inn has been built on the ...urch square. The two-story cloister is ...e of the largest in the city.

...ONASTERY OF SAN FRANCISCO. This ...anciscan monastery, which has stood ... the site since 1543, was completed in ...25. The church has been rebuilt several ...es. Its façade is decorated like a ...able, with stuccoed columns, and is ...nked by two massive towers. The altars ...ar the side entrance illustrate scenes ...m the Old Testament. The retables ...d the cherubs on the ceiling are fine ...mples of local Baroque.

...ONASTERY OF SANTO DOMINGO. Built in ...42, this monastery was the largest and ...althiest in the city, as well as the ...ellectual center. Its ruins have been ...ned into a hotel and restaurant (Casa ...nto Domingo) where some of its ...nishings and works of art remain.

A RELIGIOUS CITY
From top to bottom: the churches of San Francisco, a neighboring village and Los Remedios, the arch of Santa Catalina, the church of La Merced and Antigua cathedral.

...NVENT OF LAS CAPUCHINAS. This was ...e last convent to be built in Antigua. ...e increasing influence of the Capuchin ...der was interrupted by the earthquake ... 1773 and the vast buildings were ...cupied by only twenty-eight nuns. ...yond the main cloister, with its massive ...lumns and pointed segmental arches, ...e Torre del retiro consists of eighteen ...lls for spiritual retreats and novices. A ...aircase leads to an underground room ...ose central pillar supports the floor of ...e circular courtyard. It is thought that it ...y have been used as a pantry although ...s the only known example (cellars were ...e more common during the colonial ...riod than they are today).

...URCH OF EL CARMEN. The church's ...o-story façade is one of the most ...autiful in the city and is best admired ... the morning light. In places the brick is ...ible beneath the stuccoed geometric ...otifs on the pairs of pillars. The church ...s consecrated in 1728.

Antigua has a number of shops to interest visitors, including art galleries and jade workshops which sell jewelry and jade ornaments.

COFFEE "FINCAS"
You only have to visit the environs of Antigua to realize just how much coffee is grown on the floor and slopes of the valley. The occasional owner's residence can be seen nestling amidst the vast *fincas*, beneath the trees whose shady foliage shelters the coffee shrubs. Industrial activity is limited to the Nestlé fruit-processing plant on the outskirts of Antigua toward Ciudad Vieja, and the Hunapú cotton mill in the city.

"CASAS" OF ANTIGUA GUATEMALA ★

Although they may not have the grandeur of the religious buildings, Antigua's private residences owe their charm to their single stories, their pastel-colored façades and high, often whitewashed walls, literally overflowing with flowering shrubs. The urban landscape is characterized by massive car gateways, pinnacle turrets and high windows with iron or turned-wood grilles. Inside patios are often converted into gardens, bordered with galleries and wooden pillars. Antigua has much in common with San Cristóbal de las Casas ▲ 233.

CASA DE LOS LEONES. A beautiful door, with an entablature flanked by lions, has been added to this late 17th-century aristocratic residence. Today it is one of three restored residences functioning as a hotel.

CASA POPENOE. Built during the first half of the 17th century this private house has been restored and authentically furnished. It is open to the public.

CASA K'OJOM (MUSIC MUSEUM). The museum has a small display of pre-Hispanic instruments including conches, whistles and turtle shells, as well as Spanish musical instruments from marimbas (a kind of xylophone) to calabash (*tecomates*) and simple sound boxes● 78. There is also a reproduction of the Maximón of Santiago Atitlán ● 72 ▲ 281.

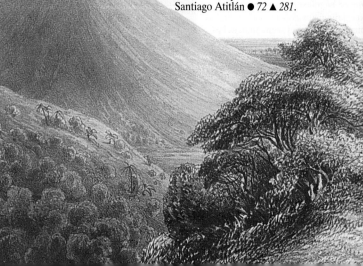

RO DEL MANCHÉN (CERRO DE LA CRUZ)
questrian statue of Santiago, the patron saint
e Reconquest, the Conquest of America and
city, stands on top of this hill which offers a
ndid view of the Antigua valley. The statue
a gift from Spain.

ROUND ANTIGUA

N JUAN DEL OBISPO. Lying at the foot
the Volcán Agua, this village developed
und the 16th-century residence built for Bishop
rroquín. The church and monastery complex has retained
original appearance.

NTA MARIA DE JESÚS. This village was founded at the end
the 16th century by the Indians brought from
etzaltenango ▲ 282. The inhabitants used to transport
od from their forests to the town, which earned the village
original name of El Aserradero (the sawmill). The village
he departure point for the ascent of Volcán Agua.

N ANTONIO AGUASCALIENTES. This village is famous for its
aving. The cloth used to make its *huipiles* ● 94 is decorated
both sides with geometric bird and flower motifs.

OTENANGO. The Pipil dialect is still spoken in the village. It
ed to be situated on the road which ran between the Agua
d Fuego volcanos and linked the colonial capital with
cuintla ▲ 269. The Baroque church dates from the end of
17th century.

N FELIPE DE JESÚS. The village church, founded in 1430,
s rebuilt in 1850 in neo-Gothic style
th stones re-used from the church of
Merced ▲ 272. It houses an
onymous recumbent Christ.
grims come here on the first Friday of
nt and throughout Holy Week.

NTIGUA TO CHIMALTENANGO

secondary road leaves Antigua via the
lle Ancha de los Herreros toward
imaltenango. It goes through the village of Jocotenango
ere the square has a fine late-17th-century baroque church.

N ANDRÉS ITZAPA. About 2 miles from the road,
e village of San Andrés Itzapa has a
nctuary dedicated to Maximón ● 72,
281 who is venerated by Indians and
dinos alike. Families visit the
nctuary to offer candles, incense
d cigarettes and ask for help,
ure, or forgiveness.

CIUDAD VIEJA
There is still
disagreement over
the exact site of the
first Spanish town.
According to one
theory Ciudad Vieja,
at the foot of the
Volcán Agua, stands
on the site of the
former capital
(1527–41). However,
recent excavations
tend to suggest that it
lay about a mile to
the east, at San
Miguel Escobar.

PATZÚN
When the Franciscans settled here in 1540 they brought with them a statue of Saint Bernardino of Siena, who became the patron saint of the village. During the Corpus Christi festival the streets of Patzún (below) are covered with flowers and colored sawdust arranged in wonderful patterns. Arches of vegetables are erected at the intersections.

This child from Sololá is wearing the local costume: striped trousers, a woollen apron and "western" style shirt.

SUMPANGO
The 16th-century parish church was badly damaged in the 1976 earthquake – its square shape, large buttresses and low towers and pediment were not enough to protect it. It has since been restored. On November 1, the inhabitants of Sumpango, like those of Santiago Sacatepéquez, fly huge kites.

SANTIAGO SACATEPÉQUEZ. This village of five thousand inhabitants is famous for its All Souls' Day (Day of the Dead) celebration ● 74. The ancient tradition of making and flying huge kites on November 1 is thought to be based on a legend which tells of demons invading the cemetery and disturbing the sleep of the dead. An old sage from the village suggested that the demons could be frightened away by the noise of rustling paper, so the decision was taken to fly kites in the rising winds of November and the custom began. Other explanations take into consideration the astronomical knowledge of the Maya, the traditional use of bright colors in clothing, art and crafts, and the climatic changes that take place in the highlands of Guatemala at the end of October. These changes are characterized by the end of the rains, strong winds, clear skies and a drop in temperature. The kites are made several weeks in advance by families and groups of friends, Indians and mestizos, using bamboo for the ribs and paper for the sails. Their diameter can be anything from 6 to 26 feet.

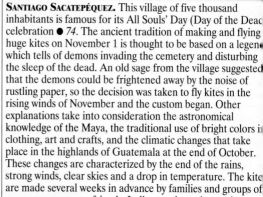

CHIMALTENANGO ▲ 275. Chimaltenango means the "town of the walls" in Nahuatl while its Cakchiquel ● 63 inhabitants call it Bocob, (meaning shield). Like all the villages on the high central plateaux, it was badly damaged by the earthquake of 1976 and rebuilt with materials paid for by foreign aid. Although they were cheaper and more resistant to earthquakes, these materials were not as comfortable or esthetic as the traditional adobe and tiles.

COMALAPA. The monastery was founded by the Clarisses in the 17th century and was designed as a place in which the monks could take refuge and store their belongings in the event of an earthquake. The building fulfilled its purpose in 1717 and 1773. All that remains is the church with its beautiful Baroque façade, badly damaged in 1976 and subsequently restored. A tradition of primitive painting ● 132 depicts the traditions and customs of everyday life in the village. These works can be seen in the village or in the galleries of Antigua and Guatemala.

IXIMCHÉ. For three years (1524–7) following the truce agreed with Alvarado ● 36, the Cakchiquel capital was also the Spanish capital. The Mayan site, an example of the Postclassic ceremonial center, was restored in the 1960's by the Guillemin. The site occupies a narrow promontory between two ravines. The promontory was dissected by an artificial moat which separated the ceremonial and aristocratic center in the east from the large area occupied by the "commoners". A series of four ceremonial squares, constituting separate groups, occupies the upper part of the promontory. Two of the groups have a ball court. Little remains of the structures, as the columns and walls were made of adobe. Polychrome paintings on a layer of stucco have been discovered on some of the surviving remains. A sacrificial stone used for tearing out hearts and an offering of skulls from decapitated victims provide evidence of human sacrifice ● 46.

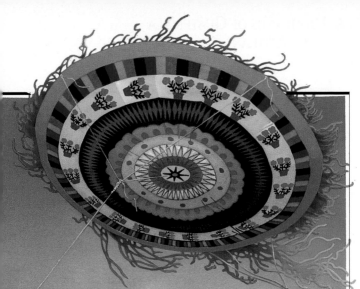

SANTA APOLONIA. Beyond this small pottery-producing village, the road winds through the valleys and along the rocky slopes of the Sierra Madre before climbing (mirador of Lake Atitlán) towards the major intersection of Los Encuentos (78 miles). Here a road to the right leads to the Quiché region ▲ *286* and about 2 miles further on is the road to Sololá and Lake Atitlán.

SOLOLA. Situated on the border of the Cakchiquel and Quiché regions, Sololá constitutes an important link between the mountain economy and the tropical production of the Pacific coast ▲ *290*. As well as the usual food crops, potatoes, carrots, radishes, beetroot, peaches and apples are grown. The large covered market is organized in sections – utensils, industrial items, meat, basic products and clothes – and gives a clear picture of the consumer habits of the rural population.

A great variety of motifs appear on the All Souls' Day kites. They may be inspired by Mayan symbols and divinities, depict scenes of everyday life or even bear images of modern-day personalities.

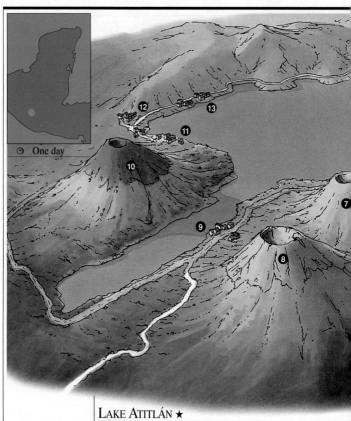

LAKE ATITLÁN ★

ORIGINS. According to some geologists, the lake was forme as a result of the appearance about eighty thousand years a; of a volcano to the west of the present depression. Three volcanos (**7, 8, 10**) emerged from the water in its crater, giv the lake its characteristic kidney-bean shape. They were followed, at the foot of Tolimán, by the smaller Cerro de O (**6**), a volcano in the process of being formed and where, according to legend, the Tzutuhils hid their treasure when t Spanish arrived. Although the depth of the lake shown on maps is in the region of 1,050 feet, surveys carried out in the 1960's estimated the depth near San Lucas Tolimán to be 1,970 feet. It is thought that the water drains by undergrour seepage toward the Pacific plain. The 1976 earthquake caus

the faults at the southeastern end of th lake to widen and the water level to dr by 16 feet.

CLIMATIC CHANGES. The prevailing win on the lake – the *xocomil* – blows in the afternoon from the southeast. Toward end of the year cold north winds clear sky, giving it the purity so sought-after photographers. *Tumberías*, whirlwinds caused by winds blowing from opposite directions, can form dangerous troughs

⊙ One day

FISH AND BOATS
Although there is an abundance of fish in the lake, there is little variety. The carnivorous blackbass, introduced in the 1960's, has wiped out all other species except the mojarra, a small fish with white flesh and very fine bones, served grilled or fried in restaurants. Fishing is done with a line, early in the

up to 6 feet deep on the lake and are much feared ɪshermen. Among the many legends ‌ting to these meteorological ‍nomena is that of a wicked giant who ‌d only be destroyed by the combined ‌ngth of the villagers. The limbs of the ‌ɪembered giant were shared out and displayed in the ‌lic squares of the villages. The village which had the head ‌w tired of the trophy and threw it into the lake. Since then, ‌ry afternoon the giant is said to take his revenge by ‌wing fiercely from the watery depths and endangering the ‌ll fishing boats.

‌ɪNOMY. The villages on the lake's eastern shore lie on the ‌der of the Cakchiquel ● 63 region. Like their Tzutuhil ‌nterparts in the south and west, they are prevented from ‌ducing large food crops by the steepness of the slopes and ‌shortage of land. Families limit their own food ‌ısumption so that they can sell more and make the ‌itional income necessary to buy indispensable industrial ‌ducts. The drop in the level of the lake has in fact released ‌ile land along its shores. Onions, introduced in the 1960's, ‌now widely cultivated and complement the traditional ‌ing industry, with mojarra and blackbass, being sold at ‌ket or direct to the restaurants of Panajachel. Another ‌ɪortant source of income is tourism, either in the form of ‌ges paid to hotel and restaurant staff or for the production ‌raditional craft items ● 84 sold on the stands lining the ‌ets of the villages, in the capital or abroad.

morning, from *cayucos*, small dugout canoes whose sides are raised with five lateral planks (top). The handles at the back are used to haul them up onto the beach, and a small bench about mid-way along gives the fisherman somewhere to sit. These boats can be seen along the lake shores, their bottoms filled with leaves to maintain humidity.

Doing the washing at San Lucas Tolimán (above).

TRADITIONAL CRAFTS
The *huipiles* and trousers of Santiago Atitlán are embroidered with animal motifs (birds, rabbits and fish), arranged between vertical and horizontal lines against a white ground (top, opposite page).

Many of the inhabitants are versed in the art of painting primitive portraits and scenes of everyday life (the market, picking coffee beans and cotton, the village streets). The master of this distinctive "school" of painting was Juan Sisay, assassinated in 1992 for taking too much interest in the development of his village community and the life of its inhabitants. The more recently developed art of wood carving produces figures of fishermen, weavers, porters or women cooking *tortillas*, birds, fish and crabs (*jaiba*), and elegant and unusually shaped little boxes with mysterious drawers.

LAKE CIRCUIT
It is possible to complete a circuit of the lake on foot. Various guides and travel agents organize excursions ◆ *366*.

ON THE SHORES OF THE LAKE

SAN JORGE LA LAGUNA. During the 19th century the inhabitants took corn and vegetables down to the Pacific pl[a] where they bartered them for cocoa and sugarcane molasse[s] The village still has its Maximón ● *72*.

PANAJACHEL. Those interested enough to climb to the mark[et] and church (below), in the village center, will discover the traditional face of the Cakchiquel village of Panajachel. Th[e] other "Pana", decried by the very visitors who contribute to [its] artificiality, has indeed become a tourist center. There are boats available fo[r] hire to take touris[ts] across the lake.

SANTA CATARINA PALOPO AND SAN ANTONIO PALOPO. Onion crops and irrigated gardens occupying tiny parcels of land ar[e] the main forms of agricultural activity. Most of the buildings are orientated in the same way, with a door on the north or south side and a small window overlooking the lake. The other main activitie[s] are weaving, for both domestic use and the local tourist industry, fishing and producing mats and cushions (*petates*) woven out of reeds (*tul*).

SAN LUCAS TOLIMAN. This important village has the advantage of being linked both to the *altiplano* road networ[k] and to the Pacific coast, which makes it the gateway to Santiago Atitlán.

SANTIAGO ATITLÁN. Santiago Atitlán, whose name means "flower of the nations", is the main town in the Tzutuhil region and successor to the capital of the ancient kingdom which shared its name. Today nothing remains of ancient Chuitinamit, which was situated on the far side of the bay. Although the village itself has become a much-visited tourist center, it is still possible to appreciate the richness and diversity of its traditional ⟨cra⟩fts. The local divinity, Maximón ● 72, has the upper hand ⟨ov⟩er the Catholic Church, although he did not make his first ⟨ap⟩pearance until the end of the 18th century. There are ⟨se⟩veral founding myths concerning his creation. For a long ⟨tim⟩e he was shrouded in mystery, only appearing to the ⟨fai⟩thful during Holy Week and always eclipsing Christ during ⟨th⟩e spectacular village ceremonies. Maximón has provided a ⟨co⟩nsiderable source of income for the members of the Santa ⟨Cr⟩uz brotherhood who display him between a recumbent ⟨Ch⟩rist and crucifixes (below). Santiago is a real hotbed of ⟨In⟩dian resistance and, like many other villages in the region, ⟨ha⟩s suffered from violent repression ⟨du⟩ring recent years. This spiritually rich ⟨vil⟩lage has about thirty chapels. There ⟨ar⟩e more than ninety, often ⟨fu⟩ndamentalist, sects in Guatemala, not ⟨to⟩ mention the original traditional ⟨bel⟩iefs, while catechization is often ⟨un⟩derpinned by fairly unsubtle forms of ⟨in⟩doctrination.

⟨SA⟩N PEDRO LA LAGUNA. The village of ⟨Sa⟩n Pedro is very similar to Santiago. ⟨It h⟩as the same houses, built of volcanic ⟨roc⟩k with corrugated iron roofs; the ⟨sam⟩e steam baths (*temascal*) in the yard, ⟨wh⟩ere the family washes in a way which ⟨is b⟩oth hygienic and ritualistic; the same ⟨tw⟩o-story houses belonging to the ⟨no⟩*uveau-riche* merchants, carriers and ⟨ém⟩igrés who have made money abroad; ⟨an⟩d, finally, the same population which ⟨is⟩ gradually opening up to outside ⟨inf⟩luences, both national and foreign. San Pedro is also ⟨po⟩pular with hippies, who consider Panajachel far too ⟨po⟩lluted by tourism.

⟨SA⟩N JUAN LA LAGUNA. This sleepy village is like an extension ⟨of⟩ San Pedro. In fact many of San Juan's peasants rent land ⟨fro⟩m the village of San Pedro. There is a modern church ⟨wh⟩ich has little aesthetic appeal, but the adjoining town hall is ⟨ch⟩arming and has retained its old, individually hand-carved, ⟨wo⟩oden pillars. The landscape surrounding San Juan la ⟨La⟩guna is dotted with coffee-drying "patios" dominated by ⟨ne⟩arby pulpers and hoppers.

⟨SA⟩N PABLO LA LAGUNA. This is a strange little village with no ⟨we⟩ekly market. Most of the houses still have their original ⟨ad⟩obe walls and thatched roofs. The agave (sisal) grown on ⟨the⟩ hillsides is the raw material for the main activity of San ⟨Pa⟩blo: rope-making.

SAN MARCOS LA LAGUNA
This lakeside village, divided in two by the football pitch and the school, lies partly on a fairly large plateau and partly on the hillside. The old adobe church has just been demolished, no doubt to make way for a new place of worship. The rows of pine and avocado seedlings on the shores of the lake are part of a reforestation project. There is also a scheme to revive the use of medicinal plants among the villagers.

NAHUALÁ
A few miles northwest of the lake, the inhabitants of Nahualá quarry the basalt used to make millstones (*metates*). The villagers also make simply decorated pine furniture and painted wood sculptures reminiscent of the colonial era.

TOTONICAPÁN

San Miguel Totonicapán is a large, busy
village situated at an altitude of 8,200
feet. It is the main town in the region of
Totonicapán and lies in the center of a
very densely populated valley. Its main
activities are traditional crafts ● *84* and
commerce. The church of San Cristóbal
Totonicapán prides itself on its 17th-

CUATRO TERMINOS
This major
intersection services
Totonicapán 9 miles
to the north and
Quetzaltenango and
its valley to the west.
The road continues
west to
Huehuetenango
▲ *284* and the border
post of La Mesilla
(Mexico), and into
Chiapas ▲ *231*. Fruit-
growers' stalls sell
organically grown
apples, pears, small
peaches (*duraznos*)
and sweet candied
fruits.

century paintings. Like all the *huipiles* in the Totonicapán
basin, the local *huipil* has retained the lace collar added by the
Spanish ● *97*. The houses of San Andrés Xecul, nestling at
the foot of the hill, still have adobe walls and tiled roofs. The
church has a multicolored dome and its naive painted enamel
façade, decorated with cherubs, tropical fruits and the lions of
the Spanish crown (above) is one of the village's main
attractions. However, the paved streets leading up to the
chapel and calvary, which stand next to a Mayan sanctuary
● *66*, are also worth a visit. In the forest beyond, the mouth of
a sacred cave where Indian priests officiate, can be seen mid-
way up the hillside. Maximón is also venerated at San Andrés
● *72*, ▲ *281*.

QUETZALTENANGO

Quetzaltenango's Quiché name, Xelajú, is still used but is
usually abbreviated to Xela (pronounced "chéla").
THE SECOND REGIONAL TOWN. Quetzaltenango has no major
attractions but is nonetheless a charming place. There is a
contrast between the impressive volcanic stone and freestone
architecture of the monuments in its main square (including
the city hall, the museum of history and natural history and
the Banco de Occidente), and the modesty of the neighboring
streets which are often still paved and lined with tiny adobe
houses. The opulent structures built during the late 19th-
century coffee boom are still characterized by a certain rural
traditionalism.

SALCAJÁ
The village of Salcajá
is situated between
San Cristóbal
Totonicapán and
Quetzaltenango. Its
church, the first to be
founded in
Guatemala, stands off
the main street, to the
right, in a pretty
square. Although it
has been renovated,
the façade still has its
original naive
decorations.

HISTORY. The town
was founded by
Pedro de Alvarado
● *36* on May 15,
1524. After the
declaration of
Independence and
the brief attachment
of the newly created

es to the Mexican empire of Agustín de Iturbide, in
8–40 western Guatemala formed the Estado de los Altos,
sixth state in the Federation of Central America. Towards
end of the 19th century the production of coffee led to the
elopment of roads and ports, and the country's oldest
k, the Banco de Occidente, was founded in
etzaltenango in 1883 (view of the town in 1896, below).
NUMENTS. The beautiful Parque de Centroamérica
tral square) is surrounded by neoclassical buildings
hedral, city hall and cultural center) built in volcanic
e. Opening onto the square is the Pasaje Enríquez,
igned in 1900 using the Parisian *passages* as a model. The
domed cathedral, rebuilt in 1899, has retained the façade
ly slightly offset) of the former Catedral del Espíritu
to, built in 1535 and destroyed by an earthquake. The
sa de la Cultura houses a small history museum on the first
or and a natural history museum on the second. The
classical theater has a beautiful, colonnaded façade.

OUND QUETZALTENANGO

RRO EL BAÚL. This hill offers a splendid view of
etzaltenango and the valley.
NIL. In the chancel of this town's huge church, the silver
oussé tabernacle and altar front date from the colonial
iod. Crops, predominately onions, are grown in the river
d which is littered with huge basalt rocks spewed out by the
cán Zunil. The impressive Cerro Quemado and Santa
ría volcanos can be seen from the valley when it is not
ouded in mist. Maundy Thursday procession in Zunil
low, opposite).
ENTES GEORGINAS. One of the
ings rising on the slopes of
Volcán Zunil has been
nneled and harnessed.
wever, the formerly
h temperatures of
source are
creasing and today
not exceed 95°F.
thing is permitted and
ommodation is
ilable.

WARD SAN MARCOS

N JUAN OSTUNCALCO. The village, the home of Jesús
stillo who composed music for the marimba ● 78,
cializes in wicker furniture.
N MARTÍN SACATEPÉQUEZ. This Mam village, at the foot of
Volcán Chicabal, was once quite an important center. In
2 San Martín and its neighbor, Concepción Chiquirichapa,
fered the worst natural disaster of their history. An
thquake in April was followed, on October 24, by the
ption of the Volcán Santa María which buried the
rounding arable lands under three feet of pumice.
LCAN CHICABAL. The summit of this squat volcano, to the
th of San Martín Sacatepéquez, can be reached on foot in
hours with the help of a guide.

ALMOLONGA
Almolonga, known locally as the "orchard of Central America", is a major center for vegetable growing. Its daily market is characterized not only by the scents of the mountains ("volcanos" as they are called here), but also by the colors of the *huipiles*, embroidered with orange, yellow and red zigzag motifs ● 94, and the *sotto voce* negotiations so typical of Indian markets ◆ 374.

CANTEL
The Cantel textile factory, founded in 1883, is the oldest industrial installation in Guatemala. It has employed as many as several thousand workers. The village also has a glass workshop, which produces attractive functional and decorative items.

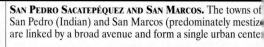

FESTIVAL OF TODOS SANTOS ★
The festival of the patron saint of Todos Santos is the occasion for spectacular celebrations lasting for several days. October 31 ends with a night of music and dancing in the costumes to be worn by the horsemen in

SAN PEDRO SACATEPÉQUEZ AND SAN MARCOS. The towns of San Pedro (Indian) and San Marcos (predominately mestizo) are linked by a broad avenue and form a single urban center.

QUETZALTENANGO TO HUEHUETENANGO

SAN FRANCISCO DE ALTO. The Friday market is the highlight of the week for this sleepy village, which specializes in home-produced traditional crafts. On October 4 the largest livestock market of the *altiplano* is held here, on the vast esplanade overlooking the square.

MOMOSTENANGO. Momostenango (bottom, center) is an important center for sheep and wool: blankets (*colchas* o *frazadas*), ponchos, jackets and shirts in white, gray or brown wool are mass-produced in its workshops and sold at markets throughout the country.

CUCHUMATANES

HUEHUETENANGO. Huehuetenango, at the foot of the Cuchumatanes range, is the successor to the ancient Mam capital Zaculeu ("white land"), and the last major town on the road to La Mesilla and the Chiapas ▲ *231* border. Its market provides an opportunity to meet inhabitants from all parts of the region.
ZACULEU. The archeological site of Zaculeu (top, left) was built on an easily defendable plateau surrounded by

the following day's races. These are held in the main street and involve trying to stay on horseback for as long as possible. Taking part in the races is a social act which gives the riders a symbolic prestige unquantifiable in terms of western society. All Souls' Day (The Day of the Dead) is spent in the cemetery ● *70*.

ravines. It was inhabited from the end of the Preclassic period, but did not reach the height of its glory until the second half of the Postclassic period when it became the Mam capital until the arrival of the Spanish in 1525. After 1,000 the temples were built in stone rather than adobe. Structure 1 was built during the Early Postclassic and consists of a single, rectangular room with a stone altar built against the back wall. Most of the other Late Postclassic temples also had a single room, although there are exceptions (Structure 4 has three rooms). There are nearly always three entrances each with two columns placed in a long opening. The bases, which are usually square, consist of large vertical steps and have staircases on one, three or four sides flanked by ramps. Other elongated structures were built on low platforms. The ball court, like the one at Mixco Viejo ▲ *269*, is in the form of an I. The decision taken by the restorers of Zaculeu to cover all the restored buildings with stucco has been much criticized. Although the present appearance of the buildings (with the exception of the colors) is probably quite close to their original state, it is unpopular because it does not correspond to the general preconception of ruins: with exposed stonework and lush green vegetation climbing all over on the walls.

The marimba, the national instrument of Guatemala, is played at all Indian and mestizo festivals ● 78.

IANTLA. Pilgrims come here ●m the neighboring regions to worship the ●ver-cloaked Virgin of la Candelaria.

ERRA DE LOS CUCHUMATANES. The Cuchumatanes range ●s thrown up from the depths of the sea by powerful ●logical forces. It reaches its highest point with the peak of ●mal (12,795 feet) where marine fossils are found in ●undance. This karstic causse, the so-called "terraced ●rdillera", is characterized by its stark relief, valleys, folded ●pes, rocky ledges and tangled, rocky peaks. The conifers ●t once covered it have been replaced by a stunted ●getation of thistles and dry grasses where coyotes, pumas, a ●v jaguars and birds of prey manage to survive. The villages ● in the warmer, but often wet, lateral valleys.

●DOS SANTOS ★. The 90 percent Mam ● 63 village of Todos ●ntos nestles in a north-facing valley which, throughout the ●ar, is shrouded in mist from the early afternoon. In recent ●ars it has experienced significant changes, due as much to a ●rthward population migration as to the increase in tourism. ●e men of Todos Santos wear one of the most interesting ●stumes in Guatemala: striped shirts with long, embroidered ●llars; black woollen over-trousers, to keep their thighs ●rm, and red and white striped trousers ● 98. Both men and ●men wear rigid straw hats. The village is dominated by the ●stclassic ruins of Tecumanché which are still used as a place ● worship. Turkeys are sacrificed around two crosses – the ●● cross is also a Mayan symbol representing the crossing of the four ways, (the four points of the compass) ● 66.

MOUNTAIN VILLAGES ★. The isolated village of San Juan Atitlán can only be reached after a very steep climb in a four-wheel drive vehicle, or on foot (about six hours). San Pedro Soloma, situated in a valley, has experienced every imaginable disaster. It was destroyed by earthquakes in 1773 and 1902 and by fire in 1884. A year later its population was decimated by smallpox. San Mateo Ixtatán is perched on the side of a desolate valley.

The central square in Huehuetenango.

SACRED SPRINGS
Deep in the valley of San Mateo Ixtatán, salt springs have been harnessed and are worked every afternoon. The collection of the water is considered a sacred event and is authorized by supernatural powers. The descent to the entrance of the mines is preceded and concluded by ritual ceremonies on the altars (*quemaderos*). The water is carried back to the village in large earthenware jars and evaporated in huge cooking pots.

285

"POPOL VUH" ● 146
The *Popol Vuh* manuscript was discovered in the Franciscan convent next to the church of Santo Tomás by Father Ximénez. One of his successors, the

Abbé Brasseur de Bourbourg, took the manuscript to Spain in 1860 and published it in Paris in 1866 ▲ 292.

SANTO TOMÁS
The church of Santo Tomás was built in c. 1540 by the Dominicans. Its vault was rebuilt after the 1976 earthquake but the parishioners refuse to have its smoke-damaged retables cleaned. The high walls are newly whitewashed for the festival of the patron saint.

CHICHICASTENANGO

In spite of the influx of tourists, Chichicastenango has not only retained its outward appearance of a mountain village, with its mudbrick walls, but also its own sense of identity as village community ● *64, 68.*

MARKET ◆ 374. On the day before the market the square is invaded by traveling merchants setting up the frames of the

stalls. At night the trading families sleep on their bundles, wrapped old blankets, givi the place a ghostl appearance. Afte all this chaos the market, which offers a good sample of crafts from all over Guatemala, comes as something of a surprise all the negotiations are conducted in low voices. It is advisa to make your way through the outer barrier of crafts of doubtful quality, which have been made specifically for tourists, to the center of the square. The villagers do their trading in the Indian market, held around the fountain.

CHURCH OF SANTO TOMÁS. The great stairway leading into the church (pictured above, during the festival of Santo Tomás) was built on top of an older place of worship, and Indian priests burn incense on an altar at the foot of the ste Other *chuchkajau* incessantly swing censers ● *70* in front of the door. It is courteous to respect the sacred nature of the place and avoid parking on the church square or using the main entrance.

INDIAN RITUALS. The architectural and artistic interest of the church is eclipsed by the rituals performed there. Families first present their bundles containing offerings of rose petal candles, alcohol and sometimes corn at the foot of the centr altar before distributing them on the altars along the main aisle. They are accompanied by an Indian priest who, kneeli on one knee, murmurs prayers addressed to the divinities, although a request sometimes involves a discussion aloud. These devotions express the complex and multi-faceted fait of a nation that has been converted willingly or by force. It i probable that the Indians are more receptive to the dialogic and sacrificial aspects of the imported religion than the abstractions of th great mysteries of a totally alien theology.

RELIGIOUS SYNCRETISM. The priest is only in charge of the church during the bilingual services (accompanied by marimba, flutes and drums), or during collective christenings.

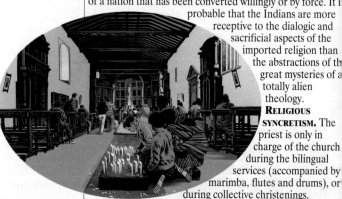

> **"WE HAVE ALWAYS LIVED HERE: IT IS ONLY JUST THAT WE CONTINUE TO LIVE IN THE PLACE THAT WE LOVE AND WHERE WE WANT TO DIE. FOR IT IS ONLY THERE THAT WE CAN BE RESTORED TO LIFE."**
>
> POPOL VUH

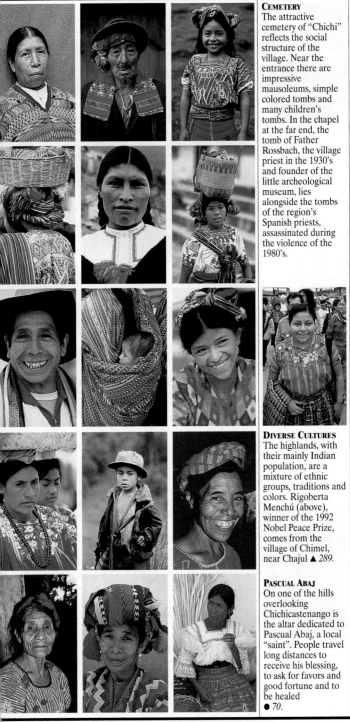

CEMETERY
The attractive cemetery of "Chichi" reflects the social structure of the village. Near the entrance there are impressive mausoleums, simple colored tombs and many children's tombs. In the chapel at the far end, the tomb of Father Rossbach, the village priest in the 1930's and founder of the little archeological museum, lies alongside the tombs of the region's Spanish priests, assassinated during the violence of the 1980's.

DIVERSE CULTURES
The highlands, with their mainly Indian population, are a mixture of ethnic groups, traditions and colors. Rigoberta Menchú (above), winner of the 1992 Nobel Peace Prize, comes from the village of Chimel, near Chajul ▲ 289.

PASCUAL ABAJ
On one of the hills overlooking Chichicastenango is the altar dedicated to Pascual Abaj, a local "saint". People travel long distances to receive his blessing, to ask for favors and good fortune and to be healed
● 70.

287

MAYAN REMAINS
Excavations carried out in the east of the Quiché region led to the discovery of a number of objects, including two Late Classic funerary urns (above and right), a ceramic vase in the form of a human skull (below), an Early Classic ceramic piece representing a monster (center) and a carved jade plaque (top, opposite).

The sanctuary belongs to the community and when priests tried, on more than one occasion, to rid it of pagan rites, they were themselves driven out. More recently the priests in charge, Indian in some cases, have been much closer to their flock and supported their rights and interests.

UTATLÁN
The Mayan city of Utatlán, built on a rocky spur, is one of the late defensive sites of the Guatemalan highlands. The ruins lie several miles west of Santa Cruz del Quiché, the regional capital.

The cemetery of the Ixil ● *63* village of Chajul, with its whitewashed tombs, is typical of the cemeteries of the region.

EAST QUICHÉ

SAN ANDRÉS SAJCABAJA, LA LAGUNITA. These mixed villages, occupied by Indians and *Ladinos*, are in the center of a region which was dramatically affected by the political violence of the 1980's. Franco-Guatemalan archeological excavations carried out under the direction of Alain Ichon at La Lagunita, a few miles from the regional capital, led to the discovery of thirty or so steles and sculpted stones, ceramic urns with lids, an effigy of the jaguar (symbol of the nocturnal sun) and four monolithic sarcophagi. Offerings, including three hundred pieces of pottery, were found in a vast artificial cavity beneath the central plaza, surrounded by four pyramids. Their date of AD 400 corresponds to La Lagunita's golden age. The site was occupied between 600 BC and AD 600.

ZACUALPA AND JOYABAJ. The intense mauves and reds of the *huipiles* ● *95* of Zacualpa are now used in huge bedspreads. The blouses of Joyabaj have a mauve background and broad, embroidered collar, decorated with rosettes of stylized flowers. The village, whose patron is the Virgen de la Asunción, celebrates its saint's festival on August 15. The pre-Columbian *palo volador* ● *77* is still performed under the Christianized name of Saint Michael's dance.

NORTH QUICHÉ

SACAPULAS. The first inhabitants of the village came from the north, following the Río Negro (or Chixoy) upstream. Sacapulas, where the Río Negro flows east-west before turning north, has for a long time been a crossroads.

CUNEN AND USPANTÁN. These villages are situated in the valley of the Río Chixoy and lie on the road linking Huehuetenango and Quiché with Verapaz ▲ 292. Uspantán was on the edge of the northern region held by the guerillas between 1979 and 1983 and was caught in the cross-fire between the rebels and the army. Rigoberta Menchú ▲ 287, from the isolated village of Chimel, to the north of Uspantán, gave an account of daily life in these rural areas and of the fierce repression brought to bear on the population during those terrible years. These accounts, together with her action to promote the rights and identity of the Indian people, won her the 1992 Nobel Peace Prize.

IXIL REGION. Nebaj, Chajul and Cotzal are three mountain villages which share the same language and are traditionally known as the Ixil Triangle. During the 1970's rebellion, this area was used as an army outpost and suffered as a consequence. It was also at the heart of the "reconquest by force" initiative of 1980–2, which employed a scorched earth strategy combined with the idea of "civil self-defence patrols" and "model villages". Once again its people found themselves caught up in a conflict which made day-to-day living conditions unbearable. There were more refugees from this region than anywhere else, with people fleeing to Mexico (almost a hundred thousand went in 1985) or the high mountain ranges. With the military maintaining an influential role, the return to a so-called civilian government in 1985 did nothing to allay fears. The CPR communities of the population in resistance) of the Sierra, more than ten thousand people, were to all intents and purposes surrounded by the army and unable to reach the areas that were ready to receive them until March 1994, under international control. During this time, the survival of the Ixil population and the reconstruction of the region were supported, at arm's length, by foreign aid and organizations.

The church of Chajul in the Ixil region.

The Late Classic Mayan remains in the *Ladino* village of Canillá (below), near La Lagunita and San Andrés, have been restored.

Indian woman from the highlands picking coffee.

HOSTILE COASTLINE
A stretch of gray sand shelving steeply beneath the water, violent breakers, currents running parallel to the shore, powerful ebb tides and sharks constitute the "charms" of the Pacific Ocean. Bathing is ill-advised.

Sculpture dating from AD 700–900, from the region of Santa Lucía Cotzumalguapa.

COFFEE "FINCAS"

The Quetzaltenango-Retalhuteu-Mazatenango triangle produces 90 percent of Guatemala's coffee. The country is th fifth largest exporter of coffee in the world and, in spite of fluctuations in the exchange rate, coffee (with an average income of three hundred million dollars), combined with tourism and the money sent home by those working abroad, accounts for most of Guatemala's foreign currency revenue. Although Brazil and Colombia are larger producers, Guatemala has the largest private coffee plantations in Lati America.

SEASONAL WORK. In the Pacific coastal region coffee is picke from August to November and requires a large additional workforce (known as *cuadrilleros*). These seasonal workers, usually Indians, come from the villages of the *altiplano*. The big landowners employ them for a few weeks and pay a derisory wage.

PACIFIC PLAIN AND COAST

The benchland proper (*boca costa*), characterized by low altitude, tropical vegetation, is succeeded by wet grassland. The road known a the Pacific Highway (CA-2) runs along the benchland at an average distance of 25 miles from the coast. The plain is intersected by rivers which are dry for part of the year and torrential for the other part.

A NATURAL HIGHWAY. The corridor formed by the alluvial plai bordering the Pacific Ocean has been a natural highway since the continent was first inhabited. All the groups that populated South and Central America crossed the continent from west to east. The inhabitants of the southern coast of Mesoamerica were simple hunters and gatherers until the Olmecs ● *31* introduced their "parent culture".

AGRI-EXPORT MODEL. For a long time after the arrival of the Spanish the mountain villages had vast communal lands on the plain. From the early 20th century the region was occupied by banana plantations. United Fruit ▲ *307*, for example, owned plantations around Tiquisate. During the 1950's and 1960's a more diverse form of agriculture was introduced. After sugarcane (shown top, opposite page), the main agricultural products today from the border of Mexico to El Salvador ▲ *314* are cattle, cotton and, to a lesser degree, sesame and soya.

RETALHULEU. This small town is the coastal counterpart of Quetzaltenango ▲ *282*. The histories of the two towns during the coffee boom of the late 19th and early 20th centuries show striking similarities. The splendid Palaci del Gobierno, which houses the town's administrative offices and city hall, is a reminder of this golden age.

ABAJ TAKALIK. In the district of EL ASINTAL, the vast site of Abaj Takalik ("the standing stone" in Quiché) extends across an area now

overed by several *fincas*. A number of archeologists have xplored the remains since the end of the 19th century. The ite is thought to have been occupied from the Middle 'reclassic period. This is indicated by the structure of the nain square, which is characterized by a form of mudbrick rchitecture found at Kaminaljuyú ▲ 268. A second phase of Mayan-style construction, during the Middle and Late 'reclassic, extended into the Classic period. In-depth xcavations have been carried out since 1987 by he National Institute of Anthropology, but nalysis has been hampered by the poor state f preservation of these fragile structures, /hich have been subjected to heavy rainfall.

ANTA LUCÍA COTZMAGUAPA. Like the eighboring communities of La Gomera and Nueva Concepción, which were the product f the division of state territory, Santa Lucía s a "mushroom town" which developed during the 1970's.

"FINCA" EL BAÚL. The owner of a sugarcane *finca* as gathered together the sculptures found on his land and placed them under one roof. Among the sculptures, which late from the beginning and the end of the Classic period, a tele with two ball-players wearing animal skins, and a stone aguar are of particular interest.

"FINCA" EL TARRO. On a hill rising out of the fields of ugarcane, a head sculpted from a large stone (c. AD 300) is et into the ground next to a stele. It has a headband ecorated with geometric disks. Mayan rituals are regularly erformed here to ask for good harvests.

BILBAO. Some fine sculptures decorate the flat surfaces of normous stones which lie scattered among the sugarcane. They are too heavy to move.

"LAS ILUSIONES". Monoliths representing figures and erpents have been placed in the courtyard of this farm where small, private museum is open to the public.

A DEMOCRACIA. Huge stones from several farms in the icinity have been gathered together in the village square. Others, too big to move, are still *in situ*. The small village nuseum has pieces of similar origin, but of more modest dimensions (10–13 inches), as well as other objects ound in the region.

PUERTO SAN JOSÉ AND PUERTO QUETZAL. ince Puerto Quetzal was built, between 978 and 1982, the old port of San osé has been virtually abandoned. However, the beaches of San osé, the most easily accessible or Guatemalans, are totally ngulfed at weekends and on public holidays. The sea long the entire length of he Pacific coast is extremely angerous and unfortunately rownings are frequent. To the east is the Monterico Nature Reserve, dominated y beautiful mangrove lanations ■ 20.

MAZATENANGO
Mazatenango is a fast-developing town at the center of a stockbreeding and cocoa- and hevea-producing region. One of the area's few carnivals, which includes dancing and cock fights, is held here in February.

MONOLITHS
The Late Preclassic sculptures of La Democracia (center) use the natural shape of the rock. This style of sculpture, found as far afield as El Salvador, is derived from the Olmecs. The sculptures include large-scale human heads and big-bellied men known as *Dioses Gordos* (fat gods). They are probably trophy heads and statues of sacrificed enemies. Statue (below) found at La Concepción (300 BC–AD 250).

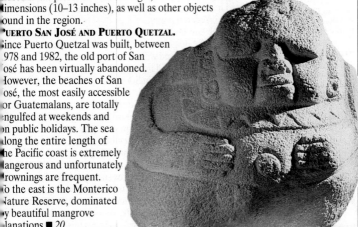

ABBÉ BRASSEUR DE BOURBOURG (1818–74)

⟡ The French *abbé* was the priest of Rabinal in 1855. He learned the Quiché language and translated the *Popol Vuh* ● *146* and the *Rabinal Achi* ● *148*, described by the 1862 French edition as "a scenic presentation of the town of Rabinal, transcribed for the first time by Bartolo Ziz, an elder from that same town". Brasseur later became priest of San Juan Sacatepéquez where he discovered the text known as *Memorial de Soledad* or *Anales de los Cakchiqueles*. The accounts descend from the oral tradition and were written after the Conquest. They are among the rare sources providing a basis for the study of kingdoms that existed before the arrival of the Spanish.

"TORITO"
This ritual, still performed in villages during the festival of their patron saint, is part of the Paabanc festival.

HISTORY

Between 1524 and 1530 the Spanish subjugated all the kingdoms that lay in their path, from Chiapas to the central highlands of Guatemala ● *36*. After 1530, their attempts to continue north and east proved more difficult. The region to the east, which for half a century had been subjected to the expansionist pressures of the Quiché kingdom, became know as the "battlefield" and until 1537, this was where the Conquerors encountered fierce resistance from the Kekchis and Chols ● *63*.

EVANGELICAL CONQUEST. In 1537 the bishop Marroquín and the governor Maldonado reluctantly signed an agreement with Bartolomé de Las Casas ▲ *234* giving the Dominicans the exclusive right to represent the Spanish presence in what was to become Verapaz. They adopted a similar evangelical policy to that used a few years earlier in the north and east of Quiché ▲ *286* and, from 1542, concentrated on converting merchants and, more especially, local chieftains (*caciques*). The Church promised to allow the latter to retain their power over the people. In 1545 seven villages, including Rabinal, Cobán and Chamelco, were converted to Christianity. Conflicts arose subsequently between the population and the overseeing religious authorities who wanted to regain control of a region which had become too free for their liking.

BAJA VERAPAZ

SIERRA DE LAS MINAS. The sierra, which straddles the regions of Alta and Baja Verapaz, El Progreso, Zacapa and Izabal, owes its name to its relatively unexploited mineral wealth. Although the ancient Maya extracted jade, the tradition was lost during the colonial period and it is only during the last twenty-five years that jade has been reintroduced into the workshops of Antigua. Some marble is mined and exported. The forest, on the other hand, is being gradually destroyed by over-exploitation, a situation which led to the sierra being declared a nature reserve and subject to the 1989 law governing protected regions.

SALAMA. The church has a 17th-century central altar, retable and statues. The neighboring village of San Jerónimo has a 17th-century church and will soon have a museum of popular traditions and arts. It will be housed in one of the earliest sugar mills in South America, currently being converted.

RABINAL. Gourds and *morros* (fruit with a thick, hard skin) made into carved or painted receptacles (*guacales*) are one of the local specialties, along with pottery and candle making.

KAJYUB. The territory of the Rabinaleb, who themselves succeeded the Poq'omab in the valley, was threatened by the expansionist ambitions of the Quichés during the fifty years prior to the arrival of the Spanish. About a mile north of Rabinal, the stone enclosure of the old fortified town of Kajyub stands at an altitude of 4,130 feet. Various entrances give access to a courtyard

containing a temple-pyramid which covers an area of 393 square feet. Pyramid staircases lead to the temple above built of flat stone slabs.

BIOTOPO DEL QUETZAL ■ *24*. This nature reserve (2,840 acres rising to an altitude of 7,545 feet) is in the heart of the Sierra de las Minas, which forms the eastern extension of the Cuchumatanes range and is a favorite haunt of the quetzal. The reserve's primary concern is the preservation of the high-altitude rain forest. Constant temperatures and levels of rainfall throughout the year maintain biological conditions making this a unique genetic "reservoir". Although the chances of seeing a quetzal are slim (dawn is the best time), there is plenty of opportunity to enjoy a walk through the forest with its varied flora and fauna.

ALTA VERAPAZ

ᴸAMÁ TO COBÁN. The village of Tactic makes a variety of ᵗraditional wares (silver jewelry, straw hats, dairy products) ᵗ is especially famous for the quality of its embroidery and ᵃving. The women here wear characteristic wide skirts ᵗᵍht in at the waist and red coral necklaces. The village is ᵐinated by the sanctuary of Chixim (with its Cristo de la ᵉricordia), a place of pilgrimage on January 15. Santa ᵘz Verapaz, founded in 1543, has a church with a rare ᵉrior apse. Further west San Cristóbal Verapaz is famed ᵗs Good Friday celebrations.

QUETZAL
The length of its tail plumes forces the quetzal to build tunnel-shaped nests in rotten tree trunks, between 10 and 16 feet above the ground. The male's green tail plumes (up to 3 feet long) are extremely decorative and used as ornamentation. Imported by the lowland Maya, they are highly prized and have long been the subject of a well-established trade. Today the quetzal (*Pharomachrus moccino*) is threatened as much by the disappearance of its natural habitat as by the trade in its feathers.

▲ HIGHLANDS OF GUATEMALA VERAPAZ

EMBALSE CHIXOY
Between 1978 and 1983 a huge, hydro-electric dam was built on the borders of Quiché and Baja and Alta Verapaz. The resulting reservoir filled the valley of the Chixoy and its tributaries (Salamá, Quixal and Carchelá). The five Quixal turbines (300 megawatts) now provide virtually all the region's electricity. The archeological survey carried out before the valley was flooded revealed an ancient and relatively dense population in the area during the pre-Hispanic period.

VALLEY OF COBÁN. Situated at 4,330 feet in the heart of the Sierra de Chamá the valley of Cobán has high levels of rainfall. Its orchid nurseries (the climate is ideal ■ 28) are open to the public. But this is above all a region o[f] cardamom and coffee. The cultivation of coffee shrubs, encouraged in the central regions from 1845, was extended into Verapaz in 1860 with the arrival of German immigrants ● 88 fleeing from the crisis in Europe. Cobán, founded by t[he] Dominicans, was granted the status of "imperial city" and received its coat of arms from Charles V in 1558. The centra[l] square is dominated by the Baroque façade of the cathedral of Santo Domingo. The village of San Pedro Carchá is famo[us] for its tanneries, wooden masks and goldsmiths. The Verapa[z] regional museum is housed in the Don Bosco college. To th[e] east the caves of Lanquín have some remarkably shaped stalactites.

TOWARD IXCÁN AND PETÉN

To the north of the Sierra de Chamá, the mountains subside[s] and give way to the *Franja Transversal del Norte*, the setting [of]

CUBULCO
Cubulco, to the west of Rabinal, is one of the few villages in Guatemala where the traditional dance of the *Palo volador* ● 77 is performed on July 25. A broad flight of steps leads to the Iglesia del Calvario.

Mayan cemetery in the highlands.

a vast agricultura[l] development project which too[k] place in the 1970['s.] The idea was to relieve the pressu[re] on the densely populated high plateaux by settli[ng] the under-populated areas of the north, using the offer of free proper[ty] rights on state territory.

RIVER AND CAVES OF LA CANDELARIA. The complex, discovered in 1971, was studied by the archeologist Patricia Carot in 1975. The river disapppears and resurges many tim[es] along a 7-mile network eroded into the limestone hills. The biggest of La Candelaria's underground chambers is almost 220 square yards with a 196-foot high vaulted ceiling[.] These caves were not used as dwellings or defensive sites b[ut] had a religious function. As symbols of life they were dedicated to the worship of the Earth and Rain gods, and a[s] underground caves, they were the domain of the dead and [the] "other world".

IXCÁN. This isolated region is particularly well known as the[ir] rear-line guerrilla base of the 1970's. The ensuing violence and repression caused more than a hundred thousand peasants to seek refuge in Mexico. Since the establishme[nt] of a constitution and the return of a civilian government in 1985, the situation is gradua[lly] becoming more stable.

LAKE OF LACHUA. This circular lake (720 feet deep) lies in the center of a national park (24,700 acres), a paradise for tropic[al] flora and fauna.

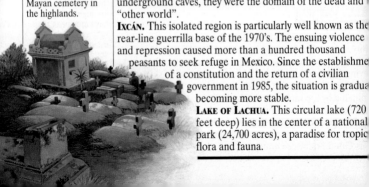

SOUTHEASTERN MAYA

▲ SOUTHEASTERN MAYA
TOWARD THE CARIBBEAN COAST

1. GUATEMALA CITY
2. SALAMÁ
3. JALAPA
4. MOTAGUA VALLEY

M aya territory extends into eastern
Guatemala and as far as Honduras
and El Salvador, where several
archeological sites can still
be seen today.

⊙ Four days

PACIFIC OCEAN

MOTAGUA FAULT
At the 140 kilometer
(87 mile) mark, the
road between
Guatemala City and
Esquipulas crosses
the fault separating
the North American
from the Central
American (tectonic)
plate. A violent
earthquake in
February 1976 caused
the plates to move to
such a degree that the
central line of the
road was displaced by
about three feet. On
the right is a
monument to the
disaster which
claimed 24,000 lives.

This area
includes eastern Guatemala
(Oriente) from the Pacific coast to the shores of the
Caribbean, the extreme west of Honduras, which has one of
the most remarkable Mayan sites (Copán ▲ 299), and the
western half of El Salvador, the smallest country in Central
America. Together they cover the southeastern section of the
Route of the Mayas.

MOTAGUA VALLEY

The main highway (CA-9) linking Guatemala City to the
Atlantic Ocean was built in the 1950's under the government
of President Arbenz. It replaced the old colonial road (Río
Dulce–Lake Izabal–Verapaz–Antigua), which ran parallel to
the north and fell into disuse following the construction of the
large Atlantic port of Puerto Barrios ▲ 310 and the

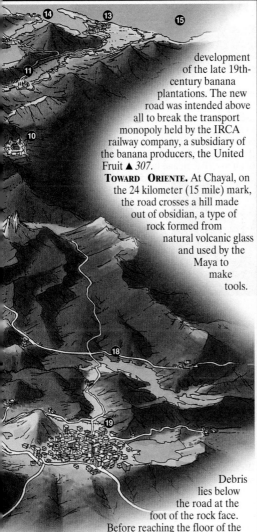

development of the late 19th-century banana plantations. The new road was intended above all to break the transport monopoly held by the IRCA railway company, a subsidiary of the banana producers, the United Fruit ▲ *307*.

TOWARD ORIENTE. At Chayal, on the 24 kilometer (15 mile) mark, the road crosses a hill made out of obsidian, a type of rock formed from natural volcanic glass and used by the Maya to make tools.

Debris lies below the foot of the rock face. Before reaching the floor of the Motagua Valley, the road follows the rugged relief of the sierra, whose desert hillsides positively bristle with cereus cacti. At the 136 kilometer (84 mile) mark, a road leads to Zacapa, Chiquimula, the track to Honduras and Copán, and finally Esquipulas.

ORIENTE

LAKES AND VOLCANOS. Oriente – a term used to designate the regions situated to the east of Guatemala City, towards El Salvador and Honduras – has tended to be neglected by short-term visitors because its mestizo population appears less "typical" than the Indian population of the western *altiplano*. It is nevertheless a region of grandiose and varied

Growing cocoa (below) in Oriente.

INDUSTRIAL PROJECTS
To the right of the bridge across the Motagua River are the remains of a huge paper factory. This was never put into

production because of a political and financial dispute between Spain and Guatemala. It was part of a wave of great infrastructure projects in the 1970's which also included the Chixoy hydro-electric dam ▲ *294*, the oil pipeline to Santo Tomás and the new port on the Pacific coast ▲ *291*. A little further on, the Guatemalan cement company, *Cementos Progreso*, stands to the left of the hairpin bends around the 40 kilometer (25 mile) mark on the CA-9. The company is now promoting the reforestation of the region, having first devastated it to maintain its industrial activity.

▲ Southeastern Maya Toward the Caribbean

The town of Esquipulas is famed fo worship of a black Christ, sculpte orange wood by the Portuguese scul, Quirio Catano in 1549, which stanc the basi

ESQUIPULAS II

un paso firme
hacia la paz

AEREO   GUATEMALA   Q.0.40

TALLER NAC. GRABADOS EN ACERO·GUATEMALA

landscapes, where volcanos alternate with mountain lakes. **"ROSARIO PARK".** Near Chiquimula and the village of Ipala, which is dominated by a volcano with a crater lake, paleontological deposits have been under excavation since April 1994. Although the bones are, unfortunately, damaged (they were either used as foundations for houses or ground into powder to fatten cattle), the deposits have nevertheless revealed sor very large bones belonging to mammoths. Others came from the ancestors of today's bears, some of which reached heigh of almost 10 feet, and to the contemporaries of the first American bears of 30,000–8,000 BC.

ESQUIPULAS. Esquipulas lay within the orbit of Copán during the Classic perio and then of the Payaqui kingdom unde the influence of Mitlán. By the time the Spanish conquerors arrived, Esquipulas was politically and militarily weakened and was finally subjugated in 1530. The river Lempa runs through the valley an crosses El Salvador on its way to the Pacific Ocean. Dominated by the distar high peak of Miramundo (5,560 feet), t town is the official seat of the Central American Parliament, a consultative tribunal created after the 1986 Esquipulas agreements and based on th European Parliament. Few sessions are held here, however. The town is also the capital of the *Trifinio*, a zone which covers the borders of Guatemala, Honduras and El Salvador, and deals with tri-national development projects. A vast neoclassic basilica (above), completed in 1795 after twenty years' work, is visited by worshippers from the surrounding regions and literally invaded around January 15, the date of the annual pilgrimage in honor of its black Christ. One distinctive feature of the event is the iridescent garlands (*toquilla*) wound around straw hats or decorating vehicles. If you continue beyond the attractive 17th-century parish church, you will come to the Franciscan monastery, perched on the hill of Belén opposite the town, from where there is a magnificent view of the town and valley.

ROAD TO COPÁN
Turn left in the village of Vado Hondo at the 178 kilometer (110 mile) mark on the CA-9. Copán is very

badly signposted, so you will need to use a map. Make sure you don't confuse the site of Copán, shown as "Copán Ruinas", with Santa Rosa de Copán (both are in Honduras) as this will result in a very long detour, albeit on a very pretty mountain road. It takes about two hours to cover the 31 miles between Vado Hondo and the frontier post at El Florido. The site of Copán lies about 8 miles across the Guatemala-Honduras border. Crossing the border to visit the site is not a problem: the authorities issue a special 48-hour visa for this purpose
◆ 356.

TOWARD COPÁN

ESTANZUELA. A small museum of paleontology has a collection of bones of prehistoric animals discovered in the region, including a fine mastodon skeleton and various items found locally. There is also a reconstruction of a pre-Columbian sepulcher.

ZACAPA AND CHIQUIMULA. The main activities of these two fairly unprepossessing and extremely hot towns are stockbreeding and, more recently, the cultivation of crops in glasshouses situated at the bottom of the valley where they cannot be seen from the road. A little further on, the landscape of the Oriente gives way to vast estates, the ancestral fiefs of *Ladino* families.

TOWARD HONDURAS. The track leading to the frontier post of El Florido and then on to Copán, passes [th]rough the Chorti villages of Jocotán ("the place where [dr]ums grow") and Camotán ("the place where sweet potatoes [gr]ow"). Here the peasants wear characteristic white shirts and [tr]ousers. The land is divided into small, individual properties [de]voted to raising livestock and producing food crops, [so]metimes using irrigation.

[C]OPÁN

[T]he floor of the Copán valley, in Honduras, is carpeted with [to]bacco plants, interspersed with wooden drying houses which [ar]e gradually being replaced by breeze-block structures. The [lo]cal cigars are renowned for their quality. Coffee is the [re]gion's other famous source of wealth and at harvest time [be]ans can be seen drying by the roadside and in courtyards. [T]he village has preserved its traditional character, with its [w]hitewashed walls, tiled roofs and checkerboard streets [ar]ound the central church square. A delightful museum [ef]fectively displays ceramics and other small objects of [in]terest found during the excavations.

SITE OF COPÁN ★
The ruins lie just outside the village, in a dry deciduous forest. Beyond the site is the Copán river whose course is followed by the road from Zacapa. A museum houses the monumental sculptures that have been replaced on the site by replicas.

1. Great Plaza
2. Ball Court
3. Court of the Hieroglyphic Stairway
4. Temple 22
5. East Court
6. West Court

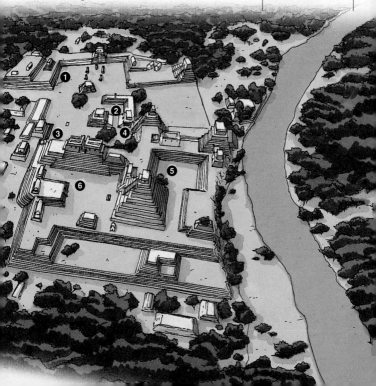

The archeological site of Copán lies close to the Guatemalan border and is one of the few Mayan sites in Honduras. The wealth of its monuments, and particularly its many elaborately decorated steles, make it one of the most important cities in Maya territory. In competition with Quirigua, about 30 miles to the north, Copán reached the height of its glory between the 5th and 9th centuries AD.

BALL GAME ● *112*

The I-shaped ball court near the Great Plaza is open to the south and closed by steps surmounted by a stele to the north. The court proper is divided by three markers placed on the central axis of the aisle. Three macaw heads, the winged symbol of the diurnal sun, are placed at the top of each of the slopes on either side of the court. The game, played by two teams, was more of a ritual than a sport and symbolized the victorious struggle of the forces of life over the forces of death.

RESEARCH

The ruins were described for the first time in 1576, in a letter written to the Spanish king by a senior colonial magistrate, Diego de Palacio (published 1860). But it was Stephens and Catherwood ● *56* who brought them to the attention of the world in 1841. In

1885 Maudslay ● *56* photographed the site (right, the east face of the collapsed Stele C, since restored). Copán has been the subject of much research and, with Tikal, is the most excavated and best known of the Mayan sites. Head of one of the *bacabs* (above) which supported the sky on the façade of Temple 11.

SCULPTURE

Sculpture appears on architectural elements as well as independent pieces such as steles and altars. Most of the steles bear a full-length portrait of the king on one of the main sides, while the rest of the monument is carved with intricate hieroglyphic inscriptions. The most ancient steles, slightly wider towards the top, are sculpted in bas-relief. The relief becomes more pronounced towards AD 700. Stele P, dated AD 623, and Stele C, AD 782 (left).

ALTARS ● *110*

With the exception of the most recent, altars usually accompany the steles. The sixteen kings of the Copán dynasty are represented round Altar Q, AD 776 (above).

HISTORY

The Copán valley was inhabited at least from the beginning of the first millennium BC, although it did not become a Mayan site until c. AD 400. The Copán dynasty, founded at about this time, came to an end at the beginning of the 9th century with the death of the sixteenth sovereign.

STELES ● *110*

Stele F, dated AD 721 (back view, above), was among the several Copán steles drawn by Frederick Catherwood ● *130*. Stele B ▲ *304* (detail, right) represents the accession to the throne of king Eighteen Rabbit as an emergence from the jaws of the terrestrial monster, thus comparing the young sovereign with the rising sun. The entire structure represents the earth in the form of a two-headed monster. On the east face is the first head, seen from the front, from which the king is emerging (right). On the west face the second head is represented as a mask seen from above. Other masks are superposed on the smaller north and south faces of the stele which form the body. Frame of the inner door of Temple 22 and Stele D, preceded by its sculpted altar in the form of a two-headed monster (left).

Copán
Stele B

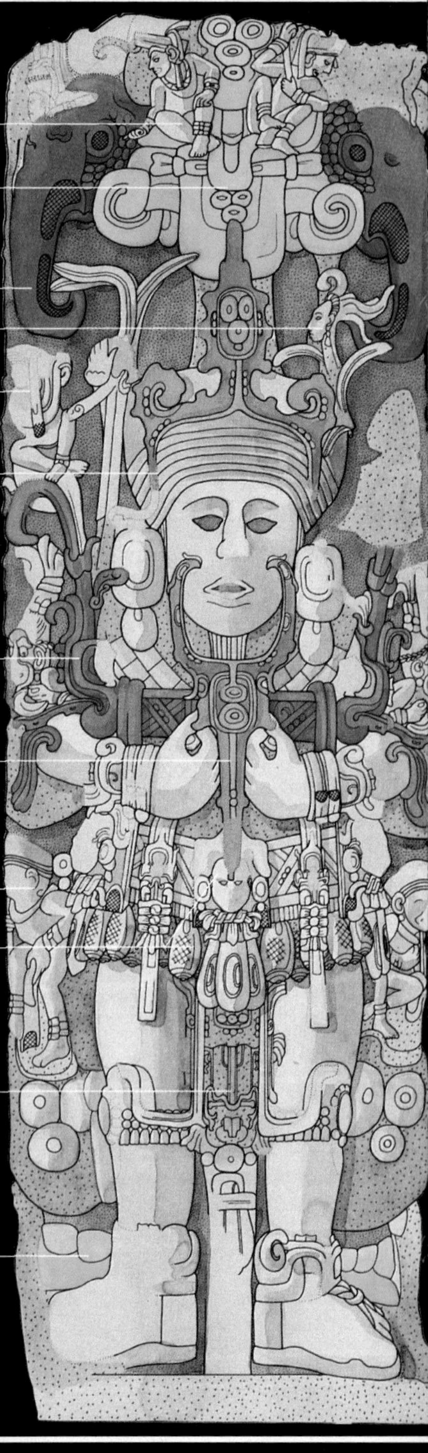
EAST FACE
First head of the terrestrial monster from which the king Eighteen Rabbit is emerging.
Ancestor
Terrestrial monster
Macaw, symbol of the diurnal sun
Personified corn
Ancestor
Royal headdress with turban
Scepter in the form of a two-headed serpent whose jaws are open on a supernatural creature marked with various sacrificial symbols
Symbolic sacrificial object
Ancestor
Belt and shells
Loin cloth with solar image
Lower jaw of the terrestrial monster

"CARVED DIRECT, IN THE ROUND, [THE SCULPTURE] TAKES ON A BAROQUE LUXURIANCE AND A REFINEMENT WHICH HAVE AROUSED ADMIRATION AND EXERTED AN IRRESISTIBLE ATTRACTION OVER ARCHEOLOGISTS." HENRI STIERLIN

WEST FACE
Second head of the monster

Founding ancestor of the dynasty, seated in the forehead cavity.

Terrestrial symbols

"In the city of Copán, the King walks his silver-coated deer in the gardens of the palace. The jeweled plume of Nahual shines on the sovereign's shoulder. On his breast he wears magic shells strung on golden threads . . .

Eyelid

Eye

Nose and ornament

.... The bamboo bracelets on his forearms are so polished that they could compete with the finest ivory...

Snout

Breath of life

Teeth

. . . A magnificent heron's plume, stands erect upon his brow."
Miguel Angel Asturias
Leyendas de Guatemala

Jaw

Terrestrial symbols

THE STELES OF QUIRIGUA ● 110
These steles are not accompanied by altars, and the few round sculptures that have been designated as such appear, because of their shape and size, to have been used for other purposes. It is also obvious that the zoomorphs cannot be described as altars. These huge sandstone blocks, between 10 and 13 feet long, represent a mythical animal while partly conserving the original shape of the rock. The two-headed terrestrial monster is often depicted with the sovereign emerging from its open jaws, symbolizing his accession to the throne. Zoomorphs O and P have a flatter rock at their base which continues the inscription of the principle monument. It also bears the image of a dancing figure wearing a jaguar mask (and thus identified with the nocturnal sun) who is about to disappear into the bowels of the earth. Together the two monuments celebrate a dynastic succession: the dead sovereign disappears into the earth while his successor, in the form of a bird (the embodiment of the diurnal sun) emerges from it.

QUIRIGUA ★

Despite its small size, Quirigua has some of the most original and beautiful sculptures in the Mayan world. Situated in the lower Motagua valley, the site lies about 25 miles from Copán ▲ 299 as the crow flies, and the history of the two sites is indissociable. The huge steles and enormous carved rocks (called zoomorphs) were briefly described by Stephens. At the end of the 19th century Maudslay ● 57 photographed, drew and made molds of them. The site has been excavated by several expeditions, the most important being that of the University of Pennsylvania in 1974–9.

HISTORY. The city was founded during the Early Classic period, as evidenced by two dated 5th-century steles. The early occupations of the site are today buried beneath several feet of alluvial deposits. Quirigua, for a long time dependent on Copán, freed itself when its king, Cauac Sky, captured and put to death the king of Copán, Eighteen Rabbit, in 737. This marked the start of a period of glory for Quirigua which lasted more than a century. The last date carved on the site (810) appears on the façade of one of the buildings of the king Jade Sky.

THE LARGEST MAYAN STELE. The layout of the principle group is like a smaller version of the Copán group, with an Acropolis to the south and a Great Plaza to the north containing a number of monuments. The steles on this site (left and center) are of impressive dimensions: the 35-foot high Stele E, erected in 771 is the largest monument of this type. The sovereign is shown from the front of these steles, standing on the mask of a terrestrial monster or a jaguar and holding

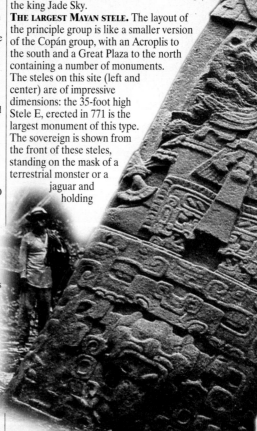

a thunder-scepter and a round shield. His headdress consists of one or more helmets, crowned with a mask and a panache of plumes. The quality of the calligraphy is superb. One cannot but admire the elegance of the text of Stele F (dedicated in 761) and of the complete glyphs of Stele D (766) ● *44*.

UNITED FRUIT COMPANY

Until the 1960's the banana plantations that stretched from Quirigua to the Caribbean coast were the property of the *Frutera* (United Fruit) company. In 1880, the government granted a land concession to a Boston company which, as a result of mergers and consolidation, became the United Fruit Company (UFCO). This company gradually gained control over all areas of economic activity to the point of becoming, with the help of successive governments, a state within a state. In 1904, Estrada Cabrera empowered it to take over the railways, under construction since 1884 by various companies under the direct influence of North

❝The heavy magnificence of the architecture of Quirigua evokes the towns of the Orient. The air of the tropics lightly brushes the impalpable delights of lovers' kisses. Balms which weaken. Mouths are hot, full and moist. Warm waters where lizards sleep on virgins' bodies. The tropics are the erogenous zones of the world! In the city of Quirigua, women wait at the door of the temple, their ears adorned with beads of amber. Tattooed, their breasts left free. Men painted in red and wearing a strange obsidian ring in their noses. And young girls painted in a raw clay wash symbolizing the virtue of grace. The priest arrives and the crowd moves aside. The priest knocks at the door of the temple with his golden finger. The crowd kneels and licks the ground to bless it.❞

Miguel Angel Asturias
Leyendas de Guatemala

Sacrificial stone among the ruins of Quirigua.

▲ SOUTHEASTERN MAYA
TOWARD THE CARIBBEAN

America. This led to the formation of an economic and financial network involving almost 217,450 acres of banana plantations, 152 miles of IRCA (International Railways of Central America) railway tracks, the quay at Puerto Barrios ▲ *310* and the maritime transport of bananas by the "great white fleet". The entire operation was exempt from export duties and harbor dues.

EXPORTING BANANAS
The Bandegua factory, situated a few hundred yards from the entrance to the site of Quirigua, offers an opportunity to see inside a banana packaging plant. The bananas are conveyed on ropes and sorted: those rejected are kept for local consumption and loaded loose into lorries, sometimes bearing El Salvador number plates. Once they have been washed and weighed (top, opposite page), the fruit is packed under chemically protected conditions into cases bearing different quality labels: United Brands for the best quality and Chiquita for inferior quality. The cases are taken by rail or lorry to the banana quay at Puerto Barrios which has just been privatized.

THE "GREEN OCTOPUS". In 1924, the "Green Octopus", as United Fruit became known in Guatemala, obtained legal authorization to grow bananas along the banks of the Motagua river, subject to the payment of $14,000 to rent this state land, plus 1 cent per bunch of bananas exported. In 1928, war almost broke out between Guatemala and Honduras when the rival Honduran Cuyamel Fruit Company tried to extend its territory by extending the border. In the same year the Compañía Agrícola de Guatemala, a subsidiary of the UFCO, began its operations on the Pacific coast, near Tiquisate. The IRCA came under United Fruit control in 1933.

LAND REFORMS. The land reforms (the famous decree 900) were decided by the Árbenz government, voted on June 17, 1952 and introduced in January 1953. They mainly involved confiscating uncultivated land from the banana company and other big landowners and redistributing it among the peasants. The UFCO lost around 173,000 acres (80 percent) of its land at Izabal and 217,450 acres on the south coast. In 1951, the banana company, the country's largest corporation, led an attempt to destabilize the government, which was being accused of communism. With a US Secretary of State as a shareholder (John Foster Dulles, whose brother was head of the CIA) the banana company had no difficulty in protecting its own interests.

REGAINING CONTROL. Árbenz refused to yield to injunctions from Washington and the country was attacked from Copán in June 1954 by a small band of armed mercenaries under the command of Colonel Castillo Armas. The government lost the support of the army and collapsed within a few days. The rebel colonel seized power and the confiscated land was returned to the *Frutera*.

END OF AN ERA.

In 1971, the plantations were sold to Del Monte which later merged with the UFCO and became United Brands. Meanwhile the banana company, which, according to the US Ministry of Justice, controlled 85 percent of all the land suited to growing bananas on the continent, was condemned in the United States for monopolistic practices and had to sell off the IRCA. United Brands, by now a multinational food company with extremely diverse interests, redeployed its fruit-growing operations in Central America, moving into Panama, Costa Rica and Honduras and withdrawing from Guatemala after the fruit there was attacked by disease. Today United Brands buys bananas from individual properties, companies and cooperatives, packages the fruit and transports it to Puerto Barrios for export.

> "As the train climbed the Motagua valley, the luxuriant strip of coastal vegetation gave way to a parched, dusty landscape. The river flowed between great, arid mountains, tawny gold except where they were tinged violet-blue by the shadow of the clouds. Here and there the landscape was tufted with brown, leafless shrubs or still bearing withered leaves hanging from their branches. Beneath the burning sun, the landscape was strangely wintry. On the bare slopes, immediately above the river, cereus cacti rose stiffly towards the sky. Not a shadow: the dust rose in clouds as we passed. "
>
> Aldous Huxley
> *Winter Cruise in Central America*

TOWARD PUERTO BARRIOS

SANTO TOMÁS DE CASTILLA. The road that forks to the left, just before Puerto Barrios, leads to the modern Atlantic port Santo Tomás de Castilla. Founded in 1604 in the shelter of the Amatique Bay, Santo Tomás de Castilla was modernized during the 1950's to compete with the banana port of Barrios, then owned by United Fruit. It gradually took over the merchandise traffic from Puerto Barrios and was equipped with cranes in the 1970's.

Puerto Barrios has many examples of Caribbean-style architecture. The houses are wooden with wide verandas and balconies.

CERRO SAN GIL NATURE RESERVE. The nature reserve of Cerro San Gil, at the eastern end of the Montaña del Mico, is administered by the private foundation Fundaeco. It has an impressive range of tropical rainforest fauna: three hundred species of birds, salamanders and other native amphibians, and twenty-eight species of mammals, including jaguars, tapirs, spider monkeys and howler monkeys ■ 24.

Chapel of Santo Tomás de Castilla, 19th century.

▲ SOUTHEASTERN MAYA TOWARD THE CARIBBEAN

House in Puerto Barrios

The Wages of Fear (1953), directed by Henri-Georges Clouzot and starring Yves Montand and Charles Vanel.

CULINARY SPECIALTY
You really must sample Livingston's *tapado*, a fish soup made with coconut milk and eaten with plantain.

The Río Dulce (below) flows into the Caribbean at Livingston. Main street (right).

PUERTO BARRIOS. As an epigraph to hi novel, *Le salaire de la peur* (*The Wages (Fear*), Georges Arnaud wrote: "Guatemala is a country that doesn't exist; I know, I have lived there." The port, founded by the liberal president Justino Rufino Barrios ▲ *265*, has developed considerably since Arnaud's apocalyptic description. Although no place names are mentioned, the novel, which describes the oil wells of Petén during the 1950's, is extremely well documented. Like the towns on the Pacific plain, Puerto Barrios experience an extremely rapid demographic and economic development. Although its black population is tending to decrease, the town and its seafront have retained certain Caribbean characteristics. Puert Barrios has many unusual features. For example, the little monument that stanc on a brackish canal at the edge of town, inscribed with a poe exalting the noble feelings, self-sacrifice and courage of the plantation worker, active from dawn to dusk; or the funerary mausoleum in the form of a maharajah's palace, probably th tomb of a Hindu immigrant; in the center of the town, the cinema–hotel–restaurant–wash house *A sus ordenes*, whose wooden walls also house many other small businesses; or, finally (and the list is by no means complete), the *Hotel del Norte*, the silent – and haunted – reminder of the "good old days" of the rail transport and merchant navy of yesteryear.

LIVINGSTON

Although situated on the mainland, Livingston can only be reached by boat from Puerto Barrios or along the Río Dulce, or by light aircraft (it has a short landing strip). The town is known locally as La Buga (the mouth), a reference to the fact that it stands on the Río Dulce estuary. Its black population, originally from Jamaica, settled here around 180 and named the town after Jamaica's governor, Louisiane Edward Livingston, the author of a code abolishing slavery. These Garinagus ● *88* are related to the Garinagus of southern Belize ▲ *343*, a region with which they have much closer family, commercial, smuggling and all other forms of

ding ties than with the rest of Guatemala. The language
oken is Garifuna: a mixture of island Creole, English and
kchi, interspersed with a few words of French, particularly
ose related to counting.

MATRIARCHAL SOCIETY. The influence of the women, who
e often in charge of matters of education, religion and
litics, is a fundamental part of Garinagu society. Women
erpret dreams and maintain the relationship with the
cestors. The matrilineal tradition is reinforced by the fact
at the men often emigrate to the United States or
nada, both countries with large
rinagu communities. The new
eeze-block and two-story
uses have been built by the
uveaux riches with dollars
rned in the North.

D OF THE WORLD. The
all township has only
ur streets – the main street
ding from the jetty and
ree others running at
ht angles to it – and as
any vehicles, two of which
e used to distribute two
ernationally famous
ands of fizzy drinks to
cal retailers. The
erchants tend to be
kchis and the Blacks
hermen, although it is
eir wives who sell the fish
the village or the *barrios*.
e festival of San Isidro,
e patron saint of these
cellent fishermen,
incides with Yurunen
ich commemorates their
rival on the continent.
vingston's attractions are
odest, but can be highly
joyable. In the evening
e streets are alive with
aying, rhythmic dancing
the sound of reggae and
lypso music, while sea
eezes cool the air. The
arby Siete Altares
terfall (non-existent in
e dry season) is well
rth a visit. It can
reached on foot, but
urneying by boat is much
ore comfortable. Village
ists devote themselves
various styles of painting,
d make locally inspired
velry, while the local
stronomy should not
missed.

LEIDEN STONE
For a long time the
jade Leiden stone
(owned by the Leiden
Museum in the
Netherlands) gave the
earliest known Mayan
date (AD 320). It was
discovered at Puerto
Barrios but most
probably came from
Tikal ▲ *322*.

311

▲ SOUTHEASTERN MAYA TOWARD THE ATLANTIC

RÍO DULCE ★

Whereas Livingston has a mainly black population, the banks of the Río Dulce are inhabited by Kekchis who live in thatched huts on the water's edge. The river (below), whose bridge lies 32 miles from Livingston, is the only communications route and, as public transport (a dugout) only "runs" once a week, on Tuesdays, each family has its own craft (*cayucos* with oars or an outboard motor). Immediately above its mouth the Río Dulce flows between two steep, limestone walls and forms numerous meanders. Beyond that it winds between two low banks, from which hot springs emerge, before opening up in a lake, El Golfete, which is 3–4 miles wide, over 12 miles long and bordered by mangroves.

BIOTOPO CHOCÓN MACHACAS. The nature reserve on the north bank, named after the two rivers that flow through it, belongs to Guatemala's San Carlos University. Its 17,800 acres cover a region of tropical rainforest, mangroves, lakes and slow-flowing rivers. A few manatees still exist in this aquatic maze which is their natural habitat. Commonly known as the "sea cow" this marine mammal is probably the source of the myth of the siren. It has a slender body, thick skin covered with short hair, a spatula-shaped tail and dense, resilient bones. As a vegetarian it controls the growth of aquatic plants and shares the same habitat as turtles, dogfish and many other species of fish. A short nature trail enables visitors to admire mahogany trees, American cedars, sapodi and custard-apple trees, as well as large numbers of parrots, toucans, golden orioles and green woodpeckers.

MANATEE
Although the Maya believed that the manatee had supernatural powers, they were not averse to butchering them for important ceremonies. Christopher Columbus sighted three of these "sirens" in January 1493: "They were as pretty as their descriptions, even though there was something human about their faces." With the arrival of the Conquerors manatees, which abounded in the region at the time, were increasingly widely hunted. The 17th-century (date of the engraving, above) chronicler Fuentes y Guzmán recorded that: "they can be hunted all year round, not only in Lake Izabal and the Río Dulce, but along the entire coast from Mexico to Nicaragua".

CASTILLO DE SAN FELIPE

From the beginning of the 16th century, goods being traded between the captaincy and the Spanish metropolis were

nsported via what was then known as the Golfo Dulce. ates had been making constant attacks along the Gulf of exico and the coast of Belize, and their increasing ursions up to the Río Dulce and into Guatemala, led to the rtification of the entrance to Lake Izabal at the point where rehouses received merchandise on its way to and from ain. In 1595 a tower was built, subsequently destroyed, and uilt in 1604. During the 1640's pirate attacks were ensified and the building was again damaged. The fort was uilt by the magistrate Lara in 1651 who called it the stillo de San Felipe de Lara, in honor of the reigning anish sovereign and so that his own name would not be rgotten.

ULTIPLE RECONSTRUCTIONS. As the threat of pirates ninished, in 1655 the building became a prison. It reverted its former use ten years later, however, when the "coastal aternity", based on Turtle Island, resumed their attacks. A awbridge and ramparts were added to e original tower, which had a thatched of and damaged beams. Over a period several decades pirates and Spanish ught numerous battles, many of which ompted further architectural erations to the fort. In the 18th ntury its defenses were considerably proved by the military engineer ndrés Ortiz de Urbina who extended e ramparts and increased the number guard posts to one hundred. Although has since fallen into ruins, the fort has tained this final layout.

AKE IZABAL ★

ne origin of the lake's name is certain. According to one of two rrent theories, "Izabal" is a Mayan ord meaning "where you sweat ntinuously", while the other maintains that the lake was med by the Spanish conquerors in honor of the sovereign of astile, Isabella la Catolica. The lake is fed by the Río olochic and is the largest lake in Guatemala, with an area of 0 square miles. Between 1978 and 1979, the nickel on its orthern shores was mined by the Exmibal company, a bsidiary of the big Canadian company, INCO. Following e highly costly construction of an ore-refining plant, world ices collapsed due to over-production and the factory was

forced to close within six months. After this, tiny boats took the concentrate to the loading terminal whose metal structure at Livingston is still used by roosting seagulls. There has always been a suspicion that the INCO was interested in these deposits because of the presence of more strategic metals than nickel. Near the lake, the cave of San Antonio is open to the public.

TOURIST SITE
The ruined Castillo de San Felipe (below) was reconstructed as a tourist attraction in 1955–6 by the architect Francisco Ferrus. It is situated at the entrance to Lake Izabal, on the northern shore, and is easily reached by boat from the bridge. The surrounding grounds have been planted with coconut palms.

RÍO DULCE BRIDGE
The Río Dulce bridge (opened in 1979) spans the river at its narrowest point. Secondary residences are springing up on the approaches to the bridge, which has become an extremely popular area among wealthy city dwellers from the capital; boatmen are keen to point out the residences of former presidents. It is also a popular place for sailing, speedboats and water skiing. The oil pipeline from Rubelsanto (Verapaz) crosses the Río Dulce below the bridge.

313

At the entrance to the town, past the craft market (below), the sta[tue]
of Salvador del Mundo (Saviour of the World), the capital's patro[n]
celebrated on August 4 to 6, blesses this martyred country.

TOURIST RESORTS
Many of the villages along El Salvador's 200-mile coastline have become tourist resorts. Visitors can enjoy fishing for tuna, groupers, swordfish and sailfish, or watersports such as surfing on the oceanic race and windsurfing. To the west, from the beach of Zunzal to Mizata, the rocks of the jagged coastline abound with oysters and

shellfish.
Further on, near the Guatemalan border, is the modern port of Acajutla, the most important in Central America.

SAN SALVADOR
In the city center, devastated by the 1986 earthquake, the beautiful neoclassical architecture of the Palacio Nacional (inaugurated in 1911) in the Plaza Libertad (top, right) contrasts with a concrete cathedral built in the 1970's. The relatively elegant Teatro Nacional (1917) was restored in 1978 and has a fresco on the ceiling of the auditorium.

One pseudo-Gothic cathedral (right), built between 1905 and 1936, is dedicated to Santa Ana, whose festival is celebrated from July 18 to 25.

El Salvador occupies the ancient territory of Cuzcatlán ("land of jewels") the home of several ethnic groups: the Pipils ▲ *316* on the coastal plain, the Chortis to the west of the Río Lempa, the Lencas and the Uluas to the north and the Pokomams on the present border of Guatemala. When Pedro de Alvarado first attempted to conquer the territory in 1524 he was wounded and defeated by Chief Atlacatl. The second attempt, led by his cousin Diego in 1528, proved more successful. El Salvador did not regain independence until 1821, following the "call" to rebellion issued by the priest José Matías Delgado on November 5, 1810. Since then the country's political development has been regularly punctuated by *coups d'état* and civil conflict ● *40*.

ROCKY TERRAIN. El Salvador has the same physical characteristics as the southern regions of Chiapas and Guatemala: from south to north, a coastal plain, three mountain ranges reaching a height of 7,930 feet, a high central plateau and interior mountain chains. The cordillera includes a line of twenty-five volcanos. The Río Lempa, whose waters have been harnessed by four hydro-electric power stations, flows through the country for a distance of 217 miles. The colonial village of Suchitoto lies on the shores of Lake Suchitlán (52 square miles). Several nature reserves, Cerro Verde, El Bosque, El Imposible, Montecristo (rainforest), El Jocatal lake and the Parque Walter Deininger, as well as signposted walks and other modest sites (rivers, lakes, hot springs and pools) offer a range of varied and interesting excursions.

SOCIETY. This densely populated country (5.5 million inhabitants in an area of 8,110 square miles) has an entirely mestizo population (in the cultural sense of the word) and an extremely polarized social structure. El Salvador is emerging from a long period of civil war with the firm intention of putting its recent and bloody past behind it and adopting a positive approach to its problems, with a view to moving toward a more equitable social and political development.

> HE AMERINDIAN CIVILIZATIONS ALL EXPRESS THIS SANCTIFICATION OF THE EARTH. FROM THE NORTH TO THE SOUTH OF THIS VAST CONTINENT, THE EARTH-MOTHER IS THE SOURCE OF ALL LIFE."
>
> JEAN-MARIE LE CLÉZIO

ECONOMY. Coffee (65 percent), sugar, cotton and prawns are El Salvador's main exports. The currency transfers of migrant workers (there are over one million in California alone), American financial aid (although decreasing) and income from tourism are invisible but very real resources. El Salvador's industrial economy, which deals mainly with the processing of agricultural products, did well during the boom years following the creation in 1963 of the Central American common market, and is now the second largest on the isthmus, after that of Guatemala.

SAN SALVADOR

San Salvador was one of the Spanish regional capitals during the Conquest. The capital epitomizes the national contradictions: its fashionable districts on the hills to the north (Escalón, Miramonte) contrast with the neglected city center where the after-effects of the 1986 earthquake can still be seen. Demobilization has merely added to the latent problem of delinquency created by social deprivation. The ever-present fear of attack, kidnapping and burglary does not prevent the wealthy and middle classes doing their shopping on the Boulevard de los Héroes or enjoying themselves at the weekend in the terraced restaurants and night clubs of the Zona Rosa.

JOYA DE CERÉN ★

This small site, discovered by chance in 1976, lies in the Zapotitán Valley, not far from the ceremonial center of San Andrés ▲ 316. The village was buried by volcanic ash following the eruption of Volcán Caldera in c. AD 600, which is why it became known as the "Pompeii of Central America". The main interest of the ruins, which have been extremely well-preserved by the lava, is that they have revealed various aspects of the daily life of Mayan peasants at the end of the 6th century. The modest adobe and mud dwellings, surrounded by fields of corn and beans, were buried beneath the first layer of lava. The ash (1067° F) which then covered the lava was accompanied by toxic gases which asphyxiated the villagers. Using radar, archeologists were able to uncover the remains of dwellings divided into several rooms with beaten-clay floors and roofs thatched with palm branches. Domestic equipment retrieved included corn mills, terracotta plates and dishes, obsidian utensils and benches, as well as food remains. The most important discovery was a codex found in a cupboard which is still being studied. Although fairly unspectacular, the site is of great historical and archeological interest.

CHALCHUAPA

Santa Ana, situated in the heart of the coffee-growing region, is the country's second largest town but has nothing of any particular interest to attract visitors. However, a little further west is Chalchuapa, a vast site

GREEN SPACES
The environs of San Salvador have a number of parks. At Planes de Renderos are the Parque Balboa and the cliffs of La Puerta del Diablo, the botanical garden of La Laguna (situated in a crater), and the waterfalls of Los Chorros. To the southwest are Parque Saburo Mirao, the Parque Zoologica and Museo de Ciencias Naturales. To the east is Lake Ilopango. The forested slopes of Volcán Izalco (possibly 500,000 years old) harbor orchids and numerous species of birds, including seventeen types of hummingbird. There is a splendid view from the summit (6,660 feet) across the Pacific plain. In 1957 Volcán Izalco inexplicably fell silent. This bare, rumbling young cone had been continuously active since it was formed in 1770 (emitting smoke and lava every half hour).

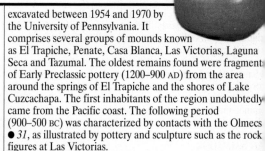

Vase found in
El Salvador.

excavated between 1954 and 1970 by
the University of Pennsylvania. It
comprises several groups of mounds known
as El Trapiche, Penate, Casa Blanca, Las Victorias, Laguna
Seca and Tazumal. The oldest remains found were fragments
of Early Preclassic pottery (1200–900 AD) from the area
around the springs of El Trapiche and the shores of Lake
Cuzcachapa. The first inhabitants of the region undoubtedly
came from the Pacific coast. The following period
(900–500 BC) was characterized by contacts with the Olmecs
● *31*, as illustrated by pottery and sculpture such as the rock
figures at Las Victorias.

EL TRAPICHE. Dating from about the same period is the first
version of the pyramid of El Trapiche, which was at the time

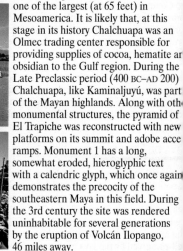

one of the largest (at 65 feet) in
Mesoamerica. It is likely that, at this
stage in its history Chalchuapa was an
Olmec trading center responsible for
providing supplies of cocoa, hematite and
obsidian to the Gulf region. During the
Late Preclassic period (400 BC–AD 200)
Chalchuapa, like Kaminaljuyú, was part
of the Mayan highlands. Along with other
monumental structures, the pyramid of
El Trapiche was reconstructed with new
platforms on its summit and adobe access
ramps. Monument 1 has a long,
somewhat eroded, hieroglyphic text
with a calendric glyph, which once again
demonstrates the precocity of the
southeastern Maya in this field. During
the 3rd century the site was rendered
uninhabitable for several generations
by the eruption of Volcán Ilopango,
46 miles away.

TAZUMAL. During the Late Classic period the small center of
Tazumal was dominated by Structure 1 (49 feet high) which
consisted of two superposed pyramidal platforms. There is
barely any trace of the temple on the summit. Excavations
have revealed six phases of construction for the lower
platform and three for the upper platform. The temple was
reached on the west side by a staircase flanked by ramps. The
platforms were built of adobe bricks or stones, set in clay and
covered with stucco. The group also includes a ball court with
two parallel mounds running east–west and with its west end
closed by a low wall. In spite of these efforts there is no doubt
that the Late Classic site of Chalchuapa is relatively
insignificant when compared with the Preclassic version.

PIPILS. After the year 1000 the Postclassic period was marked
by the arrival of the Nahua-speaking Pipils. Their presence is
evidenced by a range of characteristics of central Mexican
origin in both architecture and sculpture such as stone
chacmool and the life-size statue of Xipe Totec, the Mexican
god of the springtime. During the Late Postclassic period, the
groups of Laguna Seca and Tazumal were abandoned and
occupation was limited to the Penate group which included,
in particular, some low mounds. At the time of the Conquest
the region was predominantly occupied by Pokomam-
speaking populations ● *62*.

PETÉN

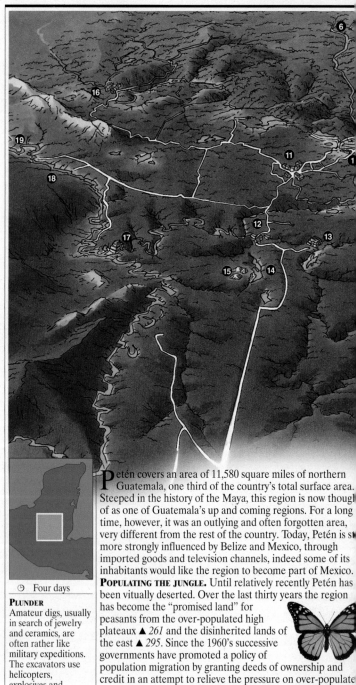

⏱ Four days

PLUNDER
Amateur digs, usually in search of jewelry and ceramics, are often rather like military expeditions. The excavators use helicopters, explosives and dinghies to achieve their ends.

Petén covers an area of 11,580 square miles of northern Guatemala, one third of the country's total surface area. Steeped in the history of the Maya, this region is now thought of as one of Guatemala's up and coming regions. For a long time, however, it was an outlying and often forgotten area, very different from the rest of the country. Today, Petén is still more strongly influenced by Belize and Mexico, through imported goods and television channels, indeed some of its inhabitants would like the region to become part of Mexico.

POPULATING THE JUNGLE. Until relatively recently Petén has been vitually deserted. Over the last thirty years the region has become the "promised land" for peasants from the over-populated high plateaux ▲ 261 and the disinherited lands of the east ▲ 295. Since the 1960's successive governments have promoted a policy of population migration by granting deeds of ownership and credit in an attempt to relieve the pressure on over-populated areas. Throughout the changing fortunes of recent years, the 300,000 new inhabitants of Petén have founded hamlets, villages, *fincas* and agricultural cooperatives. But the price h

"EL MUNDO MAYA" In 1988 the National Geographic Society proposed to the governments of those countries which share the territory of the ancient Mayan empire a common tourist development project designed to preserve their natural and cultural wealth.

en the "ecological assassination" of the continent's second gest area of tropical forest. The virgin forest has been lentlessly felled, cleared and burned so that corn and beans n be cultivated. After two or three years the fragile layer of il, often less than a foot deep, becomes exhausted. Yields l and the area is converted to use for cattle breeding ■ 22.
CONOMIC INTERESTS. Small farmers are often "relieved" of eir property deeds by large landowners or unscrupulous embers of the military. The region, which was wealthy der ancient Mayan rule, dreams of a return to that lden age of prosperity based on the felling of rare pical trees, the collection of chewing gum (chicle 330) or, more recently, the cutting of ornamental pical plants and palms (*xate*) for export. The market r rare woods brings in an annual revenue of two llion dollars ($7,000–10,000 per mahogany tree) at e cost of 123,550 acres of forest being destroyed.
OO LITTLE, TOO LATE. Despite the power and fluence of private economic interests, the thorities have finally responded to pressure from nservationists to protect this fragile and

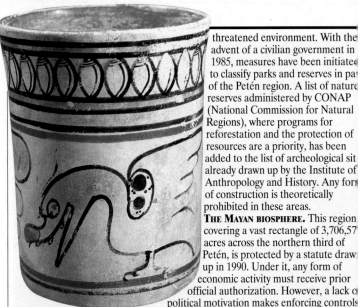

Polychrome vase with bird decoration from Petén, on display in the Museo Popol Vuh ▲ *267* in Guatemala City.

threatened environment. With the advent of a civilian government in 1985, measures have been initiated to classify parks and reserves in part of the Petén region. A list of nature reserves administered by CONAP (National Commission for Natural Regions), where programs for reforestation and the protection of resources are a priority, has been added to the list of archeological sites already drawn up by the Institute of Anthropology and History. Any form of construction is theoretically prohibited in these areas.

THE MAYAN BIOSPHERE. This region covering a vast rectangle of 3,706,57 acres across the northern third of Petén, is protected by a statute draw up in 1990. Under it, any form of economic activity must receive prior official authorization. However, a lack of political motivation makes enforcing controls and sanctions impossible.

LAKE PETÉN ITZÁ ★

With increasing levels of rainfall recorded over the past fifteen years, the inhabitants of this area face a worrying situation that can only be resolved by digging an artificial canal to drain water from the lake into the Río San Pedro to the northwest. Neither the local authorities nor the government appear to have the funds to finance the project. In the long term the nearby airport is under threat, but here as elsewhere, it is hoped that international aid will save the day. The causeway between Flores and Santa Elena is periodically raised, the riverside houses are gradually being abandoned and the main street is undergoing resurfacing. In some areas, planks are used as sidewalks. The lake is still we stocked with fish and species such as the *blanco,* with its delicious white meat, and the *aletón* are especially popular.

FLORES ★

Flores, surmounted by its small cathedral, is an island in La Petén Itzá. Since the 1970's Flores and the mainland village of Santa Elena and San Benito have undergone major, if somewhat haphazard, development. However, Flores, the regional capital since the 19th century, is threatened by the

EL REMATE
Lake Petén Itzá (below and above right). El Remate, to the east of the lake, is the starting point for the road which runs round the northern shore of the lake, toward the Cerro Cahuí and San Andrés reserves ▲ *329.*

...ters of the lake. It is an attractive town of single-story ...vellings, with adobe or brightly painted wooden walls ...though an aerial view reveals an expanse of corrugated ...n roofs). The central square is decorated with steles from ...e surrounding area. As a result of international interest in ...e protection of the tropical forest, a number of ...nservation agencies have set up bases on the island.

...AYASAL. The site of the ancient Itzá capital, Tayasal lies ...pposite Flores and at the western end of the peninsula ...hich cuts the lake in two. It was here, in the heart of Petén, ...at the long Itzá migration came to an end. The Itzás, ...iginally from central Mexico, settled in Yucatán in the 10th century (during the renaissance of Chichén Itzá ▲ 205) and remained there for more than two hundred years before continuing southwards. According to tradition, Hernán Cortés ● 36 passed through the region in 1525, on his way to Honduras and left his wounded horse at ...yasal. The Itzás, who had never seen such an animal, ...ified it and offered it delicacies such as flower petals. The ...orse couldn't resist these choice offerings and died. The ...dians made an effigy in its honor, which scandalized ...anciscans later destroyed. Remote from Spanish influence ...d hidden in the forest, the Indians survived at Tayasal until ...e end of the 17th century. Their defeat by Martín de Ursula ...n March 13, 1697 marked the end of the last Indian ...ngdom. The terrified Itzá warriors fled in panic into the ...ke and were drowned. According to one theory, the high ...nestone content of the waters of the lake may have petrified ...eir skeletons. The mirador at the ...p of the peninsula, named after the last ...zá king, Canek, offers a splendid view ...f the lake.

...AVE OF ACTÚN CAN. Underground ...osion caused by the penetration of ...inwater into the karstic hills (*mogotes*) ... the south of Flores has created caves. ...earest to Flores is the cave of Actún ...an on the southern edge of Santa ...lena. The large rocky chambers are evocatively named after ...e striking shapes of the many stalactites and stalagmites ...at adorn them.

...HE ROAD TO TIKAL

...his road, tarmacked in 1983, is the only surfaced road in ...etén. It crosses green pastureland and even an archeological ...te, Ixlú, whose ruined pyramids can be seen to the right. ...bout 18 miles from Flores, a road turns off toward Melchor ...e Mencos ▲ 334 and the border of Belize ▲ 335. Craftsmen ... the village of El Remate, on the eastern shore of Lake ...etén Itzá, work in tropical woods such as American cedar ...obillo).

...ERRO CAHUÍ CONSERVATION PARK. This 1,600-acre warm ...btropical rainforest is a conservation area dedicated to this ...pe of natural habitat and its flora and fauna, administered ... the research and conservation department of Guatemala's ...an Carlos University.

POACHING
Rainforest covers between 10 percent and 15 percent of the total area of Central America and contains 10 percent of the world's species. The jaguar and ocelot are still hunted shamelessly for their beautiful skins, while coati and rare breeds of deer are served in the restaurants of Flores.

ISLAND OF PETÉNCITO
The island's zoological gardens contain alligators, jaguars, coatis, weasels, peccaries, macaws and parrots. It is easily reached by boat.

SANTA ELENA AND SAN BENITO
On the mainland, opposite the island of Flores, the two villages of San Benito and Santa Elena form a single center, linked by an avenue which crosses them from east to west. The international airport lies to the east, on the road to Tikal. Near San Benito are the caves of Nojojnaj. Large pre-Hispanic steles stand in Santa Elena's central square.

TIKAL ★

With Copán ▲ *299*, Tikal is one of the best-known Mayan sites. Many of its monuments were photographed at the end of the 19th century by Alfred Maudslay (such as that below) and Teobert Maler ● *56*. Later, plans were made of the site and its inscriptions studied. In 1956 a team from the University of Pennsylvania began a serie of systematic excavations. Their work wa continued in 1970 by Guatemalan excavation and restoration teams.

HISTORY. Tikal was occupied from the Middle Preclassic period (900–600 BC) and reached the height of its glory durin the Late Classic period (AD 550–950). The earliest stele on the site (Stele 29) bears a date equivalent to AD 292, while the latest (Stele 11) is dated AD 869. It has been estimated that, during its peak, Tikal had around ten thousand inhabitants within a radius of thirty minutes walk from the center. However, defensive moats and embankments, as well as other remains, have been found even further afield. The town was situated almost at the center of Maya territory, o the route between Campeche and Belize, which could be the reason for its extraordinary development.

LAYOUT. The city has some of the highes temples in Maya territory, comparable to those of El Mirador ▲ *329*. Temple 4 (230 feet) is the tallest of Tikal's temples which are characterized by the steepness of their staircases and, above all, by thei roof crests decorated with stuccoed relie ● *108*. The monuments are organized around the Great Plaza, bordered by Temples 1 and 2 and the North Acropolis. A number of perfectly restored groups of structures, scattered in the forest, are linked by paths or broa

HERITAGE
In 1979 the site was declared a monument and placed on UNESCO's international cultural heritage list.

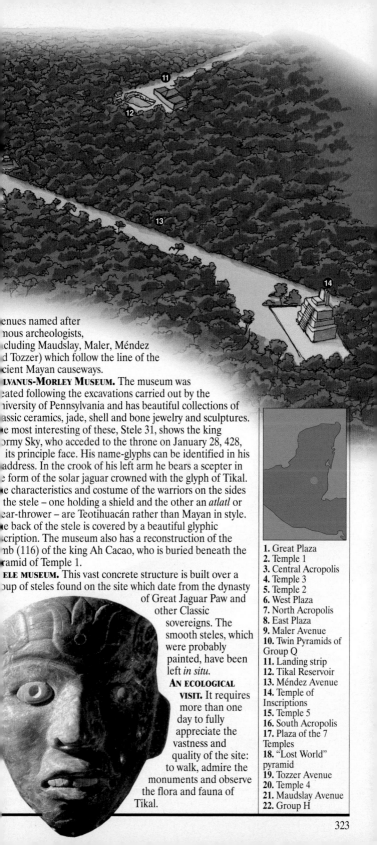

...enues named after
...nous archeologists,
...cluding Maudslay, Maler, Méndez
...d Tozzer) which follow the line of the
...cient Mayan causeways.

...LVANUS-MORLEY MUSEUM. The museum was
...ated following the excavations carried out by the
...niversity of Pennsylvania and has beautiful collections of
...assic ceramics, jade, shell and bone jewelry and sculptures.
...e most interesting of these, Stele 31, shows the king
...ormy Sky, who acceded to the throne on January 28, 428,
...its principle face. His name-glyphs can be identified in his
...address. In the crook of his left arm he bears a scepter in
...e form of the solar jaguar crowned with the glyph of Tikal.
...e characteristics and costume of the warriors on the sides
...the stele – one holding a shield and the other an *atlatl* or
...ear-thrower – are Teotihuacán rather than Mayan in style.
...e back of the stele is covered by a beautiful glyphic
...scription. The museum also has a reconstruction of the
...mb (116) of the king Ah Cacao, who is buried beneath the
...ramid of Temple 1.

...ELE MUSEUM. This vast concrete structure is built over a
...oup of steles found on the site which date from the dynasty
of Great Jaguar Paw and
other Classic
sovereigns. The
smooth steles, which
were probably
painted, have been
left *in situ*.

**AN ECOLOGICAL
VISIT.** It requires
more than one
day to fully
appreciate the
vastness and
quality of the site:
to walk, admire the
monuments and observe
the flora and fauna of
Tikal.

1. Great Plaza
2. Temple 1
3. Central Acropolis
4. Temple 3
5. Temple 2
6. West Plaza
7. North Acropolis
8. East Plaza
9. Maler Avenue
10. Twin Pyramids of
Group Q
11. Landing strip
12. Tikal Reservoir
13. Méndez Avenue
14. Temple of
Inscriptions
15. Temple 5
16. South Acropolis
17. Plaza of the 7
Temples
18. "Lost World"
pyramid
19. Tozzer Avenue
20. Temple 4
21. Maudslay Avenue
22. Group H

The center of the city is built on a series of hills, at an altitude of around 165 feet above the swampy depressions that lie to the east and west of the site. Most of the structures date from the Late Classic period, the golden age of Tikal, but there are some older structures which were not renovated during this period. These include the so-called "Lost World" pyramid, from the Late Preclassic, and a number of Early Classic pyramids in the North Acropolis. Tikal also has architectural groups known as the Twin Pyramid Groups, a feature peculiar to this site and that of Yaxhá. They were the setting for the celebrations of the end of the *katun*.

JADE MASK
The many objects, including masks, figurines and jewelry, found in the tombs of Tikal include this jade, pyrites and shell mask dating from the Early Classic period (AD 527).

TWIN PYRAMIDS
Each group consists of four structures surrounding a central plaza (1): to the north, an enclosure sheltering a stele and its altar (2); to the east and west, a pyramid with four staircases (3); and to the south, a long, rectangular building pierced by nine doors (4). The Group A E-4 formerly known as Group Q (above), was built by the king C to celebrate the end of the seventeenth *katun* (AD 771) ● *44.*

The northern enclosure contains Stele 22 and its altar ● *111* (above and opposite). These elements are almost all sculpted.

MULTITUDE OF STRUCTURES

Tikal consists of a great many structures, from the temples in the central plaza to the groups linked by *sacbeob*. The largest structures in the center of the city are grouped around the triangle formed by the Maler, Maudslay and Tozzer causeways.

NORTH ACROPOLIS

When the site was abandoned, this vast platform (109 yards by 87 yards) supported eight funerary temples, which were the result of three hundred years of architectural activity. Beneath the platform older remains were discovered, some dating from the 3rd century BC.

RITUAL

Stele 22 shows the king C during the celebration of the end of the *katun*. With his right hand he is scattering pearls or seeds while in his left hand he is holding a scepter. A supernatural creature is hovering above his head.

THE MEANING OF THE TWIN PYRAMIDS

These complexes were built to celebrate the end of the *katun* ● 44. They undoubtedly had a cosmological significance since the various structures always follow the same layout and are always found in the same place and facing in the same direction. Thus although the exact use of this group of buildings is not known (nor the nature of the rituals performed or the identity of the participants), it is reasonable to assume that the complex represented a microcosm visited by the king or his representatives to summarize the passage of time. These ambulations guaranteed universal order before embarking upon a new period of uncertainty.

SOVEREIGNS OF TIKAL

Curl-Nose is depicted on Stele 4 (below).

The glyph Stormy Sky represents the element "sky" and is surmounted by a smoking axe, flanked with two arms (yellow glyphs).

The earliest known Tikal steles already bear the portrait of the sovereign accompanied by an inscription in which his name appears as the principle subject. The first identified sovereign is Great Jaguar Paw who ruled in the first half of the 4th century and whose successor is still unknown. Then came Curl-Nose (AD 379–426) and his son Stormy Sky (426–57). The principle face of Stele 31 (AD 445) bears a portrait of Stormy Sky surmounted by the protecting figure of his father. A long inscription on the back of the monument establishes his line of descendance and mentions, as well as his own name, those of Curl-Nose and Great Jaguar Paw.

Curl-Nose is dead (indicated by the hand closing his jaw) and is therefore shown in the sky.

The father and predecessor of Stormy Sky is called Curl-Nose –a name indicated by the monster in the headdress.

The serpent clasped to his breast is the insignia of royal power.

In his right hand Stormy Sky is holding a royal emblem consisting of a chain of jade disks extended by a serpent's head and a garland. In the crook of his left arm is a scepter made of a jaguar head whose headdress incorporates a tied package, the emblem of Tikal. Above the king, in the sky, is the recumbent bust of Curl-Nose, identified by the name-glyph in his headdress.

The name of Stormy Sky (marked in yellow) consists of the glyph for the sky surmounted by the bust of the mythical figure representing lightning with his distinctive symbol: a smoking axe embedded in his forehead.

The name-glyph of the first king identified at Tikal is a jaguar paw, surmounted by the element signifying "bone" and another affix (marked in orange).

To make them easier to identify, the name-glyphs have been highlighted in different colors (which do not appear in the actual steles).

The name-glyph of Curl-Nose, Stormy Sky's father, comprises the head of an animal with a "curled" muzzle, at the end of which is the affix *yax* ("new"). This head is surmounted by a knot (red glyphs).

WALL PAINTINGS
Reproduction
(below), painted in
1959 by Antonio
Tejeda Fonseca
● *128*, of the wall
paintings at Uaxactún
(above).

UAXACTÚN ★

Like Tikal, 18 miles to the south, Uaxactún (meaning
"eight stones") was inhabited during the Middle Preclassic
period and finally abandoned during the 10th century.
Early research undertaken by the Carnegie Institution
between 1926 and 1937 laid the foundations of the archeolo₉
of the central Mayan lowlands. Uaxactún's chronology was
established by means of the dates on its inscriptions, and the
historical evidence supplied by its ceramics and
architecture.

FIVE HILLS. Groups of stone structures built on fiv
hills constituted the heart of the city. These we
surrounded by scattered platforms for houses.
Archeological surveys of the land around the
ceremonial and political center have revealed tha
the major Mayan sites were veritable cities with ₐ
large, permanent population.

MONUMENTS. The step pyramid in Group E date₅
from the Late Preclassic period. Like the "Lost
World" pyramid at Tikal, it has a staircase on each
of its four sides and masks of cosmic creatures. A
structure made of perishable materials, indicated
today by stake holes, was built on this stucco-
covered base. The entire structure was covered
during the Classic period by a new pyramid
which has not survived, faced on the east side
by a rectangular platform supporting three
small temples. From the top of the pyramid it w
possible to see the sun rise behind the central
temple on the spring and autumn equinoxes. The su₁
rose behind the left-hand temple on June 21 (the
summer solstice) and behind the right-hand
temple on December 21 (the winter solstice). These
remarkable astronomical positions were undoubtedly
celebrated by rituals held on the pyramid. A wooden
tower in Group A offers a splendid view of the ruin
of Structure A-5.

ummingbird, tree
rn and an opossum:
ree examples of the
idely varied flora and
una of Petén ■ 24.

ÍO AZUL

bout 28 miles east of Dos Lagunas, the site of Río Azul,
hich can be reached only by four-wheel-drive vehicle, has
een plundered several times since it was discovered in 1962.
ven so, between 1983 and 1987, a team from the National
eographic Society and the University of
exas discovered some magnificent items
hich yielded valuable information on
e Early Classic period. More than five
undred edifices, the tallest of which is
54 feet high, cover an area of just over a
quare mile.

URIED TREASURE. Among the many
pulchers of Río Azul, thirty-two of
hich have been plundered, Tomb 1
D 417) was undoubtedly one of the
chest. Tomb 12 is decorated with painted glyphs in which the
mbols representing the four points of the compass are in
eir exact position and are accompanied by their respective
atrons: the Sun (east), Venus (south), Darkness (west) and
e Moon (north).

CITY IN DECLINE. Río Azul seems to have been abandoned
c. 535, probably following a civil war. It was reoccupied in
e 8th century, under the control of a family bearing the
me name as that which had ruled two hundred years earlier.
he city would soon have re-established itself as the frontier
ost for Tikal, but in c. 830 Río Azul was the victim of a raid
om the Puuc region and the city once again became a
ilitary outpost.

OWARD EL MIRADOR

he road that skirts round Lake Petén Itzá to the west passes
rough the village of San Andrés, the last surviving pocket of
e Itzá language ● 62. From here the road continues round
e lake, offering some splendid views *en route*, while a track
eads 56 miles due north to Carmelita (the journey on this
ack takes at least four to five hours).

XPEDITION. Carmelita is the departure point for an
xcursion to the ruins of
l Tintal, El Mirador and
akbé. This trip should only be
ttempted between February
nd April. Hiring a mule is less
ring than walking and a more
isurely way of appreciating the
orest and its remarkable flora
nd fauna ■ 24.

L MIRADOR ★. The site of
l Mirador is thought to date
om the Late Preclassic period.
s huge pyramids (the eighteen-
ory Tigre pyramid stands 197
et high) were built before the
ldest stone structures of Tikal
, 322 and Uaxactún. Public art
as designed to consolidate the
ocial order. At El Mirador it was

A WILD REGION
The two roads
leading north from
Flores (toward Tikal
▲ 322 and San
Andrés, on the shores
of Lake Petén Itzá,
above) enter the
Mayan biosphere, the
wildest region in
Petén. This is the
world of the *chicleros*
▲ 330, *xateros* and the
grave robbers.

Vase with glyph and
number (below, left)
and vase depicting an
audience scene
(below), from
Uaxactún.

DOS LAGUNAS
This "jewel" of the
Mayan biosphere is
situated 31 miles north
of Uaxactún. Many
non-governmental
organizations involved
in conservation
programs for the
tropical environment
are based at Dos
Lagunas.

CHICLE
The *chicleros* set off into the forest at the height of the rainy season, between September and January, when the sap of the sapodilla tree is at its most plentiful. They build a basic camp of huts made of branches to shelter beds, cooking pots and heating facilities for the latex. Moving outward from these temporary camps, the peasants (left to right, top) climb the sapodilla trees to make incisions in the bark and then make regular collections of the liquid that is exuded. It is heated to solidify it and molded into white latex bricks. The

the impressive size of the architecture which was important and not, as would later be the case, the glorification of great deeds and rulers.

Climbing to the top of the Danta (Tapir) pyramid, the taller twin of the Tigre, is an experience which is hard to describe. Like the temples of Tikal, it offers a magnificent view across vast expanse of the forest.

NAKBÉ

The site of Nakbé was identified during a reconnaissance flig in the 1930's by archeologists from the University of Pennsylvania. It lies about 8 miles southeast of El Mirador ar is linked to that site by a Mayan causeway (*sacbé*) built durin the Middle Preclassic period (between 1000 and 400 AD). In 1962 Ian Graham of the University of Harvard plotted the fir plan of the site which he called Nakbé ("on the way" in Yucatecan Maya). The ruins were dated in 1987. The monumental platforms and structures that can be seen today built between 500 and 300 BC, cover structures built several hundred years earlier. The tallest temple in the West Group i

147 feet high, while the tallest in the Eas Group is 98 feet high. The stone building have no interior rooms and stand on soli rock bases.

FOUR GIANT MASKS. One of the major archeological discoveries was the four huge masks, carved in stone and decorated with stucco, found at the foot of Structure 1 in the West Group. Three were covered up again, due to the absence of any means of preserving ther

bricks are then transported from the camp by pack mules which return with food supplies. In spite of the development of synthetic gums there are still export outlets for the natural chicle gum, primarily in Japan.

but the one that is still visible is remarkable for its size and craftsmanship. The mask is 36 feet wide and 16 feet high and represents a head with a 5-foot long muzzle.

"CORAL" GROUP. The group consists of five structures, two of which are surmounted by three rooms, furnished with stone benches and decorated with wall paintings. Places of worship and dwellings were discovered beneath numerous small mounds. A complete ball court ● *112*, one of the three Preclassic courts in Petén, is though to have covered an earlier court dating from 500 BC making it the earliest court known to date.

SOUTHWEST OF FLORES

The other route to the highlands, besides the one linking Petén with the Río Dulce ▲ 312, follows the track maintained by the oil companies to take the crude oil extracted in the Río San Pedro region south via La Libertad, Sayaxché and Yalpemech (the "northern transversal fringe"), before climbing the foothills of the Sierra de Chamá to Cobán ▲ 294. From Sayaxché a fleet of small craft travel up and down the rivers.

SAYAXCHÉ. The town of Sayaxché developed as a result of the waves of migration from the north which affected southwest Petén. It has become a small regional capital, particularly with the transport of crude oil from the fields of El Naranjo. It stands at the confluence of the Ríos Pasión and Petexbatún and on the only road between Petén and Verapaz ▲ 292. It is also the departure point for excursions to the sites of El Ceibal, Aguateca and Altar de los Sacrificios. Apart from the spectacle of a transporter ferry moved by a ridiculously small dugout canoe, the only local item of any interest is the stele in front of the town hall.

CEIBAL ★

HISTORY. The site of Ceibal (Structure A-3, left) lies at the heart of the Río Pasión region and was relatively unimportant during the Classic period. It experienced its golden age from 830, probably after the arrival of the Putúns who followed the Usumacinta upstream. Ceibal is the historic site of Chakanputún, founded by the Itzás, a Putún Maya group who adopted a number of Mexican characteristics. Its architecture and sculpture reveal Yucatecan traits and the new sovereigns of Ceibal were certainly foreigners judging from the characteristics of the figures on the steles. The role played by Ceibal in the 9th century as the most important city of the southern lowlands is indicated on

A NEW STYLE
Putún influence can be seen on the steles of Ceibal. The principle figures on Steles 10 and 11 (AD 849) do not have the usual cranial deformation in which the forehead extends the line of the nose, ▲ 248 and they also have a moustache. After 870, monuments moved even further from the Classic tradition. The sculpted figure on Stele 13 has long hair and is not wearing the characteristic high and complicated Mayan headdress.

Early Classic tetrapod vase (center) and bowl (below) from Petén.

Torso of figure on Stele 6 (AD 687) at Piedras Negras.

Stele 10 which mentions four cities, including Ceibal, Tikal and Calakmul. The site was abandoned just after 900. **MONUMENTS.** The site was excavated during the 1960's Group A, in the center of the site, has two plazas. The north plaza has a ball court. In the centre of the south plaza stands Structure 3-A: a platform with four staircases and a stele at the bottom of each one. The architecture and sculpture reveal the influence of the Mexican features introduced by the Putún Maya. Later edifices are characterized by a cladding of thin slabs, reminiscent of Puuc stonework ▲ *220*, while a round structure preceded by an altar in the form of a jagu stands at the end of a *sacbé* to the south of Group

RÍO PETEXBATÚN ★

To the west of Sayaxché is the Río Petexbatún region, named after the river that flows through it which has always been a communications route. **MAYAN ARCHITECTURE.** The construction of ceremonial centers on elevated ground is a recurrin feature of the region and is particularly evident at Arroyo de Piedra, Aguateca, Quim Chilijan and D

PIEDRAS NEGRAS
It is a two-day voyage from Sayaxché, along the Ríos Pasión and Usumacinta, past the Mexican border, and Yazchilán ▲ *248*. Piedras Negras lies downstream past several sets of rapids (whose crossing on

Pilas. Archeologists have also observed the predominance o a plaza layout consisting of a group of three or more rectangular structures, arranged symmetrically round a central court. Contrary to those in central Petén, however, there is no ritual structure on the east side. This type of layo relates particularly to groups of dwellings, although it has al been employed in districts reserved for the elite. Ball courts are rare and are only found at Dos Pilas, Punta de Chimino and Ceibal ● *112*.

DOS PILAS

HISTORY. Dos Pilas dominated a vast area since its territory lay in the rectangle delineated by the Ríos Pasión and Salinas and which also included the towns of Cancuen and La Amelía. The city was founded by a member of the Tikal royalty, exiled in c. 600. Although the three successive sovereigns ruling from 698–760 successfully consolidated the military power of the city, Dos Pilas was nevertheless defeated by the satellite town, Tamarindito, during the reign of the last sovereign. This reversal of fortune provoked the collapse of the metropolis which was abandoned in 760. The two concentric defensive walls with stakes on their summits were not resistant enough to prevent the fall of the city.

the return journey is hazardous), and can only be reached by dinghy. There are few remains on the site – most have either been bought by collectors or are in the archeological museum in Guatemala City ▲ *267*.

The ocelot (above) is one of the protected species in the Mayan biosphere.

ONUMENTS. The unfinished hieroglyphic stairway was
errupted in c. 700. The sculpted motifs depict a crouching
stage, but the end of the text is missing. It is thought to
present the capture of the sovereign of Ceibal who was
crificed seventeen years earlier. Funerary enclosures with
lls made of thin stone slabs and covered with stones to
rm a flat roof were discovered, as well as two tombs, one of
ich was not found until 1991 and contained the remains of
e second sovereign. Also concealed in this sepulcher was a
de, shell and mother-of-pearl
address, pottery decorated with glyphs
d thousands of slivers of obsidian.

GUATECA

guateca (right) stands on a cliff
erlooking the Río Petexbatún. After an
tial period of occupation during the
te Preclassic it probably experienced a
naissance. The structures and steles

at can be seen today are products of this second era. The
val family occupied a sort of acropolis situated to the east
the central plaza but, because the city was in a permanent
te of conflict, moved to a more strategically secure
ucture, built to a new design and with new materials.
near defense walls were constructed with greater care
an those at Dos Pilas and were thicker
ound the area occupied by the royal
nily. The city center represented
e deified sovereign, and the
otection of his person was of
ramount importance. An
ropolis which stood on a
atform on the west side of
e central plaza is one of the
w examples of this type of
mplex in the region. The
ulpture on the steles
picts some of Aguateca's
lers: the sovereign Shield
rtle is featured on a
ulpture dated 640; Stele 8
50) shows a sovereign
th jaguar paws for hands
d feet; Stele 13 (860) is
corated with seven
rpents; Stele 17 shows a
guar at the feet of the
inciple figure; Stele 4
00) bears a motif of a
onkey or a man dressed
a monkey skin. Like the
ole of southwest Petén,
e town was invaded in
e early 10th century.
e finest pieces can be
en in the archeological
useum in Guatemala
ty ▲ 267.

USUMACINTA
Below the site of
Altar de los
Sacrificios the Río
Pasión flows into the
Usumacinta (above,
19th century) which
forms the border with
Chiapas ▲ 248.

**CONSTRUCTION
TECHNIQUES ● 106**
Hieroglyphic
stairways and
sculpted panels
flanking flights of
access steps are one
of the region's
architectural
characteristics. They
are present on the
major sites of Dos
Pilas, Tamarindito
and Ceibal, while at
Aguateca smooth
panels occupy the
same position next to
the steps. After the
fall of Dos Pilas,
Aguateca and Ceibal
used larger stones
sculpted on several
sides, as well as
employing similar
techniques and
layouts to those used
in central Petén for
structures built for
the elite.

**STELES OF PIEDRAS
NEGRAS**
Stele 40 (center),
dated 746, and Stele
12 (left), dated 795.

Corn cobs drying in a
village in Petén.

" As for Mayan
architecture . . . it
is a collection of
pyramids, flat walls
divided into
rectangular panels,
and broad, regular
flights of stairs.
As such, it is a
materialization
of the most
characteristically
human imaginings of
Man, and the most
unnatural. **"**
Aldous Huxley
*Winter Cruise in
Central America*

LAKE YAXHÁ
Mid-way between
Flores and Belize, a
track leads to Lake
Yaxhá (below), a
favorite haunt of
crocodiles. Its
limestone bottom
gives a gray tinge to
its waters.

FLORES TO BELIZE

Beyond Tikal the road running eastward from Flores towar
Belize becomes a track. During the rainy season muddy
potholes often make it impassable.

YAXHÁ. The archeologist Teobert Maler ● *56* was the first t
explore the ruins of this site in 1904 and published his
discoveries in 1908. Few Mayan cities have revealed such ar
urban network of streets, side streets and sidewalks.
nine acropolises with a total of five hundred
structures are still largely unrestored. In Plaza
Structure 90, a promontory supporting the
remains of six pillars, is original. To the east of
the plaza, Temple 216 stands on an acropolis ar
offers a spectacular view of the forest, the lakes
Yaxhá and Sacnab and the island of Topoxté.
Plaza A is a complex with twin pyramids, like those of Tikal
▲ *324*. A huge, ten-tonne stone lies mysteriously abandone
on its side.

TOPOXTÉ. The island can be reached by boat or on foot in t
dry season. Built during the Postclassic period, three main
structures are aligned on a meridional axis: a pyramid with
platform and no temple to the south, the principle pyramid,
with a staircase visible on its west face, in
the center, and a smaller pyramid to the
north. Facing the pyramids and to the west
are the altars and steles decorated with
small circles.

BIENVENIDO
SITIO
Arqueológic
YAXHA

NAKUM. Nakum, about 12 miles north of
Yaxhá, is reached via a track running across swampy
depressions (*bajos*), which are flooded during the rainy
season. Its buildings, used for astronomical observations, be
the dates 771, 810 and 849. Palace D, positioned on a vast
plaza bordered by massive structures, is unusual in that it ha
forty-four rooms. The monoliths opposite Temple A were
erected to celebrate solstices and equinoxes. They were buil
of limestone which is now badly eroded. The plaza and the
other buildings, to the east and west, form the group known
as the "Solstice observatory", and are built along similar lin
to the astronomical mounuments at Yaxhá and Uaxactún.

NARANJO. The ruins cover a large area. Thirty-six of its forty
seven steles are sculpted.

MELCHOR DE MENCOS AND THE BELIZE BORDER. The borde
zone is deeply indicated in the illegal trade of rare tropical
woods. The inhabitants of Melchor de Mencos, the last villa
in Guatemala (39 miles from Flores), report periodical
incursions by soldiers from Belize trying to move the border
markers.

BELIZE

▲ BELIZE

In 1981 British Honduras became independent and joined the Commonwealth as Belize (national flag, below).

"Walking through the streets [of Belize City], there was little evidence of the terrible catastrophe of 1930, when a hurricane unleashed the full force of a huge tidal wave upon the city. It is true that a pile of bricks was all that remained of the principle house of God; but Mammon, Caesar and the Penates had been raised, fresh and shining, from their ruins. Nearly all the dwellings, all the government buildings, all the shops and warehouses had been rebuilt or repaired. On the whole the city looked remarkably clean and well kept. Even a tidal wave has its good side: at least it clears away the slums fairly effectively. Our governments and local authorities are less brutal; but they are also, unfortunately, considerably less effective."

Aldous Huxley
*Winter Cruise in
Central America*

Belize, bordered to the north by Mexico and to the west by Guatemala, extends for 180 miles along the Caribbean coast. The country has an average width east to west of just 68 miles and a total surface area of 8,866 square miles, not including its two hundred or so islets and reefs. While the northern and coastal regions are flat, the mountains in the south and west reach heights of above 3,300 feet (Victoria Peak rises to 3,680 feet). The climate varies slightly from one district to another and the rainy season takes place between June and September. Between September and December, the north winds can become violent hurricanes, like those which destroyed Belize City in 1930, 1955 and 1961, causing the capital to be moved to Belmopán. A number of rivers cross Belize from west to east: the most important are the Río Hondo, which forms the border with Mexico ▲ *188*, and the Belize and Sarstún Rivers.

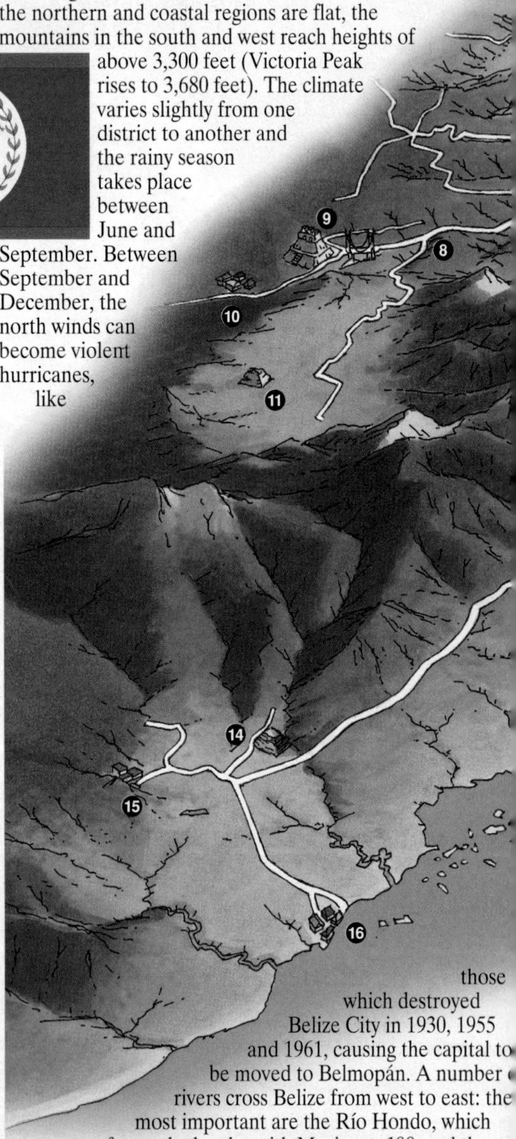

ECONOMY. During recent years the chicle gum market ▲ *330* has declined, and Belize has had to diversify its economy. It exports mahogany, pine, cocoa, fruit and tobacco as well as lobsters, prawns and oysters. It also produces corn, rice, bananas and cattle. Tourism is an important source of income

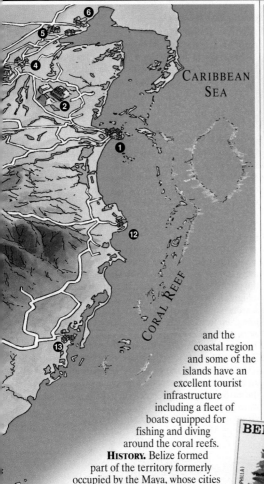

CARIBBEAN
SEA

CORAL REEF

🕒 Four days

**ROADS AND
DISTRICTS.**
Belize is divided into
six districts: Corozal,
Orange Walk, Belize,
Cayo, Stann Creek
and Toledo. After
Belize City and
Belmopán, the major
towns are Corozal,
San Ignacio,
Placencia and Punta
Gorda. The 1,370-
mile road network
consists of the

and the
coastal region
and some of the
islands have an
excellent tourist
infrastructure
including a fleet of
boats equipped for
fishing and diving
around the coral reefs.

HISTORY. Belize formed
part of the territory formerly
occupied by the Maya, whose cities
there included Altún Ha, Lubaantún,
Caracol, and Xunantunich. At the end of
the 9th century the urban centers were
[ab]andoned and ancient knowledge forgotten.
[A] renaissance during the Postclassic period was little
[m]ore than a prelude to the final collapse provoked
[b]y the arrival of the Spanish. Enforced migrations,
[te]rritorial incursions and imported European
[di]seases decimated the last remaining survivors of
the great Mayan civilization.
Until the 17th century
missionaries
based at Bacalar
▲ 185 paid sporadic
visits to Tipu,
the most
important
village in the
region.

BELIZE

(SWIETENIA MACROPHYLLA)

MAHOGANY TREE

$1
BELIZE
INDEPENDENCE 21 SEPTEMBER 1981

Western Highway
(toward Guatemala),
the Northern
Highway (toward
Mexico), the
Hummingbird
Highway and the
Southern Highway.
The international
airport is 10 miles
from Belize City.

337

▲ BELIZE

TOWARD THE REEFS
From Belize City, the principal areas
of interest along the coast can be
reached by sea. Amateur divers
should visit the Cayes.

AN ETHNIC MOSAIC

THE LAST OF THE MAYA. The corsair and pirate vessels that
scoured the coast forced the last of the Maya to seek refuge
the forests of the interior where they were joined during th
Caste War ▲ 186 by groups of Maya fleeing from Yucatá
In modern Belize the Maya form three different linguisti
groups: the Kekchis, from Guatemala, who have come to
work in the sugarcane plantations in the south of
the Toledo district; the Mopáns, in the upper
valley of the Belize River; and the Yucatecs in th
district of Corozal to the north of Orange Walk.
Altogether, they represent 10 percent of the
population ● 62.

A SECOND LINGUISTIC GROUP. The first British settlers on the
coast of Belize came to exploit its hardwoods. They brought
with them black African slaves and Carib Indians from the
Antilles. The descendants of the black slaves, known as
Creoles, speak the Creole language, which is a mixture of
English, African dialects, Mayan, Carib and Spanish, as well
as English. They represent 60 percent of the population and
are concentrated in Belize City. The Spanish-speaking
mestizos, are of mixed Spanish–Mayan descent. The rest of
the population consists of refugees from the Caste War and
emigrants from Guatemala and Central America.

A MULTICULTURAL SOCIETY ● 88. The descendants of workers
imported from the West Indies (between 1844 and 1917) to
work on the sugarcane plantations still live in the districts of
Toledo and Corozal. They usually speak Spanish, Creole and
English. Merchants from India settled in Belize City (Hindu
temple, left) and Orange Walk. They no longer speak Hindi
and so have lost contact with the country of their forebears.
the early 20th century Chinese emigrants settled in Belize an
were followed by Syro-Lebanese who formed a tightly knit
group of traders. The last group of immigrants were German
speaking Mennonites, now   farmers and stockbreeders.

**GARINAGUS ● 88
▲ 342**
African slaves
shipwrecked in the
Antilles formed an
independent group
on the island of St
Vincent and adopted
the language and
customs of the
Caribbean. These
Garinagus (who

spoke Garifuna)
supported the French
republican rebellion
and were exiled by
the British to Roatán
in 1797. From there
they settled along the
coast of Honduras,
Nicaragua,
Guatemala and
Belize (in the Stann
Creek district).
Driven back by the
Bay Men, who feared
their rebellious and
libertarian spirit, they
were not officially
acknowledged by the
community until
November 19, 1832.
This date has now
become a national
festival.

Port of Belize City,
late 19th century.

BELIZE CITY

Belize City stands on the estuary of the Belize River and is dissected by Haulover Creek. For a long time it was the capital of a country with a population of around 200,000, but was replaced by the centrally located city of Belmopán due to the frequent hurricanes which threatened the inhabitants and administrative infrastructures. Today it has 50,000 inhabitants and is still the country's main economic and cultural center.

FORT GEORGE. This former British fort was built on an island separated from the mainland by a narrow channel. This was filled in during the 1920's when a monument to the memory of Baron Bliss, one of the country's benefactors, was also erected. Today the Fort George Hotel stands on the site. It was built after World War Two and is one of the city's best hotels.

SOUTHERN PART OF THE CITY. The most characteristic part of the city lies south of the Swing Bridge. It is an old district of narrow streets, wooden houses and small shops. A fresh produce market is held there every Saturday. Regent Street and Albert Street, the only streets to have survived from 18th-century Belize, house large companies and the business sector. The town clock, on its metal scaffolding, shows a different time on each of its four faces. A flea market now occupies the site of the former Court House, which was destroyed by fire in 1918.

GOVERNMENT HOUSE. The building was abandoned following the Hurricane Hattie disaster and the foundation of Belmopán. The wooden edifice was built on the Southern Foreshore between 1812 and 1814 by the British architect Christopher Wren and is now used as a VIP visitors' residence.

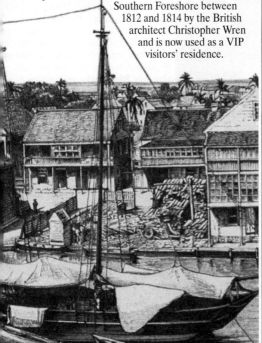

ST JOHN'S ANGLICAN CATHEDRAL
The typically English Protestant church (below) was built in 1812 by black slaves with the bricks used as ballast by ships coming to load up with wood.

HOTEL MONA LISA
The hotel (above) was used in Peter Weir's film, *Mosquito Coast* (1986), starring Harrison Ford.

BRIDGES IN BELIZE CITY
Belize City is linked to the mainland by Belcan Bridge upstream, and the old Swing Bridge at the mouth of the river. On the other side of the Swing bridge, the Fort George district offers a splendid view of the port.

JAMAICANS
Rastafarians have mainly settled in Belize City. They believe in the redemption of the Black Race and its return to Africa, and worship the Negus Haile Selassie I, under the name of Ras Tafari. They can be recognized by their long hair (dreadlocks) that their religion forbids them to cut.

LAMANAÏ ★

Of all the Mayan sites, Lamanaï was occupied for the longest period: 500 BC to the 19th century. The site is unmaintained and is reached by following the New River upstream from Orange Walk for about 18 miles. During the dry season there is also a track from San Felipe. The oldest pottery shards on the site date from 500 BC. Four centuries later the tallest Mayan pyramid

(108 feet) of that period was constructed. There is a Late Classic ball court, as well as houses built over ceremonial structures and Postclassic temples over Classic houses.

ALTÚN HA

Archeologists from the Ontario Royal Museum in Canada, who excavated the site (right) between 1964 and 1971, translated the name Rockstone Pond into Mayan: Altún Ha.

NORTHERN ARCHEOLOGICAL SITES

A lack of roads makes it difficult to reach the many archeological sites discovered, but as yet relatively unexplored, in the northern region of Belize. Only seven sites are open to the public and none of them have any facilities, so it is essential to take drinking water. As these visits often involve crossing areas covered with high grass, visitors should wear boots, trousers tucked into socks, long-sleeved shirts and a hat as protection against the tropical sun.

SANTA RITA. The present town of Corozal, in the extreme north of Belize, is built on part of the site of Santa Rita, occupied by the Maya when the Spanish arrived. The surviving Mayan structures are about one mile from the town. Stucco decorations and two sepulchers have been found dating from the Early Classic period. The buildings are from the Late Postclassic period (1350–1530). In 1985 Diane and Arlen Chase discovered a tomb and a skeleton covered with pieces of jade and mica. One of the buildings has been reconstructed and is the only one which can be visited.

CERROS. The site of Cerros lies across the bay from Corozal. It can be reached by boat and, in the dry season, by road via Chunos, Progreso and Copper Bank. Cerros was an important site during the Late Preclassic period (350 BC–AD 250). Stucco masks nearly 8 feet high flanked the staircases of two structures. The tallest edifice stands 72 feet high, but the residential area is often flooded. During its prime, Cerros controlled the trade along the Río Hondo and the New River and a canal was dug around the town to facilitate the traffic of large dugouts.

NOHMUL. Situated about a mile from San Pablo, in the direction of Orange Walk, this major site consists of two groups linked by a *sacbé*. It was occupied at the end of the

XUNANTUNICH
The site (left) was occupied in the Classic period (150–900). The 147-feet-high Castillo, opposite the central plaza, is a monumental Mayan structure. On its south face, a stucco frieze, restored in 1972, is a cosmological composition on several levels representing the earth and the sky in the form of a celestial band supported by *bacobs* (detail above).

...eclassic period, and then at the end of the Classic period ...00–900). There are less significant sites, such as San ...steban and San Antonio, near Orange Walk.

...LTÚN HA ★. The Mayan city of Altún Ha, which lies about 28 ...iles north of Belize City and 7 miles from the coast, can be ...ached via the Northern Highway. Restored in the 1970's, ...is is the most explored site in Belize. It was occupied from ...e Early Preclassic period (c. 1000 BC), but most of the ...sible structures date from the Late Classic period. Altún Ha ...ust have had a population of about ten thousand. The ...nter consists of two adjoining plazas, one to the north ...d the other to the south. Its water came from a huge, ...ay-lined reservoir with a stone and clay dam at ...e southern end to prevent water escaping ...to the swamps. In the stone Temple of the ...ltars, which is covered by a later structure, ...oken pieces of carved jade were discovered, ...hile excavations of a tomb unearthed almost ...ree hundred jade objects and the ...ecomposed remains of a codex. Like ...ubaantún ▲ 343, Altún Ha has no steles or ...onolithic altars.

Lemboglossum rosii orchid.

...HAN CHICH. Chan Chich lies near the Guatemalan ...order and can be reached by road or charter aircraft from ...elize City. The site is ideal for observing tropical flora and ...una, especially birds ■ 26 or for simply relaxing in its chalets ... restaurant-bar. The complex, which dates from the Classic ...eriod, consists of two large plazas surrounded by structures. ...hen they were discovered, the temples had already been ...artially plundered. In the south of Orange Walk, between ...amanaï and Chan Chich, the sites of Las Milpas, El Infierno, ...akabish and San José have also been found, but are difficult ... get to. They date from the same period and have not yet ...en excavated.

KINICH AHAU
A royal tomb at Altún Ha contained the largest piece of sculpted Mayan jade ever discovered: the head of Kinich Ahau, the Sun.

XUNANTUNICH. The Western Highway runs from Belize City t Flores ▲ *320* in Guatemala. Near the border it crosses a region which was densely populated until the 18th century. Xunantunich is situated about 8 miles from San Ignacio, the most important town in western Belize. Three carved steles stand in Xunantunich's central square. In 1959 Evan Mackie proved that the site, which consists of three plazas surrounde by structures, had been partially destroyed by an earthquake during the Late Classic period. From the top of the Castillo there is a splendid view of the Petén jungle ▲ *317*, the Mayan mountains and the district of Cayo. Several other sites can be visited near San Ignacio, including Barton Ramie, El Pilar and, to the south of the Western Highway, Tipu and Mucnal Tunich. To date, they are all relatively unexplored and overgrown.

CARACOL. The Mayan city of Caracol, also in the district of Cayo in western

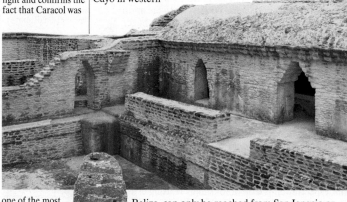

one of the most important centers of the Mayan civilization.

Belize, can only be reached from San Ignacio or Georgeville. A track enters the Pine Ridge natur reserve and runs south to Caracol via Augustine and San Luis. Prior authorization must be obtained from the Department of Archeology or the Forestry Department Western Division before visiting the area. The site of Caracol, probably the largest site in Belize, stands on the Plateau of Chiquibil in the Chiquibil Forest Reserve, at the heart of the region. The tallest temple on the site is slightly taller than the Castillo at Xumantunich and its base is slightly larger than that of the temples of Tikal ▲ *322*. Caracol and Tikal, about 43 miles away, were both Classic sites and were constantly at war with each other. Following a conflict in 562, Caracol dominated the region for more than a century.

TOWARD THE SOUTH

DANGRIGA, A GARINAGUS VILLAGE ● *88* ▲ *338*. A poorly maintained mountain road, the Hummingbird Highway, runs from Belmopán into southern Belize and the village of Dangriga (opposite) which means "stagnant waters" in Garifuna. In 1802 a Garinagus community was founded at the mouth of Stann Creek River and was later augmented by runaway slaves. In 1823 other Garinagus from Honduras,

The Caribbean influence can be seen in the cuisine of the Garinagus. Thin pancakes, known as cassava bread, are a specialty and are made by grating manioc and passing the flour through large cylindrical sieves made from plaited palms.

der the command of Alejo Bani, settled in uthern Belize. They grew crops and sold their getables in Belize City where they were only owed to stay for forty-eight hours at a time. The arinagus still preserve certain African traditions, pecially music, dancing and food, and continue to actice their animist religion called *obeah*. On ovember 19 they celebrate the anniversary of eir recognition by the Belize authorities. The stival, a cultural feast is extremely popular.

NEXPLORED WEALTH. There are a number of explored sites in the forests around Dangriga. e Southern Highway passes the sites of Pomoná d Kendal and, further south, Alabama, all in the ann Creek district, as well as Kuchil Balum in the ockscomb Basin Forest Reserve.

VADERS. South of Dangriga the track enters the strict of Toledo and continues to Punta Gorda. e region – which has numerous remains of its rmer Mayan inhabitants and no direct mmunications routes with its neighbor, uatemala – was invaded by American onfederates who came to buy weapons from the itish during the Civil War. After the defeat of the uth, some confederates set up sugarcane antations here, but, unused to the climate and ing conditions, soon returned to the United ates. Their lands were taken over by newcomers every ethnic origin: Garinagus and Hindus, kchi and Mopán Maya, Chinese, Europeans and estizos.

NTA GORDA. Punta Gorda lies at the southern d of Belize and can be reached by plane from lize City and Dangriga and by boat from vingston and Puerto Barrios in Guatemala ▲ 309. nta Gorda has a Saturday market, remarkable its colors and the variety of the products sold, d where the colored cloth ● 89 of Guatemala has

pride of place. The departure point for visiting the archeological sites in this district is San Pedro, about 11 miles north of Punta Gorda. The inhabitants of San Pedro, San Antonio, Santa Cruz, Aguacate and others are Kekchi and Mopán Maya ● 62 refugees from the Guatemalan coffee plantations. They have eserved their Indian languages and traditions, luding weaving. Guides are available, offering nducted tours of the Hokeb Ha and Blue Creek ves. The ruins of Hokeb Ha, Pusilha and benka can only be visited on horseback.

BAANTÚN ★. Work on the site of Lubaantún lace of the fallen stones"), about a mile from n Pedro, was carried out by a series of mainly itish archeologists between 1903 and 1970, from omas Gann to Norman Hammond. The latter

Tropical forest near Lamanaï.

CAVES OF SAINT HERMAN
About 11 miles from Belmopán in the direction of Dangriga, the caves of Saint Herman form a remarkable underground network once occupied by the Maya. These labyrinthine caves, where narrow passages open onto huge chambers several dozen yards high, offer an extraordinarily beautiful and spectacular display of stalactites and stalagmites, underground rivers and "windows" where rays of light penetrate into the very bowels of the earth.

KINKAJOU
This Central American monkey is mainly active at night, eating fruit, eggs, several varieties of insects and honey.

discovered that the site was founded just after AD 700 and abandoned less than two hundred years later. Its architecture is extremely original and consists of pyramidal platforms, with staircases, on which edifices were built in perishable materials. The tallest structure on the site is 36 feet high. The Mayan vault was not used here and there doesn't appear to be any form of stone decoration. The stonework was entirely dry, without mortar, and usually consisted of small elements, perfectly adjusted and arranged to create the best esthetic effect. Terraces were also built using large blocks known as megaliths. No sculpted steles have been discovered at Lubaantún. The site consists of over one hundred structures grouped around twenty plazas. There are three concentric zones: a central religious zone, a belt of ceremonial structures including ball courts and edifices whose function is unclear, and a residential zone. The ceramic figurine-whistles discovered on the site are extremely varied and include a unique figure wearing a sort of helmet with a single vent opening. The site is not maintained and visitors are advised to go suitably equipped and wearing boots and trousers.

UXBENKA. Uxbenka, near Santa Cruz, was not discovered until 1984. The site has yielded twenty dated Early Classic steles, seven of which were sculpted.

NIM LI PUNIT. Midway between Punta Gorda and Dangriga near Indian Creek, Nim Li Punit was discovered in 1970 not far from Xnaheb. Architecturally, the site can be linked with Lubaantún. Among the twenty-five steles, (dated between 64 and 800) discovered here one was 10 feet high; the largest stele yet found in Belize. Although, like most of the other sites, Nim Li Punit had been plundered, the tomb excavated in 1986 by R. Leventhal was intact. There are probably several dozen undiscovered sites, hidden in the jungles of Belize. Each new discovery enriches the archeological map of this tiny country.

Robin Haddon

Strategic

PRACTICAL INFORMATION

A trip to Central America should be organized carefully. To avoid any disasters or a premature return, it is best to make the following arrangements: firstly, contact your doctor and find out which vaccinations you will need and when you will need to have them, then apply for any necessary visas, and finally decide what to pack be well prepared if you are traveling during the rainy season.

HEALTH

Before traveling to any tropical country, you will need to take certain health precautions. The elderly, young children, pregnant women and those with a medical condition are advised to take particular care, as emergency medical treatment may not always be available outside the major cities.

VACCINATIONS

Vaccinations are not compulsory although you are recommended to have vaccinations against tetanus, typhoid-paratyphoid and polio, meningitis, hepatitis A and B, malaria, cholera, yellow fever and rabies. You will usually need a course of vaccinations starting a minimum of one month before you travel. Missing any of these vaccinations by even a day can lead to a three-month delay.

MALARIA

The parasite responsible for malaria is transmitted by a mosquito bite and can cause repeated attacks of malaria accompanied by high fevers. Preventative treatment is indispensable and is taken either daily or weekly throughout your stay (it is usually commenced one week before arriving in the affected area and continued for several weeks on returning). Anti-malarial tablets are only available on prescription. You are recommended to protect yourself against mosquito bites as much as possible by wearing long sleeves, long trousers and insect repellent at all times.

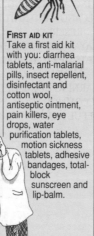

FIRST AID KIT

Take a first aid kit with you: diarrhea tablets, anti-malarial pills, insect repellent, disinfectant and cotton wool, antiseptic ointment, pain killers, eye drops, water purification tablets, motion sickness tablets, adhesive bandages, total-block sunscreen and lip-balm.

TIME DIFFERENCES

The time in four major cities at midday in Mayan countries

summertime *am*

wintertime *am*
• *the following day*

summertime *pm*

wintertime *pm*

ON ARRIVAL

Should you need to purchase any medication after you arrive, always buy it from a pharmacy and not a market. *Lemotil* is for stopping attacks of diarrhea and *Entocid* for upset stomachs (a bottle costs around $2). Insect repellents are often more effective than imported products.

TREATMENT

If you are undergoing a course of medication remember to bring prescription with you stating clearly the actual scientific name of the drugs you are taking as the commercial name often varies from one country to another.

AIDS

As in other tropical countries, the Aids virus has been slowly spreading throughout central America.

WATER

Drink bottled liquids where possible – mineral water, beer, soft drinks – and avoid drinking any tap water (when ordering drinks always ask for them without ice, as it may have been made from tap water). Belize City has a modern water purification system and many hotels in Cancún and Belize also have their own purification systems.
Avoid salads as these may have been rinsed in tap water and eat only cooked vegetables and thick-skinned fruits that you peel yourself.

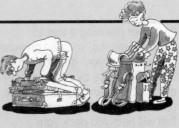

INGUAT

VISAS AND PASSPORTS

MEXICO

There are no visa requirements for US or UK visitors. US citizens do not require a passport, though proof of citizenship is needed.

US:
EMBASSY OF MEXICO
1911 Pennsylvania Avenue, N.W.
Washington, DC
20006
Tel. (202) 728 1600
MEXICAN CONSULATE
GENERAL
8 East 41st
New York, NY 10017
Tel. (212) 689 0456

UK:
MEXICAN EMBASSY
60/61 Trafalgar Sq
London WC2N
Tel. (0171) 839 6586

EL SALVADOR

US citizens require a visa (available free from the consulate). There are no visa requirements for UK visitors.

US:
EL SALVADOR EMBASSY
2308 California Street
Washington, DC
20008
Tel. (202) 265 9671
SALVADORAN
CONSULATE
46 Park Avenue
New York, NY 10016
Tel. (212) 889 3608

UK:
EL SALVADOR EMBASSY
AND CONSULATE
1st Fl, 5 Gt James St
London WC1N
Tel. (0171) 430 2141

GUATEMALA

All visitors from the US and the UK require a valid passport and a visa.

US:
CONSULATE GENERAL
OF GUATEMALA
57 Park Avenue
New York, NY 10016
Tel. (212) 686 3837
GUATEMALAN EMBASSY
2220 R. Street, N.W.
Washington,
DC 20008
Tel. (202) 745 4952

UK:
GUATEMALAN EMBASSY
13 Fawcett Street
London SW10
Tel. (0171) 351 4042

BELIZE & HONDURAS

All visitors must have a valid passport. There are no visa requirements for US or UK citizens.

US:
EMBASSY OF HONDURAS
3007 Tilden St, N.W.
POD 4-M Washington,
DC 20008
Tel. (202) 966 7702
EMBASSY OF BELIZE
2535 Massachusetts Avenue, N.W.
Washington, DC
20008
Tel. (202) 332 9636

UK:
BELIZE HIGH
COMMISSION
10 Harcourt Houses
19a Cavendish Sq.
London W1M
Tel. (0171) 499 9728
HONDURAN EMBASSY
115 Gloucester Pl.
London W1H
Tel. (0171) 486 4880

PHOTOGRAPHY

Because of the humidity of the climate you may wish to take silica capsules to place in your camera bag to absorb damp and possibly an isothermal box to protect your films.

Make sure you take the correct film and filters (ones that are designed for use in strong sunlight). Print film (35mm) is readily available all along the Route of the Mayas, main outlets being pharmacies, hotels, and camera stores. You are advised, however, to check that the film is not out of date before purchasing.

WHAT TO PACK

Whatever the season, do not forget that the nights can get extremely cold in places of high altitude.

Take a bathing-costume, t-shirts, shorts, lightweight trousers, a light sweater or jacket, sunglasses, a hat, a raincoat for the wet season, good hiking boots, plastic sandals (for showers where you have doubts about the level of cleanliness, and also in case you need to walk in or through water). Pack a flashlight with extra batteries, a pocket knife, a money belt and toiletries (cosmetics can be very expensive). It is preferable to use a waterproof bag or case that can be padlocked. Leave jewelry or valuables at home.

MAYA TRAILS AND SPECIAL-INTEREST HOLIDAYS

Many specialist tour operators offer small-group or special-interest holidays with fixed itineraries. Some may even be prepared to design a tour specially for you. These usually last between 14 to 24 days and will take you through ancient lands of the Mayas, visiting the major highlights. Usually starting from Mexico or Cancún, they frequently include visits to Guatemala, Chichén Itzá, Antigua and Flores and often finish with several days at a beach resort.

DRIVER'S LICENSES

Should you wish to rent a car you will require a valid passport and a current driver's license. If traveling from the UK you will need an International Driver's License, which is available from the Automobile Association Haymarket London W1 Tel. (0171) 839 4355

If you are planning a visit to Central America, you can prevent the holiday of your dreams turning into a nightmare by taking account of the climate and customs of the countries you will be visiting. The first will help you pack your suitcase and the second ensure that you return with it.

CLIMATE

The tropical climate of the Mayan countries means that you will have good weather during your visit, regardless of the time of year. In the rainy season (June–September) it only rains in the late afternoon which does not interfere too much with visits or excursions. Temperatures tend to vary more with altitude than with season. If you visit the Caribbean coast don't underestimate the strength of the sun which is often disguised by a warm breeze.

YUCATÁN PENINSULA (MEX.)
It is always warm on the Yucatán Peninsula with temperatures often reaching 104° F. Brief but violent storms (*nortes*) can occur in the late afternoon, even during the dry season.

TABASCO (MEX.)
The low altitude of the state of Tabasco means the climate is warm and wet throughout the year. It is more pleasant during the dry season.

CHIAPAS (MEX.)
The mountainous regions of Chiapas are swept by cool winds and are cold at night, hence their name: *terra fria* (cold land).

GUATEMALA
Temperatures in the Guatemalan highlands are very cool at night and sometimes even during the day in winter. The Pacific coast and the Petén jungle have a hot, wet, tropical climate.

BELIZE
The inland climate is similar to that of Yucatán. The islands are swept by sea breezes and are extremely pleasant throughout the year.

From top to bottom: Mexico, Guatemala, Belize, Honduras, El Salvador.

RECOMMENDED
Plan your visit for November and enjoy the magnificent All Souls' Day celebrations in the highlands, relatively few tourists and a cloudless sky.

THE BEST TIME TO VISIT											
JAN.	FEB.	MARCH	APRIL	MAY	JUNE	JULY	AUG.	SEP.	OCT.	NOV.	DEC.
☀	☀	☀	☀	☁	🌧	🌧	🌧	🌧	☁	☀	☀
🚶🚶🚶	🚶	🚶🚶	🚶	🚶🚶	🚶	🚶🚶	🚶🚶🚶	🚶🚶	🚶	🚶	🚶🚶🚶

☀ Dry Season	🌧 Rainy Season	☁ Intermediate Season	🚶🚶🚶 No. of tourists

ECONOMIC SITUATION

EXICO
he rigorous
conomic policies of
e Mexican
overnment in recent
ears appear to be
earing fruit with
flation reduced to
ound 12 percent in
e early 1990's.
exico is now setting
s sights on the great
orth American
arket.

UATEMALA
ter Mexico,
uatemala has the
eatest wealth of
atural resources
specially coffee, of
hich it is the world's
xth largest
oducer. The
uerilleros who held
vay in the highlands
e gradually being
absorbed into the
ommunity.

BELIZE
Former British
Honduras still
maintains strong ties
with Britain through
the Commonwealth –
Queen Elizabeth II
remains the Head of
State of Belize. Its
Gross Domestic
Product per head of
population is the
highest in Central
America, with the
exception of Mexico.

HONDURAS
This essentially
agricultural country
produces the
traditional products of
the region: coffee and
fruit destined for the
North American
market.

EL SALVADOR
In 1992 this tiny
country adopted a
new presidential
constitution and since
then it has been
making a concerted
effort to maintain
internal stability. After
twelve years of civil
war the country is
experiencing its first
years of peace.

SAFETY

TOWNS AND CITIES
The shanty towns
surrounding the
capitals, such as the
narrow side streets of
Belize City, have
nothing to offer
tourists and are best
avoided during the
day as well as at
night. The centers of
the more tourist-
orientated towns
(Mérida, Cancún,
Antigua, Flores and
San Cristóbal) are
safe even at night.
However, visitors are
advised not to walk
out after dark in
Guatemala City and
San Salvador.

BANDITS
Many isolated and
forested regions are
notorious for bandits.
These places should
not be visited alone
and especially not
after dark. Tourist
offices issue
warnings concerning
certain excursions
which could prove
dangerous and these
should be listened to.

POLICE
A form of "legal"
highway robbery, in
which drivers of
private vehicles can
be stopped by the
more unscrupulous
members of the
national police
force, is
becoming fairly
common practice.
A mind-boggling
list of imaginary
offenses is read out
which the driver is
invited to "clear" by

making a "voluntary
contribution"
(*mordida*). If this
should happen to
you, pay up with
good grace and lodge
your complaint later,
but only at the tourist
office or with the
tourist police.
Although common
practice in
Guatemala and
Mexico, this type of
incident is less
frequent in the other
countries on the
"Ruta Maya".

PICKPOCKETS
The most common
type of crime against
tourists is the classic
pickpocket. So take a
few simple
precautions: use
traveler's cheques,
keep photocopies of
official documents
(passport, plane
tickets) in a safe
place, and only carry
the amount of money
needed for a
particular day or visit
(leave the rest
somewhere safe).

IDENTIFYING THE MAYAN COUNTRIES					
	BELIZE	**GUATEMALA**	**HONDURAS**	**MEXICO**	**EL SALVADOR**
CAPITAL	BELMOPAN	GUATEMALA CITY	TEGUCIGALPA	MEXICO CITY	SAN SALVADOR
SURF. AREA (sq.miles)	8,865	42,042	43,278	759,529	8,124
POPULATION (millions)	0.19	9.47	5.26	87.80	5.38
DENSITY (inhabitants/sq. mile)	3.3	33.5	18.1	17.3	98.8
LIFE EXPECTANCY (years)	67	65	66	70	67
LITERACY (% of population)	95	55.1	63.1	63	63

aero**mexico**

Cancún is the most common point of entry to the Route of the Mayas, although each area does have its own international airport. The cost of an air ticket can vary greatly, depending on the time of year and the particular destination. Tour operators offer a wide range of different types of holidays. For the hardened traveler or those with plenty of time it is even possible to travel from the US to Mexico by train or bus.

BY AIR

Most international flights arrive in Cancún, Guatemala City, Mexico or Belize City. From there take connections to many of the other towns and cities in Central America. Tegucigalpa and San Salvador, situated on the periphery of the Route of the Mayas, have their own international airports. For travelers with a limited amount of time it is probably best to stay based in Cancún and take

trips from there. For those with more time at their disposal and who wish to explore the south of the region, most companies with flights to Central America (Taca in particular) will fly to San Salvador.

FROM THE US

American Airlines and United Airlines offer roundtrips from New York to Guatemala City and New York to Mexico City. American Airlines and

Continental Airlines offer roundtrip flights from New York to Cancún. Prices range from $1700 (business or first class) to $499 (coach class) for a ticket to Guatemala City, $1336 (first class) to $330 (coach class) for a ticket to Mexico City and $1638 (first class) to $396 (coach class) for a ticket to Cancún.

FROM THE UK

British Airways and American Airways offer direct flights from London Heathrow to Mexico City. Roundtrip ticket prices range from £579 to £629 according to season. Roundtrip fare to Cancún via Mexico City costs £806 to £844, and to Guatemala City via Miami costs from £1,029 to £1,131

	Main roads
	Air routes
	Railways

BIENVENIDOS

A LA CIUDAD DE MEXICO
CAPITAL DE LA NACION

according to season.
British Airways
reservations
Tel. 0345 222111.

BY TRAIN
It is possible to travel
to Central America by
train from Mexico or
the US, although as
there is no American
train company which
travels to Mexico you
will need to change at
the border. Allow a
minimum of thirty
hours to travel from
Los Angeles or
Houston to Mexico
City and between
twenty-four and
thirty hours for the

journey from Mexico
City to Mérida. For
information and
reservations
contact:
Ferrocarriles
Nacionales de
Mexico, estación
central de
Buenavista,
Tel. (5) 547 85 45
or 547 58 19

BY BUS
Greyhound Bus
Lines travels to
Mexico City.
Tickets from New
York to Mexico are
available at a cost of
$149 (one-way) and
$298 (roundtrip).

TOUR OPERATORS
Many specialist tour
operators offer
different types of
holidays throughout
the Route of the
Mayas. Tours, leisure
trips, activity holidays
and special interest
holidays are all
available.

US
AMERICAS TOUR AND
TRAVEL
Tel. (800) 238 4467
ARCHEOLOGICAL TOURS
Tel. (212) 986 3054
CULTURAL TOURS OF
MEXICO
Tel. (800) 487 4783
DESIGN TRAVEL &
TOURS
Tel. (800)
543
7164

ELEGANT VACATIONS
Tel. (800) 451 4398
GLOBETROTTERS
Tel. (800) 321 2835
GREAT ADVENTURE
TRAVEL
Tel. (800) 874 2826
GRAND CIRCLE TRAVEL
Tel. (800) 321 2835
GREAT TRIPS
Tel. (800) 552 3419
MAYA CARIBE TRAVEL
Tel. (800) 223 4084
MAYA WORLD TOURS
Tel. (800) 392 6292
QUESTERS WORLDWIDE
NATURE TOURS
Tel. (800) 468 8668
SPANISH HERITAGE
TOURS
Tel. (800) 221 2580
SOUTHERN HORIZONS
Tel. (800) 333 9361
UK
EXODUS
Tel. (0181) 675 7996
EXPLORE WORLDWIDE
Tel. (0125) 231 9448
KUONI WORLDWIDE
Tel. (0171) 499 8636
SOUTH AMERICAN
EXPERIENCE
Tel. (0171) 976 5511
TWICKERS WORLD
Tel. (0181) 892 8164

New York

Europe

Atlantic Ocean

Miami

Europe

Havana

CUBA

DOMINICAN
REPUBLIC

JAMAICA

HAITI

CARAGUA

Caribbean Sea

San José

VENEZUELA

Panama City

PANAMA

COLOMBIA

Although travel is not always simple, the various means of transport in the Mayan countries will certainly feature among the more picturesque memories of your visit. Flying is the quickest and most comfortable way to travel. Buses are widely used by the local people and are a lively and convivial form of transport, although if you are visiting only one of the five countries you may well prefer to drive. Some isolated sites, such as lakeside villages and small Caribbean islands, can only be reached by boat.

INTERNAL AIRLINES

The Mayan countries have a highly developed internal airline network. Most flights are daily and reasonably priced. The large number of national airports in each of the five countries enables you to visit most places and make best use of your time. Remember that during high season, and over national holidays and other special events flights will need to be reserved in advance. Always confirm flights 2 days before departure.

ISLAND LINKS

In Belize the small planes of the local Island Air company operate daily services between the islands of Cay Caulker, Ambergris Cay (San Pedro) and Belize City international airport.
ISLAND AIR
Ambergris Cay
Tel: (026) 2484
Cay Caulker
Tel: (022) 212
or (212) 213.

"MAYAN PATH"

The *Mayan Path* is an option offered by the airline companies Aviateca and Taca, based in Paris, Tel. (33) 1 44 51 01 64 or 1 44 51 01 65 Fax 1 40 07 12 72. It is designed to enable visitors to take advantage of the regular air services to travel quickly and at competitive prices within the Mayan countries.

HOW IT WORKS

Choose your itinerary from the selection of towns and cities serviced by the companies. Each stage costs one or two coupons. Calculate the number of coupons required for your itinerary: it must be worth at least four coupons to qualify for the *Mayan Path* option. Calculate the cost of your trip by multiplying the number of coupons by US$65.

0   30

Bus routes:
28 miles / 1 hr   Distance journey t

Air services:
— — Mayan Pa
——— Other rou
✈ Internatio airport

MEXICO ◀

Veracruz
VILLAHERM◯
94 m
2 ½ hrs

Oaxaca

TUXTLA
GUTIERREZ
53 miles
2 hrs
Oaxaca   San Cris
de las C

Cuauhté
City

MEXICO ◀

Tapachula

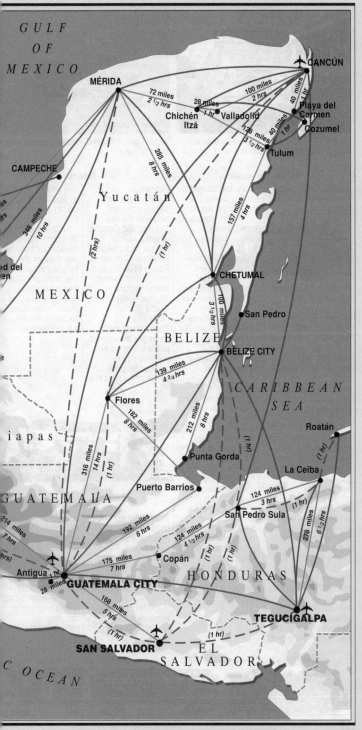

Buses are colored and often decorated with icons and good-luck charms.

Motor boats link the Caribbean islands with the mainland.

INTERCITY BUSES

A highly developed bus network makes it possible to reach

nearly all the villages, even the most isolated ones, in the Mayan countries. Journey times vary according to the road, the vehicle and, above all, the weather. Prices vary between $4 and $6 per 100 km (62 miles).

FIRST-CLASS BUSES
The fir-class buses run by private companies are more spacious than the second-class buses run by the national bus company, although not necessarily particularly comfortable. They do, however, offer a more rapid service between the main towns and cities for virtually the same price as the public buses. Tickets are paid for in advance at the company office where you can also reserve a seat on the day before departure.

Prices and timetables are displayed. These buses often run at night, especially on long journeys.

SECOND-CLASS BUSES
Second-class buses, usually old American school buses, are uncomfortable and normally packed. Put your trust in the driver: he is in complete control of his vehicle. An extremely agile young man is responsible for taking on passengers, shouting out the destination at each intersection, and letting them out at the right "stop". He also puts heavy luggage on the roof and collects the transport tax (*tasa*) from passengers. As the cost of transport varies, ask among local passengers. These buses run mainly in the morning, from 5am onward, but are less frequent in the afternoon.

BOATS

FERRIES
A passenger ferry service operates between the Isla Mujeres and Cancún (Puerto Juárez), the Isla de Cozumel and Playa del Carmen or Puerto Morelos, and links Puerto Barrios and Livingston (Guatemala) to Punta Gorda (Belize).

"LANCHAS"
These small motor boats are a means of public transport and will take you to isolated lakeside villages and sites that

can only be reached by boat (for about US$2). Regular services are often interrupted in the late afternoon. Out of season you have to negotiate on the spo for a *lancha privada* The price, preferably return, should be agreed before you leave. It can be up to ten times the price o a public *lancha*.

TRAINS

The rail network is used more for merchandise than passengers. Trains are fairly slow and dangerous (keep an eye on your luggage) and are a far from ideal means of transport.

MEXICAN NETWORK
Mexico is the only

one of the five Maya countries to have an extensive and efficient rail network. As first-class seats are extremely reasonable, avoid traveling second class. Beware of the during the night in sleeping compartments.

Guatemalan buses are often old American school buses.

This curious and typical tricycle is ideal for weaving through the narrow streets of Belize City.

CITY TRANSPORT

BUSES
Only large urban centers such as Guatemala City, San Salvador, Mérida and Cancún have an urban bus network. The number indicated on the front of the bus corresponds to its route (information is available from the tourist office). There are no fixed stops, although buses tend to slow down at intersections to take on or set down passengers. Just indicate to the driver that you want to get off. A journey never costs more than US$1, payable when you get on.

have negotiated the cost of the journey, and don't pay until you have reached the agreed destination.

ROAD SIGNS

Stop: *alto*
Slow down: *despacio*
Danger: *peligro*
Give way: *ceda el paso*
Parking: *estacionamiento*
Maximum height: *altura maxima*
Maximum width: *ancho libre*
No turning: *no voltear*
Cul de sac: *no hay paso*

COLECTIVOS"
These minibuses or light trucks carry around ten passengers and operate between airports (or ports) and the city center. This rapid service costs, on average, only a tenth of the equivalent taxi fare.

TAXIS
The famous Mexican "beetles" and other cars sporting a taxi sign have two things in common: they are rare and it is unusual for them to have a meter. Make sure you agree the cost of the journey before you set off.

HITCHHIKING
This service is usually provided by light trucks, open at the back, known locally as pick-ups. Don't climb aboard these joyful convoys before you

CARS

Cars can be hired in all the large towns and cities and at the international airports (where they are more expensive) of all the five Mayan countries.

HIRING A CAR
Make sure you have

an international driving license ♦ 346. If you pay by

banker's card (accepted everywhere) allow for an additional charge of 5 percent. A supplement is charged to leave a car in a town other than the place of hire. Hire vehicles may not be taken into Petén, in northern Guatemala, except to the Flores/Santa Elena airport.
AGENCE KOKA
Tel: 50 12 33 or 50 05 26.
It is also forbidden to cross borders in hire vehicles unless they are from the Dollar and Avis agencies who, subject to a supplement (US$20), allow you to cross from Guatemala into Honduras.

DRIVING ON THE "RUTA MAYA"

Once you leave the main roads, road surfaces are poor (especially in Guatemala) and signposting often non-existent. Good maps are available from the American Automobile Association (AAA) in Texaco and Esso gas stations. Do not leave valuable items in the car. If you are driving in town, avenues have priority over streets. The

maximum speed is 50 km/h (30 mph). Gas is extremely cheap in all five countries (around $1.50 per gallon). Gas stations are few and far between off the main roads.

Crossing borders between the Mayan countries can be an adventure in itself. It is prohibited, and dangerous, to cross a border in a hire vehicle so public transport is the only option. A number of airline companies operate daily services between the main towns o the various countries. Unlike the first-class buses, economy-class buses do not cross borders. Once the customs formalities are over, you can continue your journey by bus or pick-up in the next country

LOCAL TRANSPORT: BUSES, BOATS, TRAINS AND PLANES

GUATEMALA/MEXICO

◆ INTERCITY BUSES
A number of border posts allow buses to cross between Guatemala and Mexico. The border towns (and their Mexican counterparts) of Tecún Umán (Ciudad Hidalgo), El Carmen (Talisman) and La Mesilla (Ciudad Cuauhtemoc) are the most frequently used.

◆ BOATS
It is also possible to cross directly from Petén (Guatemala) into Chiapas (Mexico) by *lancha* ◆ 354 (prices and frequency variable) along the Río San Pedro and the Río de la Pasión. This is a long and physically demanding trip, best undertaken in a group.

◆ TRAINS
A railway line links Puerto Barrios –Guatemala City –Tecún Umán (Mexican border) and continues toward the United States along the Mexican Pacific coast.

EL SALVADOR / GUATEMALA

◆ BUSES
There is a direct, first-class bus service between San Salvador and Guatemala City (the King Quality bus from the Hotel Presidente). There is also a daily, economy-class service from San Salvador's Occidente terminal. Some buses only go as far as the border where you can catch a Guatemalan bus to Guatemala City. Others go to Puerto Barrios (Guatemala) and the Guatemalan–Mexican border.

GUATEMALA / BELIZE

◆ FERRIES
A boat leaves Puerto Barrios (Guatemala) on Tuesdays and Fridays at 7.30am, stopping at Livingston (Guatemala) at about 9am before continuing to Punta Gorda (Belize). It makes the return trip on the same day, leaving at 2.30pm. Tickets can be bought on the day of departure before boarding. Get there at least two hours beforehand to be sure of a seat and to allow enough time for customs and immigration formalities.

◆ BUSES
There are direct daily links between Flores (Guatemala) and Chetumal (Mexico) via San Ignacio, Belize City and Orange Walk (Belize). The bus leaves Flores at 5am (reservations at the Hotel San Juan, Santa Elena).

EL SALVADOR / HONDURAS

◆ BUSES
The border post of El Amatillo, in the east of El Salvador, is the most frequently used and the safest for Honduras. The buses for El Amatillo arrive and leave from the Oriente terminal in San Salvador. For passengers in the south of the country, a more direct route takes them to Copán (Honduras). However, it is advisable to ask for information on safety at tourist offices as there is still the possibility of disturbances in the region.

MEXICO / BELIZE

◆ BUSES
Chetumal (Mexico) is the departure and arrival point for buses to and from Belize. Batty Brothers and Venus operate a daily return service from Belize City to the north: Chetumal–Belize Cit via Corozal and Orange Walk.

◆ AIR LINKS
There are daily services from Belize City to Cancún and Mérida.

VISITING COPÁN (HONDURAS) FROM GUATEMALA
The quickest way is to go direct from Guatemala City to Chiquimila (105 miles) by first-class bus: Rutas Orientale (19 Calle 8–18, Zona 1, Guatemala City). Take the Transporte Vilma bus from the Chiquimila terminal t the border, in the direction of El Florido The last bus that will enable you to cross the border (which closes at 5.30pm) leaves at 2.30pm. T cross the Guatemala–Hondura border (open 6am–5.30pm), take the minibus (the last bus is at 3.30pm) to Copán. If you miss the last minibus, you can take a pick-up.

Loading luggage: an extremely picturesque operation.

El Salvador welcomes you at the border with Guatemala.

CROSSING A BORDER

Customs formalities are carried out at the border post. This involves showing your passport, having it stamped by the customs official for the country you are leaving

and paying an exit tax. The procedure is repeated at the customs post of the country you are entering where you pay customs duty. You will also be asked how long you plan to stay in the country (maximum length of stay is

3 months). The time taken by these formalities varies according to the number of people crossing (allow 20 minutes on average) and the time spent waiting for the bus to continue your journey.

	CUSTOMS DUTIES	AIRPORT TAX
BELIZE	$B 1 (US$ 0.5)	US$ 10
GUATEMALA	10 Quetzals (US$ 2)	US$ 10
HONDURAS	10 Lempira (US$ 1.5)	US$ 10
MEXICO	6 Pesos (US$ 2.5)	US$ 17
EL SALVADOR	15 Colones (US$ 2)	US$ 17

PRINCIPLE AIRLINE COMPANIES IN THE TOWNS AND CITIES OF THE MAYAN COUNTRIES

	CANCÚN	CHETUMAL	MÉRIDA	VILLAHERMOSA	GUATEMALA C.	BELIZE CITY	SAN SALVADOR	TEGUCIGALPA
AÉROCARIBE	84 20 00	2 66 75	28 67 90	14 32 02				
AÉROMEXICO	84 35 71		27 95 66	12 43 89				
AÉROCANCÚN	83 31 44							
AÉROCOZUMEL	86 01 62		28 67 90					
AVIACSA	84 42 14	2 77 65	26 91 73	14 47 55				
AVIATECA	84 39 38		24 94 77		38 14 79			
LACSA	87 31 01				34 69 05		24 62 22	37 01 56
MEXICANA	87 44 44		24 67 54	16 31 32				
TROPIC AIR	87 64 46					02 456 71		
TAESA			26 99 13					
AÉROLITORAL				14 36 13				
AÉROQUETZAL					36 52 14			
AÉROVIAS					31 96 33	02 754 45		
COPA					36 62 56		23 92 25	52 06 28
SAHSA					35 26 71	02 770 80	24 03 40	
TACA					31 91 72		23 22 44	
TAPSA					31 48 60			
TRASLADOS					34 71 05			
ISLAND AIR						02 311 40		
MAYA AIRWAYS						02 723 12		
SKY BIRD						02 325 96		

◆ CURRENCY

Years of soaring inflation have taught the inhabitants of the Mayan countries to be extremely cautious where money is concerned. It is a region where the dollar rules and European currency is only changed in the large towns and cities.

MEXICAN PESO

On January 1, 1993, following a period of high inflation, the "new peso" (N$), divided into 100 *centavos*, replaced the "old peso" ($) which is still in circulation. A new peso is worth 1,000 old pesos. The new coins are bi-colored, and smaller and lighter than the old ones. Bank notes are in new and old pesos. Notes of equivalent value have the same design and color, only the denomination is different. Prices are marked in new pesos (N$) and cheques and credit card slips must be made out in new pesos.

QUETZAL

The local currency of Guatemala is named after the quetzal bird which is also the national emblem. The quetzal is divided into 100 *centavos*.

Coins are rarely used.

	LOCAL CURRENCY	EQUIV. US$
BELIZE	Belize Dollar	B$ 2
GUATEMALA	Quetzal	Q 5.80
HONDURAS	Lempira	£ 8
MEXICO	Peso	N$ 3.35
EL SALVADOR	Colón	C 8.72

BELIZE DOLLAR

The currency of Belize is the Belize dollar (B$).

Unlike its neighbors, where the rate of exchange fluctuates fairly significantly, Belize operates a "one for two" rate, where US$1 is equivalent to $B2

DOLLAR AND PESO

The symbol for the US dollar (S with two bars) and the peso (S with one bar) are very similar. Look carefully at prices for the big hotels, luxury goods, etc. as they are often marked in US dollars, especially in Yucatán.

LEMPIRA

The currency of Honduras is the lempira, divided into 100 *centavos*.

COLÓN

Like the other currencies, El Salvador's colón is divided into 100 *centavos*.

SOME PRICES

1 MEAL AT A MARKET: US$ 1	1 DOUBLE ROOM: US$ 50	A ONE-WEEK SPANISH COURSE: US$ 65	ONE DAY'S CAR HIRE (4x4): US$ 70

ENTRANCE TO A MAJOR MAYAN SITE: US$ 6	GOOD QUALITY "HUIPIL" (EMBROIDERED INDIAN TUNIC): US$ 30	1 ROOM WITH HAMMOCK: US$ 5	1 DIVING EXCURSION (INCLUSIVE): US$ 50

EXCHANGE

The US dollar is the most easily exchanged form of currency (bank notes or traveler's cheques). These can be exchanged in banks (Monday–Friday 9am–1pm), in Bureaux de Change (most numerous in Mexico and open at night), or in most big hotels (poor exchange rate but useful in the evening or at weekends).

BLACK MARKET EXCHANGE

It is possible to exchange money and traveler's cheques on the black market, in the city-center streets of the capitals and at border posts. Although the rate of exchange is poor, it is one way of getting rid of the currency of the country you are leaving since banks in the neighboring country do not necessarily accept it.

METHODS OF PAYMENT

US DOLLAR

In Belize you can pay for purchases with US dollars. In the other Mayan countries the dollar is the only foreign currency accepted, but it can't be used for small purchases.

CREDIT CARDS

(tarjeta de crédito)
Automatic cash dispensers accepting international credit cards are few and far between and it is difficult to withdraw money after the banks have closed. Cards are readily accepted in major hotels, restaurants and stores but usually involve an additional charge of about 5 percent. Visa, American Express and Diner's Club cards are the most widely accepted.

TIPPING

Tips in restaurants are usually in the order of 10 percent. You are expected to fill in the *Tips* or *Propina* section and write the total at the bottom of the invoices and checks given to you. If you want, the proprietor or storekeeper will do it for you. In hotels tips are calculated on the basis of length of stay. Give at least US$1 to the cleaner, the chamber maid and the child who has patiently watched over your car without you asking.

COST OF LIVING

The cost of a holiday in Central America varies from country to country. Holidays in Guatemala are relatively inexpensive. El Salvador, Honduras and Mexico are more costly and Belize is the most expensive of all. Prices on the sites and in major towns and cities tend to be higher than in the rest of the country. Prices for leisure activities and hotels are between 15 percent and 25 percent lower during the rainy season. The cost of your holiday will depend on how you travel.

VAT

When paying checks don't confuse tips and VAT (*IVA*). The latter is 15 percent on standard consumer products (including all hotel and restaurant expenses) and 20 percent on luxury products.

Patience and discretion are two of the qualities required, and always rewarded, during a journey through the Mayan countries. Allow at least one hour to make a call from an international telephone center and two to four weeks for a letter to reach Europe. Communications are not only slow and laborious but also expensive – international telecommunications charges in Central America, and especially Guatemala, are among the highest in the world.

TELEPHONE

International calls (*larga distancia*) are extremely expensive from Central America (on average US$25 for three minutes). Collect calls (*por cobrar*) can be made from Mexico (dial 09) and Belize (dial 115) but are not so easy from Guatemala, El Salvador and Honduras. In some cities you can use AT&T's US Direct which accesses you

to an AT&T operator who will help you place a call to the US, or you can call directly with the use of a calling card (Belize 555, Guatemala 190, Honduras 123, El Salvador 190, Mexico 95 + 800 + 462 + 4240).
All towns have telecommunications centers where you can make national and international calls, send telegrams, telexes and faxes (sending a one-page fax costs half as much as a three-minute telephone call). Opening hours are usually very convenient with most centers staying open until midnight.

MEXICO

Only Mexico has phone boxes that take phone cards (blue for international calls and orange for national calls). Cards cost 10 or 30 pesos.

FROM THE US

Calls to Central America cost from $1.00 to $2.46 per minute.

FROM THE UK

Calls to the region cost from £1.14 to £1.39 per minute.

MAIL

RECEIVING MAIL

The most reliable method is to have mail sent *poste restante* to the main post office of the relevant town (preferably a capital or major center) where it will be easiest to collect.

SENDING MAIL

The Central American postal service is extremely slow and unreliable. It is best to send mail from the main post offices in the capitals or large towns. Have it weighed before you send it so that any additional tarifs may be paid in advance, avoiding extra delay.

STAMPS

The stamps from the five Mayan countries are among the most beautiful in the world. Collectors will find a wide range of stamps on sale in the central post offices of Guatemala City and Belize City in particular.

ELECTRICITY

The current is 110 volts and sockets need flat American plugs, so take an adapter. Only the large hotels have 220 volts. Some regions (e.g. Honduras, Guatemalan highlands and Tulum in Mexico) have frequent restrictions on the use of electricity.

TELEPHONE CODES FROM AND TO THE US AND UK				
	FROM US	FROM UK	To US	To UK
BELIZE	011-501	00-501	00-1	00-44
GUATEMALA	011-502	00-502	00-1	00-44
HONDURAS	011-504	00-504	00-1	00-44
MEXICO	011-52	00-52	98-1	98-44
EL SALVADOR	011-503	00-503	0-1	0-44

5a. Avenida Arco Gucumatz

FINDING YOUR WAY AROUND

CHI UXE KAJAM B'E

Most of the towns are built around a central square (Plaza Mayor or Zócalo) and crossed from north to south by avenues (avenidas) and from east to west by streets (calles).

STREET SIGNS
Streets and avenues have either a name or number, and sometimes both. Street names may be indicated on two superposed plaques: one in Spanish and the other in Maya.

STREET LAYOUT
In El Salvador, Honduras and Antigua Guatemala, streets and avenues are numbered in relation to the central square. Streets to the east of the square are called Calle Oriente, and to the west Calle Poniente. Similarly, avenues to the north are Avenida Norte, and to the south Avenida Sur. For example: 3 Calle Oriente, no. 10 is the address of no. 10 on the third street to the east of the central square.

IN BELIZE
Most of the towns in Belize do not conform to this grid layout and use the English terms street, avenue, lane, etc. to designate the winding streets which often follow or lead to the coast.

ADDRESSES IN GUATEMALA CITY
The capital is divided into over twenty zones (zonas), each with the same street and avenue numbers. First locate the zone in question. The first figure after the (numbered) street indicates the nearest avenue; similarly, the first figure after the (numbered) avenue indicates the nearest street. The second figure indicates the distance in meters between the place you are looking for and the intersection with the nearest avenue or street. For example, the INGUAT tourist office:
7a Avenida 1–17 Zona 4
is situated in zone 4, on 7th avenue, 17 meters from the intersection with street no.1.

TAKING PHOTOGRAPHS

Taking photographs on the "Ruta Maya" is, first and foremost, a continual process of tact and respect. A telephoto lens is invaluable since it avoids disturbing the local inhabitants, although it is always preferable to ask their permission. In certain Maya villages and during certain ceremonies, photographs are strictly prohibited. Do observe these restrictions which are always clearly indicated. On some sites a charge is made for the right to take photographs and this is paid at the entrance. A charge is always made for movie cameras on archeological sites in Mexico.

GOING OUT

Bars close just after midnight. In Mexico, where the night life is more lively, many bars have "happy hours" when they offer two drinks for the price of one. On the Atlantic coast, in Cozumel, Playa del Carmen and Livingston, there are sometimes open-air discos. In Guatemala it is an offense to drink alcohol in the street. The national police forces are totally unsympathetic toward cannabis smokers: abstinence is the simplest and best form of precaution.

NEWSPAPERS

Local newspapers are in Spanish, except in Belize where they are in English. The dailies (below) are thick and heavy and usually provide good coverage of international events. You will find the *Herald Tribune* in the big hotels and you can read national newspapers in the relevant embassies.

Markets are a feast for the eyes as well as a source of snacks throughout the day.

On the coast buy fish direct from the fishermen when they return to shore.

Corn, chicken and black beans form the basis of a local cuisine deeply rooted in the Mayan culture. Although it cannot be described as gourmet cooking, it is sufficiently varied to be enjoyable. Bear in mind, however, that food is the prime carrier of a number of infections so it is essential to take a number of basic precautions.

CORN AND "TORTILLAS"

Corn is the basis of the local cuisine and is found in a large number of dishes: the *tortilla*, for example, is a flat maize pancake which serves as bread, plate, spoon and serviette. This unique dish is served filled with cheese or mince (*enchiladas*), covered with melted cheese (*quesadillas*), or filled and fried (*tacos*). It can also be rolled up and dipped in *guacamole* (a thick puree of avocado, chilies and onions, and flavored with coriander). El Salvador has a variation on the *tortilla*: the *pupusa* is a smaller pancake

filled with cheese, sausage and black beans.

BEANS AND CHICKEN

Red and black beans (*frijoles*) and white rice (*arroz*) are served with most dishes. Beef is rare in the region and poultry is the only meat eaten in any quantity. Chicken (*pollo*) and turkey (*guajolote*) are served in a brown, chocolate-based sauce (*mole*), which has an incredible twenty different ingredients and is seasoned with hot spices.

FISH AND SHELLFISH

Very much in evidence in the coastal regions are shrimps and prawns (*camarones*) and oysters (*ostiones*) from September to April, and lobsters (*langosta*) from June to February. A salad of raw fish (*ceviche*) marinated in lemon juice is also a classic dish. Shark and barracuda are among the deep sea fish on the menu.

BREAD

Although introduced relatively recently, a wide variety of breads are available including: bread rolls (*bollilos*), wholemeal or black bread (*pan negro*), coconut bread (*pan coco*) sweet bread (*pan dulce*) and salted bread (*pan frances*).

DESSERTS

Dessert often consists of a fresh fruit salad: grapefruit, oranges, bananas, melon, mangos and papaws all grow in abundance in the region. Restaurants offer a variety of different flans and ice creams (*helados*). Don't be caught out by *tortas*: in Central America (Mexico) they are filled sandwiches, not pies

Local beers are light. The rum, on the other hand, should be treated with caution and drunk in moderation.

"Mercados de la comida" are a pleasant and inexpensive alternative to "tourist" restaurants.

DRINKS

Don't drink tap water. Always ask for bottled mineral water, which will be opened when served. Some hotels leave a carafe or container of drinking water in the rooms for guests. The delicious fruit juices, sold in the

street and squeezed while you wait, are perfectly alright, although the same cannot be said for the local drinks made from freshly squeezed fruit, water, corn juice or coconut milk. You can always use water purifying tablets, but it takes several hours before the water is drinkable. Ironically in these great coffee-producing countries, the black coffee is often mediocre: thin and very sweet. You need to specify if you drink coffee without sugar (*sin azûcar*).

SPECIALITIES

Barbaco: a piece of mutton or goat's meat wrapped in banana leaves and cooked on charcoal.
Carnitas: little pieces of fried pork, eaten hot.
Chicharron: fried pork rind, eaten cold. *Ciles rellenos*: peppers stuffed with meat, fish or cheese. The *tamales* eaten in Mexico are made from polenta (ground corn) and meat.

SOMETHING DIFFERENT

Poc-chuc consists of strips of fillet pork marinated in orange juice and served with a sauce and spicy onions.
Pollo pibil is a dish consisting of chicken pieces marinated in a non-spicy sauce (annatto seeds, orange juice, garlic, salt and pepper), wrapped in banana leaves and cooked in the oven.

PRECAUTIONS

Raw vegetables and fruit sold in the street should be peeled or washed before eating. If possible only eat pre-cooked pork: locally prepared dishes are ideally suited to the potential problems associated with some foods. Only take water, ice creams, sorbets and ice cubes in the big hotels. Only buy milk in sealed bottles with a "pasteurized" label (*pasterizada*). In this tropical climate food is spicy. Very spicy food is described as "hot" (*calientes*) and less spicy food as "moderate" (*templados*).

Although chilies are recognized as having antiseptic properties, a western palate can find them hard to handle. You can always make it clear when placing your order that you want dishes without spices (restaurants are used to such orders).

MEAL TIMES

Breakfast (*desayuno*), served until 10am, is a very rich meal consisting of a choice of several different egg dishes, including *huevos rancheros* (fried eggs in a chili sauce, served on a *tortilla*) and *huevos a la mejicana* (scrambled eggs with tomato and chili). Lunch (*comida* or *almuerzo*) is served up to 3pm and dinner (*cena*) up to 10pm. Dinner is often replaced by a tea (*merienda*) consisting of sweet bread and coffee. If you decide to adopt the local eating habits you will snack throughout the day and only eat one full meal at lunchtime.

WHERE TO EAT

Every village has a *mercado de la comida* where you can eat on the spot, up to 3pm, at ridiculously low prices (around US$1 for a hot dish, a drink and a coffee). To ring the changes, you can eat Italian or Mexican food in most of the larger towns. Belize has a number of Chinese restaurants and El Salvador has several vegetarian restaurants.

When you have exhausted the secrets of local, everyday life, why not try a tour designed to reveal the main Mayan sites or some of the more original aspects of the Mayan countries. These tours can be organized and combined to suit your particular needs. The minimum time indicated should be extended during the rainy season. The cost varies according to the regions visited, the means of transport and the type of accommodation.

CLASSIC TOUR
(2 WEEKS)
Leaves from and returns to Cancún, stopping at Chichén Itzá, Mérida, Uxmal, Palenque, Chichicastenango, San Cristóbal de las Casas, Panajachel, Antigua, Tikal and Belize City. The tour enables you to see the major Mayan sites and three countries: Mexico, Guatemala and Belize. It can be extended by any of the following options.

DIVING EXTENSION
(+ 5 DAYS)
Leaves from Belize City with accommodation on the island of Ambergris Cay and/or Cay Caulker and various excursions to, for example, the underwater caves of the Blue Hole or the depths of the Marine Reserve.
The tour is designed for diving and leisure enthusiasts, who will discover one of the most beautiful coral reefs in the world on the Caribbean coast of Belize. Prices in San Pedro (Ambergris

Cay) are high and you should avoid staying there if you want to spend your money on diving.

EL SALVADOR EXTENSION
The tour leaves from Guatemala City and visits the site of Joya de Cerén. The two-day trip into El Salvador can be made from Honduras (border incidents are minimal since the end of the civil war).

COPÁN–LIVINGSTON –POPTÚN EXTENSION
(+ 7 DAYS)
This tour enables you to visit the site of Copán (Honduras), discover the village of Livingston with its Caribbean atmosphere, and visit the Ixobel *finca* at Poptún (Guatemala) where you can help to pick coffee beans at harvest time. The tour takes a minimum of one week but the time spent in each place can vary. For example, it is possible to go from Guatemala City to Copán, visit the ruins and return to Guatemala in one day ◆ 356. However, to avoid having to rush, it is better to allow two days for this trip, staying overnight in Copán.

ADVENTURE TOUR
(21 DAYS)
Leaves from and returns to Cancún, passing via Tikal, Sayaxché, Bonampak, Palenque and Mérida. This demanding and original (and rather costly) route is ideal for would-be adventurers. It takes you through the jungle in a dug-out and enables you to visit the more inaccessible sites. It can be undertaken individually but is rather difficult to organize.

YUCATECAN SITES TOUR
(1 WEEK)
The tour leaves from and returns to Cancún, crossing Yucatán via Chichén Itzá, Mérida, Uxmal and Palenque (Chiapas). It is ideal if you are short of time and want to visit the major Mayan sites in Mexico and enjoy the beaches of the Caribbean coast.

or people who like peace, quiet and relative solitude, there are numerous "lost paradises" in the more secluded corners of the Mayan countries: Punta Allen, Lake Montebello (Mexico), Río Petexbatún, the Biotopo de Monterico (Guatemala), the Volcán Cerro Verde (El Salvador) and, of course, the many almost deserted islands of Belize.

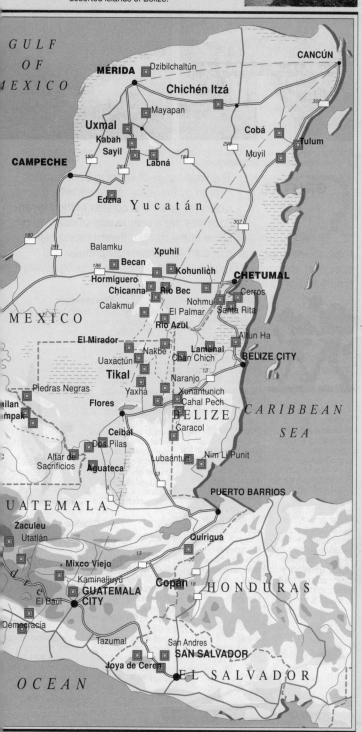

GULF OF MEXICO

CANCÚN

MÉRIDA · Dzibilchaltún

Chichén Itzá

· Mayapan

Uxmal

Cobá

Kabah

Tulum

Sayil

Muyil

CAMPECHE

Labná

Yucatán

Edzna

Balamku

Xpuhil

Becan

Kohunlich

Hormiguero

CHETUMAL

Chicanna

Río Bec

Cerros

Calakmul

Nohmul

Santa Rita

MEXICO

El Palmar

Río Azul

Altun Ha

El Mirador

Lamanai

Nakbe

Chan Chich

BELIZE CITY

Uaxactún

Tikal

Naranjo

Piedras Negras

Yaxhá

Xunantunich

Flores

Cahal Pech

BELIZE

Caracol

CARIBBEAN SEA

ilan

Ceibal

mpak

Dos Pilas

Lubaantun

Nim Li Punit

Altar de Sacrificios

Aguateca

PUERTO BARRIOS

GUATEMALA

Zaculeu

Quiriguá

Utatlán

· Mixco Viejo

Kaminaljuyú

Copán

HONDURAS

GUATEMALA CITY

El Baúl

Democracia

Tazumal

San Andres

SAN SALVADOR

Joya de Cerén

EL SALVADOR

OCEAN

The many lakes in the Mayan countries provide an ideal focus for walks and excursions.

Sunset from the shores of Lake Atitlán.

GRUTAS
Tarifa
TURISTA EXT. Q7.00
TURISTA NAC. Q.2.00
NIÑOS MEN. 10 A. 1.00 C.
" ¡BIENVENIDOS! "
BIOENERG.

The wide range of sporting opportunities offered by the volcanos, waterfalls, nature reserves, lakes and oceans of the Mayan countries are a unique way of discovering some of the many different facets of this region. Green tourism is becoming increasingly popular and specialist agencies in Guatemala and Belize are offering quality "sport-and-nature" tours.

WALKING

Walking is an enjoyable way of discovering a region at your own pace, and off the beaten track. The Mayan countries have some of the most volcanic highlands in the world. Climbing the volcanos ◆ 370 will delight any traveler, while committed long-distance walkers can enjoy the beautiful landscape of the vast plains and plateaux which stretch between the villages.

RIVERS AND WHITE-WATER RAFTING

Excursions are organized in Belize from San Ignacio and Belize City, and in Guatemala from Flores, Antigua and Guatemala City. The Usumacinta, the longest river in the Mayan countries, flows from Guatemala into the Gulf of Mexico. It used to be one of the Mayas' main trade routes, which explains why there are so many Mayan sites along its banks. Here you are far from the more easily accessible sites, with only the cries of monkeys to disturb you. The three other navigable waterways are the Grijalva, the Hondo and the Motagua.

WINDSURFING

Windsurfing enthusiasts can surf on Lakes Atitlán, Petén Itzá and Izabal in Guatemala and Lake Coatepeque in El Salvador, as well as off the coast. Equipment can be hired at each site. At Panajachel (Lake Atitlán) Luis René Portillo organizes day excursions and *mañanas aquaticas* (nautical mornings) on the lake as well as hiring out equipment, such as pedalos, rowing boats,

windsurfing boards and canoes.

CAVING

There are a number of underground caves and rivers that were once the setting for sacred Mayan ceremonies.

POPTÚN AND ITS ENVIRONS

Visits to the caves in the vicinity of Poptún (mid-way between Flores and Río Dulce) are organized from the Ixobel *finca* (Poptún) ◆ 364.

LA CANDELARIA

It is advisable to organize your visit to the caves of La Candelaria with a tour operator or La Candelaria agency. The caves and river (33 yards wide in places) form an underground network over 7 miles long. The visit lasts for at least two hours and made partly on foot and partly by boat along the river.

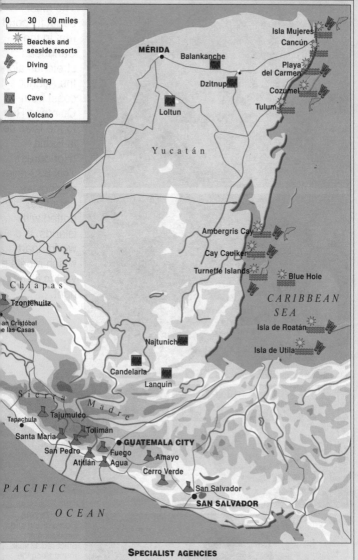

Map legend:
0   30   60 miles

☀ Beaches and seaside resorts
🤿 Diving
🐟 Fishing
⬛ Cave
🌋 Volcano

MÉRIDA   Balankanche
Dzitnup
Loltun

Isla Mujeres
Cancún
Playa del Carmen
Cozumel
Tulum

Y u c a t á n

Ambergris Cay
Cay Caulker
Turneffe Islands   Blue Hole

C H I A P A S
Tzontehuitz
an Cristóbal
e las Casas

C A R I B B E A N
S E A

Isla de Roatán
Isla de Utila

Najtunich

Candelaria
Lanquin

S i e r r a   *M a d r e*

Tapachula   Tajumulco
Santa María   Tolimán
San Pedro   Fuego
Atitlán   Agua   **GUATEMALA CITY**
Amayo
Cerro Verde
San Salvador
SAN SALVADOR

P A C I F I C

O C E A N

SPECIALIST AGENCIES

HORSERIDING,
OLCANOS, EXCURSIONS
URISMO EK CHUAH
, calle 6–24, Zona 2
uatemala City 01002
el. / Fax: 2-24375
BUNGY JUMPING,
HITE WATER RAFTING
AYA EXPEDITIONS
ammy Ridenour)
5, calle 1–91,
ona 10
uatemala City
1010
el / Fax: 374666

◆ SAILING (LAKE
IZABAL, LIVINGSTON,
BELIZE)
VIAREAL (Real
Desrosiers)
4, calle Oriente, no. 7,
Antigua Guatemala
Tel: 323228
IZABLA ADVENTURE
(Alfredo Torriello)
La Galleria, 7 Av.
14–44, Zona 10
Guatemala City
Tel: 340323/24
Fax: 317912

◆ EXCURSIONS IN
PETÉN
EXPLORE
(Carlos Jiménez)
Av. Centroamérica,
Flores, Guatemala
Tel / Fax: 500655
12–51, Zona 10
Guatemala City
Tel: 316243
Fax: 341179
◆ CAVING
CANDELARIA (STP)
2 Av. 7–78,
Zona 10

Guatemala City
01010
Tel: 346235/36
Fax: 346237
◆ HORSERIDING,
CANOEING, CYCLING
(BELIZE)
MAYA MOUNTAIN
LODGE P.O. Box 46,
San Ignacio, Cayo,
Belize
Tel: 92-2164
Fax: 92-2029
Freephone:
1-800-344-MAYA

The most beautiful coral reef in the Caribbean stretches along the Atlantic coast from Quintana Roo to the Islas de la Bahia (Honduras). This 620-mile ecological paradise, dotted with islands, is a world apart which merits a visit in its own right.

DIVING
Scuba diving and snorkeling are practiced all year round along the Caribbean coast. The barrier reef, the longest in the world after the Great Barrier Reef of Australia, is a marine reserve which harbors an infinite wealth of underwater flora and fauna. It is strictly prohibited to take coral from the reef.

SNORKELING

you don't have a
ver's certificate you
n hire a mask,
ppers and breathing
be for about US$3
r day and admire
e coral and fish at
allow depths. The
a de Cozumel has
number of reserves
r divers, such as
nankanaab
ark, while day
ps in a motor
at offer an
portunity to see the
oals. The skipper
ovides a mask and
eathing tube to
able you to explore
ch site. Cost:
ound US$25.

DIVER'S CERTIFICATE

ou can take your
ternational diver's
rtificate while on
liday. It takes three
five days and
volves five dives
d a written test.
ost: from less
an US$150 (the
eapest
rtificate in the
orld is at
ila,
onduras) to
S$350.
verage cost of
o 45-minute
ves (including
ansport and
quipment): US$50.

CANCÚN AND ISLA MUJERES
The "sleeping shark"
reserve is 3 miles
north of the island (at
a depth of 75 feet).
The low level of
oxygenation in the
underground caves
makes the sharks
lethargic and, in
theory, harmless.

DIVING SITES

PLAYA DEL CARMEN AND COZUMEL (MEX.)
More than
twenty-five
diving sites
around the Isla
de Cozumel and
off the Playa del
Carmen are
remarkable for
their
colorful
corals.

CAULKER, AMBERGRIS AND OTHER CAYS (BELIZE)
◆ Blue Hole:
Plunging to a depth
of 130 feet off the
Turneffe Islands, this
formation, studied by
Jean-Yves
Cousteau, is the only
one of its kind in the
world. By torchlight it
reveals underwater
caves barred by
huge stalagmites and
stalactites. Allow five
hours to get there
from Cay
Caulker.
◆ Hol Chan
Marine:
This
submerged
canyon, at
a depth of
98 feet, is
covered
with coral
and teems
with fish.

◆ Half Moon Cay
(Lighthouse Reef):
About 70 miles east
of Belize City lies
one of the Northern
Hemisphere's only
three atolls (coral
islands formed by
an emerged ring of
land around a
lagoon).

BAY ISLANDS: ROATÁN, UTILA AND GUANAJA
The diving sites of
Honduras afford the
same quality of
underground
landscape as the
northern sites at a
substantially lower
cost.

FISHING

Underwater fishing is
practiced in the rivers
and sea. For those
who like something
more exhilarating,
there is always game
fishing which involves
long trials of strength
with deep-sea fish,
such as tarpon, tuna,
swordfish and
porgies, before
returning them to the
water. The less
daring may prefer to
fish for prawns and
shrimps in the
shallows of Belize.
On the islands
restaurants are
happy to cook the
fruits of your fishing
trips. The lobster-
fishing season is
between June 15 and
March 15.

FISHING CALENDAR

	J	F	M	A	M	J	J	A	S	O	N	D
LUE MARLIN	○	○	◐	◐	●	●	●	●	○	○	○	○
WHITE MARLIN	○	○	◐	●	●	●	●	◐	○	○	○	○
LYING FISH	○	◐	●	●	●	●	●	●	●	○	○	○
UNA	○	○	◐	●	●	●	●	●	●	○	○	○
ARRACUDA	●	●	●	●	●	●	●	●	◐	●	●	●
ONITO	○	◐	●	●	●	●	●	●	●	◐	◐	◐
ORGY	●	●	●	●	●	●	●	●	●	●	●	●
HARK	●	●	●	●	●	●	●	●	●	●	●	●

● large number	◐ not many	○ none

369

◆ VOLCANOS AND NATURE RESERVES

The high plateaux of El Salvador and Guatemala have a remarkably dense concentration of volcanos. As well as offering some magnificent views, these active giants give the most spectacular *son et lumière* display in the world. For those who prefer less strenuous walks, the Mayan countries have nature reserves open to the public which offer the chance to encounter a wealth of wildlife.

ACTIVE VOLCANOS

PACAYA (8,373 feet) is the most famous active volcano in Guatemala. Allow a 2-hour drive by minibus and a 2½-hour walk to reach the summit. At night the boiling magma spews its lava into the cold, dark sky.

SANTIAGUITO AND FUEGO
These are Guatemala's other two active volcanos. Fuego can be reached from Antigua.

TWO GIANTS

TAJUMULCO
At 13,845 feet this is the highest volcano in Guatemala. It is popular with walkers as it is easy to climb in spite of its impressive size.

TACANA
Tacana ("the house of fire") is the second highest volcano (13,425 feet) in the Mayan countries. It lies on the border of Mexico and Guatemala and is one of the few active volcanos in the region.

CLIMBING A VOLCANO

◆ Never climb a volcano alone. You run the risk of getting lost or being the victim of one of the numerous attacks recorded every year in these dangerous places.
◆ In the towns which are the departure points for these excursions there are a number of agencies and guides available. Descents are often at night to enable you to watch the sunset from the summit and, on the active volcanos, to see the luminous lava the dark.
◆ Take something to eat and drink and some warm clothing. It is cold in the mountains, especially at night with the only warmth coming from the very hot ground near the active craters.

VOLCANOS OF EL SALVADOR

In El Salvador excursions to climb the Izalco, Cerro Verde and Santa Ana volcanos are organized from Santa Ana or San Salvador.

CERRO VERDE
One of the most beautiful national parks in El Salvador lies on the slopes of this huge, extinct volcano, above Lake Coatepeque. On either side of the Cerro Verde are the Izalco and Santa Ana volcanos.

IZALCO
The Volcán Izalco is still listed as an active volcano as its last eruption was in 1966. Its history is famous in El Salvador. Until February 1770 the present site of Izalco was occupied by a hole emitting a column of sulphuric steam. Then a cone began to form around the edge of the smoke, growing at an amazing rate until it reached a height of 6,135 feet. Izalco went on spewing out fire, a spectacle visible for several miles around, which earned it the name of the Lighthouse of the Pacific. In 1957 all activity suddenly ceased and the small eruption of 1966 has been its only sign of life since then. Its slopes have become fresh, peaceful and incredibly fertile.

CLIMBING IZALCO
A marked path leads from the car park at the entrance to the Cerro Verde National Park. The excursion takes 3–4 hours from start to finish.

VANTAGE POINTS
The best point from which to view Izalco is from the top of the Cerro Verde volcano which, at 6,660 feet above sea level, allows you to look down on its crater. Another famous vantage point is the Hotel de Montaña, built to offer guests unique view of an active volcano. It was completed in 1957, the year in which, after two hundred years of activity, the volcano suddenly fell silent.

Lake Izabal offers an opportunity to admire a wide variety of rare tropical species.

Hut on the banks of the Río Dulce, reached from Livingston or Lake Izabal.

DIFFICULT CLIMBS (GUATEMALA)

SAN PEDRO
The Volcán San Pedro (9,908 feet) is one of the three volcanos of Lake Atitlán. In Cakchiquel Maya it is called "Choyjuyub" meaning "volcano of the lagoon". From the summit, "El Mirador", there is a magnificent view of the lake and the other two volcanos, Tolimán and Atitlán.

TOLIMÁN
The Volcán Tolimán (10,360 feet) is covered with a profusion of dense vegetation. The difficulty experienced in finding a way through the undergrowth is outweighed by the pleasure of walking in such wild, natural surroundings.

AGUA
You can go down into the very deep crater of the Volcán Agua

(12,388 feet) to a mountain refuge which can accommodate up to thirty people.

SANTO TOMÁS
The Santo Tomás volcano (11,499 feet) is one of the hardest to climb in the region. Two paths lead to the summit: allow 6–8 hours walking time if you take the *Las Georginas* path and 8–10 hours via the *Cumbre de Alaska*. Don't consider attempting it without a guide.

NATURE RESERVES

GUATEMALA
CERRO CAHUI CONSERVATION PARK
The park, on the northern shore of Lake Petén Itzá, is reached from Flores. Its fauna includes jaguars, howler monkeys and peccaries.
BIOTOPO CHACÓN MACHACA DEL MANATI
Near Livingston. The tapir and jaguar are its most impressive inhabitants.
BIOTOPO DEL QUETZAL
About 100 miles from Guatemala City, on the road to Cobán and near the village of Purulhá. The largest nature reserve for this sacred bird.

MEXICO
SIAN KA'AN BIOSPHERE RESERVE
About 68 miles of coral reefs and 1,284,950 acres of jungle and mangroves inhabited by pumas, jaguars and tapirs make this the most diverse nature reserve in all the Mayan countries. It can be reached from Felipe Carrillo along the road between Tulum and

Chetumal.
CALAKMUL BIOSPHERE RESERVE
Over 180 species of birds live in the jungle and savanna of the reserve, crossed at the northern end by the Escárcega–Chetumal road.

BELIZE
COCKSCOMB BASIN WILDLIFE SANCTUARY
This 101,310-acre sanctuary has a large jaguar population. It is reached from Dangriga.
HALF MOON CAY RESERVE
This manatee sanctuary is reached

from Cay Caulker.

EL SALVADOR
CERRO VERDE NATIONAL PARK
On the slopes of the Cerro Verde volcano, this forest has many species of birds and animals. The volcano offers a great view of Lake Coatepeque and Volcán Izalco.

CLIMBING VOLCANOS				
VOLCANO	HEIGHT	DIFFICULTY	CLIMBING	POINT OF DEPARTURE
PACAYA	8,373 feet	easy	3 hours	Antigua Guatemala
FUEGO	12,346 feet	difficult	4 hours	Antigua Guatemala
SAN PEDRO	9,908 feet	difficult	3–4 hours	Panajachel (Lake Atitlán)
TOLIMÁN	10,360 feet	very difficult	5 hours	Panajachel (Lake Atitlán)
AGUA	12,388 feet	difficult	3–4 hours	Antigua Guatemala
SANTO TOMÁS	11,499 feet	very difficult	6–10 hours	Quetzaltenango
IZALCO	6,070 feet	easy	3 hours	Cerro Verde (San Salvador)

Most Mayan festivals celebrate the patron saint of the community or the founding of the village. The villagers take part in religious processions and traditional dances, wearing the magnificent ceremonial costumes of their own particular region. The Guatemalan highlands have the largest Indian community in Central America and the most authentic Indian festivals ● *72, 74, 76.*

EASTER IN ANTIGUA GUATEMALA

During Holy Week in Antigua, the Passion of Christ is re-enacted with great fervor. The paved streets are strewn with flowers and long, brightly colored ribbons. On the night of Maundy Thursday, before Easter Day, a carpet of colored sawdust is spread on the ground by the families of Antigua. They then decorate it using stencils of all kinds of geometric designs, flowers and animals. On Good Friday, the sawdust carpets disappear as the procession, consisting of a hundred or so costumed participants, passes through the streets. The ensuing festival lasts until dawn.

FEAST OF THE ASSUMPTION AT SOLOLÁ

On August 15 the Indians of the Cakchiquel and Tzutuhil communities

of Sololá celebrate the Assumption of the Blessed Virgin. The day begins with the traditional market of Sololá, with the women wearing red flowered *huipiles* and blue striped skirts. Mass is followed at 11am by a grand procession in honor of the Virgin Mary. The members of twelve brotherhoods, dressed in ceremonial costume, take part in the procession and perform religious rites accompanied by music and masked dancers.

ALL SAINTS DAY AT TODOS SANTOS

The festival of Todos Santos begins on October 31 with masked dances (*bailes de la Conquista*) to the sound of marimbas in the church square. A horse race is held outside the village the following day. From dawn until dusk, about fifteen horses (ridden in turn by the inhabitants) compete over a course of a hundred yards or so until they are ready to drop. On November 2, religious ceremonies are followed by a costumed procession which makes its way drunkenly to the cemetery where families give free rein to demonstrations of laughter and tears. Todos Santos, lost in the mountains of the Sierra de los

Cuchumatanes (at an altitude of more than 8,200 feet), can only be reached by bus once a day from Huehuetenango. The bus leaves at 2pm but make sure you reserve your seat in the morning. The same bus does not return until 5am the following morning. Allow three days for the return journey and the visit to Todos Santos ▲ *285.*

CHRISTMAS IN THE MAYAN COUNTRIES

Christmas Day is preceded by weeks of processions, the *posadas,* that re-enact Mary and Joseph's search for shelter. The festival is celebrated in all the Mayan countries by costumed dances and music. The festivities of Chichicastenango in Guatemala, where they also celebrate the festival of the patron saint from December 13–21, are undoubtedly some of the most spectacular. The more daring can even climb the *palo volador* and "fly"

upside down around this huge pole. This spiritual rather than physical test represents the movement of the stars around the sun ● *76.*

Planning your trip to the Route of the Mayas around a particular holiday or festival is an ideal way of joining in the local spirit. Holy Week (the week before Easter) is the most important holiday. Local people have a week off work and often take a trip to a beach or resort so buses and hotels tend to be packed for the whole week. It is worth remembering too that during festivals virtually all businesses and government agencies are closed.

JANUARY

1 Día del Año Nuevo (New Year's Day)
Throughout the Mayan countries

6–10 Día de los Reyes Magos (Epiphany)
Guatemala and Mexico

7–15 Fiesta de Cristo de Esquipulas
*Throughout the Mayan countries,
in particular Esquipulas, Guatemala.*

15-31 San Sebastián
Mexico, Honduras and El Salvador

28–31 Candalario (Candlemas)
Campeche, Mexico

FEBRUARY

1—2 Candalario (Candlemas)
Mexico, Honduras and El Salvador

1–5 San Felipe
Yucatán, Mexico

11–23 Campeche Carnival
Campeche, Mexico

21 National holiday
Mexico

Weekend preceding Lent– Carnival
Mardi Gras
Mexico and Guatemala

MARCH

1–6 Regional holiday
Chiapas, Mexico

9 Baron Bliss Day
Belize

16–21 Festival of Spring
Quintana Roo, Mexico

19 San José
Copán, Honduras

21 Vernal Equinox, Chichén Itzá
Yucatán, Mexico

24 San Gabriel
Chiapas, Mexico

Easter Semana Santa, Holy Week
*Throughout the Mayan countries
in particular Antigua, Guatemala*

APRIL

15 Ascension Day
Yucatán, Mexico

11–25 Festival of Spring
*Commemoration of the foundation of the town of
San Cristobál de Las Casas,
in Chiapas, Mexico*

25 San Marcos
*San Marcos La Laguna,
Sololá, Guatemala*

29 Festival of the Three Crosses
Yucatán, Mexico

MAY

10 Saint Helen of the Cross
*Throughout the villages in Santa Cruz,
Mexico and Guatemala*

24 Commonwealth Day
Belize

30 San Ferdinando
Honduras

JUNE

22–9 San Antonio de Padua
Yucatán, Mexico, and Honduras

22–4 San Juan Bautista
San Juan La Laguna, Guatemala

22–9 San Pedro and San Pablo
Mexico and Guatemala

24 San Juan Chamula
*San Juan Chamula
Chiapas, Mexico*

29 San Pedro La Laguna
Sololá, Guatemala

30 Army Day
Guatemala

End of June Festival of Corpus Christi
Guatemala

JULY

17 Fiesta de San Cristóbal de las Casas
Chiapas, Mexico

19 Festival of the Sacred Heart of Jesus
Puerto Barrios
Izabal, Guatemala

25 Santiago Apóstolo
Throughout the Mayan countries

AUGUST

4 Fiesta de Santo Domingo de Guzman
*Cobán, in Alta Verapaz,
Guatemala*

4–6 Festival of the Divine Savior
Divino Salvador del mundo
San Salvador

10–16 Traditional Mexican festivals
*Yucatán, Campeche
and Tabasco, Mexico*

15 Festival of Guatemala
Guatemala City

20–30 San Juan Chamula, San Augustino
and San Miguel
Chiapas, Mexico

SEPTEMBER

10 National holiday
Belize

15 and 16 Independence Day
Guatemala (Sept. 15), Mexico (Sept. 16)

14–20 Civil week
Honduras

OCTOBER

4 Fiesta de San Francisco de Asisi
*Panajachel in Sololá and San Francisco
El Alto in Totonicapán, Guatemala*

12 Día de la Raza (Columbus Day)
Throughout the Mayan countries

NOVEMBER

1 Todos Santos, All Saints' Day
Huehuetenango, Guatemala

1–30 Festival of Our Lady of the Martyrs
Honduras

2 Day of the Dead
Throughout the Mayan countries

5 Independence Day
El Salvador

13 San Diego
Yucatán, Mexico

19 Garifuna Settlement Day
Belize

30 Pilgrimage and Festival of Xmatkuil
Mexico

30 San Andreas Apostolo
Chiapas, Mexico

DECEMBER

1 Feast of the Immaculate Conception
Quintana Roo and Campeche, Mexico

7 Burning of the Devil
Totonicapán, Guatemala

8 Saint Nicolas
Noche Buena Chiquita

10–12 Feast of Our Lady of Guadalupe
Mexico and Honduras

21 Saint Thomas
Chichicastenango, Guatemala

16–24 Procesions de las Posadas
Mary and Joseph's search for lodgings
Throughout the Mayan countries

19–26 Festival of the Nativity
Throughout the Mayan countries

A profusion of colors in the fruit and vegetable markets where the women sell their produce.

The finest markets on the Route of the Mayas are, once again, found in the Guatemalan highlands. The markets of the *altiplano* are brightly colored showcases of local crafts, offering an ideal opportunity to buy traditionally made clothes, woven items and other everyday objects at reasonable prices ● 82.

SOME GUATEMALAN MARKETS		
	TOWN	**REGION**
MONDAY	Antigua	Sacatepéquez
	Chimaltenango	Chimaltenango
	Zunil	Quetzaltenango
TUESDAY	Comalapa	Chimaltenango
	Patzún	Chimaltenango
	Sololá	Sololá
	San Lucas Tolimán	Sololá
	Santa Clara la Laguna	Sololá
	Tucuru	Alta Verapaz
WEDNESDAY	Huehuetenango	Huehuetenango
	Momostenango	Totonicapán
	Palín	Escuintla
	Patzicia	Chimaltenango
	Sacapulas	El Quiché
THURSDAY	Antigua	Sacatepéquez
	Chimaltenango	Chimaltenango
	Chichicastenango	El Quiché
	Nebaj	El Quiché
	Patzún	Chimaltenango
	Sacapulas	El Quiché
	San Mateo Ixtatán	Huehuetenango
	San Miguel Ixtahuacán	San Marcos
	Santa Cruz del Quiché	El Quiché
	Tecpán Guatemala	Chimaltenango
	Totonicapán	Totonicapán
	Tucuru	Alta Verapaz
FRIDAY	Comalapa	Chimaltenango
	Palín	Escuintla
	San Andrés Itzapa	Chimaltenango
	San Lucas Tolimán	Sololá
	San Pedro Sacatepéquez	Guatemala
	Santiago Atitlán	Sololá
	Sololá	Sololá
SATURDAY	Patzicia	Chimaltenango
	Santa Cruz del Quiché	El Quiché
	Santa Clara la Laguna	Sololá
	Santiago Sacatepéquez	Sacatepéquez
	Todos Santos	Totonicapán
SUNDAY	Chichicastenango	El Quiché
	Esquipulas	Chiquimula
	Momostenango	Totonicapán
	Rabinal	Baja Verapaz

Markets begin early in the morning. It is best to arrive in the village the afternoon before, so that you are on the spot first thing in the morning. In this way you will avoid the mass of tourists who tend to arrive late in the morning. Of course, all prices are negotiable. Always divide the first price quoted by two to give yourself a basis for negotiation.

Markets are an important part of Indian economic and social life. They provide an opportunity to meet friends and acquaintances. For many inhabitants it is the only time they come down from the mountains.

These dolls are sold by children as good luck charms.

The stylized bird appears on most embroidered textiles.

Unlike Mexican markets, the markets of the Guatemalan *Altiplano* have retained their authenticity, remaining primarily Indian markets.

Seven of the most interesting are mentioned in the following list and offer a wide range of different products:
◆ brightly colored, hand-woven textiles and clothes whose motifs and materials are specific to their village of origin;
◆ ceramics (at Santa Cruz Chinautla, Jalapa, Huehuetenango, Totonicapán, Antigua);
◆ classic Mayan jewelry in jade and carved stone, now found in many jewelers (Antigua);
◆ straw hats with colored bands (characteristic of Todos Santos, Cuchumatán, Huehuetenango);
◆ musical instruments and objects made of carved wood;
◆ ritual masks in painted wood, representing gods, devils and animals.

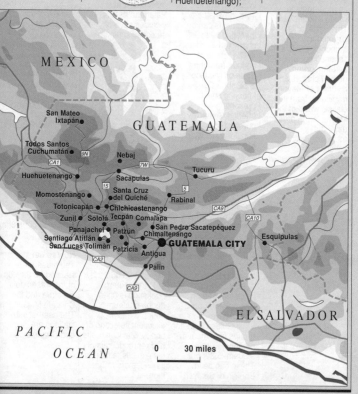

Mexico has the largest museum of pre-Columbian art in Latin America. It offers an excellent introduction to the Mayan culture for those starting their visit in Mexico City (allow at least one day). The museums of the other main towns and cities in the region are also well worth a visit. Collections of Mayan art in Europe and North America are a good starting point when preparing for your visit.

MUSEO DE ANTROPOLOGIA (MEXICO CITY)

The museum, which has the most complete collection in Latin America, offers an excellent introduction to Mayan history and culture and, more generally, to all the civilizations of Mesoamerica. At the entrance to the first floor is a relief map showing the area covered by Mayan culture as well as an exhibition of the different geographical environments in which it flourished. The first floor is devoted to archeology, while the second floor presents an ethnographic view of the richness and diversity of Mayan traditions, from the classic world of the Mayas to the present day. The archeological collection is extremely impressive.

NOT TO BE MISSED

◆ The collection of figurines from Jaina ▲ 230, an island off the coast of Campeche. These terracotta miniatures (sometimes polychrome) represent various important figures and constitute one of the most complete and realistic records of the social hierarchy and costumes of the Mayan culture. Warriors, women from the aristocracy and priests can be identified by their characteristic attire.
◆ The "stone of Jonuta" from the State of Tabasco ● 52 shows a kneeling priest presenting an offering. A macaw is perched on his shoulder. His typically Mayan profile is clearly visible.

◆ The collection of steles and lintels constitutes a major record of social and religious life. The remarkably preserved steles on display illustrate the official art form and propaganda medium of the Mayan sovereigns.
◆ The collection of funerary objects and bas-reliefs from the Temple of the Inscriptions at Palenque ● 108, includes several stuccoed sculptures, a

reproduction of the funerary chamber and its sarcophagus and the famous bas-relief of the Temple of the Cross at Palenque.
◆ In the gardens is a reconstruction of the Temple of Hochob, in the State of Campeche, with a huge mask of the terrestrial monster forming the entrance. There is also a reproduction of the Temple of the Frescos at Bonampak ▲ 249, ▲ 243, containing copies of its famous wall paintings.
◆ Finally, there is a collection of everyday items, richly decorated ceramics and musical instruments.

USEFUL INFORMATION

The Museo de Antropología: Open Tues.–Sat. 9am–7pm, Sun. and public holidays 10am–6pm. Closed Mon. Tickets are on sale until 6pm. Admission 16 pesos, free on Sun. and public holidays.
◆ Guided tours for groups (minimum five persons): 9.30am–5.30pm. These can be in English or Spanish

(no charge for Spanish). No guided tours on Sundays. For large groups it is possible to reserve a guide.
INFORMATION
Tel: 553 63 86
◆ The museum bookshop is open during museum hours. It has an excellent selection of books, Mexican crafts and reproductions of the exhibits, although its prices are rather high.

◆ The museum library is open Mon.–Fri. 9am–8pm

HOW TO GET THERE
The museum is situated on the corner of the Paseo de la Reforma and the Calzada M. Gandhi. The nearest subway stations are *Auditorio* and *Chapultepec*.

Central patio of the museum and the column decorated with bronzes by Chavez Morado.

The façade of the reconstruction of the Temple of Hochob in the museum gardens.

AN ARCHITECTURAL MASTERPIECE

The Museo de Antropología, designed by the architect Pedro Ramirez Vazquez, was opened on September 17, 1964. A vestibule leads into a central patio where a huge column, covered in bronze bas-reliefs by Chavez

Morado, supports a monumental roof. All the first-floor rooms open onto this central patio which enables visitors to choose the order of their visit. Modern Mexican art is renowned for its murals: the entrance hall and the introductory rooms to the anthropological and Mesoamerican culture sections are decorated with frescos by Rufino Tamayo, Jorge Gonzalez Camarena and Raúl Anguiano.

MAYAN COLLECTIONS IN THE MUSEUMS OF THE WORLD

◆ **UNITED STATES:**
The finest collections of Mayan art are housed in the museums of North America.
METROPOLITAN MUSEUM OF ART
5th Avenue and E 82nd Street
New York
AMERICAN MUSEUM OF NATURAL HISTORY
Central Park West 79th Street
New York
THE BROOKLYN MUSEUM OF ART
200 Eastern Parkway
New York
DUMBARTON OAKS
1703 32nd Street

Washington D.C. 20007
UNIVERSITY MUSEUM
University of Pennsylvania
33rd and Spruce Streets
Philadelphia PA 19104
Steles from Piedras Negras ▲ 332.
PEABODY MUSEUM OF ARCHEOLOGY AND ETHNOLOGY
Harvard University
Cambridge
Massachusetts
◆ **GREAT BRITAIN:**
BRITISH MUSEUM, MUSEUM OF MANKIND
6, Burlington Gardens

London
The museum has the finest collection of Mayan art in Europe.
◆ **SWITZERLAND:**
MUSEUM FÜR VÖLKERKUNDE
Augustiner Gasse 2
4001 Basel
Wooden lintels from Tikal ▲ 320.

ON THE "RUTA MAYA"

◆ **MEXICO:**
MUSEO LA VENTA
Av. Adolfo Ruíz Cortinez S/N
Villahermosa
Open daily 8am–4.30pm. Collection of Olmec statues.
MUSEO DE HISTORIA
Corner of Calle de Juárez and 27 de Febrero
Villahermosa
Open daily 9am–6pm.
MUSEO REGIONAL DE ANTROPOLOGIA
511, av. Carlos Pellicer
Villahermosa
Open daily 9am–8pm.
MUSEO DE ARQUEOLOGIA
Paseo de Montejo y Calle 41
Mérida
Open 8am–8pm. Closed Mon. and Sun. after 2pm.

◆ **GUATEMALA:**
MUSEO SANTIAGO DE LOS CABALLEROS
Plaza Mayor
Antigua
Open daily 9am–12pm and 2pm–6pm.
MUSEO DEL LIBRO ANTIGUO
Plaza Mayor
Antigua
Open daily 9am –12pm and 2pm–6pm.
MUSEO DE ARTE COLONIAL
Calle de la Universidad and Avenida Norte
Antigua
PALACIO NACIONAL
Zona 1
Guatemala City
Open daily 8am–4pm.
MUSEO NACIONAL DE ARQUEOLOGIA
Edificio 5, La Aurora, Zone 13

Guatemala City
Open Tues.–Sun. 9am–4pm. Closed Mon. and w/e noon–2pm.
MUSEO DE ARTE MODERNO
Edificio 6, La Aurora, Zona 13
Guatemala City
Open Tues.-Sun. 9am–4pm. Closed Mon. and w/e noon–2pm.
MUSEO IXCHEL
4, Av. 16–27
Zona 10
Guatemala City
MUSEO POPOL VUH
Av. La Reforma 8–60, Zona 9
Guatemala City
◆ **HONDURAS:**
INSTITUTO HONDUREÑO DE ANTROPOLOGIA E HISTORIA
Villa Roy, Barrios
Buenos Aires
Tegucigalpa D.C.

In spite of the continued survival of the Mayan languages and the increasing use of English with the development of the tourist industry, Spanish remains the first spoken language in the Mayan countries. If you have the time, why not start your visit to Central America with a Spanish course? Learning Spanish *in situ* can be combined with lodgings in a host family, which in no way restricts your opportunities of discovering the country. On the contrary, it will enhance the experience.

The towns of Quetzaltenango and Antigua, in Guatemala, and San Cristóbal de las Casas, in Mexico, are the main centers for learning Spanish. However you can learn the basics or brush up your Spanish in all the towns of Guatemala, Mexico and Honduras (there are two schools at Copán).

The average cost of a one-week, four hour-a-day private course is US$65 (or about US$100 with lodgings). If you are interested in this type of course you should allow a minimum of seven days. You will find the most highly recommended schools in the towns cited in the list of useful addresses ◆ 386–406. But there are others, so ask the local tourist office or former pupils who are still in the region.

Common expressions ◆

Yes: *sí*
No: *no*
Please: *por favor*
Thank you: *gracias*
Pardon/Sorry: *perdón*
Excuse me: *disculpe* or *con su permiso*
At your service: *a sus ordenes*
Good morning: *buenos días*
Good afternoon (evening): *buenas tardes*
Goodnight: *buenas noches*
Of course: *¡Cómo no!*

Today: *hoy*
Tomorrow: *mañana*
Yesterday: *ayer*
Allowed/Permitted: *autorisado*
Forbidden/Prohibited: *prohibido*
I am English/American: *soy inglés (a)/ norteamericano (a)*
I don't understand: *no entiendo*
Can you help me?: *¿me puedes ayudar?*
What time is it?: *¿Qué hora(s) es(son)?*
It is 3pm: *son las tres de la tarde*

Days of the week ◆

Monday: *lunes*
Tuesday: *martes*
Wednesday: *miercoles*
Thursday: *jueves*
Friday: *viernes*
Saturday: *sábado*
Sunday: *domingo*

Months of the year ◆

January: *enero*
February: *febrero*
March: *marzo*
April: *abril*
May: *mayo*
June: *junio*
July: *julio*
August: *agosto*
September: *septiembre*
October: *octubre*
November: *noviembre*
December: *diciembre*

Numbers ◆

One: *uno*
Two: *dos*
Three: *tres*
Four: *cuatro*
Five: *cinco*
Six: *seis*
Seven: *siete*
Eight: *ocho*
Nine: *nueve*
Ten: *diez*
One hundred: *cien*
One thousand: *mil*

◆ People ◆

Mestizo: *ladino*
Indian: *indigena* (the term *indio* is pejorative)
Woman: *mujer*
Man: *hombre*
Surname: *apellido*
What is your name?: *¿Cómo te llamas?*
First name: *nombre*
Mother: *madre*
Father: *padre*
Daughter: *hija*
Son: *hijo*
Sister: *hermana*
Brother: *hermano*
Aunt: *tía*
Uncle: *tío*

◆ Travel ◆

To travel: *viajar*
Plane: *avión*
Airport: *aeropuerto*
Luggage: *equipaje*
Ticket: *boleto*
Change: *cambio*
Customs: *aduana*
Departure: *salida*
Arrival: *llegada*
Travel agency: *agencia de viaje*

Finding your way around ◆

Where is ...?: *¿Dónde se encuentra ...?*
Is it near here?: *¿Está cerca de aquí?*
Is it far from here?: *¿Está lejos de aquí?*
Straight on: *todo recto*
On the left: *a la izquierda*
On the right: *a la derecha*
How long by car?: *¿Cuánto tiempo en coche?*
How long on foot?: *¿Cuánto tiempo caminando?*
How many kilometers?: *¿Cuántos kilómetros son?*

Getting around ◆

Bus: *camión* (Mex.) or *camioneta* (Guat.)
Luxury bus: *camión de lujo* or *pullman*
First class: *primera clase*
Second class: *segunda clase*
Bus station: *terminal* or *central des autobuses*
Car: *coche* or *carro*
Small car: *cochecito* or *carro compacto*
Four-wheel drive: *cuatro-cuatro* or *doble tracción*
To hire: *alquilar* or *rentar* (Mex.)
Insurance: *seguro*
Unlimited mileage: *kilometraje libre*
Driving license: *licencia de conducir*
Gas station: *gasolinera*
Gas: *gasolina*
Oil: *aceite*
Tire: *llanta*
Taxi: *taxi*

Collective taxi: *collectivo*

◆ At the hotel ◆

Hotel: *hotel*
Room: *cuarto* or *habitación*
Single room: *cuarto sencillo*
Double room: *cuarto doble* or *matrimonial*
Key: *llave*
Bed: *cama*
Shower: *ducha*
Toilets: *baños* or *servicios*
Hot water: *agua caliente*
Cold water: *agua fría*
Soap: *jabón*
Bathroom: *cuarto de baño*
Towel: *toalla*
Where is the nearest hotel?: *¿Dónde se encuentra el hotel más cercana?*
I have reserved a room: *tengo un cuarto reservado*
I would like a room: *quisiera un cuarto*
I would like to see the room: *quiero ver el cuarto*
Can you wake me up?: *¿me puede despertar?*
To camp: *acampar*

◆ At the restaurant ◆

Restaurant: *restaurante*
Table: *mesa*
Plate: *plato*
Knife: *cuchillo*
Fork: *tenedor*
Spoon: *cuchara*
Glass: *vaso*
Purified water: *agua purificada*
Red wine: *vino tinto*
White wine: *vino blanco*
Beer: *cerveza*
Real coffee: *café de cafetera*
Instant coffee: *Nescafé*
Coffee with milk: *café con leche*
(Black) tea: *té (negro)*
Fruit juice: *jugo*
Diluted fruit juice: *agua de fruta*
Fruit juice with milk: *licuado con leche*
Breakfast: *desayuno*

Lunch: *comida*
Today's menu: *comida corrida*
Dinner: *cena*
Menu: *carta*
Chili: *chile*
Especially no chili: *sobre todo sin chile*
Soup: *sopa caldo* or *sopa de verduras*
Eggs: *huevos*
Scrambled eggs: *huevos revueltos*
Fried eggs: *huevos estrellados*
Toast: *pan tostado*
Butter: *mantequilla*
Jam: *marmelada*
Sandwich (meat salad, tomato): *torta*
Kidney beans: *frijoles*
Corn pancake: *tortilla*
Filled corn pancake: *taco*
Meat: *carne*
Beef: *carne de res*
Fried chicken and chips: *pollo frito con papas*
Fried chicken and rice: *pollo frito con arroz*
Pork fillet: *lomo de puerco*
Pork chop: *chuleta de cerdo*
Steak and chips: *bistek con papas*
Fish: *pescado*
Avocado puree: *guacamole*
Green tomato sauce: *salsa verde*
Vegetables: *verduras*
Salad: *ensalada*
Cheese: *queso*
Dessert: *postre*
Cake/pastry: *pastel*
Ice cream: *helado*
Ice cream made with milk: *helado de leche*
Fruit: *fruta*
Dish of fruit: *plato de frutas*
Banana: *plátano*
Orange: *naranja*

Papaw: *papaya*
The check, please: *la cuenta, por favor*
Tip: *propina*
Service included: *servicio incluido*

◆ Visits ◆

To visit: *visitar*
Open: *abierto*
Closed: *cerrado*
Ticket: *boleto*
Town: *ciudad*
Village: *pueblo*
District: *barrio, zona* or *colonia*
Street: *calle*
Avenue: *avenida*
Boulevard by the sea: *malecón*
House: *casa*
Garden: *jardín*
Theater: *teatro*
Cinema: *cinema*
Museum: *museo*
Archeological site: *ruinas* or *sitio arqueológico*

At the post office

Post office: *oficina de correos*
To telephone: *telefonear* or *hacer una llamada*
Collect call: *por cobrar*
Fax: *fax*
Stamp: *estampilla, sello* or *timbre*
For Europe: *para Europa*
Telegram: *telegrama*
Envelope: *sobre*
Air mail: *por avión*
Letter: *carta*
Post card: *postal*

◆ Emergencies ◆

State police: *policía federal*
Municipal police: *policía municipal*
Fire brigade: *bomberos*
Hospital: *hospital*
Pharmacy: *farmacia*
Doctor: *doctor*
Call the doctor please: *llama al doctor, por favor*

◆ Money shopping ◆

Bank: *banco*
Credit card: *tarjeta de crédito*
Traveler's checks: *cheques de viajero*
In cash: *en efectivo*

Price: *el precio*
How much is it?: *¿Cuánto vale?* or *¿Qué precio?*
It's too expensive: *es demasiado caro*
Receipt: *comprobante*
Packet of cigarettes: *cajetilla de cigarros*
Newspaper: *periódico*
When does the shop open?: *¿A qué hora abre la tienda?*
When does the shop close?: *¿A qué hora cierra la tienda?*
Where can I find . . . ?: *¿Dónde se puede encontrar . . . ?*

"Cabana" with a palm roof on the beach of Playa del Carmen.

Houses on stilts, built on the beaches of the cays (Belize).

The Mayan countries tend to organize their day around the sun, which rises very early and sets around 6pm. Don't wait until it gets dark to think about accommodation. Reservations are not the best way of ensuring a room in a hotel. It is better to get there early and take possession of the room before it is offered to someone else. Only the big hotels operate a reservation system. The "Ruta Maya" offers a wide range of different types of accommodation at vastly differing prices, from the most luxurious to the most basic.

RESERVATIONS AND ADVERTIZED PRICES

There is no point in reserving rooms in advance during off-peak periods or in other than the largest hotels. Your room will be offered, with no misgivings, to the first guests to arrive. It is better to get to your destination before sunset to allow time to choose your hotel and especially your room – ask to see it first. The price of a room in a small hotel, out of season, can be negotiated.

DIFFERENT TYPES OF ACCOMMODATION

HOTELS AND MOTELS
The largest international hotels in the region are in Villahermosa, Guatemala City, Belize City and Cancún. The high prices (US$100–US$400 for a double room) are justified by the extremely high quality of service. Away from these cities the quality of accommodation

varies greatly, but prices are reasonable.

YOUTH HOSTELS
(*Albergues de la juventud*)
Youth hostels are few and far between in Guatemala and Belize, but more common in Mexico. They are run by the CREA (*Consejo Nacional de Recursos para la Atención de la Juventud*) in association with the international Youth Hostel Association. Students must have an international student card to benefit from the special rates available.

CAMPING
Camping is allowed on most beaches. Supervised camp sites charge between US$1 and US$10 per night. Two camp sites well situated for visiting Mayan temples at sunrise are those at Chichén Itzá (Mexico) and Tikal (Guatemala).

"CABANAS" AND HAMMOCKS
This typical Central American accommodation consists of a hut or *cabana* with a palm roof and equipped with hooks for

suspending hammocks. This apparently very basic accommodation, with candles the only form of lighting and a sand floor, is often ideally situated – facing the sea or in natural surroundings. If you don't travel with a hammock you can always hire one on the spot. Prices per night vary from US$1 (communal accommodation) to US$10 (private *cabana* with hammock provided).

Useful addresses

AGUATECA ▲ 333

Guatemala
Accessible by *lancha*
from Sayaxche.
*Guide compulsory to
gain access.*

ALTAR DE SACRIFICIOS ▲ 331

Guatemala
At the confluence of the
Usumacinta River and
the Rio de la Pasión,
4 hours by *lancha* from
Sayaxche.

ALTÚN HA ▲ 341

Belize
25 miles north of Belize
City on the Old Northern
Highway. Accessible to
four-wheel-drive vehicles
(track signposted).
Open 9am–5pm

BALAMKU ▲ 194

Mexico
Not far from the village
of Conhuas, 36 miles
from Escarcega on
highway 186.

BECÁN ▲ 191

Mexico
1½ miles from the village
of Xpuhil on highway 186.
Open 8am–5pm
*Bus from Chetumal and
Escárcega to the village
of Xpuhil.*

BONAMPAK ▲ 249

Mexico
A very isolated site. Tour
operators can take you
from Palenque or San
Cristóbal by plane or by
track and *lancha*. Make
inquiries in advance.
*Take supplies, water
and a torch. Conditions
at the site are very
primitive.*

CAHAL PECH ▲ 342

Belize
2 miles from San Ignacio
on the San Antonio road.

CALAKMUL ▲ 230

Mexico
Track restricted to four-
wheel-drive vehicles, off
the Chetumal-Escárcega
road.
*A very isolated site
which can only be
reached by this track.*

CARACOL ▲ 342

Belize
36 miles by track from
San Ignacio, restricted to
four-wheel-drive vehicles
*Prior permission
required.*

CEIBAL ▲ 331

Guatemala
From Sayaxché by a
track restricted to four-
wheel-drive vehicles or
by river 1 hour by *lancha*.

CERROS ▲ 340

Belize
From Corozal, the last
town before Chetumal by
boat.

CHAN CHICH ▲ 341

Belize
20 miles north of
Belmopán, by a track
restricted to four-wheel-
drive vehicles during the
wet season.

CHICANNÁ ▲ 192

Mexico
2½ miles outside Xpupil
on the Chetumal-
Escárcega road.

CHICHÉN ITZÁ ▲ 205

Mexico
1 mile from the village of
Piste on the Mérida-
Valladolid road (no. 180).
Open 8am–5pm
*There are plenty of buses
from Cancún and Mérida.
It is possible to charter a
plane in Cancún with
Aerocaribe.* Son et
lumière *every evening at
7pm in Spanish and at
9pm in English.*

COBÁ ▲ 182

Mexico
25 miles from Tulum on
the Nuevo Xcan road,
half a mile from the
village.
Open 8am–5pm

COPÁN ▲ 299

Honduras
Half a mile from the
village. Open 8am–4pm.
*Several buses a day
from the Guatemalan
border and Tegucigalpa
or San Pedro Sula.*

DOS PILAS ▲ 332

Mexico
Inland, on the road to
Aguateca from Sayaxche.

DZIBILCHALTÚN ▲ 216

Mexico
10 miles from Mérida on
the Progreso road, then
take a right turn toward
Conkal for 6 miles. The
site is on the right-hand
side, a few hundred
yards from the road.

EDZNÁ ▲ 226

Mexico
From Campeche,
through the village of
San Antonio Caya on
highway 261, soon after
which is the junction with
the Edzná road.
Open 8am–5pm
Bus from Campeche

EL BAÚL ▲ 291

Guatemala
20 miles from Escuintla,
coming from Guatemala
City on highway 2. Turn
right at the village of
Santa Lucia
Cotzumalguapa. The El
Baúl *finca* is a few miles
further on the left.
Key from the warden.

EL MIRADOR ▲ 329

Guatemala
Bus from Flores to San
Andrés, from there hitch a
ride to Carmelita then on
foot or by mule (track
accessible to four-wheel-

drive vehicles).
*Take supplies and wat[er]
purifying tablets. Guide
recommended.*

HORMIGUERO ▲ 19[?]

Mexico
A 10-mile track from
Xpuhil. Restricted to fou[r]
wheel-drive vehicles.

IXIMCHÉ ▲ 276

Guatemala
2 miles from the town o[f]
Tecpán, Guatemala (30
miles from Guatemala
City on the Panamerica[n]
Highway toward Lake
Atitlán).

JOYA DE CERÉN ▲ 31[?]

El Salvador
On the San Juan Opico
road, 5 miles north of th[e]
Panamerican Highway.
Open 9.30am–4.30pm.
Closed Sat.
*Bus from Guatemala
City or San Salvador.*

KABÁH ▲ 220

Mexico
8 miles south of Uxmal
on highway 261.
*The highway passes
right through the middl[e]
of the site. Buses from
Mérida and Campeche*

KAMINALJUYÚ ▲ 268

Guatemala
On the outskirts of
Guatemala City.
Accessible by public
transport.

KOHUNLICH ▲ 189

Mexico
From highway 186,
coming from Chetumal,
just before the village of
Francisco Villa, take a
turning toward the south.
The site is 4 miles from
the village.
Open 8am–5pm
*This site is difficult to get
to without a rented
vehicle.*

LABNÁ ▲ 221

Mexico
4 miles from Sayil.
*The Puuc road passes
in front of the entrance
to the site.*

A DEMOCRACIA ▲ 291

Guatemala
0 miles from Escuintla,
oming from Guatemala
ty on highway 2. Turn
ft at the village of
quinalá. The ruins are
the square.

AMANAÍ ▲ 340

Belize
½ hours by *lancha* from
range Walk.

UBAANTÚN ▲ 343

Belize
bout 12 miles north of
unta Gorda on the San
edro road. 1 mile
utside San Pedro.
pen 8am–5pm

AYAPÁN ▲ 212

Mexico
he ruins are 1 mile
utside the village of
echalquillo, 20 miles
om Mérida on
ghway 18.
pen 8am–5pm

IXCO VIEJO ▲ 268

Guatemala
5 miles north of
uatemala City,
2 miles outside San
uan Sacatepequez.
uses pass the entrance
the site from the bus
ation in Zone 4.

UYIL ▲ 184

Mexico
his site is also called
hunyaxche.
alf a mile from the
llage of Muyil.
pen 8am–5pm
miles from Tulum on
ghway 307 toward
hetumal.

AKBÉ ▲ 330

Guatemala
the Dos Lagunas
ational Park.
uide essential. Arrange
our visit through a tour
perator.

ARANJO ▲ 334

Guatemala
rom Melchor de Mencos,
n the Flores-Belize City
ad, a 10-mile track
ccessible to four-wheel-
rive vehicles.
uide recommended.

NIM LI PUNIT ▲ 344

Belize
12 miles north of Punta
Gorda (signposted).
Bus from Punta Gorda.

NOHMUL ▲ 340

Belize
2 miles north of Orange
Walk on the Northern
Highway

PALENQUE ▲ 243

Mexico
4 miles from the small
town of Palenque.
Open 8am–5pm
*Bus from Villahermosa
and San Cristóbal. The
Mexico–Mérida train
stops at Palenque.*

PIEDRAS NEGRAS ▲332

Guatemala
On the banks of the Río
Usumacinta, accessible
from Sayaxché on certain
days by *lancha*.
*Guide recommended.
Arrange your visit
through a tour operator.*

QUIRIGUA ▲ 306

Guatemala
About 4 miles off the
Guatemala City-Puerto
Barrios road. Get out at
Los Amates, from where
there are taxis and
frequent buses.

RÍO AZUL ▲ 329

Guatemala
By a 60-mile track from
Uaxactún restricted to
four-wheel-drive vehicles.
*Take supplies and
water purifying tablets
with you.*

RÍO BEC ▲ 192

Mexico
10 miles from Xpuhil by
track.
*Only accessible to four-
wheel-drive vehicles.
To visit this site you will
need a permit which you
can obtain on your way
through the village of 20
de Noviembre.
Guide compulsory.*

SAN ANDRÉS ▲ 316

El Salvador
The site is near Joya de
Ceren on highway 1
between San Salvador
and Guatemala City.

SANTA RITA ▲ 340

Belize
A few miles from the
village of Corozal, on the
Chetumal road.

SAYIL ▲ 221

Mexico
2 miles from Kabah, turn
right on the Puuc road.
The site is 2 miles further
on. Open 8am–5pm

TAZUMAL ▲ 316

El Salvador
500 yards from
Chalchuapa, 10 miles
from Santa Ana.
Open 9am–5pm
Closed Mon.
*Regular buses from
Santa Ana and San
Salvador.*

TIKAL ▲ 322

Guatemala
Tarmac road from
Flores
Open 6am–5.30pm.
*Many buses and taxis;
plane as far as Flores
from Guatemala City.*

TONINÁ ▲ 242

Mexico
5 miles from Ocosingo
on a good track, off the
Palenque–
San Cristóbal road.
Open 9am–4pm.
*Accessible to all types
of vehicle. Numerous
buses.*

TULUM ▲ 177

Mexico
Half a mile from El
Crucero on highway 307.
Open 8am–5pm
*Numerous buses take
highway 307 throughout
the day. Catch one at
El Crucero for the return
journey. An early-
morning visit is
advisable as this is a
very popular site.*

UAXACTÚN ▲ 328

Guatemala
By bus from Flores via
Tikal or by a track
restricted to four-wheel-
drive vehicles.

UTATLÁN ▲ 288

Guatemala
1 mile from Santa Cruz
del Quiché by car.

UXMAL ▲ 222

Mexico
35 miles from Mérida
on highway 261.
Open 8am–5pm
*Buses run all day from
Mérida and stop at the
entrance to the ruins.
Son et lumière at 7pm
in Spanish and at 9pm
in English.*

XPUHIL ▲ 190

Mexico
5 miles outside the
village of Xpuhil on
highway 186.
Open 8am–5pm
*Track restricted to four-
wheel-drive vehicles.
Visits to the site require
a permit which you can
obtain at the Rancho
San José. Guide
compulsory.*

YAXCHILÁN ▲ 248

Mexico
Like neighboring
Bonampak, this site calls
for a well-planned visit.
See Bonampak.

YAXHÁ ▲ 334

Guatemala
Accessible by the
Flores–Belize City road,
then by a signposted
track restricted to four-
wheel-drive vehicles.

XUNANTUNICH ▲ 341

Belize
From San Ignacio, just
before the Guatemalan
border.
Open 8am–5pm
Bus from San Ignacio.

ZACULEU ▲ 284

Guatemala
On the way out of the
town of Huehuetenango.
Taxis or bus from the
town center.

RESTAURANTS (MEALS)
*   < $15
** $15 to $25
***   > $25

CAMPECHE

Dialing code 981

USEFUL INFORMATION

BANK AND BUREAU DE CHANGE
BANAMEX
Calle 10, no. 15
Open Mon.–Fri.
9am–1pm
BANCOMER
Calle 59, no. 2A
Open Mon.–Fri.
9am–1pm

TOURIST OFFICE
OFICINA DE TURISMO
ESTATAL
Pl. Moch-Cuouh and
Calle 61
Tel. 660 68
or 660 767

MAIN POST OFFICE
OFICINA DE CORREOS
Ave. 16 de Septiembre
and Calle 53
Tel. 621 34
Open Mon.–Fri.
8am–7pm, Sat. 8am–1pm,
Sun. 8am–2pm

TRANSPORT

AIRLINES
AEROCARIBE
Ave. López Portillo S/N
Tel. 129 08
AEROMEXICO AIRPORT
Tel. 658 78 or 666 56
Fax 649 25

CAR RENTAL
HERTZ RENT A CAR
Baluartes Hotel
Ave. Ruiz Cortínez
Tel. 639 11
JAINA RENTE UN AUTO
Ramada Hotel
Ave. Ruiz Cortínez, no. 51
Tel. 622 33
KALAKMUL
TRANSPORTES
TURISTICOS
Calle 8, no. 201
Tel. 140 20
Fax 139 40

RESTAURANTS

** **RESTAURANTE IRAMAR**
Calles 8 and 61
Tel. 628 83

Campeche's most renowned seafood restaurant.

** **RESTAURANT AND BAR MARGANZO**
Calle 8, no. 265
Overlooking the sea,
between Calles 57
and 59
Tel. 623 28
Open lunchtime and
evening (until late).
*Mexican cuisine and
seafood.*

HOTELS

*** **RAMADA HOTEL**
Ave. Ruiz Cortínez, no. 51
Tel. 622 33
Fax 116 18

** **HOTEL ALHAMBRA**
Ave. Resurgimiento, no.85
Tel. 668 22

** **POSADA DEL ANGEL**
Calle 12, no. 189
Next to the cathedral.
Tel. 677 18

* **HOSPEDAJE TERESITA**
Calle 53, no. 31
3 blocks from the
Plaza Central.

CANCÚN

Dialing code 98

USEFUL INFORMATION

CONSULATES
AMERICAN CONSULATE
Ave. Náder, 40
Tel. 842 411
Open 9am–2pm
and 3–6pm
CANADIAN CONSULATE
Pl. Mexico, no. 312
2nd floor
Tel. 843 716
Open 11am–1pm
FRENCH CONSULATE
Instituto Internacional
de Idiomas
Ave. Xel-Ha - SM 25
Tel. 846 078
GERMAN CONSULATE
Punta Conoco, no. 36
SM 24
Tel. 841 898
ITALIAN CONSULATE
La Mansión Costa
Blanca Shopping Center
Tel. 832 184
SPANISH CONSULATE
Cielo 17, Depto 14,
SM 4
Tel. 841 895

CANCÚN

0   100   500   yards

to Puerto Juarez and Mérida

avenida G. de la Torre

avenida Chichén Itzá

avenida

calle roble
calle
calle Palmera
calle
taurel
Uxmal

avenida Bonampak

bus terminal

monumento al historia del México

avenida Tankah

calle Turbayab

calle Punta
calle Tankah
calle Yoxchén
calle Allen
C.-Nichchenabin
calle rosos
calle

calle Sunyaxchen

calle azucenas
calle jazmines
calle
avenida
calle

oficinas de aviateca

ayuntamiento (town hall)

comisaría de policía

correos

avenida Xel-Ha
avenida Xel-Ha

mercado municipal

avenida Xel-Ha

avenida Tankah

calle Tough
calle gladiolas

calle Yaxchilan

calle tulipanes

calle

calle claveles

calle crisantemas

monumento al diálogo entre Norte y Sur

av. Cobá

avenida Cobá

hospital

mercado

avenida Náder

centro federal de turismo

avenida Kukulcán

to beaches and hotels

HOTELS (DOUBLE ROOM)

* < $25
** $25 to $75
*** > 7$75

BANK AND BUREAU DE CHANGE
UNEX CASA DE CAMBIO
Ave. Tulum, no. 13
Close to Ave. Cobá
Open 9am–9pm

TELEPHONE
TELMEX
Ave. Cobá et Alcatraces
Ave. Uxmal

TOURIST OFFICE
DELEGACION ESTATAL DE TURISMO
Ave. Tulum, no. 26
Cancún Centro
Tel. 848 073

MAIN POST OFFICE
OFICINA DE CORREOS
At the western end of Ave. Sunyaxchén, near Ave. Yaxchilán
Open Mon.–Fri.
8am–7pm
Open Sat. and holidays
9am–1pm
International money orders can be collected up to one hour before closing.

TRANSPORT

AIRLINES
AEROCANCUN
Oasis Building
Bd Kukulcán
and Calle Cenzontle
Zona Hotelera
Tel. 833 144
or 832 319
AEROCARIBE
Ave. Tulum, no. 29,
SM 5
Cancún Centro
Tel. 842 000
or 860 083
Fax 841 364
AEROCOZUMEL
Ave. Tulum, no. 29
Cancún Centro
Tel. 842 000
or 860 162
AEROMEXICO
Ave. Cobá, no. 80
Cancún Centro
Tel. 843 571
or 840 151
AVIACSA
Ave. Cobá, no. 55
Cancún Centro
Tel. 844 214
or 844 211
Fax 846 599
AVIATECA
Ave. Tulum, no. 200,
Plaza Mexico
Cancún Centro
Tel. 843 938 or 871 386
LACSA
Ave. Bonampak
and Ave. Cobá

Edificio Atlantis SM 4
Cancún Centro
Tel. 873 101
or 875 101
MEXICANA
Ave. Cobá, no. 13
Cancún Centro
Tel. 874 444
or 872 769
TROPIC AIR
Ave. Cobá
Plaza America
Cancún Centro
Tel. 876 446

CAR RENTAL
AVIS
Aeropuerto Internacional
Tel. 860 147
Fax 860 238
BUDGET
Ave. Tulum, no. 214,
Cancún Centro
Tel. 844 101
or 846 955
Fax 845 011
DOLLAR
Ave. Tulum
Cancún Centro
Tel. 840 708
or 840 619
Fax 849 090
HERTZ
Calle Reno, no.20,
SM 20
Cancún Centro
Tel. 841 326
or 846 624
NATIONAL
Ave. Uxmal, no. 12
Cancún Centro
Tel. 864 490
or 864 492
Fax 864 493

RESTAURANTS

*** LA HABICHUELA
Margaritas, no. 25
Parque las Palapas
Tel. 843 158
Open 1–9pm
Interior garden in an elegant Mayan setting. Superb local dishes.

*** ROSA MEXICANA
Calle Claveles, no.4
Tel. 846 313
One of Cancún's largest restaurants, built in the style of a hacienda. Local cuisine.

** LA LANGOSTA FELIZ
Avenida Tulum, no. 33 C
Cancún Centro

Open 7am–10.30pm
Seafood.

** LOS BRACERITOS
Ave. Yaxchilán, no. 35
Open 24 hours
Local cuisine.

** PIEMONTE PIZZERIA
Ave. Yaxchilán, no. 52
Good value Italian specialties. Delicious snacks.

** LOS ALMENDROS
Ave. Bonampak
and Calle Sayil
Tel. 840 807
A popular restaurant. Specialties include "pocchuc" (pork with onion, lemon and pimento) and "papadzules" (tortillas with an egg-and-tomato sauce).

* 100% NATURAL
Opposite the Caribe Internacional Hotel
Ave. Yaxchilán and Ave. Sunyaxchén
Tel. 843 617
Large café with pleasant pastel-colored surroundings. Local vegetarian cuisine.

NIGHTLIFE

CARLOS "N" CHARLIES
Tel. 831 304
Bd. Kukulcán.
This bar-restaurant is very popular with American tourists. Offers a festive atmosphere.

SEÑOR FROG'S
Bar situated right next door to Carlos "n" Charlies, and very similar in style.

HOTELS

ON THE BEACH

*** CAMINO REAL CANCÚN
Punta Cancún
Tel. 830 100 or 831 200
Fax 831 730

*** CLUB MÉDITERRANÉE
Punta Nizuc
Tel. 842 900
Fax 842 409

*** MARRIOTT'S CANCÚN RESORT
Bd. Kukulcán
Tel. 852 000
Fax 851 731

*** SHERATON CANCÚN RESORT
Bd. Kukulcán
Tel. 831 988
Fax 831 450

TOWN CENTER

** HOTEL HACIENDA CANCÚN
Ave. Sunyaxchén, no. 39
Tel. 841 208

** HOTEL PARADOR
Ave. Tulum, no. 26
Tel. 841 310

** HOTEL ANTILLANO
On the corner of Calle Claveles and Ave. Tulum
Tel. 841 532
One of the best value hotels found in Cancún.

* HOTEL KOMSAVER
Ave. Yaxchilán, no. 15
Tel. 841 650

* HOTEL UXMAL
Ave. Uxmal. Just before Ave. Chichén Itzá
Tel. 842 266

SPORT

SCUBA DIVING
SCUBA CANCUN
P.O. Box 517
Cáncún, QROO

PONY TREKKING AND DIVING
XCARET
25 miles south of Cancún, on the coast.
Tel. 830 654 or 830 743
Open 9am–6pm
Closes 5pm, Oct.–Mar.
Pony trekking and scuba diving. It is possible to explore the archeological conservation area on the coast between Cancún and Tulum.

CHETUMAL

Dialing code 983

USEFUL INFORMATION

GUATEMALAN CONSULATE
Obregón, no. 342

On the corner of Rafael
Melgar
Tel. 213 65
Open Mon.–Fri.
9am–2pm

BANK AND BUREAU DE CHANGE
BANCO DEL ATLANTICO
Calle 50, no.406
Open Mon.–Fri.
9am–1pm

TOURIST OFFICE
CASETA DE INFORMACION TURISTICA
Ave. de los Heroes
and Efrain Aquilar
Tel. 236 63

MAIN POST OFFICE
OFICINA DE CORREOS
Plutarco Elias Calles 2 A
Tel. 200 57

TRANSPORT

AIRLINES
AEROCARIBE Airport
Tel. 266 75
AVIACSA
Hotel del Prado
On the corner of Ave.
de los Heroes and
Chapultepec
Tel. 277 65
or 276 54

CAR RENTAL
AMEN RENTE UN AUTO
Ave. Carmen O.
de Merino, no. 208-A
Tel. 284 52
NATIONAL RENT A CAR
Ave. de los Heroes,
no. 138
Tel. 205 42

RESTAURANT

* LA CABAÑA AZUL
Ave. 5 de Mayo, close
to the seashore.
Local cuisine.

HOTELS

** HOTEL EL MARQUES
Ave. Lázaro Cardenas,
no. 121
Tel. 229 98

** LOS COCOS
Heroes de Chaputelpec,
no. 138
Tel. 205 44

* HOTEL UCUM
Calle Gandhi, no. 4
Tel. 207 11

CHICHÉN ITZÁ

Dialing code 985

HOTELS

*** HOTEL MAYALAND
200 yards from the
entrance of the ruins
Tel. 252 342
Fax 257 022
*The best hotel in
Chichén Itzá.
Magnificent view of the
Caracol. Air
conditioning, gym and
tennis courts.*

** HOTEL DOLORES ALBA ★
Between the
Balankanché caves and
the ruins.
Tel. 213 745 (Mérida)
*Swimming pool. The
proprietor will take you
to the site in the
mornings.*

** PIRÁMIDE INN AND TRAILER PARK
Half a mile from the
west entrance to the
ruins.
*Swimming pool, air
conditioning.*

CAVES

BALANKANCHE
Two miles from Chichén
Itzá (signposted)
Hourly guided tours.
Open 9am–4pm
Closed Mon. and Sun.
1pm

COBÁ

Dialing code 985

HOTEL

*** VILLA ARQUEOLÓGICA COBÁ
Next to Lake Cobá
Tel. 425 74
*Houses an extensive
library specializing in
Mayan culture.
Swimming pool, good
restaurant.*

COZUMEL

Dialing code 987

TRANSPORT

AIRLINES
AEROCARIBE /
AEROCOZUMEL
Airport
Tel. 205 03 or 209 28
MEXICANA
Ave. R. Melgar Sur,

---

no. 17
Tel. 201 57 or 201 33
Fax 204 05

CAR RENTAL
A. MONTEJO BUDGET
5a Ave., no. 8
Tel. 209 03
ALGO RENT/AVIS
20 Ave., no. 220
Tel. 219 23
HERTZ
Ave. Juárez, no. 181
Altos
Tel. 221 36
THRIFTY
Corner of Calle 1
and 5a Ave.
Tel. 213 08

RESTAURANTS

*** PEPE'S GRILL
Ave. Rafael Melgar
and Calle Adolfo
Rosado Salas
Tel. 202 13
*One of the best menus
in Cozumel. Seafood,
langoustines, unusual
and delicious dishes.*

** LA CHOZA
Calle Adolfo Rosado
Salas, no. 198
On the corner of Ave.
10 Sur
*Reasonably priced for a
Cozumel restaurant.
Local dishes.*

* RESTAURANTE LAS PALMERAS
On the main square
Tel. 205 32
*Regional dishes served
on a charming terrace.*

* PIZZA ROLANDI
Ave. Rafael Melgar
between Calles 6 and
8 Norte
*Extremely popular,
good value.*

SPORT

SCUBA DIVING
★ BLACK SHARK
DIVE SHOP
5a Ave. Ent. Rafael E.
Melgar and 3 Sur
P.O. Box 462
Tel. 203 96 or 232 82
Fax 203 96
*Groups limited to a
maximum of seven
people. Offers diving
certificates (PADI).*
BLUE BUBBLE DIVERS
At the intersection of
5a Ave.and Calle 3 Sur
Tel. 218 65 (local)
or 011 52 987 (USA)
CARIBBEAN DIVERS
39 B Melgar Av.

(Hotels *Melia Mayan
Cozumel* and *Sol
Cabanas del Caribe*)
Tel. 210 80
214 26 or 211 45
DIVE PARADISE
Waterfront
601 Melgar Ave.
Tel. 210 07
or 213 66
DIVING ADVENTURE
Calle 5, no. 2
P.O. Box 78 - Cozumel
Quintana Roo
Tel. 230 09
Fax 230 09
FREDDY CONTREAS
Adolfo Rosado Salas
and 5a Ave. Sur
Tel. 241 23
SNORKOZUMEL
Melgar Ave., no. 471
(Lobby of the
Soberamis hotel)
Tel. 241 66
For keen snorklers.

FISHING AND SCUBA DIVING
WILD CAT DIVERS
5a Ave.
Between Calle 2
and Calle 4 Norte
Tel. 210 28
or 239 21
Fax 210 28

HOTELS

*** STOUFFER COZUMEL
Carretera a Chankanab
four miles
Tel. 203 22
Fax 213 60
*Two swimming pools,
tennis courts and boat
hire.*

** HOTEL PLAZA
Calle 2 Norte 3,
San Miguel
Tel. 200 66
*Roof pool and air-
conditioned rooms.*

* HOTEL MARY-CARMEN
Ave. 5 Sur 4, San Miguel
Tel. 205 81
*This hotel has a very
Spanish atmosphere
with its rooms
overlooking an
illuminated patio.*

NIGHTLIFE

CARLOS "N" CHARLIES
On the sea front
Tel. 201 91
Open noon–dusk.
*Mexican-American bar-
restaurant. Friendly
atmosphere. Prices tend
to be high.*

DOS OJOS

SPORT

RAMBLING, TREKKING AND DIVING
DIVERS OF THE HIDDEN WORLDS
"Dos Ojos Jungle Adventure"
A.P.66, Tulum, Quintana Roo
Tel. 744 081

ESCARCEGA

Dialing code 982

HOTELS

** HOTEL ESCARCEGA
In the city center
Tel. 401 86
Half a mile from ADO station.

ISLA MUJERES

Dialing code 987

RESTAURANTS

** GOMAR
Madero
Tel. 201 42
Specialty: seafood

* CAFÉ CITO
Matamorros, no. 42
Tel. 704 38
Delicious breakfasts served in unusual surroundings.

HOTELS

*** HOTEL DEL PRADO
Tel. 200 29 or 200 43
Luxury hotel with good facilities. The beach here is excellent for diving.

** HOTEL PERLA DEL CARIBE ★
Madero, no. 2
Tel. 204 44 or 203 02
Friendly and charming atmosphere. Tastefully decorated, spacious, clean rooms.

* HOTEL LAS PALMAS
Guerrero, no. 20
Tel. 204 16
Light, clean rooms.

MÉRIDA

Dialing code 99

USEFUL INFORMATION

CONSULATES
CONSULATE OF BRITAIN AND BELIZE
Major A. Dutton
Calle 58-53, no. 450
Tel. 286 152
CANADIAN CONSULATE
Ave. Colón, no. 309
Tel. 256 419
CONSULATE OF THE UNITED STATES OF AMERICA
Paseo Montejo, no. 453 and Ave. Colón
Tel. 255 011

BANKS AND BUREAUX DE CHANGE
BANAMEX
Pl. Mayor

387

Palacio Montejo
BANAMEX
Calle 56 and Calle 59
Open Mon.–Fri.
9am–1pm and 4–5pm
CASA DE CAMBIO
Calle 56, no. 491
Between Calle 57
and Calle 59.
Open Mon.–Sat.
9am–5pm
*Tends to offer better
rates than the bank.*

DOCTOR
DOCTOR AH PUGA
NAVARRETE
Calle 13, no. 210
Between Calle 26
and Calle 28
Tel. 250 509
Open 4–10pm
English spoken.

BOOKSHOPS
HOLLYWOOD LIBRERÍA
Calle 60, no. 496
To the north of the Plaza
Central
Tel. 213 619
*International
newspapers and
magazines, novels and
travel guides.*
LÍBRERIA DANTE PEÓN
Teatro Peón Contreras
On the corner of
Calle 60 and Calle 57
Tel. 249 522
Open Mon.–Sun.
*Books in English,
French and Spanish.*

MAIN POST OFFICE
OFICINA DE CORREOS
On the corner of Calle
65 and Calle 56.
(between Calle 56
and Calle 56 A)
Tel. 212 561
Open Mon.–Fri. 7am–
7pm, Sat. 9am–1pm

TRANSPORT

AIRLINES
AEROCARIBE
Paseo Montejo, no. 500
Tel. 286 790
Fax 249 559
Airport:
Tel. 461 361
Fax 461 333
AEROCOZUMEL
Paseo Montejo, no. 500

Tel. 286 790
Fax 249 559
Airport:
Tel: 461 361
Fax 461 333
AEROMEXICO
Paseo Montejo
Tel. 279 566
or 279 000
Fax 264 732
AVIACSA
Airport:
Tel. 269 173
or 263 954
Fax 263 253
AVIATECA
Airport:
Tel. 249 477
or 243 605
Fax 244 354
MEXICANA
Calle 58, no. 500, on
the corner of Calle 61
Tel. 246 754
Fax 242 937
TAESA
Calle 15, no. 92 B
Tel. 269 913

CAR RENTAL
AVIS
Paseo Montejo, no. 500
Tel. 282 828
or 236 191
Fax 236 007
BUDGET
Prol. Paseo Montejo,
no. 49
Tel. 272 708
HERTZ
Calle 55, no. 479, on the
corner of Calle 54
Tel. 242 834
Airport:
Tel. 249 187
MEXICO RENT A CAR
Calle 60, no. 495
Tel. 274 916
NATIONAL RENT A CAR
Calle 62, no. 483 A, on
the corner of Calle 57
Tel. Airport: 247 068

RESTAURANTS

*** LA CASONA
Calle 60, no. 434
Tel. 238 348
*Good Italian and
Mexican cuisine.*

***** PORTICO
DEL PELEGRINO**
Calle 57, no. 501
(between Calle 60
and Calle 62)
Tel. 216 844
Open lunchtime
noon–3pm, evenings
6–11pm.
*Specializes in local
dishes (pavo poc-chuc).*

**** CAFETERÍA
EL MESÓN**
In the Hotel Caribe

Calle 59, no. 500
(behind Hidalgo park).
Tel. 219 232
*Local dishes, self-
service.*

** CEDRO DEL LIBANO
Calle 59, no. 529
(between Calle 64 and
Calle 66).
Tel. 237 531
Open 11.30am–
11.30pm
*This Lebanese
restaurant offers a
selection of delicious
dishes from the
Middle East.*

** LOS ALMENDROS
Pl. de Mejorada,
Calle 50 (between Calle
57 and Calle 59)
Open 11am–11pm
*Varied cuisine, Yucatán
specialties often
featured, good cocktails.
Very popular air-
conditioned restaurant.*

* EL LOUVRE
Calle 62, no. 499
(on the corner of Calle
61, on the northwest
corner of the Plaza
principale)
Tel. 213 271
Open every day from
morning until night.
*Fast-food, good quality.
Restaurant located in
the town center.*

HOTELS

***** HOLIDAY INN
MÉRIDA**
Ave. Colón 498
Tel. 256 877
*Luxury hotel with good
facilities.*

** GRAN HOTEL *
Calle 60
(between Calle 61
and Calle 59).
Tel. 236 963 or 247 730
Fax 247 622
*Situated on the most
attractive plaza in
Mérida. Magnificent
colonial building with
galleries connecting two
floors of rooms,
mosaics, and a patio
covered in greenery.*

American Express not
accepted.

**** HOTEL DOLORES
ALBA**
Calle 63, no. 464
Tel. 285 680
or 283 163
*Patio and pool. There is
also another Hotel
Dolores Alba at
Chichén Itzá
(reservations can be
made from Mérida).*

* HOTEL LAS MONJAS
Calle 66a, no. 509
Tel. 219 862

NIGHTLIFE

EL TUCHE
Calle 60
To the north of the Plaza
Central
*Cabaret with local live
band and dancing
(salsa), reasonably
priced good food.*

TROVADOR BOHEMIA
Santa Lucía park
*Guitar trios featured.
Bar open from 9pm.*

CULTURE

PARC SANTA LUCÍA
On the corner of Calles
55 and 60.
*Folk dance performed
every Thursday starting
around 9pm.*

**TEATRO PEÓN
CONTRERAS**
Calles 60 and 57
*Folk dancing, Tuesdays
at 9pm.*

**ARCHEOLOCIAL
MUSEUM**
Paseo de Montejo
and Calle 41
Open 8am–8pm.
Closed Mon. and Sun.
from 2pm.

OCOSINGO

HOTEL

** HOTEL CENTRAL
Ave. Central, no. 1
Tel. (967) 300 39

PALENQUE

Dialing code 934

TRANSPORT

CAR RENTAL
AUTO RENTAS YAXCHILÁN
Jiménez, no. 7
On the corner of 5 de
Mayo
Tel. 500 20

RESTAURANTS

*** LA OAXAQUEÑA
At the entrance to the
town coming from the
ruins.
*Good food, rather
expensive.*

***** RESTAURANT-BAR
HARDY'S OR LA SELVA**
On the road to the ruins
100 yards from the
Maya statue.
Tel. 503 63
Regional cuisine.

**** LA PALAPA
DE APOHEL**
Ave. 5 de Mayo
between
Independencia
and Abasolo).
Comfortable

*surroundings, good
food. Seafood a
specialty.*

* GIRASOLES
Juárez, no. 189
Open morning,
lunchtime and evening.
*A popular meeting place
for visitors.
Regional cuisine.*

* MONTES AZULES
Juárez, no. 120
*Generous portions,
friendly welcome, music
(marimba) on Fri., Sat.
and Sun. Local cuisine.*

HOTELS

** HOTEL LA CAÑADA
Close to Maya
Tulipanes

Tel. 50 102
*Bungalows dotted
through the forest.
Spacious, clean, double
rooms.*

** HOTEL PALENQUE
Ave. 5 de Mayo, no. 15
Tel. 50 188

** HOTEL EL PARAÍSO
1½ miles from Carretera
de las ruinas
Tel. 50 033/045
*Beautiful rooms
overlooking a patio and
a quiet garden.*

PLAYA DEL CARMEN

Dialing code 987

RESTAURANTS

***** RESTAURANTE
MASCARAS**
Plaza Central.
*The oldest and most
famous city in Playa del
Carmen.*

** DA GABI *
Calle 12 (behind the
Blue Parrot)
*Good fast service.
Regional, Italian and
European cuisines.*

HOTELS

**** BLUE PARROT
INN ***
(by the beach to the left
of the Embarcadero).
*The most pleasant
place in Playa del
Carmen, with happy
hours (two drinks for the
price of one) almost all
day. Original décor: the
bar seats have been
replaced by swinging
chairs. Good restaurant.*

** MAYA BRIC
Ave. 5 between Calle 8
and Calle 10.
*Rooms around a flower-
covered patio.
Swimming pool.
Very quiet.*

SAN CRISTÓBAL DE LAS CASAS

Dialing code 967

USEFUL INFORMATION

TELEPHONE CENTER
BOUTIQUE
SANTO DOMINGO
Esquina Paniagua
*Credit cards accepted.
Reverse charge calls
possible.*

HOSPITAL
CROIX ROUGE
(CRUZ ROJA)
Ave. Insurgentes
(close to Centro
Recreativo Municipal).
Tel. 807 12
SAN CRISTÓBAL
CENTRO DE SALUD
Ave. Insurgentes, no. 24
(Opposite the Fray
Bartolomé Park).
Tel. 807 70
*24-hour emergency
service*

BOOKSHOPS
EL MURAL
Crescencio Rosas, no. 4
*Books and magazines
in English and Spanish .
Daily newspapers –
enquire when you
arrive.*
LIBRERÍA EL RINCÓN
Diego de Mazariegos
*Secondhand books –
exchange two for one.*
LIBRERÍA SOLUNA
24-D Real de
Guadalupe, to the east
of Pl. Principale.
*Some English books
but mostly stocks books*

*in Spanish. Possible to
exchange two books for
one.*

MAIN POST OFFICE
OFICINA DE CORREOS
Cuauhtémoc, no. 13
(between Crescencio
Rosas and Hidalgo).
Tel. 807 65
Open Mon.–Fri.
8am–7pm,
Sat.–Sun., holidays
9am–1pm

TRANSPORT

CAR RENTAL
AUTO RENTA
RICCI DIESTEL
Ave. 5 de Mayo, no. 6-A
On the corner of
Guadalupe
and Victoria
Tel. 809 88
BUDGET/AUTO RENTAS
YAXCHILÁN
Diego de Mazariegos,
no. 36
Barrio la Merced
Tel. 818 71
Fax 831 00

CULTURE

CASA DE LA CULTURA
At the intersection of
Hermanos Domínguez
and Hidalgo
(Opposite *El Carmen*).
*Concerts, films,
lectures, exhibitions.*

**ROBERTO RIVAS
BASTIDAS**
Centro Bilingüe
Ave. Insurgentes,
no. 57
Tel. 841 57
Fax 837 23
Language courses.

**UNIVERSIDAD
AUTÓNOMA
DE CHIAPAS**
Ave. Hidalgo
Departamento
de Lenguas
Language courses.

HOTEL D'MÓNICA
Ave. Insurgentes,
no. 33
*Live Latin-American
music every Friday
evening.*

RESTAURANTS

*** EL TEATRO
Calle Primero de Marzo,
no. 8
Tel. 831 49
Open 11am–11pm
*Magnificent view of the
town. Excellent food,*

particularly the
steak châteaubriand,
wood-fire cooked pizzas
and best of all the fillet
steak San Cristóbal.

*** LA PARRILLA
Ave. Belisario
Dominguez, no. 32
Closed Sat.
Saloon-style décor,
wood fire. Regional
cuisine: good cheeses
and grilled meats.

** TULUC
Ave. Insurgentes, no. 5
Tel. 820 90
Open morning,
lunchtime and evening.
Breakfast served from
6.30am
Good restaurant, but
rather expensive.
Regional and French
cuisine.

* RESTAURANT
AND PANADERÍA
MADRE TIERRA
Ave. Insurgentes, no. 19
Open 8am–9.30pm
Regional cuisine
(very good coffee).

HOTELS

*** HOTEL
CASA MEXICANA
Calle 28 de Agosto,
no. 1
Tel. 806 98
or 806 83
Fax 826 27
In a large renovated
colonial house.
Beautifully planted
patio.

*** HOTEL
FLAMBOYANT
Calle Primero de Marzo,
no. 15
Tel. 805 14
Once a colonial house.
Tends to be full of
groups of tourists during
high season.

** HOTEL EL PARAÍSO
Ave. 5 de Febrero,
no. 19
Tel. 800 85

Pleasant little hotel with
modern decoration.

** HOTEL ESPAÑOL
Calle Primero de Marzo,
no. 16
Tel. 804 12
To the north of the
cathedral in a colonial-
style building with two
small interior
courtyards. Each room
has its own fireplace

* HOTEL FRAY
BARTOLOMÉ
DE LAS CASAS
Calle Niños Heroes,
no. 2
Tel. 809 32
Fax 835 10
This basic hotel has a
pretty flowered patio.

TULUM

Dialing code 987

RESTAURANT

* CABAÑAS
DON ARMANDO ★
500 yards to the south
of the ruins, on the
beach.
Open 8am–noon.
Bar and dancing every
evening.
Regional cuisine.

HOTELS

** HOTEL EL PARAÍSO
One mile to the south of
the ruins.

** HOTEL EL FAISAN
Y EL VENADO
Opposite the access
road to the ruins.

* HOTEL CABAÑAS
DON ARMANDO ★
On the beach.

TUXTLA
GUTIÉRREZ

Dialing code 968

USEFUL
INFORMATION

TELEPHONE CENTER
LADATEL
Ave. 1 Sur and
Calle 2 Or.
Open 9am–10pm

MAIN POST OFFICE
OFICINA DE CORREOS
To the east of the Plaza
Central.
Open Mon.–Sat.
8am–6pm, and Sun.
9am–noon, for stamps
only.

MUSEUM

REGIONAL
ANTHROPOLOGICAL
MUSEUM
Calzada de los hombres
illustres de la
Revolución
Madero Park
Tel. 204 59

TRANSPORT

CAR RENTAL
AUTO BADIA
Hotel Flamboyant
Bd Dr Belisario
Dominguez, km 1081
Tel. 108 88
or 109 99
O.K. AUTO RENTAL /
DOLLAR
5a Norte Poniente,
no. 2260
Tel. 289 32
Airport: Tel. 229 20
Q.R. RENT A CAR
Hotel Bonampla
Bd Dr Belisario
Dominguez, no. 2510
Tel. 255 06
Airport: Tel. 255 59

AIRLINES
AEROCARIBE
Bd Belisario
Dominguez, no. 180
Tel. 220 32
or 114 90 / 220 53
Fax 377 59 / 220 53
MEXICANA
Ave. Central Poniente,
no. 206
Tel. 271 08
Fax 216 92

RESTAURANTS

** LA PARILLA
NORTEÑA
Calle 14 de Septiembre
and Calle 11 Oriente
Norte
Large dining room with
walls covered in
frescos. Specialties:
grills and kebabs.

* RESTAURANTE
LAS PICHANCHAS
Ave. 14 de Septiembre,
Ote 857

Tel. 253 51
Open-air restaurant
enlivened by marimba
playing. Varied menu
featuring regional
cuisine.

* RESTAURANTE
EL GRAN CHEFF
Ave. Central Poniente,
no. 226 and Calle 1
Poniente Norte.
Regional cuisine,
comida corrida (fast
food).

HOTELS

*** HOTEL
FLAMBOYANT
Bd Belisario Dominguez
Tel. 10 888
Fax 112 36
Comfortable rooms
situated around a
swimming pool. Disco,
tennis courts, restaurant
and bar.

** HOTEL REGIONAL
SAN MARCOS
Calle 2 Or. Sur, no. 176
Tel. 31 940
Basic, air-conditioned
rooms.

* GRAN HOTEL
OLIMPO
Ave. Sur Ote, no. 215
Tel. 20 295 or 31 770
Very basic.

UXMAL

Dialing code 99

CAVES

LOLTUN
Four miles to the south
of Oxkutzcab
Guided tours 9.30am,
11am, 12.30pm and
2pm. Closed Mon.

HOTELS

** HACIENDA UXMAL HOTEL
500 yards from the ruins, on the opposite side of the road.
Tel. 471 42
Very quiet with a beautiful patio and pleasant swimming pool. Generous breakfasts.

*** HOTEL VILLA ARQUEOLÓGICA
A Club Méditerrannée hotel. Next to the site.

** RANCHO UXMAL
Coming from Mérida, 2 miles before the ruins, on the right.
Rooms with hot water, fan and mosquito net.

VALLADOLID
Dialing code 985

CAVES

DZITNUP
Four miles from Valladolid, taking the road to Chichén Itzá then the dirt track, one mile on the right.
Open Mon.–Sun.
9am–5pm.
Bus and taxi from Valladolid.It is advisable to take a torch.

HOTELS

** HOTEL EL MESÓN DEL MARQUES
Calle 39, no. 203
Tel. 630 42
Fax 622 80
Superb, beautifully planted patio and extremely comfortable rooms. No hot water in the evening.

** HOTEL DON LUIS
Calle 39, no. 191
Tel. 6 20 08
Air-conditioned rooms around a shaded swimming pool.

* HOTEL MARÍA DE LA LUZ
Calle 42, on the zócalo.
Tel. 620 71
Pleasant surroundings, swimming pool in a verdant setting.

RESTAURANTS

** RESTAURANTE CASA DE LOS ARCOS
Calle 39, between Calle 38 and 40.
Tel. 624 67
Beautiful well-lit setting, perfect for enjoying a choice of delicious Yucatán specialties.

* EL PAPILLON
Calle 42, sur lo zócalo.
Small, basic and very popular restaurant.

VILLAHERMOSA
Dialing code 93

USEFUL INFORMATION

BANK AND BUREAU DE CHANGE
BANCOMER
On the corner of Zaragoza and Juárez.
Tel. 237 00
Open Mon.–Fri.
9am–1.30pm
CAMBIARIA DEL CENTRO
Saenz, no. 222
Tel. 430 53 or 430 54
Open Mon.–Fri.
8.30am–2pm and
4–6.30pm
Service tends to be faster than the bank.

TOURIST OFFICE
SECRETARIA
DE TURISMO DEL ESTADO
Ave. Paseo de tabasco,
no. 1504
Tel. 636 33
Fax 628 90

MAIN POST OFFICE
OFICINA DE CORREOS
Saenz 131
Zona Remodelada
Tel. 210 40

Open Mon.–Fri.
8am–5.30pm
(stamps available until 7pm)
Open Sat. 9am–noon
(stamps available until 1pm)
Closed Sun.
BANAMEX
On the corner of streets Madero and la Reforma
Tel. 289 94
Open Mon.–Fri.
9am–1.30pm

TRANSPORT

AIRLINES
AEROCARIBE
Fco. Javier Mina, no. 901
Tel. 143 202
or 143 203
AEROLITORAL
Airport
Tel. 143 613 or 143 614
AEROMEXICO
CICOM
Avenida Carlos Pellicier
Camara no. 511
Tel. 124 389 or 129 475
Fax 121 528
AVIACSA
Fco. Javier Mina,
no. 1025-2
Tel. 144 755
Airport: Tel. 145 770
or 145 780
MEXICANA
Ave. de los Ríos,
no. 105
Tabasco 2000
Tel. 163 132 to 138.

CAR RENTAL
AUTO RENT
Ave. Ruiz Cortinez,
no. 1201
Tel. 128 003
AVIS
Juan Alvares, no. 602a
Tel. 129 214
DOLLAR RENT A CAR
Hotel Holiday Inn,
Paseo Tabasco, no.
1407
Hotel Viva: Ave. Ruiz
Cortinez, on the corner
of Paseo Tabasco.
Tel. 134 400
or 150 000
HERTZ RENT A CAR
Hotel Maya Tabasco
Ave. Ruiz Cortinez
Tel. 121 111
SANMAR AUTO RENT /
BUDGET
Paseo del Malecón,

no. 761
Tel. 143 790

MUSEUMS

HISTORY MUSEUM
On the corner of Calle de Juárez
and 27 de Febrero.
Open daily 9am–6pm

MUSEO REGIONAL DE LA ANTROPOLOGÍA
Ave. C. Pellicer, no. 511
Open daily 9am–8pm

PARC DE LA VENTA
Av. Adolfo Ruíz Cortinez
S/N
Open daily 8am–4.30pm
Collection of Olmec statues.

RESTAURANTS

** CAPITÁN BEULO
On the quay opposite the Museo Regional de la Antropología.
Departures–1.30pm,
3.30pm and 9.30pm
Floating restaurant which departs for a one and a half hour tour of the Río Grijalva. The food is less

interesting than the cruise itself. Regional cuisine.

** RESTAURANTE LA PLAYITA
Constitución, no. 202
Seafood.

HOTELS

*** HOTEL EXALARIS HYATT REGENCY
Laguna de las Ilusiones,
Juarez, no. 106
Tel. 134 444
Fax 155 808

** HOTEL DON CARLOS
Madero, no. 418
Tel. 122 493
Fax 124 622

* HOTEL PALMA DE MALLORCA
Madero, no. 516

391

Tel. 120 144
*Well located, basic
rooms. Often full.*

XPUHIL
GUIDED WALKS

Contact Serge Riou,
called Checo.
Apartado Postal 27,
CP 24640 Xpuhil,
Campeche.
Fax–Chetumal:
983 21 251
*This French resident of
Xpuhil is an excellent
guide for visits to the
sites in the Río Bec.*

◆

*Dialing codes:
2 for the capital,
9 for other towns*

ANTIGUA
GUATEMALA

USEFUL
INFORMATION

BANKS AND BUREAUX
DE CHANGE
BANCO DEL ARGO
To the north of the Plaza
Central.
Open 9am–2.30pm
*Only banks are open on
Saturdays.*
LLOYD'S BANK
4a Ave. and 4 Calle
Open Mon.–Fri.
9am–2.30pm

HOSPITAL
HOSPITAL PEDRO
DE BETANCOURT
3a Ave. and 6 Calle
Tel. 320 301

BOOKSHOPS
LIBRERÍA MARQUENSE
5a Ave. Sur, no. 9
LIBRERÍA DEL PENSATIVO
5a Ave. Norte, no. 29
*English and Spanish
books.*

★ UN POCO DE TODO
Plaza Central.
Open Mon.–Fri.
9.30am–1pm
*Travel guides, books in
English and Spanish,
maps, postcards.
English spoken*

TOURIST OFFICE
OFICINA DEL INGUAT
Palacios de los
Capitanes Generales
5a Calle Oriente
and 4a Ave. Sur
Tel. 320 763

MAIN POST OFFICE
OFICINA DE CORREOS
4 Calle Poniente
Alameda Santa Lucía
Open Mon.–Sat.
8am–noon and 2–8pm

TRANSPORT

MOTORBIKE RENTAL
MOTO-RENT
Hotel Los Capitanes
9a Ave. Sur
*Motorbikes to rent
(Yamaha 200).*

SPANISH COURSES

★ CENTRO DE
ESPAÑOL "DON PEDRO
DE ALVARADO"
4 Calle Poniente, no. 27
Open 8am–1pm
or 1–6pm
*Cost of Spanish
courses: $65 per week
(four hours per day for
five days).
Accommodation is*

available, with access to
a kitchen, in a house
with garden.

CHRISTIAN SPANISH
ACADEMY (CSA)
6a Ave. Norte, no. 15
P.O. Box 320
Tel. 323 922
Fax 323 760
Closed Sat. and Sun.
*Individual Spanish
tuition for four to five
hours per day, Mon. to
Fri. Classes held in the
garden. Accommodation
available with a family.*

EL QUETZAL
7 Calle Poniente
Appartado Postal
no. 428
*Accommodation can be
arranged with a family
($40 per week.)*

ESCUELA DE ESPAÑOL
ATABAL
1a Ave. Norte, no. 6
Tel. 320 791
*Small school, friendly
atmosphere.*

INSTITUTO ANTIGÜEÑO
1a Calle Poniente,
no. 33

MAYA ESCUELA
DE ESPAÑOL
5 Calle Poniente, no. 20
*Cost: $70 per week.
(Accommodation with a
family $50 per week.)*

POPOL VUH
7a Ave. Norte, no. 34
Tel. 323 343

PROYECTO
LINGÜISTICO
"RIGOBERTA MENCHU"
5a Ave. Sur, no. 11C
Tel. 322 931

PROYECTO
LINGÜISTICO
"FRANCISCO
MARROQUÍN"
4 Ave. Sur, no. 4
Apartado Postal no. 237

Tel. 320 406
Fax 320 406
*Up to seven hours of
classes per day.
Accommodation
available (with an
Antiguan family).
Cost: $150 per week.*

QUICHÉ
3 Ave. Sur, no. 15 A
(Behind the cathedral,
2½ blocks to the south.)
Tel. 320 575
Fax 320 575
*Very popular with
students. Friendly
atmosphere.*

TECÚN UMÁN
6 Calle Poniente, no. 3
Tel. 322 792
Fax 322 792
*Individual tuition. A tour
of local sites of interest
can also be organized.*

PROFESSIONAL
SPANISH LANGUAGE
SCHOOL
7 Ave. Norte, no. 82
Tel. 320 161
*Director: Roberto King,
author of "Spanish, an
easy way".
Individual classes of
two, four or six hours
per day for a week.*

RESTAURANTS

*** CAFE OPERA
6a Ave. Norte, no. 17
*Café-Bar-Restaurant.
Italian cuisine.
Friendly atmosphere,
classical music.*

*** EL SERENO
6 Calle Poniente, no. 30
Tel. 320 073
Open Wed. to Sun.
noon–3pm and
6.30–10pm.
*Beautiful restaurant in
an old colonial-style
house. Children under 8
years are not accepted.
Booking recommended
particularly on Sun.
Regular music recitals
Mon. and Tue. Local
crafts for sale. Regional
cuisine.*

★★ WELTEN
Calle Oriente, no. 21
Tel. 320 630
Closed Tues.
Excellent menu but
fairly expensive.
Pleasant surroundings
(attractive garden) and
rooms shown in the
evening.

★★ FONDA
E CALLE REAL ★
5 Ave. Norte, no. 5
Guatemalan cuisine.
Good restaurant,
attractive décor.
Specialty: cheese
fondues.

★ KATOK
7 Ave. Norte, no. 7
In a small patio.
Guatemalan cuisine.

★ QUESOS Y VINO
5a Ave. Norte, no. 32A
A good pizzeria which
also serves pasta and
wine. Specializes in a
Parmesan-style
cheese.

★ RESTAURANTE CAFÉ
5a Ave. Norte, no. 14
Within the La Casa de
los Gárgolas building,
this restaurant is
located in a flowered
courtyard with a
fountain. Regional
cuisine.

★ DOÑA LUISA
Calle Oriente, no. 12
(1½ blocks to the east of
the square).
A large colonial
residence with a patio,
destroyed several times
by earthquakes and
completely rebuilt.
Today it is a tea house
and bakery. The perfect
place for a delicious
breakfast.

CAFÉ CONDESA
5 Ave. Norte, no. 4
Parque central
Tel. 323 322
Open throughout the
day for breakfast, coffee
and snacks. Situated in
a courtyard behind a
bookshop on the Plaza
Central opposite the
church.

RESTAURANTE
ITALIANO EL
CAPUCHINO
6a Ave. N., no. 10
between 4 and 5 Calles
Poniente
Tel. 320 613

A small, inexpensive
restaurant which serves
delicious Italian food.

HOTELS

★★★ CASA SANTO
DOMINGO ★
3a Calle Oriente, no. 28
Tel. 320 140
or 322 102
Fax 320 102
A former convent which
has been magnificently
restored. Delightful
setting.

★★★ RAMADA HOTEL
9 Calle Poniente and
Carretera Ciudad Vieja
Tel. 322 929
Fax 323 001

★★ HOTEL ANTIGUA
8a Calle Oriente
and 4a Ave. Sur
Tel. 320 331
or 320 288

★★ POSADA
DE DON RODRIGO ★
Calle del Arco 5a
and Ave. Norte 17
Tel. 320 291
An impressive colonial
building around an
interior courtyard.
Marimba band on Sat.

★★ HOTEL EL
DESCANSO
5a Avenida Norte, no. 9
Tel. 320 142
Small hotel in a family
house. Five pleasant
rooms for 2, 3 or 4
persons.

★ POSADA LAS ROSAS
6a Avenida Sur, no. 8
Tel. 320 644
Steam baths and
generous breakfasts.

SPORT

SAILING
VIAREAL (REAL
DESROSIERS)
4 Calle Oriente, no. 7
Tel. 323 228

Organized excursions to
Lake Izabal, Lívingston
and the Cayes of Belize.

VOLCANA
EXPEDITIONS
QUETZAL VOLCANO
EXPEDITIONS
Alameda Santa Lucía
Sur, no. 6
Excursions to the
volcanos of Pacaya,
Agua, Fuego,
Acatenango.

★ POPEYE TOURS
INGUAT BUILDING
4a Calle Poniente,
no. 38
Take warm clothes and
waterproofs for the
three-hour climb to the
top of the Pacaya
volcano. Groups of a
minimum of five
people.

MUSEUMS

MUSEUM SANTIAGO
DE LOS CABALLEROS
Plaza Mayor
Open daily 9am–noon
and 2–6pm

MUSEUM OF ANCIENT
BOOKS
Plaza Mayor
Open daily 9am–noon
and 2–6pm

MUSEUM OF COLONIAL
ART
On the corner of the
Calle de la Universitad
and de Ave. Norte

NIGHTLIFE

★ BAR PICASSO
7a Ave. Norte
(between 2a Calle
Poniente and 3a Calle
Poniente)
Open daily,
7pm–midnight.
Closed Wed.
Good music, very
popular.

CAFÉ FLOR CINEMA
4a Ave. Sur, no. 1
(Half a block from the
Plaza Central)
Closed Sun.
Three screenings a day

except Sun. (films in
English and Spanish).

CINE GEMINIS
5a Calle Oriente, no.
11a
Three screenings a day,
four at the weekend.
Films in English or
Spanish with subtitles.

CINEMALA
3a Ave. Norte, no. 9
Behind Doña Luisa
Two or three screenings
a day.

JAZZ GRUCIA
Cal. Santa Lucía, no. 17
Jazz bands once or
twice a week.

MOSCAS Y MIEL
5 Calle Poniente, no. 6
A good place to dance
or just to listen to music.
Also a nightclub.

MISTRAL
4 Calle Oriente, no. 7
Bar/cinema which is
extremely popular with
visitors.

RAINBOW VIDEO
7a Ave. Sur, no. 8
On the corner of
6a Calle
Three screenings every
day except Wed. Films
in English or with
subtitles.

CHICHICAS-
TENANGO

HOTELS

★★★ MAYAN INN ★
Near the market plaza
Tel. 561 176
or 561 202
Fax 561 212
Superb colonial-style
rooms with fireplaces.
Restaurant and good
service.

★★★ HOTEL
SANTO TOMAS ★
7a Ave. 5-32
Tel. 561 061
Delightful colonial-style
hotel with an elegant
patio and arcades.

** HOTEL VILLA GRANDE
Tel. 561 053
This modern hotel has a swimming pool and is situated on the outskirts of the town.

* HOTEL GIRÓN
6a Calle
Built around a small interior courtyard. This is the cheapest hotel to be found in the center of town.

* PENSIÓN CHUGUILÁ
5a Ave., to the north of the Plaza Central.
Tel. 561 134
The rooms of this hotel overlook a pleasant interior courtyard. Several of the suites have individual fireplaces. Good restaurant.

COBÁN

RESTAURANTS

** HOTEL LA POSADA
1 Calle 4-12 Zona 2
Tel. 511 495
Regional cuisine.

* CAFÉ CENTRO
1 Calle between 1a Ave. and 2a Ave.
Tel. 512 192
Offers a varied and reasonably priced menu.

HOTELS

** HOTEL LA POSADA
1 Calle 4–12, Zona 2
Tel. 511 495
Well located in the center of town. A colonial-style residence with pleasant well-appointed rooms.

* HOTEL OXIB PECK
1 Calle 12-11, Zona 1
Tel. 511 039
Windowless rooms with showers.

BETWEEN ANTIGUA AND SOLOLÁ

RESTAURANTS

** CHICHOY I
(63 miles on the Panamerican Highway)
Local cuisine.

** CHICHOY II
(45 miles on the Panamerican Highway)

** KATOK
(54 miles on the Panamerican route)
Grilled food in a typical hut.

FLORES

USEFUL INFORMATION

BANK AND BUREAU DE CHANGE
BANCO HIPOTECARIO
On the Isla Flores (near the church).
Open Mon.–Fri. 8.30am–2.30pm
It is also possible to change money at hotel receptions.

TRANSPORT

TOUR OPERATORS/ TRAVEL AGENTS
EXPLORE
(CARLOS JIMÉNEZ)
Ave. Centroamerica
Tel. 500 655
Fax 500 655
Office situated at Flores airport/ Santa Elena and in Guatemala City.
Ave. La Reforma 12–51, Zona 10
Guatemala City
01010
Tel. 316 243
Fax 341 179
Other operators which cover Mexico, Belize and Guatemala.
EL TUCAN
Hotel, restaurant and travel agent
Calle Centroamérica.
Tel. 500 577
VIAJES Y REPRESENTACIONES ÍTZA

Near Flores in Santa Elena
Fax 500 624
SAN JUAN TRAVEL
Santa Elena, Flores.
Take buses from here to Tikal, Ceibal, Uaxactún, Chetumal and Guatemala City.

CAR RENTAL
KOKA
Flores Airport
Tel. 501 233
or 500 526
RENTA VEHICULOS
Hotel *Tayasal*
Opposite the *Gasolinera* Chevron
Tel. 500 333

RESTAURANTS

*** EL JACAL
Calle Flores
On the left on arriving in Flores
Delicious house specialties, good soups and salads. Meals are served under a straw canopy with bamboo walls decorated with various interesting objects.

** EL TUCAN ★
Calle Centro América
Flores.
Tel. 501 380
or 500 577
Fax 501 380
Closed Sun.
Excellent food served in very pleasant surroundings. Superb view over the lake, especially in the evening. Regional cuisine.

** LA MESA DE LOS MAYAS
Flores
(On the left coming from Santa Elena).
Tel. 501 240
Fax 501 240
Open daily. Regional cuisine.

HOTELS

*** HOTEL MAYA INTERNACIONAL
Near Santa Elena airort
Tel. 501 276
Situated right on the shore of the lagoon, these bungalows are reached via a footbridge. Restaurant under a large straw canopy overlooking the lake.

0 100   500 ya

GUATEMALA CITY NORTH

ZONA 3

CEME GENE

río La Barranca

anillo   pu

Martín

30a calle
31a calle
32a calle
33a calle

7a ave

** HOTEL DEL PATIO-TIKAL
Near Santa Elena airport
Tel. 501 229
A recently built colonial-style building which offers comfortable and reasonably priced rooms.

** HOTEL PETÉN
Flores
Tel. 500 662
Fax 500 662
A friendly hotel with well-maintained, comfortable rooms. The owner has a minibus and is happy to drive guests to Tikal on request.

★ **LA CASONA
E LA ISLA** ★
ores
l. 500 692
ax 501 258
newly built hotel with
art décor and
peccable rooms.

★ **HOTEL YUM KAX**
the end of San Benito
narf
l. 811 386

A hotel with little
character but a few of
the rooms have a view
of the lake.

GUATEMALA
CITY

USEFUL
INFORMATION

**EMBASSIES,
CONSULATES**
EL SALVADOR EMBASSY
12 Calle 5-43, Zona 9
Tel. 325 848 or 362 441
AMERICAN EMBASSY
Ave. la Reforma 7–01,
Zona 10
Tel. 311 541
HONDURAS EMBASSY
15a Ave. 9-16, Zona 13

Tel. 373 919 or 371 921
MEXICO EMBASSY
16 Calle 0–51, Zona 14
Tel. 680 769 or 682 485
BRITISH EMBASSY
7a Ave. 5–10 (8th floor),
Zona 4
Tel. 321 601 (602 and
604)

**BANK AND BUREAU DE
CHANGE**
VISA/MASTERCARD
7 Ave. 6-26,
Zona 9
Tel. 317 436
Open 8am–8pm

HOSPITALS
CENTRO MÉDICO
6a Ave. 3-47,
Zona 10
Tel. 323 555

HOSPITAL HERRERA
LLERANDI
6a Ave. 8–71, Zona 10
Tel. 366 771 (775)
or 320 444 (448)

TOURIST OFFICE
INGUAT
7a Ave. 1–17, Zona 4
Tel. 311 333
Fax 318 893

MAIN POST OFFICE
OFICINA DE CORREOS
7 Ave. and 12 Calle,
Zona 1
Open Mon.–Fri.,
8am–4.30pm
*Stamps, poste
restantes, possible to
send packages
weighing more than 4lb
(the only post office in*

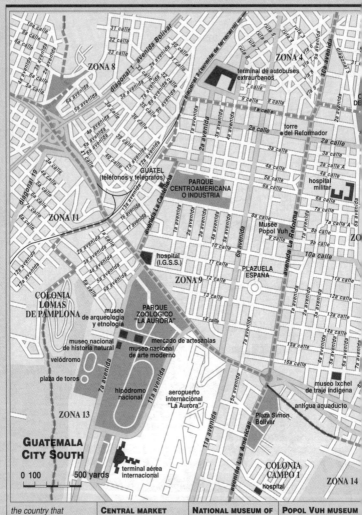

ZONA 8

ZONA 4

terminal de autobuses
extraurbanos

torre
del Reformador

GUATEL
(teléfonos y telégrafos)

ZONA 11

PARQUE
CENTROAMERICANA
O INDUSTRIA

hospital
militar

Musée
Popol Vuh

hospital
(I.G.S.S.)

PLAZUELA
ESPANA

ZONA 9

**COLONIA
LOMAS
DE PAMPLONA**

museo
de arqueologia
y etnologia

PARQUE
ZOOLOGICO
"LA AURORA"

museo nacional
de historia natural

mercado de artesanías

musée nacional
de arte moderno

velódromo

plaza de toros

hipódromo
nacional

aeropuerto
internacional
"La Aurora"

museo Ixchel
de traje indigena

antigua aquaducto

ZONA 13

Plaza Simon
Bolivar

**GUATEMALA
CITY SOUTH**

terminal aérea
internacional

**COLONIA
CAMPO 1**

ZONA 14

hospital

0 100   500 yards

---

the country that
operates this service).

CULTURE

LIBROS LUNA Y SOL
12 Calle, Zona 1
Tel. 514 967
International bookshop.

CENTRAL MARKET
Just behind the
cathedral on Ave. 9,
between Calles 6 and 8.
A market with plenty
of character. Local
crafts and souvenirs at
reasonable prices.

NATIONAL PALACE
Zona 1
Open daily: 8am–4pm

**NATIONAL MUSEUM OF
ARCHEOLOGY AND
ETHNOLOGY**
Edificio 5, La Aurora,
Zona 13
Open Tue.–Sun.
9am–4pm. Closed Mon.
and weekends
noon–2pm

**NATIONAL MUSEUM
OF MODERN ART**
Edificio 6,
La Aurora,
Zona 13
Open Tue.–Sun. 9am–
4pm. Closed Mon.
and weekends
noon–2pm

IXCHEL MUSEUM
4a Ave. 16–27,
Zona 10

POPOL VUH MUSEUM
Ave. La Reforma 8-60,
Zona 9

TRANSPORT

AIRLINES
AEROQUETZAL
Ave. Hincapie, on the
corner of Calle 18,
Zona 13 Hangar no. 8
Tel. 365 214
\or 347 693
AEROVIAS
Ave. Hincapie, on the
corner of Calle 18,
Zona 13
Tel. 319 633
or 325 686
AVIATECA
10 Calle 6–39,
Zona 1
Tel. 814 79 or 814 15

Tel. 314 860
or 319 180
TRASLADOS
Ave. Hincapie, 18 Calle,
Zona 13
Hangar no. 30
Tel. 347 105
or 347 783

MOTORBIKE RENTAL
MOTORENT
11 Calle, Zona 9
*Hondas for rent from
around $20 for a day
(Honda XL 185).*

CAR RENTAL
AHORRENT
Bd Liberación 4–83,
Zona 9
Tel. 320 544
Fax 320 548
Airport: Tel. 326 491
AVIS
12 Calle 2–73,
Zona 9
Tel. 316 990
or 324 594
Fax 321 263
Airport: Tel. 310 017
BUDGET
Ave. la Reforma 15–0,
Zona 9
Tel. 316 546
Fax 312 807
Airport: Tel. 310 273
DOLLAR
Ave. la Reforma 6–14,
Zona 9
Tel. 348 285
Fax 326 745
HERTZ
7 Ave. 14–76,
Zona 9
Tel. 322 242
Fax 311 711
Airport: Tel. 311 711
NATIONAL
14 Calle 1–42,
Zona 10
Tel. 680 174
Fax 370 221
Airport: Tel. 318 365
TIKAL RENT A CAR
2 Calle 6–56,
Zona 10
Tel. 324 721

**TOUR OPERATORS/
TRAVEL AGENTS**
SERVICIOS TURÍSTICOS
DEL PETÉN (STP)
2 Ave. 7–78,
Zona 10
Tel. 346 235
or 346 236
Fax 346 237
EL TUCÁN
Travel agent, hotel and
restaurant.
6a. Ave. 10–36,
Zona 1
Tel. 501 380
Fax 286 61
CLARK TOURS
Tel. 514 172

IZABAL ADVENTURE
TOURS
(ALFREDO TORRIELLO)
Edificio La Galería, 7
Ave. 14–44, Local 35,
Zona 10
Tel. 340 323
or 340 324
Fax 317 912
*Izabal region,
Río Dulce.*
JAGUAR TOURS
Hotel *Radisson
Villa Magna*
1 Ave. 12–46
Tel. 329 780
Fax 347 479
Cobán region, Verapaz.
TURISMO EK CHUAH
(JEAN-LUC BRACONNIER)
3 Calle 6–24,
Zona 2
Tel. 243 75
Fax 243 75

RESTAURANTS

***** CHEZ MICHEL
RIVE GAUCHE**
2a Calle 15–92,
Zona 13
Tel. 319 215
*Good French
restaurant, but fairly
expensive. There is
another "Chez Michel"
in Flores and one in
Tikal.*

*** PUERTO BARRIOS
7a Ave. 10–65,
Zona 9
Tel. 341 302 or 324 646
Fax 318 377
*Fashionable restaurant
with attractive prices.
Décor might not be to
everyone's taste.
Specializes in fish and
seafood dishes.*

** COSTA BRAVA
15 Ave. 7–79,
Zona 13
Tel. 311 288

*International cuisine;
the Spanish dishes are
particularly good.*

** EL GRAN PAVO ★
13 Calle 4–41,
Zona 1
*The menu offers every
imaginable Guatemalan
specialty.*

** EL PARADOR
12 Calle 4–17,
Zona 9
Tel. 316 774
*Excellent local cuisine
("platos típicos").*

** EL RODEO
7a Ave. 14-84,
Zona 9
Tel. 314 928

*One of the best
steakhouses in Poptún,
very popular with the
local people.*

** LOS ANTOJITOS ★
Ave. la Reforma 15-02,
Zona 9
Tel. 313 066
*Guatemalan cuisine.
Specializes in the
preparation of typical
dishes from the
country's various
different regions.*

** MESÓN DE QUIJOTE
11 Calle and 5 Ave.,
Zona 9
*Live bands every
evening, reasonable
prices, closes late.
Spanish food.*

* TÍPICO MONTUFAR
4a Ave. 11–55,
Zona 9
Tel. 315 937
Guatemalan cuisine.

* NAIS
7a Ave. 6–52,
Plaza 6–26, Edificio
Plaza, Zona 9
Tel. 319 095
*Cheese fondues, grilled
steaks. Very
reasonable.*

* LOS CEBOLLINES
12 Calle 6–36,
Zona 9
Tel. 317 065
*Other Los Cebollines
restaurants can also be
found in Zona 1 and
Zona 10 (6 Ave. 9-77).
Mexican food.*

* ZURICH
4a Ave. 12-09,
Zona 10
Tel. 363 312
*Very pleasant café ideal
for afternoon teas (tea,
coffee, pastries).*

SPORT

**WALKING AND PONY
TREKKING**
TURISMO EK CHUAH ★
(JEAN-LUC BRACONNIER)
3 Calle 6–24,
Zona 2
Tel. 243 75
Fax 243 75
*Walks and pony treks,
with excursions to the
top of volcanos,*

*excursions in the Petén
(archeology, nature),
and tourist routes
around the sites of main
interest (Guatemala and
neighboring countries).*

**BUNJEE JUMPING
AND RAFTING**
MAYA EXPEDITIONS
(TAMMY RIDENOUR)
15 Calle 1-91,
Zona 10
Tel. 374 666
Fax 374 666

SCUBA DIVING
PANA DIVERS
16 Calle 7–15,
Zona 9
Tel. 343 870
Fax 343 871
On Lake Atitlán.

**SCUBA DIVING AND
FISHING**
EXCURSIONES SPROSS
2 Ave. 3–25,
Zona 9
Tel. 323 594
Fax 323 594
*Fishing and diving in the
Cayes south of Belize
(two hours from
Livingston and on the
islands).*

POT-HOLING
CANDELARIA
Reservations: Servicios
Turísticos del Petén
2 Ave. 7–78,
Zona 10
Tel. 346 235
or 346 236
Fax 346 237
*Discover the caves of
Candelaria and Verapaz
(Mucbilhá, Raxrujá)
seven hours by road
from Cobán in a four-
wheel-drive vehicle.*

NIGHTLIFE

CONCIERTO DE LOS 60
7 Ave. and 8 Calle,
Zona 1
*Entrance is free and
drinks are affordable in
this popular bar.*

EL ESTABLO
Ave. la Reforma 11–83,
Zona 10
Bar with good music.

HOTELS

***** HOTEL
CAMINO REAL**
Ave. la Reforma
and Calle 14, Zona 10
Tel. 334 663
*International luxury
hotel. Expensive.*

***** HOTEL
GUATEMALA FIESTA**
1a Ave. 13-22, Zona 10
Tel. 322 555
*Luxury hotel with
heated swimming pool.*

***** HOTEL
DEL CENTRO**
13 Calle 4–55, Zona 1
Tel. 812 81
or 812 82
*Less expensive than the
Hotel Guatemala Fiesta.
Comfortable, well-
equipped rooms.*

***** HOTEL
EL DORADO**
7a Ave. 15–45, Zona 9
Tel. 317 777
Fax 321 877

***** HOTEL
LAS AMÉRICAS ★**
Ave. Las Americas
9–08, Zona 13
Tel. 370 601
or 334 633
*Close to the airport.
High-class hotel with a
swimming pool.
Excellent service.*

***** HOTEL CORTIJO
REFORMA**
Ave. la Reforma 2–18,
Zona 9
Tel. 366 712
or 366 716
*Rooms have minibar,
kitchenette and balcony;
some have a view over
the volcanos
surrounding the town.*

**** HOTEL
CENTENARIO**
6a Calle 5–33, Zona 1
Tel. 803 813
Fax 820 39
*Comfortable, clean
rooms.*

** HOTEL COLONIAL
7a. Ave. 14-19,
Zona 1
Tel. 267 22- 229 55
- 812 08
*Charming colonial hotel,
very clean and quiet.*

**** HOTEL
PAN AMERICAN ★**
9a Calle 5-63, Zona 1
Tel. 518 709
or 518 715
Fax 264 02

**** HOTEL RESIDENCIA
REFORMA "LA CASA
GRANDE"**
Ave. La Reforma 7-67,
Zona 10
Tel. 310 907
or 317 893
Fax 322 736
*White, square building,
with a marked Spanish
influence. Beautiful light
rooms with shower and
toilets.*

**** HOTEL RITZ
CONTINENTAL**
6a Ave. 10-13, Zona 1
Tel. 816 715
or 818 715
*Comfortable rooms and
a good restaurant.*

**** HOTEL
VILLA ESPAÑOLA**
2a Calle 7-51, Zona 9
Tel. 365 417

or 365 611
*Next to the tower of the
Reformer, a discreet
imitation of the Eiffel
Tower. Charming,
Spanish-style hotel.*

** POSADA BELÉN
13 Calle A 10-30, Zona
Tel. 292 26
or 845 10
*Superb colonial building
in a quiet street in the
city center. Booking
essential.*

*** HOTEL
CHALET SUIZO**
14 Calle 6-82, Zona 1
Tel. 513 786
*A typical and friendly
hotel. Rooms with or
without bathrooms,
around a small
courtyard lacking in
charm.*

* HOTEL SPRING ★
8a Ave. 12–65, Zona 1
Tel. 266 37
or 514 207
Fax 201 07

Large, airy rooms with windows overlooking an enormous patio.

HUEHUE-TENANGO

RESTAURANTS

** LAS VEGAS
At the Huehuetenango crossroads (next to the service station).
Local and international cuisine.

* EBONY RESTAURANT ★
2 Calle 5–11 at the corner of the Plaza Central).
Open morning, lunchtime and evening. The patron is a good source of local information and will gladly provide details of local activities, special events, timetables, and available transport. Local cuisine. Serves good breakfasts and fruit juices.

HOTELS

** HOTEL DEL PRADO
Canton San José, Zona 5
Tel. 642 151
Situated at the entrance to the town, coming from the Panamerican highway. A fairly new hotel which provides a good standard of service.

** HOTEL ZACULEU
5a Ave. 1–14
Tel. 641 086
An attractive colonial building which has been recently restored. The hotel also has a very good restaurant.

LAKE IZABAL

HÔTEL

** HOTEL IZABAL TROPICAL
At the edge of Lake Izabal, close to Fort Castillo, San Felipe.
Tel. 478 115

LIVINGSTON

RESTAURANTS

* AFRICAN PLACE
Just before the Flamingo Hotel, twenty minutes from the wharf market place
A hotel and restaurant. Fairly comfortable rooms. The restaurant is excellent. Creole cuisine.

* EL MALECÓN
100 yards from the wharf.
A large restaurant which serves very good grilled fish. Try the "tapado" (fish and seafood cooked in coconut milk).

HOTELS

** HOTEL TUCAN DUGU
Tel. 481 572 or 481 588
Book from Guatemala City on: 347 813.
Livingston's chic hotel. Very comfortable rooms.

* CASA ROSADA
On the beach.
Tel. 171 121
Impeccably clean, fairly comfortable with communal shower.

PANAJACHEL

USEFUL INFORMATION

TOURIST OFFICE
OFICINA DEL INGUAT
Calle Santander
Tel. 621 392

TRANSPORT

MOTORBIKE RENTAL
MOTO-RENT
Calle Principal and Calle Los Arboles
Bicycle and motorbike hire by the hour, the day or the week. (Honda, Suzuki and others). A good way of exploring the neighboring towns and villages (Sololá, Chichicastenango). Note, it is not possible to do a complete tour of Lake Atitlán by motorbike.

RESTAURANTS

** AL CHISME
Calle Los Arboles, on the northwest coast of Calle Principal.
Simple food such as salads and sandwiches. Very popular with tourists.

** RESTAURANTE LA LAGUNA
On the corner of Calle Principal and Calle Los Arboles
Regional cuisine and amazing breakfasts.

** THE LAST RESORT
On Ave. Santander, on the left before the beach.
Excellent and moderately priced. A popular place for Americans to meet for an evening drink. Not to be missed.

HOTELS

*** HOTEL ATITLÁN ★
At the edge of Lake Atitlán, one mile from the center of town on the road to Los Encuentros.
Tel. 621 4 16 or 621 441
The best hotel in Panajachel. Comfortable rooms, heated swimming pool and a very good restaurant. Superb view of the lake and gardens.

*** HOTEL DEL LAGO
Next to Calle Rancho Grande beach (at the end of Lake Atitlán).
Tel. 621 555 or 621 556
Well-equipped, comfortable rooms with bathrooms and balconies. Swimming pool, restaurants and attractive gardens.

*** PLAYA LINDA
In the port.
Excellent rooms with fireplaces.

** HOTEL PRIMAVERA
Calle Santander
Tel. 621 157
A small, friendly hotel with restaurant and garden.

* HOTEL GALINDO
Calle Principal next to the Banco Agricola Mercantil.
Tel. 621 168
Restaurant and hotel situated in a pleasant tropical garden.

POPTÚN

CAVES

NAJ TUNICH
Approximately 18 miles from Poptún
On a dirt track accessible only by four-wheel-drive vehicle. A guide is absolutely essential, information available in Poptún.

HOTELS

* HOTEL MARÍA ROSA
Opposite the Texaco service station at the exit from the village toward Flores.
Reasonable rooms with shower.

* FINCA IXOBEL ★
One mile to the south of Poptún, on the road to Río Dulce.
Several rooms with shower. Very basic.

Meeting point for visitors taking excursions to the surrounding caves. Four-day pony treks into the jungle organized from the finca.

PUERTO BARRIOS

HOTELS

** HOTEL DEL NORTE
On the seafront.
Quaint, colonial and charming hotel with a good restaurant in its extensive dining room.

* HOTEL EUROPA
8a Ave. between Calles 8 and 9.
Clean rooms with shower and with or without a fan. Pleasant dining room.

RÍO PETEXBATÚN

HOTELS

** POSADA MATEO ★
Take a boat from Sayaxche.
Tel. 234 03 23
Fax 231 79 12
To organize in advance contact the Posada Caribe Agency in Sayaxché. There are several bungalows overlooking the Río Petexbatún, situated in the heart of the countryside, but nevertheless with a certain amount of luxury.

* POSADA CARIBE
Take a boat from Sayaxche.

Cost: $160 per week ($130 low-season).

Somewhat more spartan than Posada Mateo.

QUETZAL-TENANGO

USEFUL INFORMATION

EMBASSY, CONSULATE
CONSULAT DU MEXICO
9 Ave. 6-19, Zona 1
Tel. 612 547
Open Mon.–Fri.
9am–11am

BANK AND BUREAU DE CHANGE
BANCO DE GUATEMALA
12 Ave. 5-12, Zona 1
Open Mon.–jeu.
8.30am–2pm
Open Fri.
8.30am–2.30pm
Open Sat.
8.30am–2pm

TELEPHONE CENTER
GUATEL
12a Ave. (between Calle 7 and Calle 8).
15 Ave. and 3 Calle,
Open until midnight

TOURIST OFFICE
OFICINA DEL INGUAT
Casa de la Cultura
7a Calle 11–35, Zona 1
Tel. 614 931

MAIN POST OFFICE
OFICINA DE CORREOS
15a Ave. and 4 Calle,
Zona 1.

LANGUAGE COURSES

CASA XELAHU DE ESPAÑOL
9 Calle 11–26, Zona 1
Tel. 612 628
Fax 612 628

CENTRO DE ESTUDIOS DE ESPAÑOL POP WUH
1 Calle 17–72
and 5 Calle 2-40,
Zona 1
Tel. 618 286
Cost: $120 per week.

CENTRO DE LENGUAJE AMÉRICA LATINA
19 Ave. 3-63, Zona 3
Tel. 616 416
Cost: $120 per week.

ENGLISH CLUB & INTERNATIONAL LANGUAGE SCHOOL
3 Calle 15–16, Zona 1
Courses in Spanish and Mayan.

GUATEMALENSIS
19 Ave. 2-41, Zona 1
Cost: $120 per week.

INSTITUTO CENTRO AMÉRICA (ICA)
1 Calle 16-93, Zona 1
Tel. 616 786
Cost: $120 per week.

MINERVA SPANISH SCHOOL
24 Ave. 4-39, Zona 3
Cost: $135 per week.

SAB SPANISH CENTER
1 Calle 12-35, Zona 1
Tel. 612 042
Full-board accommodation is available.

SPANISH SCHOOL JUAN SISAY
15 Ave. 8-38, Zona 1
Cost: $120 per week.

RESTAURANTS

*** EL KOPETÍN
14 Ave. 3–31
Specializes in seafood.

** ROYAL PARIS
16 Ave. 3–05,
Zona 3, Benito
Juárez park
Small restaurant with a very pleasant atmosphere. Reasonably priced for the quality of the food. Chocolate crêpes are highly recommended. French and European cuisine.

* RESTAURANTE SHANGHAI
4 Calle 12–22, Zona 1
Tel. 614 154

A Guatemalan version of Chinese cuisine.

* CAFE BAVIERA ★
5a Calle 12-50,
Zona 1
Open throughout the day (closes at 8pm).
Coffee shop serving cakes, tea, coffee, house specials and drinks. Open all hours.

HOTELS

** PENSIÓN BONIFAZ
On the corner of Calle 4
and Ave. 11

Tel. 614 241 or 614 229
Superb ancient surroundings, combined with a high standard of service.

** VILLA REAL PLAZA
4a Calle 12–22, Zona 1
Tel. 614 045
or 616 270
Fax 616 780

* HOTEL MODELO
14a Ave. A 2–31,
Zona 1
Tel. 612 715
Built around a beautiful flower garden with a gallery leading to spacious, well-equipped rooms.

NIGHTLIFE

CINEMA ALPINO
Pl. Ciani, 24 Ave.
and 4 Calle, Zona 3

CINEMA CADORE
13 Ave. and 7 Calle,
Zona 1

CINEMA ROMA
14 Ave. A and Calle A,
Zona 1

RÍO DULCE

HOTEL

* CATAMARAN ISLAND HOTEL
Ten mins. from Río Dulce by boat, at the edge of Lake Izabal. Make reservations from Guatemala City on Tel. 364 450. Swimming pool, tennis courts and restaurant.

SANTA CATARINA PALOPÓ

HOTELS

* HOTEL BELLA VISTA
Tel. 621 566
2 miles from Santa Catarina on the road to San Antonio.

* HOTEL VILLA SANTA CATARINA
Tel. 621 291
On the road from Panajachel to Santa Catarina.
Rooms with a view of Lake Atitlán, some with a view of the San Pedro volcano. At the edge of the lake with a swimming pool and restaurant.

SANTO TOMÁS DE CASTILLA

HOTEL

*** CAYOS DEL DIABLO
Four miles from Livingston coming from Puerto Barrios
Tel. 482 276
Make reservations from Guatemala City on:
Tel. 371 963.
Fax 506 114

SAYAXCHÉ

TRANSPORT

TOUR OPERATORS/ TRAVEL AGENTS
VIAJES LA MONTAÑA/POSADA CARIBE
Calle principal
Tel. 506 114
Fax 506 114
Regions: Ceibal, Petexbatún zone, Usumacinta. This is the best place to get information about

traveling to Posada Mateo which is only accessible by boat (see Río Petexbatún).

HOTEL

* HOTEL GUAYACAN
Tel. 506 111
Basic but comfortable rooms. Arranges trips to the sites of Piedras Negras, Ceibal, Aguateca, Yaxchilán and the Altar de Sacrificios.

TIKAL

HOTELS

*** HOTEL CAMINO REAL
Halfway between Flores and Tikal, in the village of El Remate.
Tel. 500 207
Fax 500 222
Ideally situated at the edge of Lake Petén Itzá. This hotel does not really merit its high prices. Expensive.

** JAGUAR INN
At the entrance to the site, close to the museum.
Best to reserve in advance either in writing or by telephone. Four bungalows only, with shower and toilet.

** JUNGLE LODGE
Close to the entrance to the site.
Reserve from

Guatemala City on Tel. 760 294.
Two types of accommodation are offered, with different levels of comfort: new rooms in small bungalows and refurbished rooms with showers and toilets.

RESTAURANTS

*** RESTAURANTE PARQUE TIKAL
In the concrete building of the Stele Museum.
Local dishes.

** COMEDOR TIKAL
One of the first comedores on the right when entering the Tikal site.
Open throughout the day.
One of three or four comedores which are all in competition with each other to feed the hungry tourists after their four-hour visit to the ancient site. The Comedor Pirámide is without doubt the best and cheapest of all of these. Good regional cuisine.

UAXACTÚN

HOTEL

** HOTEL RESTAURANTE CAMPAMENTO "EL CHICLERO"
Basic but comfortable rooms. Friendly proprietor. (The price of the room includes three meals).

YAXHÁ

SPORT

RAMBLING AND PONY TREKKING
LODGE EL SOMBRERO (JUAN JOSÉ DE LA HOZ

AND GABRIELA)
Yaxha, Melchor de Mencos
Excursions from Yaxha to Río Axul, with accommodation in bungalows.

◆

AMBERGRIS CAYE

RESTAURANTS

*** LILY'S RESTAURANT
At the eastern end of Caribeña Street (facing the sea).
Tel. 20 59
Open daily lunchtime and evening.
The best seafood restaurant in the town

** ELVI'S KITCHEN ★
Pescador Street (near Ambergris Street)
Tel. 21 26
Open lunchtime 11.30am–2pm and evening 6.30–10pm.
Popular meeting place. Typical Belize dishes.

** MARINO'S
Pescador Street (close to Bucaneer Street)
Good bar-restaurant where one can eat very cheaply – sandwiches and salads, or, for a little more, langoustines and other seafood.

** THE HUT
Tarpon Street, on the south side of Barrier Reef Drive.
A variety of dishes and local specialties.

HOTELS

*** RAMON'S VILLAGE RESORT
In San Pedro
Tel. 20 71

or 22 13
Fax 22 14
Cabañas overlooking the beach, bar surrounded by coconut trees, sailing boats and watersports. Very relaxed atmosphere.

*** LILY'S CARIBBEAN LODGE
To the east of the Caribeña facing the sea.
Tel. 20 59
Rooms with terraces overlooking the sea.

** EL PESCADOR
On the Punta Arena beach, 5½ miles north of San Pedro.
Tel. 23 98

** MARTHA'S HOTEL
San Pedro village.
Tel. 20 39

* MILO'S HOTEL
San Pedro village.
Tel. 20 33
Fairly quiet and very reasonably priced. Often fully booked.

SPORT

SCUBA DIVING
OUT ISLAND DIVERS
P.O. Box 7, San Pedro
Tel. 21 51
UNIVERSAL TRAVEL AND TOURS
Spindrift Hotel,
Barrier reef drive

BELIZE CITY

USEFUL INFORMATION

BANK AND BUREAU DE CHANGE
AMERICAN EXPRESS
Global Travel

41 Albert St.
Tel. 771 85
or 773 63 (364)
BARCLAY'S BANK
21 Albert St.
Tel. 772 11
Open Mon.–Fri.
8am–1pm and 3–6pm
THE BELIZE BANK
Albert St., 60 Market Sq.
(Opposite Swing Bridge).
Tel. 771 32 (133/4/5)
Open Mon.–Thurs.
8am–1pm. Fri. 8am–1pm and 3–6pm

TELEPHONE CENTER
BELIZEAN TELECOMMUNICATION, LTD (B.T.L.)
no. 1 Church St.
Open Mon.–Sat.
8am–9pm,
Sun. 8am–noon

TOURIST OFFICE
THE BELIZE TOURIST BOARD
83 North Front St.
Tel. 772 13 or 732 55
Fax 774 90

MAIN POST OFFICE
POST OFFICE
Queen St. and N. Front St.
Open Mon.–Fri.
8am–noon and 1–5pm
(Fri. 1–4.30pm)
Stamps for sale, possible to send packages to a poste restante.

TRANSPORT

AIRLINES
AEROVIAS
Airport Philip Goldson
Tel. 275 445
ISLAND AIR
Airport Municipal
Tel. 231 140
or 262 180
MAYA AIRWAYS
Airport Municipal
Tel. 272 15
SAHSA
Airport Philip Goldson
Tel. 277 080
SKY BIRD
Airport Municipal
Tel. 232 596
or 252 045
TROPIC AIR
Airport Municipal
Tel. 245 671
or 262 012

CAR RENTAL
BUDGET RENT A CAR
771 Bella Vista
Tel. 232 435
or 230 237
CRYSTAL AUTO RENTAL

1½ miles along Northern Road
Tel. 231 600
Fax 231 900
MELMISH MAYAN RENTALS
Airport Philip Goldson
P.O. Box 934
Tel. 245 221
Fax 277 681
NATIONAL CAR RENTAL
Airport Philip Goldson
Tel. 231 586
THE CITY AND THE SEA
Tourist Auto Rental LTD
2 Hutson Street
Tel. 277 569
Fax 277 569

CENTRAL BUS STATION
BATTY BROS.
BUS SERVICE
54 E. Collet Canal
Tel. 022 025
Daily departures, connections to the west and the north of the country.
JAME'S BUS
Pound Yard Bridge
Connections to the south of the country.
URBINA BUS
Cinderella Pl.
Connections to Belize City-Orange Walk.
VENUS BUS LINE
Magazine Road
Tel. 023 354
or 027 390
Connections to the north and west of the country.
Tel. Corozal: 0421 32.

RESTAURANTS

*** GRILL
164 Newton Barracks
Tel. 450 20
Considered to be one of the best restaurants in Belize City. International cuisine. Varied menu.

*** NEW CHON SAAN
55 Euphrates Ave.
Tel. 727 09
Pleasant atmosphere. One of the best Chinese restaurants in Belize City. Also offers a takeaway service.

** MARLIN
11 Regent St.
Tel. 739 13
Facing Belize River. Good fish and seafood restaurant. Varied menu.

* MACY'S
18 Bishop St.
Tel. 734 19
Open lunchtime and

evening until 10pm.
Closed Sun.
Different menu each day. Manageress is very friendly. Local creole cuisine.

* MOM'S TRIANGLE INN
11 Handyside St.
P.O. Box 332
Tel. 450 73
or 453 32
Open 6am–10pm
Closed Sat.
Large cafeteria which tends to attract a mixed clientele. Lively, friendly atmosphere. Music.

* SHEN'S PEKING PANDA
Queen Street,
opposite no. 3
Chinese restaurant which serves delicious food at reasonable prices.

HOTELS

*** RAMADA ROYAL REEF HOTEL
P.O. Box 1728,
Newton Barracks
Tel. 326 70
Fax 326 60
Luxury hotel. Extremely expensive.

*** RADISSON FORT GEORGE HOTEL
2 Marine Parade
Tel. 774 00
Fax738 20
Luxury hotel with swimming pool, several restaurants and bars.

** GLENTHORNE MANOR
27 Barrack Road
Tel. 442 12
An attractive large white wooden house run by a friendly family and offering eight clean rooms with shower and toilets.

** HOTEL CHATEAU CARIBBEAN
6 Marine Parade
Tel. 308 00
Fax 309 00
A former hospital, this building has been converted into a reasonably comfortable

"The publishers have just been informed that telephone numbers in El Salvador have been changed:

Numbers beginning with 1 remain the same.
Numbers beginning with 2, 7, 8 or 9 should be prefixed by a 2.
Numbers beginning with 3 should be prefixed by a 3.
Numbers beginning with 4 and 5 should be prefixed by a 4, and numbers beginning with 6 should be prefixed by a 6.

We are sorry that this information reached us too late to be included in the book."

hotel with fully air-conditioned rooms and a good restaurant.

** FORT STREET GUEST HOUSE
4 Fort St.
Tel. 456 38
Breakfast included in the price of the room.

* SEA SIDE GUEST HOUSE
3 Prince St.
Tel. 783 39
Wooden house in a quiet neighborhood on the sea front.
Clean and basic.

SPORT

FISHING
ACTION BELIZE
23 Regent St.
Tel. 26 52 or 450 65
Freshwater and night fishing (tarpon).
BLUE MARLIN LODGE
P.O. Box 1158
Tel. 23 31
Fishing on the lagoon and coral reef.
KELLERS CARIBBEAN
SPORT, LTD
P.O. Box 459
Tel. 20 02
Fishing.
MANATEE LODGE
Jamie & Amparo
Claiborne
P.O. Box 1242
Tel. 23 31
Specializes in inland freshwater fishing.

SCUBA DIVING AND FISHING
DISCOVER BELIZE, LTD
P.O. Box 507
Tel. 022 157
EL PESCADOR
P.O. Box 793
Tel. 022 312 or 02 72 12
M.V. LUCRETIA B.
Vic & Cathy Barothy
P.O. Box 1076
Tel. 025 2017
PRINCESS CHARTERS
Captain Baguette
P.O. Box 521
Tel. 458 41
TURNEFFE ISLAND LODGE
P.O. Box 480
Tel. 23 31

Fishing and island tours of three to seven days.

PONY TREKKING
MOUNTAIN EQUESTRIAN
TRAILS
Mile 8 Mountain Pine
Ridge Rd.
Cayo District
P.O. Box 1158
Tel. 022 331

BOAT TRIPS
TIKI TOURS
23 Regent St.
Tel. 26 52 or 450 65
Discover the sites by boat. River route leads right up to the ruins.

NIGHTLIFE

LINDBERGH'S LANDING
164 A Newton Road
Outdoor bar with pleasant atmosphere (overlooking the sea).

LOUISVILLE DEMOCRATIC BAR
69 Hyds Lane
Small friendly bar in a rather dangerous area of the city. Take a taxi back to your hotel.

BELMOPÁN

HOTELS

** BELMOPÁN CONVENTION HOTEL
2 Bliss Parade
Tel. 221 30
Fairly expensive but very comfortable.

* HOTEL EL REY INN
23 Moho St.
Tel. 234 38

CAYE CAULKER

RESTAURANTS

** MARIN'S RESTAURANT
To the west of Tropical
Paradise Hotel.
Closed Sun.
Indoor and open-air restaurant. The

excellence of the food makes up for the slow service.

** THE SANDBOX ★
Front Street
Open every evening.
Closed Sun.
Varied international menu. Food is good and portions are generous. Indoor and outdoor restaurant with a pleasant view over the sea.

** ABERDEEN RESTAURANT
To the south of Martínez
Hotel.
Tel. 21 27
Regional and Chinese cuisine.

** MARTÍNEZ CARIBBEAN INN
On Front Street next to
the Miramar Hotel.

HOTELS

** RAINBOW HOTEL
On the beach.
Tel. 21 23
Basic but clean rooms.

** TROPICAL PARADISE ★
On the beach.
Tel. 21 24
Clean, airy rooms.
Restaurant and bar.

* TOM'S HOTEL
Facing the sea.
Tel. 21 02
Very clean and reasonably priced.

SPORT

SCUBA DIVING
FRENCHIES DIVING
Daytime and night dives. Diving certificates awarded (PADI).

COROZAL

SPORT

WALKING AND POT-HOLING
ADVENTURE BELIZE, LTD
P.O. Box 35
Tel. 042 187

ORANGE WALK

HOTELS

** BARON'S HOTEL
40 Main St.
(Belize Road)
Tel. 225 18

* JANE'S HOTEL
2 Baker's St.
Tel. 224 73

PLACENTIA

SPORT

FISHING
KINGFISHER SPORT
FISHING
Tel. 062 046

SCUBA DIVING
RUM POINT DIVERS
Tel. 061 381

SCUBA DIVING AND FISHING
THE COVE RESORT
Point Placencia
Tel. 062 024

PUNTA GORDA

TRANSPORT

CAR RENTAL
ALISTAIR KING
Texaco Service Station
Tel. 072 126

HOTELS

* HOTEL FOSTER'S
19 Main St.
Tel. 072 117

* BELIZE ADVENTURE TRAVEL
65 Front St.
Travel agency and also a hotel and restaurant.

RESTAURANT

* MIRA MAR
95 Front St.
Pleasant Chinese restaurant.

SAN IGNACIO

USEFUL INFORMATION

BANK AND BUREAU DE CHANGE
BELIZE BANK
Burns Ave.
Open Mon.–Fri.
8am–1pm,
Fri. 3–6pm

TELEPHONE CENTER
BELIZE
TELECOMMUNICATION,
LTD (B.T.L.)
Burns Ave.
Cano's Gift Shop
Building
Open Mon.–Fri.
8am–noon and
1–4pm,
Sat. 8am–noon
Closed Sun.

HOSPITAL
HOSPITAL
At the top of Waight's
St. (west of the city
center)
Tel. 20 66

MAIN POST OFFICE
POST OFFICE
Government House
Buena Vista Road
(2nd floor)

RESTAURANTS

** SERENDIB
27 Burns Avenue
*Good Sri Lankan
cuisine.*

*** EVA'S RESTAURANT
AND BAR ★**
22 Burns Avenue
Tel. 092 22 67
Open morning, afternoon
and evening.
*This pleasant restaurant
is an ever-popular
meeting point for
travelers and is an
excellent information
center for the whole
area.*

*** MAXIM'S
CHINESE
RESTAURANT**
On the corner of Far
West and Bull Tree
Roads
Open lunchtime
11.30am–2.30pm.
Evening 5pm–midnight.
*A rather dismal location,
but the Asiatic
specialties are
excellent.*

HOTELS

**** SAN IGNACIO
HOTEL**
18 Buena Vista St.
Tel. 20 34 or 21 25
Fax 21 34
*Situated on a hillside
with a superb view over
the rainforest and river.
Pleasant and very
friendly hotel with a
restaurant, bar and
swimming pool. Often
fully booked.*

**** MAYA MOUNTAIN
LODGE**
P.O. Box 46
San Ignacio Caye
Tel. 21 64
*Bungalows in the jungle
with bed, bathroom and
toilets. Visit the ruins of
Tikal and Xunantunich,
take a trip in a kayak, or
simply explore the
breathtaking mountains
and rainforest. Meals
are included in the price
of the bungalows.*

SPORT

**WALKING AND
DIVING**
EXPLORE BELIZE TOURS /
MAYA MOUNTAIN LODGE
P.O. Box 46
Tel. 922 164

PONY TREKKING
CHAA CREEK COTTAGE
P.O. Box 53
Tel. 922 501

◆

CERRO VERDE

RESTAURANT

***** MONTAÑA
HOTEL RESTAURANT ★**
Tel. 281 903
or 181 981
*Specially constructed in
order to make the most
of the breathtaking
view over the Izalco
volcano.*

LAKE COATEPEQUE

RESTAURANT

***** RESTAURANT OF
THE HOTEL DE LAGO ★**
Tel. 469 511
*Pleasant restaurant with
a stunning view of the
lake. Local dishes.*

HOTELS

*** HOTEL DEL LAGO
Tel. 782 873
*Swimming pool. The
best hotel in the area.*

**** HOTEL
TORREMOLINOS**
Tel. 411 859
*Swimming pool and
restaurant.*

SAN SALVADOR

USEFUL
INFORMATION

**EMBASSIES AND
CONSULATES**
AMERICAN EMBASSY
Bd Santa Elena
Urb. Santa Elena
Tel. 981 666
Fax 982 336
BELIZE EMBASSY
Condominio Médico,
Local 34 (3º floor)
Bd Tutunichpa,
Urb. La Esperanza
Tel. 258 499
HONDURAS EMBASSY
7 Calle Poniente and 83
Ave. Norte, no. 4326
Col. Escalón
Tel. 789 524
MEXICAN EMBASSY
Paseo General Escalón,
no. 3832
Tel. 981 176
or 981 174 (179)
NICARAGUAN EMBASSY
71 Ave. Norte and 1
Calle Poniente, no. 164
Col. Escalón
Tel. 237 719
BRITISH EMBASSY
Paseo General Escalón,
no. 4828
Tel. 240 473

**BANK AND BUREAU DE
CHANGE**
CITY BANK
Edif. Sisa (3rd floor)
(Close to Pl. El Salvador
d'El Mundo).
CREDOMATIC
Edif. Cidena
Alameda Roosevelt
and Calle 51
Open 9am–1pm
and 1.30–4pm

*Money can be changed
using Visa or
Mastercard.*

TOURIST OFFICE
INSTITUTO SALVADOREÑO
DE TURISMO
Calle Rubén Darío, no.
619
Tel. 220 960

MAIN POST OFFICE
OFICINA DE CORREOS
Centro del Gobierno
Open Mon.–Fri.
7.30am–5pm
Open Sat. 7.30am–noon
Poste restante
Mon.–Fri. 8am–noon
and 2.30–5pm
*Note! Address poste
restante mail to
"Republica de El
Salvador, Centro-
América" as there are
several "El Salvadors"
throughout the world.*

TRANSPORT

AIRLINES
COPA
Ave. Roosevelt,
on the corner of 55 Ave.
Norte
Tel. 239 225 or 232 042
Fax 240 572

LACSA
43 Ave. Norte, no. 216
Tel. 246 222
Fax 233 745
SAHSA
71 Ave. Sur and Calle
Nueva no. 2, Casa no. 4
Tel. 240 340 or 235 830
Fax 245 226
TACA INTERNATIONAL
AIRLINES
Edificio Caribe,
2a Planta
Tel. 232 244
Fax 233 757

CAR RENTAL
AVIS
43 Ave. Sur, no. 137
Tel. 242 623
Fax 246 272
BUDGET
79 Ave. Sur, no. 6
Col. La Mascota
Tel. 231 668
or 983 342

ax 244 674
OLLAR RENT A CAR
3 Ave. Sur,
o. 134-A
ol. Flor Blanca
prolongación Calle
rce no. 2226)
el. 233 108
r 792 064
ax 792 138
ERTZ
alle Los Andes no. 16
olonia Miramonte
el. 268 099
ax 258 412
UPERIOR RENT A CAR
a Calle Poniente and
5 Ave. Norte, no. 828
el. 229 111
ax 210 453

CULTURE

**SCUELA DE IDIOMAS
ALVADOR MIRANDA**
orreo Centro
e Govierno
.O. Box 3274
el. 221 352
*anguage courses.
ost: $150 for a week's
uition.*

RESTAURANTS

** MEDITERRANÉE
d El Hipódromo, no.
31
ol. San Benito.
el. 236 137
*Seafood. Many other
imilar restaurants
earby (Marcelino's,
a Ola, Chili's,
aradise).*

*** LA PAMPA
RGENTINA**
inal Paseo
General Escalón
el. 791 185
*rgentinian cuisine
nd grills.*

** LA ZANAHORIA
1144 Calle Arce
(between le 19a
and le 21a Ave. Norte).
Open Mon.–Fri.
8am–6pm,
Sat. 8am–2pm.
*Large, open-air café-
restaurant. Vegetarian
cuisine.*

** SIETE MARES
Paseo General Escalón
Cond. Bálam Quitzé.
Tel. 243 031
or 243 763
*Good fish and seafood
restaurant. International
cuisine.*

* DON PAVO
Paseo General Escalón
and condominio
Balám Quitzé
Rancho Alegre,
Metro Sur.
Tel. 243 923
*Typical El Salvador
cuisine.*

*** ENTREMESES
DE FEDERICO**
1a Calle Poniente, no.
822
(between 13a
and 15a Ave. Norte).
Open lunchtime only
noon–3pm.
Closed Sun.
*Housed in the
Actoteatro building.
Large outdoor
buffet.*

* KORADI
9a Ave. Sur, no. 225
(close to the intersection
with 4a Calle Poniente).
Tel. 212 545
Open Mon. to Fri.
8am–5pm.
Sat. 8am–3pm.
Closed Sun.
*Tiny but excellent
vegetarian restaurant-
pâtisserie well located
right in the center of
town (near the ISTU
tourist office).*

HOTELS

***** HOTEL
CAMINO REAL**
Bd de los Heroes
Tel. 793 888
Fax 235 660

**** HOTEL
EL SALVADOR**
Calle Poniente, no. 11
and Ave. Norte,
no. 89
Tel. 790 177
Fax 232 901

**** HOTEL
PRESIDENTE**
Ave. La Revolución,
San Benito
Tel. 982 044
Fax 234 912

**** HOTEL
RAMADA INN**
Ave. Sur, no. 85 and
Paseo General
Escalón
Tel. 791 820
Fax 791 889

*** HOTEL
SAN CARLOS**
Calle Concepción,
no. 121
Tel. 224 808
or 228 975

*** HOTEL
CENTRO**
10a Ave. Sur,
no. 410
Tel. 715 045
*Well-kept and pleasant
hotel with comfortable
rooms at reasonable
prices.*

◆

COMAYAGUA

TRANSPORT

AIRLINES
SAHSA
Aeropuerto Toncontín
Tel. 333 333
TACA INTERNATIONAL
AIRLINES

Edificio Interamericana,
Bd Morazan
Tel. 312 469
or 312 472

HOTEL

* HOTEL QUAN
Situated very close
to the Caridad
Church.
Tel. 720 070

RESTAURANT

* POLLOS CHALO 3
Between the main
square and the market.
*The best chicken in
Comayagua.*

COPÁN

USEFUL
INFORMATION

**BANK AND BUREAU
DE CHANGE**
BANCO DEL OCCIDENTE
South corner of the
Plaza Central.
Open Mon.–Fri.
8am–noon and 2–4pm,
Sat. 8am–11am

HOSPITAL
MEDICAL CLINIC
LUIS A. CASTRO M.D.
Next to Banco del
Occidente
Open Mon.–Sat.
8.30am–noon and
2–5pm
English spoken.

CULTURE

**IXBALANQUE
SPANISH SCHOOL**
Copán Ruinas
Tel. 983 432
Fax 980 004
*Weekly courses offered
with individual tuition
(five days a week, four
hours a day).
Accommodation with a
local family can be
arranged.*

MUSEO REGIONAL
Copán Ruinas.

HOTELS

** HOTEL MARINA ★
Close to Plaza Central.

Tel. 983 070
The best hotel in town.

**** HOTEL MAYA
COPÁN**
Opposite the museum.
*Well-maintained rooms
and restaurant. Local
cuisine.*

*** HOTEL
LOS GEMELOS ★**
100 yards from the
Plaza Central, toward
the station.
*Clean and good value.
Popular with visitors.*

* HOTEL POPUL NAH
Plaza Central.

SPORT

**WALKING, POT-HOLING
AND RAFTING**
GO NATIVE
ADVENTURE TOURS
1½ blocks to the west of
Plaza Central.
Tel. 983 432
Fax 980 004
XUKPI TOURS
(JORGE BARRAZA)
Copán Ruinas
Central Park
Tel. 983 435
Open Mon.–Sat.
8am–noon and 2–5pm
Closed Sun.

RESTAURANTS

**** RESTAURANT OF
THE HOTEL MARINA**
To the east of Plaza
Central.
Tel. 983 070
Open morning,
lunchtime and evening
*Large dining room
overlooking the hotel's
swimming pool. Local
and international
cuisine.*

**** TUNKUL BAR
AND RESTAURANT**
Tel. 983 410
Open all day
*Excellent food, good
value for money.
Patronized by tourists
who enjoy its friendly
atmosphere (happy
hour 6–8pm, meals are*

served at the bar or at
small tables. Music
every evening. Local
and international
cuisine.

*** LA LLAMA
DEL BOSQUE**
To the west of the Plaza
Central
(The first street on the
right after the museum)
Tel. 983 431
Open morning,
lunchtime and evening
*Large restaurant,
friendly atmosphere,
varied menu, local
cuisine.*

BAHÍA, ROATÁN ISLANDS

HOTELS

**** HOTEL
LOST PARADISE**
West End Village
Tel. 451 306
Fax 451 388

** HOTEL SUNRISE
Sandy Bay
Tel. 310 911
(from Tegucigalpa)
578 011
(from San Pedro Sula)
451 265 (from Roatán)
*Comfortable rooms,
bar, restaurant on the
beach.*

BAHÍA, UTILA ISLANDS

HOTEL

** UTILA LODGE
Utila harbor
Tel. 453 143

BAHÍA, GUANAJA ISLANDS

HÔTEL

** HOTEL ALEXANDER
South West Cay
Tel. 454 326
*Superb location with a
restaurant and diving
facilities.*

LA CEIBA

HOTELS

**** HOTEL
PARTENON BEACH**
Sur la plage.
Tel. 430 404
*Air-conditioned rooms,
swimming pool and bar.*

** GRAN HOTEL PARIS
Parque Central
Tel. 422 371
or 432 91
*Bar, swimming pool,
restaurant, discotheque
and tour operator.*

RESTAURANTS

*** CAFETERÍA
EL PASTEL**
Ave. San isidro
and 6a Calle
Closes 9pm.

* CRIC-CRIC BURGER
In the town center.
*American-style fast-
food (hamburgers,
chicken) open-air
restaurant.*

SAN PEDRO SULA

HOTELS

** GRAN HOTEL SULA
Calle 1 and Ave. 3 and
4

* HOTEL SAN PEDRO
3a Calle and Ave. 1a
and 2a
Tel. 531 513

TEGUCIGALPA

USEFUL INFORMATION

TOURIST OFFICE
INSTITUTO HONDUREÑO
DE TURISMO
Centro Guanacaste,
Barrio Guanacaste
Tel. 226 618
Fax 533 576

TRANSPORT

AIRLINES
COPA
10 Ave. 2,
Calle S.O.
Tel. 520 628
Fax 528 009
LACSA
Edificio San Miguel
4 Piso
Tel. 370 156

CAR RENTAL
AVIS RENT A CAR
Honduras Maya Hotel
Tel. 320 888

BUDGET RENT A CAR
Aeropuerto Toncontín
Tel. 335 170
or 335 171
NATIONAL RENT A CAR
Col. El Prado
Tel. 332 653

RESTAURANTS

**** RESTAURANTE
DUNCAN MAYA**
Ave. Cristóbal Colón
to the west of Plaza
Central.
*Basic, but good-quality
food.*

**** RESTAURANTE
EL PATIO**
Calle Los Dolores 1024
*Excellent meat dishes
and cheese fondues. A
good restaurant with a
bar where one can
listen to music.*

*** RESTAURANTE
AL NATURAL**
Behind the cathedral.
*Specializes in fresh
pasta and seafood
dishes.*

HOTELS

**** HOTEL
PLAZA SAN MARTÍN**
Pl. San Martín,
Col. Palmira

**** HONDURAS
MAYA HOTEL**
Ave. Republica de Chile
Col. Palmira
Tel. 323 191

*** HOTEL
NUEVO BOSTON**
Ave. Jeréz 321
Tel. 379 411
*Clean and comfortable
rooms. Communal
lounge with television.
Close to the Plaza
Central.*

MUSEUMS

**INSTITUTO
HONDURENO
DE ANTROPOLOGIA
ET HISTORIA**
Villa Roy,
Barrio Buenos Aires.

APPENDICES

◆ Bibliography

Essential
◆ Reading ◆

◆ Baudez (C.) and Picasso (S.), *Lost Cities of the Maya*, Thames & Hudson, London, 1992.
◆ Coe (M.D.), *The Maya*, Thames & Hudson, London, 1993.
◆ Eric (J.) and Thompson (E.), *The Rise and Fall of Maya Civilisation*, Pimlico, London, 1993.
◆ Henderson (J.), *The World of the Maya*, Cornell, Ithaca, 1981.

General
◆ Interest ◆

◆ Bernal (I.), *Ancient Mexico*, Thames & Hudson, London, 1968.
◆ Brainerd (G.W.), Morley (S.G.), and Sharer (R.J), *The Ancient Maya*, Stanford, 1983.
◆ Brunhouse (R.L.), *In Search of the Maya*, Univ. Of New Mexico Press, Albuquerque, 1973.
◆ Davies (N.), *The Aztecs*, Macmillan, London, 1973.
◆ Davies (N.), *Voyages to the New World*, W. Morrow, New York, 1979.
◆ Graham (J.A.), *Ancient Mesoamerica*, Peak Publications, Palo Alto, 1966.
◆ Riding (A.), *Distant Neighbors: A Portrait of the Mexicans*, Alfred A. Knopf, New York, 1985.
◆ Sanders (W.T.) and Price (B.J.), *Mesoamerica: The Evolution of a Civilization*, Random House, New York, 1968.
◆ Simpson (L.B.), *Many Mexicos*, Univ. of California Press, Berkeley and Los Angeles, 1964.
◆ Stuart (G.S) and Stuart (G.E.), *Lost Kingdoms of the Maya*, National Geographic Society, 1993.
◆ Townsend (R.F.), *The Aztecs*, Thames & Hudson, London, 1992.
◆ Wauchope (R.) Ed., *Handbook of Middle American Indians*, vols. 2 and 3, Univ of Texas, Austin, 1965–84.
◆ Weaver (M.P.), *The Aztecs, Maya and Their Predecessors*, Academic Press, New York, 1981.

◆ History ◆

◆ Adams (R.E.W.), *The Origins of Maya Civilization*, Albuquerque, 1977.
◆ Barrera Vasquez (A.) and Morley (S.G.), *The Maya Chronicles*, Carnegie Institution of Washington, 1949.
◆ Brainerd (G.), *The Maya Civilization*, Southwest Museum, Los Angeles, 1954.
◆ Carver (N.F.), *Silent Cities: Mexico and the Maya*, Shokokusha, Tokyo, 1966.
◆ Chamberlain (R.S.), *The Conquest and Colonization of Yucatán*, Carnegie Institution of Washington, Pub. 582, 1948.
◆ Clendinnen (I.), *Ambivalent Conquest. Maya and Spaniards in Yucatán*, Carnegie Institution of Washington, 1948.
◆ Coe (M.D.), *Breaking the Maya Code*, Thames & Hudson, London, 1992.
◆ Collis (M.), *Cortés and Montezuma*, Faber & Faber, London, 1954.
◆ Culbert (T.P.) ed., *The Classic Maya Collapse*, Univ. of New Mexico Press, Albuquerque, 1973.
◆ De Fuentes (P.), *The Conquistadores: First-Person Accounts of the Conquest of Mexico*, Orion Press, New York, 1963.
◆ Flannery (K.V.), *Maya Subsistence*, New York, 1982.
◆ Gibson (C.), *The Aztecs Under Spanish Rule*, Stanford Univ. Press, Stanford, 1964.
◆ Hammond (N.), *Ancient Maya Civilization*, Rutgers, New Brunswick, 1982.
◆ Jones (G.D.), *Anthropology and History in Yucatán*, Univ. of Texas Press, 1977.
◆ Pasztory (E.), *Middle Classic Mesoamerica, AD 400–700*, Univ. of Columbia, New York, 1978.
◆ Prescott (W.H.), *History of the Conquest of Mexico*, George Allen & Unwin, London, 1913.
◆ Ricard (R.), *The Spiritual Conquest of Mexico*, Univ. of California, Berkeley, 1966.
◆ Schele (L.) and Miller (M.), *A Forest of Kings. The Untold Story of the Ancient Maya*, W. Morrow, New York, 1990.
◆ Stuart (G.S.) and Stuart (G.E.), *The Mysterious Maya*, National Geographic Society, 1977.
◆ Thompson (J.E.S.), *Maya History and Religion*, Univ. of Oklahoma Press, Norman, 1970.
◆ Thompson (J.E.S.), *The Dresden Codex*, American Philosophical Society, 1972.
◆ Weaver (M.P.), *The Aztecs, Mayas, and their predecessors*, New York, 1981.

Religion
◆ and Society ◆

◆ Aveni (A.F.), *Skywatchers of Ancient Mexico*, Univ. of Texas, Austin, 1981.
◆ Boone (N.), *Ritual Human Sacrifice in Mesoamerica*, Washington, 1983.
◆ Bowditch (C.P.), *The Numeration, Calendar Systems and Astronomical Knowledge of the Mayas*, Cambridge Univ. Press, 1910.
◆ Bricker (V.R.), *The Indian Christ, the Indian King*, Univ. of Texas Press, 1981.
◆ Brenner (A.), *Idols Behind Altars: The Story of the Mexican Spirit*, Beacon Press, Boston, 1970.
◆ Burland (C.) and Forman (W.), *Feathered Serpent and Smoking Mirror: Gods and Fate in Ancient Mexico*, Orbis Publishing Ltd., London, 1975.
◆ Carmack (R.M.), *The Quiché Mayas of Utatlán*, Univ. of Oklahoma Press, 1981.
◆ Castaneda (C.), *Journey to Ixtlan: The Lessons of Don Juan*, Simon & Schuster, New York, 1972.
◆ Castaneda (C.), *A Separate Reality: Further Conversations with Don Juan*, Simon & Schuster, New York, 1971.
◆ Coe (M.D.), *Lords of the Underworld*, Art Museum, Princeton, 1978.
◆ Coe (M.D.), *The Maya Scribe and his World*, Grolier Club, New York, 1973.
◆ Coggins (C.) and Shane (O.C.), *Cenote of Sacrifice: Maya Treasures from the Sacred Well of Chichén Itzá*, Univ. of Texas Press, 1986.
◆ Durán, Fray (D.), *Book of the Gods and Rites and the Ancient Calendar*, TRANS. AND ED. Horcasitas (F.) and Heyden (D.), Univ. of Oklahoma Press, Norman, 1971.
◆ Flanner (K.V.) and Marcus (J.) EDS., *The Cloud People: Divergent Evolution of the Zapotec and Mixtec Civilizations*, Academic Press, New York, 1983.
◆ Helfritz (H.), *Mexican Cities of the Gods*, Praeger, New York, 1970.
◆ Léon-Portilla (M.), *Aztec Thought and Culture*, Univ. of Oklahoma Press, Norman, 1963.
◆ Miller (M.E.) and Taub (K.), *Gods and Symbols of Ancient Mexico and the Maya*, Thames & Hudson, London, 1993.
◆ Nicholson (I.), *Mexican and Central American Mythology*, Hamlyn, London, 1967.
◆ Ramos (S.), *Profile of Man and Culture in Mexico*, Univ. of Texas Press, Austin, 1962.
◆ Robicsek (F.) and Hales (D.), *The Maya Book of the Dead. The Ceramic Codex*, Univ. of Virginia Museum, 1982.
◆ Robicsek (F.), *Copán: Home of the Maya gods*, New York, 1972.
◆ Roys (R.L.), *Ritual of the Bacabs*, Univ. of Oklahoma Press, Norman, 1965.
◆ Scholes (F.V.), *The Maya Chontal Indians of Acalan-Tixchel*, Washington, 1948.
◆ Teeple (J.E.), *Mayan Astronomy*, Carnegie Institute of

Washington, 1931.
◆ THOMPSON (J.E.S.),
Maya History and
Religion, Univ. of
Oklahoma Press,
Norman, 1970.
◆ TOMPKINS (P.),
Mysteries of Mexican
Pyramids, Thames &
Hudson, London, 1991.

POLITICS
◆ AND ECONOMY ◆

◆ BARRY (T.), Roots
of Rebellion. Land
and Hunger in Central
America, South End
Press, 1987.
◆ CARMACK (R.M.),
ED., Harvest of
Violence. The Maya
Indians and the
Guatemalan Crisis,
Univ. of Oklahoma
Press, 1988.
◆ CULBERT (T.P.), The
Classic Maya
Collapse,
Albuquerque, 1973.
◆ FARRISS (N.M.),
Maya Society under
Colonial rule: The
Collective Enterprise
of Survival, Princeton
Univ. Press, 1984.
◆ FLETCHER (L.),
FOLAN (W.J.) and
KINTZ (E.), Copán: A
Classic Maya
Metropolis,
New York, 1983.
◆ MANZ (B.), Refugees
of a Hidden War.
The Aftermath of
Counter-insurgency in
Guatemala, Univ. of
New York Press,
1987.
◆ MARCUS (J.),
Emblem and State
in the Classic Maya
Lowlands,
Washington, 1976.
◆ SIMON (J.M.),
Guatemala, Eternal
Spring, Eternal
Tyranny, Norton and
Company, 1987.
◆ SULLIVAN (P.),
Unfinished
Conversations. Mayas
and Foreigners
between two wars,
New York, 1989.

ART AND
◆ ARCHITECTURE ◆

◆ ANDREWS (G.F.),
Maya cities:
Placemaking and
Urbanization, Univ.
of Oklahoma Press,
Norman, 1974.
◆ BAUDEZ (C.F.), Maya
Sculpture of Copán:
The Iconography.
Univ. of Oklahoma
Press, Norman, 1994.
◆ BULLARD (W.J.),
Maya Settlement
Patterns in

Northeastern Petén,
Guatemala,
American Antiquity,
Vol. 25, no. 3, 1960.
◆ COE (M.D.), Lords
of the Underworld.
Masterpieces of
Classic Maya
Ceramics, Princeton
Univ. Press, 1978.
◆ COE (W.R.), Tikal,
a handbook of the
ancient Maya ruins,
Univ. Museum,
Philadelphia, 1967.
◆ CHARLOT (G.),
The Mexican Mural
Renaissance
1920–1925,
Yale Univ. Press,
New Haven, 1967.
◆ COVARRUBIAS (M.),
Indian Art of Mexico
and Central America,
Alfred A. Knopf,
New York, 1957.
◆ DOCKSTADER (F. J.),
Indian Art of Central
America, Cary, Adams
and Mackay,
London, 1964.
◆ GREEN ROBERTSON
(M.) and RANDS (R.L.),
Maya Sculpture
of the Southern
Lowlands, Highlands
and Pacific
Piedmont, Lederer,
Street & Zens,
Berkeley, 1972.
◆ GRUZINSKI (S.),
Painting the Conquest
– The Mexican
Indians and the
European
Renaissance,
Thames & Hudson,
London, 1992.
◆ HANKS (W.) and
RICE (D.), EDS., Word
and Image in Maya
Culture, Univ. of Utah
Press, 1989.
◆ HEYDEN (D.) and
GENDROP (P.),
Pre-Columbian
Architecture of
Mesoamerica,
Faber & Faber,
London, 1980.
◆ KELEMEN (P.),
Medieval American
Art: Masterpieces of
the New World before
Columbus, Macmillan,
New York, 1943.
◆ KUBLER (G.),
Art and Architecture
of Ancient America,
Pelican Books,
Harmondsworth,
1975.
◆ KUBLER (G.),
Mexican Architecture
in the Sixteenth
Century, Yale Univ.
Press, New Haven,
1948.
◆ LONGYEAR (J.M.),
Copán Ceramics,
Carnegie Institution
of Washington, Pub.
597, 1952.

◆ LOTHROP (S.K.),
Tulum: an
Archeological Study
of the East Coast of
Yucatán, Carnegie
Inst. of Washington
Pub. 335, 1924.
◆ MILLER (A.G.), On
the Edge of the Sea:
Mural painting at
Tancah-Tulum,
Washington, 1982.
◆ MILLER (M.E.), The
Murals of Bonampak,
Princeton, 1986.
◆ MORLEY (S.G.),
Inscriptions at Copán,
Carnegie Institute,
Washington DC, 1920.
◆ PROSKOURIAKOFF
(T.), An Album of
Maya Architecture,
Carnegie Institution,
Washington DC, 1946.
◆ PROSKOURIAKOFF
(T.), A Study of
Classic Maya
Sculpture, Carnegie
Institution,
Washington DC, 1950.
◆ RAMIREZ (P.) et al.,
Mexico: Art,
Architecture,
Archeology,
Ethnography. The
National Museum of
Anthropology, Harry
N. Adams, New York,
1968.
◆ RIVET (P.), Maya
Cities: Ancient Cities
and Temples, Putnam,
New York, 1962.
◆ ROJAS (P.), The Art
and Architecture of
Mexico, Hamlyn,
Feltham, Middlesex,
1968.
◆ SABLOFF (J. A.),
The Cities of
Ancient Mexico –
Reconstructing
a Lost World,
Thames & Hudson,
London, 1990.
◆ SAYER (C.), Arts &
Crafts of Mexico,
Chronicle Books, San
Francisco, 1990.
◆ SCHELE (L.) and
MILLER (M.), The
Blood of Kings.
Dynasty and ritual in
Maya art, George
Brazillier Inc., 1986.
◆ SMITH (B.), Mexico:
a History in Art,
Phaidon Press,
London, 1975.
◆ SPINDEN (H.J.),
A Study of Maya Art,
Peabody Museum
Harvard, Cambridge,
1913.
◆ SUTTON (A.), Among
the Maya Ruins,
Rand-McNally, 1967.
◆ THOMPSON (J.E.),
A Preliminary Study
of the Ruins of Copán,
Carnegie Institution of
Washington, 1932.

◆ THOMPSON (J.E.S.),
Maya Hieroglyphics
without Tears, British
Museum Publications,
London, 1972.
◆ THOMPSON (J.E.S.),
Maya Hieroglyphic
Writing: An
Introduction, Univ. of
Oklahoma Press,
Norman, 1971.
◆ TOUSSAINT (M.),
Colonial Art of Mexico,
REV. AND TRANS. Wilder
Weisman (E.), Univ. of
Texas Press, Austin,
1967.

◆ LITERATURE ◆

◆ ASTURIAS (M.A.),
Men of Maize, TRANS.
Partridge (F.),
Gollancz. 1963 /
Atheneum, New York,
1969.
◆ BARRERA VASQUEZ
(A.) and MORLEY
(S.G.), The Maya
Chronicles, Carnegie
Institution of
Washington, 1949.
◆ BECKETT (S.) TRANS.
AND ED., Mexican
Poetry, Calder &
Boyars, London,
1970.
◆ EDMONSON (M.),
Heaven Born Mérida
and Its Destiny: The
Book of Chilam Balam
of Chumayel, Univ. of
Texas Press, Austin,
1986.
◆ TEDLOCK (D.), Popol
Vuh. The Mayan Book
of the Dawn of Life,
New York, 1985.

TRAVELERS'
◆ TALES ◆

◆ GAGE (T.), Thomas
Gage's Travels in the
New World, ED.
Newton (A.P), George
Routledge & Sons,
London, 1928.
◆ MAUDSLAY (A.C.),
A Glimpse at
Guatemala,
Murray, 1899.
◆ NORMAN (B.M.),
Rambles in Yucatán,
Carey and Hart, 1849.
◆ PARKER (F.D.),
Travels in Central
America 1821–1840,
Univ. of Florida Press,
1970.
◆ SEXTON (J.),
Campesino: The diary
of a Guatemalan
Indian, Univ. of
Arizona Press, 1985.
◆ STEPHENS (J.L.),
Incidents of Travel in
Central America,
Chiapas and Yucatán,
ED. Predmore (R.L.),
Rutgers Univ. Press,
New Brunswick, 1949.

◆ LIST OF ILLUSTRATIONS

INDEX ·

◆ MUSEUMS ◆

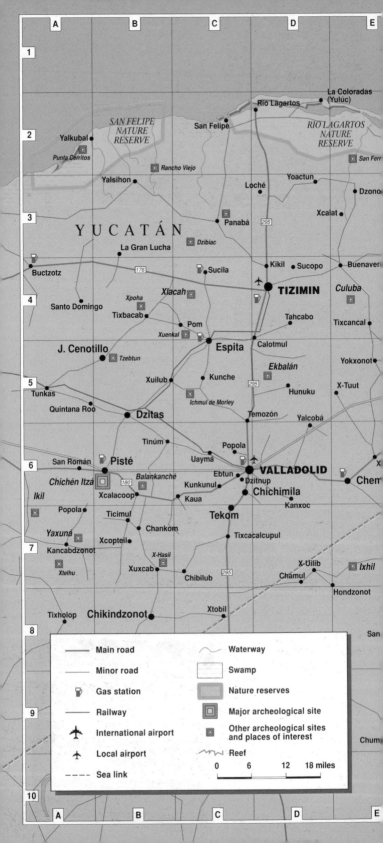